C000051565

SELF AND SOCIAL IDENTITY IN EDUCATIONAL CONTEXTS

This innovative volume integrates social identity theory with research on teaching and education to shed new and fruitful light on a variety of different pedagogical concerns and practices. It brings together researchers at the cutting edge of new developments with a wealth of teaching and research experience.

The work in this volume will have a significant impact in two main ways. First and foremost, the social identity approach that is applied will provide the theoretical and empirical platform for the development of new and creative forms of practice in educational settings. Just as the application of this theory has made significant contributions in organisational and health settings, a similar benefit will accrue for conceptual and practical developments related to learners and educators – from small learning groups to larger institutional settings – and in the development of professional identities that reach beyond the classroom. The chapters demonstrate the potential of applying social identity theory to education and will stimulate increased research activity and interest in this domain. By focusing on self, social identity and education, this volume investigates with unprecedented clarity the social and psychological processes by which learners' personal and social self-concepts shape and enhance learning and teaching.

Self and Social Identity in Educational Contexts will appeal to advanced students and researchers in education, psychology and social identity theory. It will also be of immense value to educational leaders and practitioners, particularly at tertiary level.

Kenneth I. Mavor is Lecturer in Psychology in the School of Psychology and Neuroscience at the University of St Andrews, UK. His research focuses on the cognitive underpinnings of self and identity and the implications of social identity in a variety of contexts including education, religiosity, collective action and health.

Michael J. Platow is Professor of Psychology at the Australian National University and a Fellow of the Academy of Social Sciences in Australia. His research examines leadership and social influence, fairness and trust, prejudice and intergroup relations, and group identities and learning. His teaching has been recognised by a Commonwealth Office of Learning and Teaching Carrick Citation.

Boris Bizumic is Senior Lecturer in Psychology in the Research School of Psychology at the Australian National University. His research expertise is in social, personal and political psychology. He has published widely in the areas of ethnocentrism, prejudice, group identity, education, personality, attitudes, cross-cultural research and scale construction.

SELF AND SOCIAL IDENTITY IN EDUCATIONAL CONTEXTS

*Edited by Kenneth I. Mavor, Michael J. Platow
and Boris Bizumic*

Routledge
Taylor & Francis Group

LONDON AND NEW YORK

First published 2017
by Routledge
2 Park Square, Milton Park, Abingdon, Oxon, OX14 4RN

and by Routledge
711 Third Avenue, New York, NY 10017

Routledge is an imprint of the Taylor & Francis Group, an informa business

© 2017 selection and editorial matter, Kenneth I. Mavor, Michael J. Platow and Boris Bizumic; individual chapters, the contributors

The right of Kenneth I. Mavor, Michael J. Platow and Boris Bizumic to be identified as the authors of the editorial material, and of the authors for their individual chapters, has been asserted in accordance with sections 77 and 78 of the Copyright, Designs and Patents Act 1988.

All rights reserved. No part of this book may be reprinted or reproduced or utilised in any form or by any electronic, mechanical, or other means, now known or hereafter invented, including photocopying and recording, or in any information storage or retrieval system, without permission in writing from the publishers.

Trademark notice: Product or corporate names may be trademarks or registered trademarks, and are used only for identification and explanation without intent to infringe.

British Library Cataloguing-in-Publication Data
A catalogue record for this book is available from the British Library

Library of Congress Cataloging in Publication Data
A catalog record for this book has been requested

ISBN: 978-1-138-81513-1 (hbk)
ISBN: 978-1-138-81515-5 (pbk)
ISBN: 978-1-315-74691-3 (ebk)

Typeset in Bembo
by RefineCatch Limited, Bungay, Suffolk

We would like to dedicate this book to our families.

They have acted as educators to us and to others in one form or another, and all helped shape the identities we now adopt.

Some have passed away in the course of editing this book, so we remember them by name.

Louisa Adele Webb (Mavor) – 1967–2012

Lola Dell Mavor (Green) – 1938–2014

Ian George Mavor – 1938–2015

CONTENTS

ILLUSTRATIONS

Figures

Tables

Boxes

CONTRIBUTORS

Catherine E. Amiot, Département de psychologie, Université du Québec à Montréal, Canada

Sarah V. Bentley, School of Psychology, University of Queensland, Australia

Boris Bizumic, Research School of Psychology, Australian National University, Australia

Ana-Maria Bliuc, School of Social Sciences, Monash University, Australia

Kathryn L. Boucher, School of Psychological Sciences, University of Indianapolis, USA

David Bromhead, Education Directorate, ACT Department of Education, Australia

Bryan Burford, School of Medical Education, Newcastle University, UK

Tegan Cruwys, School of Psychology, University of Queensland, Australia

Robert A. Ellis, Institute for Teaching and Learning, University of Sydney, Australia

Amber M. Gaffney, Department of Psychology, Humboldt University, Germany

Peter Goodyear, Faculty of Education and Social Work, University of Sydney, Australia

Diana M. Grace, School of Psychology, University of Canberra, Australia

Katharine Greenaway, School of Psychology, University of Queensland, Australia

S. Alexander Haslam, School of Psychology, University of Queensland, Australia

Aarti Iyer, Department of Psychology, University of Sheffield, UK

Jolanda Jetten, School of Psychology, University of Queensland, Australia

Siân E. Jones, Department of Psychology, Goldsmiths College, University of London, UK

Girish Lala, School of Social Sciences and Psychology, Western Sydney University, Australia

Eunro Lee, Research School of Psychology, Australian National University, Australia

Andrew G. Livingstone, School of Psychology, University of Exeter, UK

Winnifred R. Louis, School of Psychology, University of Queensland, Australia

Craig McGarty, School of Social Sciences and Psychology, Western Sydney University, Australia

Kathleen G. McNeill, Research School of Psychology, Australian National University, Australia

Anthony S. R. Manstead, School of Psychology, Cardiff University, UK

Kenneth I. Mavor, School of Psychology and Neuroscience, University of St Andrews, UK

Conal Monaghan, Research School of Psychology, Australian National University, Australia

Lynn V. Monrouxe, Chang Gung Medical Education Research Centre, Chang Gung Memorial Hospital, Taiwan

Mary C. Murphy, Department of Psychology and Brain Sciences, Indiana University, USA

Anne Pedersen, School of Psychology and Exercise Science, Murdoch University, Australia

Michael J. Platow, Research School of Psychology, Australian National University, Australia

Charlotte E. Rees, Faculty of Medicine, Nursing and Health Sciences, Monash University, Australia

Katherine J. Reynolds, Research School of Psychology, Australian National University, Australia

Emma Rich, Department of Health, University of Bath, UK

Harriet E. S. Rosenthal-Stott, Department of Psychology, Durham University, UK

Yvonne Skipper, School of Psychology, Keele University, UK

Joanne R. Smith, School of Psychology, University of Exeter, UK

Lillian Smyth, Medical School, Australian National University, Australia

Stefanie J. Sonnenberg, Department of Psychology, University of Portsmouth, UK

Avelie Stuart, School of Psychology, University of Exeter, UK

Emina Subasic, School of Psychology, University of Newcastle, UK

Mark Tarrant, Medical School, University of Exeter, UK

Emma F. Thomas, School of Psychology and Exercise Science, Murdoch University, Australia

Louisa Webb, School of Sport, Exercise and Health Sciences, Loughborough University, UK

Airong Zhang, Adaptive Social and Economic Systems, Commonwealth Scientific and Industrial Research Organisation, Australia

PART I

Introducing social identity in educational contexts

1

INTRODUCING SELF AND SOCIAL IDENTITY IN EDUCATIONAL CONTEXTS

Promoting learning, managing conflict, facilitating change

Michael J. Platow, Kenneth I. Mavor and Boris Bizumic

The *self*, in one way or another, is a concept that pervades the education literature. Self and learning are, in fact, intertwined, with self often understood as the outcome of learning (Prosser and Trigwell, 1999; Ramsden, 2003) but also as an antecedent to learning (Abouserie, 1995; Kwan, 2009; Schmeck, Geisler-Brenstein and Cercy, 1991; Thomas and Gadbois, 2007). At times in the literature, the concept of self is explicitly examined and developed (Pajares and Schunk, 2002; Zimmerman, 2000); at other times, however, it is used in a manner that, at best, assumes a shared understanding with readers (Kuznetsov and Kuznetsova, 2011; Rodicio, Sánchez and Acuña, 2013; Wintre, Dilouya, Pancer, Pratt, Birnie-Lefcovitch, Polivy and Adams, 2011). In social psychology, the concept of the self, too, plays a profound role in explaining behaviours (Terry, Hogg and White, 1999), shaping attitudes (Greenwald, Banaji, Rudman, Farnham, Nosek and Mellott, 2002) and, indeed, guiding learning (Trautwein, Lüdtke, Köller and Baumert, 2006).

The work of social psychologists, however, seems often not to percolate too deeply into the education literature; this is not to suggest that the education literature has percolated deeply into social psychology – it has not, and to social psychology's detriment. It is with this recognition that the current volume was conceived and written; specifically, it represents an attempt by social psychologists to introduce a set of *social-psychological* concepts and thinking into the broader education literature. 'Introduce' may be a bit presumptuous, of course, as many of the authors of the current volume (and, indeed, others) have been working on their independent research lines, each trying to make a mark within education. So, possibly more accurately, this book represents an attempt to provide a single focal point in which individual authors each review their diverse work in a forum that allows for a collective voice.

Two things come to mind as we pen these words. First, readers will quickly realise that the diversity of work we allude to above is mirrored in this volume.

On the one hand, this diversity represents the more or less idiosyncratic foray into the world of education and learning that has thus far taken place. On the other hand, it reflects, in part, the genesis of this book itself: several of the authors were contributors to one of the Australian National University's annual Spring Workshops in Social Psychology, a forum in which we strive to assemble researchers conducting like-minded research for intense and focused discussions. When planning this workshop, we sought a common intellectual theme. In this case, we realised that a particular analysis of self and identity – one in which these concepts are situated explicitly within a social context, are fluid and dynamic, and are both personal and social – was percolating into the realm of education, but in a rather *ad hoc* manner. The workshop, and this volume as one outcome of it, provided an opportunity to actualise a common voice that underlay the variety of work people were already doing. We describe relevant assumptions of this analysis below; they are also explicated in considerable detail by Haslam in Chapter 2 and, of course, by all of the authors in their own chapters as they highlight aspects that are relevant to their work.

Second, we are fully aware of the caution with which many educators and researchers in learning and teaching approach psychological analyses. Much criticism has been levied against traditional psychological models of learning from within the education literature (e.g., Billington and Williams, 2015; Bird, 1999; Bredo, 1997; Entwistle, 1997). But to our readings, many of these criticisms seem to be levied against *particular* psychological approaches. For example, Entwistle took issue with aspects of traditional behaviourist approaches to learning, analyses of intelligence, and cognitive-psychological learning theories. Although he recognised how and why it may be useful for psychologists (and others) to understand how, say, associations are learned between behaviours and external contingencies, and the processes by which memory operates, Entwistle felt that these approaches left unanswered key questions that many educators seek to answer. Indeed, educators have often sought to understand humans' subjective understandings (e.g., Soltis, 1984), meaning-making (e.g., Tang, Delgado and Moje, 2014) and integration of ideas (e.g., Biggs, 1987; Songer and Linn, 2006) and may have (undoubtedly, some certainly have) found the explorations offered by psychologists to be lacking.

In the current volume, we intentionally and explicitly move beyond the models considered by authors such as Entwistle (1997) by invoking the self and identity as fundamental processes inseparable from learning. Indeed, as we outline more fully below, the contributions of this book provide conceptual and empirical analyses of how, why and when the self: (1) enables learning and produces motivation; (2) serves as both a conduit and a boundary to the management of conflict both within and between individuals and groups (including in the classroom); and (3) provides a means for change in both one's own self (reflexively) and between individuals and groups.

Some assumptions underlying the social identity approach

Before we consider the manner in which the chapters of this volume provide insight into these three processes, we briefly review some key assumptions of the model of self and identity that underpins at least some aspect of all chapters in this volume. Again, a more full account of this model is presented by Haslam in Chapter 2. The model of self and identity that is adopted throughout this volume is based upon the combined theories of social identity (e.g., Tajfel and Turner, 1986) and self-categorisation (Turner, Hogg, Oakes, Reicher and Wetherell, 1987), collectively referred to throughout this volume as the 'social identity approach' (see also Haslam, Reicher and Platow, 2011; Haslam, van Knippenberg, Platow and Ellemers, 2003; Jetten, Haslam and Haslam, 2012). These two theories developed in particular from an established line of research and theory within social psychology but also drew inspiration from Gestalt psychology and sociology, and they were developed separately from behaviourist psychology (e.g., see Doise, 1978; Platow, Hunter, Haslam and Reicher, 2015; Robinson, 1996). Here, instead of revisiting the history of the development of the social identity approach or all of its conceptual and empirical twists and turns, or even many of its most clearly stated assumptions, we outline five key assumptions of the approach that are most relevant to the current volume.

First, the social identity approach assumes that *people pursue meaning-making, not thought minimisation*. This assumption is in explicit contrast to the 'cognitive miser' perspective (Fiske and Taylor, 1984) that has held sway in much of social cognition research; this latter perspective assumes that people have a proclivity (if not an outright preference) *not* to think if they can get away with it. Instead, and explicitly building upon the tradition developed by Bruner and his colleagues (e.g., Bruner, 1957, 1966, 1990; Bruner, Goodnow and Austin, 1956), within the social identity approach, the mind is seen as an 'interpretive' system (McGarty, 1999, p. 7). Humans seek to make sense of their environment and their place within that environment. To date, this meaning-making assumption has played its most prominent role in social identity analyses of stereotyping (e.g., Oakes and Haslam, 2001; Oakes, Haslam and Turner, 1994) and social influence (e.g., McGarty, Haslam, Hutchinson and Turner, 1994; Platow, 2007). Theoretical developments and empirical confirmations have clearly demonstrated, for example, that stereotyping is, in part, an active attempt at *understanding* and not of miserly thought processes (e.g., Berndsen, McGarty, Van der Pligt and Spears, 2001).

In the current context, moving now into the realm of education, this meaning-making assumption allows us to begin our analysis with a model of human learning as one of active growth through the *pursuit* of understanding. If we were, instead, to start our analysis of education with the premise that people simply respond to their environment with little to no thought, we would immediately limit the scope of that analysis, the breadth of questions we would ask, and the outcomes we would seek to observe. A social identity approach to education, then, assumes that *under the right circumstances*, people will actively interpret and seek to make sense of new information and experiences they encounter in their learning environments. What these 'right circumstances' are, of course, remains to be identified, with many of the subsequent chapters seeking precisely to do this.

A second assumption within the social identity approach is that *the self-concept is both to-be-explained and an explanatory principle*. On the one hand, the self is understood as the outcome of personal history, memory and expectations, a person's current state, and his or her active online assessment of the context (i.e., meaning-making). In this manner, social identity theorists and researchers require a set of principles for outlining how the self is cognitively constructed. Self-categorisation theory provides these principles (e.g., Oakes, 1987). Once again, the theory builds upon Bruner's earlier analysis that 'all perception is necessarily the end product of a categorisation process' (1957, p. 124), assuming that the self takes the form of *self-categorisations* – that is, cognitive groupings of the perceiver with (or without) others seen as the same, identical or interchangeable. How, why and when others may or may not share similarity with the perceiver remain the focus of other aspects of the theory, with some of these principles (and critical empirical tests) outlined in several chapters of this book, as well as in other (e.g., Haslam, 2004) books. A common feature, however, underlying these analyses is the view that the self-concept subsequently guides attention, creates motivation, filters information and serves as a basis for interpreting that information (e.g., Grace, David and Ryan, 2008; Haslam, Powell and Turner, 2000; Platow *et al.*, 2007). Information is, thus, assumed not to be given in a straightforward, constant manner; importantly, this refers to *all* information, including that which is about self and others and, indeed, that which is the focus of educational contexts.

Thus, the self is seen to be a reflexive system in which it is constructed through similarity and difference judgements, while these judgements are themselves influenced by individuals' currently salient self-concepts. Indeed, this reflexive process exemplifies and encapsulates the third assumption of the social identity approach, that *the self-concept is dynamic and context-dependent*. Within the social identity approach, the self is not understood to be fixed in any sense (e.g., Onorato and Turner, 2004), and this dynamic nature of the self is viewed as a normal psychological process that allows flexibility in behaviours to act appropriately in a dynamic world.

It is because of the assumption of a dynamic self-concept that we can outline a fourth assumption that, *in any given situation, the self can be cognitively (subjectively) represented at either a personal level or a collective level*. At a personal level, self is assumed to be represented as *different* from others; in self-categorisation theory terms, this reflects a cognitive representation of the perceiver categorised *with no one else*. It is what is otherwise referred to as one's personal identity and is what many psychologists from other theoretical perspectives, and lay people, understand as being the true and only self. But the social identity approach rejects any assumed stability in the self, which means that self can be represented not only uniquely (i.e., personally) but also collectively. At the collective level, self is understood by the perceiver as the same as – rather than different from – others at some level of abstraction. This is referred to as a social identity (i.e., self as a group member), and is assumed to make possible group-based behaviours (e.g., Haslam, Postmes and Ellemers, 2003; Hogg, Hardie and Reynolds, 1995). This dynamic nature of the self and its ability to vary between personal and social identities lead to a final assumption that *the personal self has no privileged status in defining a person*. That is, unlike other analyses (formal or lay), the personal self does *not* represent a 'true' self that somehow imbues social identities with meaning. Both personal and social identities are assumed to be equally valid representations of the self, representations that emerge from the very sense-making process in which people engage as they (we!) move from situation to situation throughout their (our) lives.

Together, these five assumptions thus allow us to speak meaningfully of learners not simply as isolated individuals, each with his or her own idiosyn-crasies, but as 'students' or as 'consumers' or as 'women' or as 'psychology majors'. More importantly, these terms are not just a form of shorthand for our writing – these terms are assumed to capture *meaningful* self-representations that have knowable consequences, both promotive and inhibitory. The self is not a fixed entity – it is amenable to change with variation in the social context. Importantly, it is amenable to change with variation in experience, including formal and informal learning. Finally, and critically, self is not understood as captive to the social context. People can pursue and construct identities (e.g., Reicher, Haslam and Hopkins, 2005), rebel against ones they do not value (Jetten, Branscombe, Schmitt and Spears, 2001), and be active players in considering and changing the very meanings of these identities. Each of these assumptions is broadly adopted by the authors contributing to this volume, and readers will see how they enable the authors to shed new light on the role of self and identity in educational contexts. Below, we briefly outline the chapters, organising their individual foci into broad conceptual themes.

Promoting learning, managing conflict, facilitating change

As we noted from the outset, there is considerable diversity in the content and focus of the chapters in this volume; as readers will soon realise, the chapters vary along several dimensions. In structuring the book and, indeed, in inviting authors, we chose to arrange works along dimensions in a manner that highlights the actual contexts (e.g., the classroom, the playground), stages (e.g., transitioning into university life) and mechanisms (e.g., personalities versus collective iden-tities) in and through which educational and identity processes unfold. But crossing this broad structure are at least three other key themes that are also likely to be of interest to educators: promoting learning, managing conflict and facil-itating change. We introduce the chapters below within the framework of these latter three themes even though – as readers will see – this categorisation is not mutually exclusive or exhaustive enough to cover all of the works herein.

Promoting learning

Academic social identities predict academic performance

A fundamental principle that runs through many of the chapters in this book is that academic self-concepts (e.g., academic social identities) are powerful tools yielding substantive academic outcomes. This is seen in the most direct form in the chapter by Bliuc, Goodyear and Ellis (Chapter 12). Here, the authors build upon their own prior work, and that of others (e.g., Platow, Mavor and Grace, 2013), to develop a model in which university students' social identification with their discipline promotes their own deep approach to learning; this deep approach, in turn, enhances students' learning outcomes. This is a very powerful claim as it highlights two key factors: (1) that self-involvement in the learning context yields positive educational outcomes and (2) that the self that is involved need not be restricted to a personal self. Indeed, fundamental to the assumptions of this model is that the social identity itself is imbued with *normative content*, effectively informing students of appropriate behaviours. More than that, however, it demonstrates how social identities are experienced in a deeply personal way – these identities can act as strong motivators for personal achievement.

The genesis of academic social identities

The work of Bliuc *et al.*, of course, raises the question of how these identities are developed in the first place. At least three of the chapters in this volume seek to answer this question, each in its own way. At a relatively macro level, Reynolds, Subasic, Lee and Bromhead (Chapter 3) present a compelling model in which school climate facilitates the development of students' social identification, at least with the school itself. In Reynolds *et al.*'s empirical work, they show how school kids' (seventh and ninth grade) perceptions of the overall fairness of procedures at their school, the staff–student relations, the sense of a shared mission and clear academic expectations collectively enhance students' positive social identification with their school. Critically, this social identification, in turn, actually enhances students' academic writing and numeracy performance on a national standardised test of learning outcomes. So, again, social identification (this time with the school) predicts academic performance. But now we have some insight into the genesis of that identification: positive school climate.

While we see Reynolds *et al.*'s work as a powerful demonstration of the development of social identification and its causal role, we recognise that individual teachers may find changing (or just managing) their school's climate simply to be out of their hands. Monaghan and Bizumic (Chapter 14) provide some guidance in this sphere. In their work, they show how positive performance norms within small face-to-face project groups can create a positive social identification with those groups. This identification then, as expected, positively predicts the academic performance of the groups (as wholes). This third demonstration of the role of social identifications yielding positive academic outcomes expands the analysis to include the concept of group personality, which includes students' personalities within each project group as whole. As Monaghan and Bizumic show, group personality, too, plays a significant role in producing positive academic outcomes. This is a valuable demonstration as it clearly shows how aspects of students' *personal* as well as *social* selves continue to play an important role in academic achievement.

In the third chapter that considers the antecedents of social identification, Greenaway, Amiot, Louis and Bentley (Chapter 10) also consider aspects of students' personal identities, this time in the form of individual need satisfaction. These authors were able to show that when a social group (in this case, the students' university) was seen as facilitating the satisfaction of these needs over time (i.e., longitudinally), students' social identification with that group was also enhanced over time. Although academic performance was not measured in their work, Greenaway *et al.* were able to show, *inter alia*, that enhanced university social identification positively predicted students' academic satisfaction.

Taken together, we see in these last three chapters a confirmation of a fundamental thesis that: (1) positive academic outcomes result, at least in part, from an academic-related social identity and (2) this social identity can be developed through several group-based processes from institutional factors promoting a sense of inclusion and need satisfaction to face-to-face academic interactions.

The complexity of the normative content of social identities

The power of the relationship between social identity and positive academic outcome appears simple and straightforward. Five other chapters in this volume, however, remind us of the complexity underlying this relationship and how fragile it can actually be. As we noted above, the positive academic consequences of social identity processes are premised on the assumption of an academic normative content within that identity. As we know intuitively, however, student identities are not always so academically inclined. Cruwys, Gaffney and Skipper picked up on this point in Chapter 11 by recognising that incoming university students *may* see at least some groups at university as embracing a norm of studying; and, yet, they may see other groups as embracing a norm of partying. As Cruwys *et al.* expected, when students identified with a study-oriented group, they had relatively high intentions to study themselves. However, when they identified with a party-oriented group, the students had relatively high intentions to party. Both of these effects were particularly strong when the groups were seen as highly cohesive.

Even among students whom we might traditionally view as highly achievement oriented, variability in the normative content of the student identity can be observed. Burford and Rosenthal-Stott (Chapter 16) examined the complexity of the normative content of social identifications among medical students. Among many processes, these authors considered data that show that, under certain circumstances, the normative content of the medical student social identity is relatively negative. Critically, thi   negative identity content, in turn, may lead medical students to un   Mavor (Chapter 18) also examin   authors reviewed a range of evi   normative content to the me   exclusion (interacting solely with   learning norms themselves. M   research revealing the presence   norms among the medial stud   these group-based norms may   education that ultimately supp   iveness. Whatever their cause,   which relatively high levels of   relatively strong perceptions   students' own adoption of a su

The contrast between the   norms was examined more   Chapter 13. Here, the authors review   others who examined the direct link between academic social identity, learning approaches (see Bliuc et al.'s chapter in this book). Smyth et al. realised the complexity of the normative content of social identifications and that students may be able to recognise the presence of *both* surface learning norms and deep learning norms. Smyth et al.'s results show that university students are not only able to recognise norms of both approaches among others within their disciplines, but the strength of these norms seems to have a moderating effect on the relationship between students' own discipline-related social identities and their own learning approaches. Students highly identified with their discipline do, indeed, adopt a deep approach to their learning; this effect, however, is intensified when these students also perceive there to be a discipline norm of deep learning. But, to the degree to which students perceive there to be a discipline norm of surface learning, their own deep learning approach declines substantially.

All the work we have considered thus far relating social identity to academic outcomes has focused on what we may consider to be a more traditional under-standing of academic social identification: identification as a student, as a member of a study group or as a student of a specific school/university/discipline. However, Sonnenberg (Chapter 15) reminds us that tradition, at least within the context of Anglo-American universities, is changing. Universities are beginning to be seen as service providers for customers or consumers in the role traditionally occupied by students. She makes a strong case for the reasons for this change and potential problems associated with it. But her strongest argument is simply demonstrated in the review of her own research. In her research, she questions whether the new social identity of consumer will effectively contain the appropriate normative content to enable success at university. When her respondents viewed themselves as consumers – in contrast to learners – their overall satisfaction with university studies was lowered, their motivation for studying was more external (e.g., getting a job) than internal (e.g., to increase their own knowledge), and their attributions for their poor performance were externalised (e.g., poor teaching) rather than internalised (e.g., own need to study further). This work should at least begin to give pause to the continued changing of the way erstwhile students are construed.

Taken together, we see that the relationship between social identity and positive academic outcomes is not as straightforward as we might have initially thought (or wished). The positive relationship exists when there is an *alignment* between the normative content of the social identity and the positive academic outcomes we seek to achieve.

Multiple social identities and conflicting normative alignment

At least two chapters in the current volume also recognise that the complexity of the relationship between social identity and academic achievement is enhanced once we begin to consider students' other non-academic social identities. These other social identities, too, contain normative content, but this content may be challenged or threatened in what otherwise might seem a rather banal educational context. Boucher and Murphy (Chapter 5) tackle this head-on in their examination of women's relatively low frequency of participation in Science, Technology, Engineering and Mathematics (STEM) disciplines. They put forward a compelling argument that the structure and base-rate demographics of classrooms, the learning materials themselves, and the lack of opportunities for appropriate role models simply serve to highlight women's identities *as women* instead of as students or, even more appropriately, as STEM students. By making this valued – but contextually irrelevant – alternative social identity salient, women may begin to feel threatened in the learning context. This experience of threat, in turn, may heighten their anxiety, leading them either to perform relatively poorly or simply to leave the context to reduce this anxiety. As such, women may seek out alternative disciplines of study that at least *appear* to have a greater alignment with the normative content of what it means to be a woman (in this case, stereotyped views of women flourishing in human-related endeavours, such as nursing or sociology). Although these are valid (and valuable) areas of study in their own right, women's original interests *as students* may well have lain elsewhere. And, politically, we are left with an unrepresentative gender distribution in STEM disciplines.

A similar argument is made by Jetten, Iyer and Zhang (Chapter 6) although they propose slightly different social and psychological processes. Nevertheless, the crux of their argument is that the normative content of the university student social identification is more closely aligned with that of people from higher socio-economic status (SES) rather than lower SES backgrounds. This misalignment means that students from lower SES backgrounds may not pursue higher education in higher frequencies than they currently do because they simply view it as a place not for them – regardless of their individual capacities, interests and achievements. They see themselves not only as not belonging but also as *losing* both their old identities and concomitant friendships – with the latter exacerbating the difficulties as they lose the social support that those from higher SES backgrounds maintain.

Managing conflict

Self and identity processes may, thus, enhance or limit learning and engagement in the learning context. But the personal and social identifications that people adopt do not exist in isolation from each other. They do, of course, coexist and are imbued with symbolic and material status and power differences. Managing potential conflicts that emerge from these different identities represents a second theme considered in chapters of this book. Monrouxe and Rees (Chapter 17) examine these issues in their qualitative analysis of ethical conflicts between medical students and those healthcare professionals who have greater seniority and power (e.g., doctors). The focus of their analysis is how these lower-status students manage their own identities as students and as developing professionals and how they explain the identities of others in the context of potential and actual breaches of ethical conduct. The end result is a complex but highly meaningful narrative in which students place themselves into particular roles (e.g., apprentice, caregiver, hero), other professionals into roles (e.g., eager teacher, god, bully) and the patients themselves into roles (e.g., martyr, prop, victim). Moreover, the construction of these identities simultaneously explains and guides students' behaviours in and through the ethical conflicts they encounter.

Continuing an analysis of developing professional identities among medical students, Burford and Rosenthal-Stott (Chapter 16) take an explicitly *intergroup* approach to their analysis. They identify how the content of medical student identities (expressed through stereotypes) are the outcome of specific contexts in which the students find themselves as well as their own goals and motives. While this process of self-stereotyping may provide content to students' identities, Burford and Rosenthal-Stott also point out how the development of these identities in intergroup medical contexts creates specific forms of conflict. For example, doctors may give preference to information from doctors over nurses (even if the nurses are correct), while patient gender and ethnicity may impact upon doctors' diagnoses and management of illnesses. To manage potential conflicts that emerge from these and other intergroup relations, Burford and Rosenthal-Stott propose invoking a shared (or *superordinate*) identity between members of different groups (e.g., healthcare professional). But they are quick to recognise that this very process of emphasising a shared identity can be seen as a threat to the valued subordinate identities, potentially causing further problems rather than resolving them. Ultimately, they suggest, among other things, imbuing the content of the identities (i.e., the self-stereotypes) with conflict management norms (e.g., professionalism) as a direction forward.

In the work by Jones, Livingstone and Manstead (Chapter 4), emotional and physical conflict is examined in their intergroup analysis of bullies and bullying in schools. They begin by noting that many traditional analyses approach the problem from an individualistic perspective, focusing on characteristics of bullies and victims as unique individuals. In contrast to this, however, Jones *et al.* propose that bully–victim relationships can be understood as intergroup relations in themselves and as overlying other intergroup relations as well. In either case, groups may have particular social norms promoting (or prohibiting) bullying. When they have promoting norms, group normative behaviour (in this case, bullying) is met with pride and enhanced social identification. But when they have prohibiting norms, members of bullying groups feel guilt and are inclined toward apologies. By tackling bullying behaviour from an intergroup perspective, Jones *et al.* ask readers to look no more for idiosyncratic personality factors, but systemic, social-structural variables that create and diminish bullying in schools at a broader level.

Finally, the chapter by Grace and Platow (Chapter 7) takes a very different look at the role of social identities in conflict. Their case example of the history of the colonial and postcolonial education of Indigenous Australians demonstrates how the formal education system was used by the more powerful white Australians to deny, denigrate and destroy the social identities of Indigenous Australians. While the broader political system sought to eradicate Indigenous Australians *per se*, the education system worked to re-educate Indigenous children in such a way as to eradicate their identities as Indigenous peoples. The education system did this only with those children who were thought (by white Australian authorities) to 'pass' in white society. The others were given little to no formal education at all, while attempts were still made to separate them from their traditional social identities (e.g., through religious conversion). The education system, thus, became a social identity battleground between powerful (white) and powerless (Indigenous) Australians. The conflict was not between subgroups (e.g., doctors/students, bullies/victims) but between the educational institutions themselves and those they were purportedly educating. And the conflict was not one that occurred in a benign educational context; it occurred *because* of the educational context – the identities and educational contexts did, indeed, manage the conflict, but in a way that actively promoted and perpetuated it.

In these four chapters that consider conflict management, the authors all take an intergroup approach to their chosen problem. In doing so, they have armed themselves with the conceptual and empirical tools offered by the social identity approach in its analysis of intergroup conflict and conflict resolution. These include an examination of social identity management strategies (e.g., ingroup favouritism); social identifications and the meaning of those identifications (in terms of stereotype content and social norms); the hierarchical structure (i.e., relative inclusiveness) of these identities, intergroup status and power differences, the legitimacy of these differences, and the permeability of group boundaries.

Facilitating change

The final theme that emerges from the analyses within this volume is that of facilitating change, both within the individual and at a broader societal level. At an individual level, Smith, Louis and Tarrant (Chapter 9) recognise, as many of the current authors do, that student identities are imbued with particular meanings. Importantly, these meanings are often quite broad in scope, spanning *beyond* the domains of learning, studying and the classroom *per se*. It is with this recognition that Smith *et al.* begin their analysis of change promotion among university students. They observe, specifically, that the normative content of what it means to be a university student includes, at least among the students themselves, *unhealthy* behaviour such as binge drinking. Smith *et al.* then review an emerging body of research examining the interactive role of social identification and the normative content of that identification. When, for example, students who identify highly as students perceive the student identity as containing, in part, the norm of binge drinking, they are more likely to do this themselves (note the similarities with the work of Smyth *et al.*, this volume, in the domain of learning approaches). This type of normative influence occurs regardless of whether the norms are descriptive or prescriptive. Fortunately, Smith *et al.* are also able to identify similar patterns for more healthy behaviours. Their lesson is, as we have seen throughout this review of chapters, that the content of people's social identities is very important in guiding behaviour. In the case of Smith *et al.*'s analysis, this content can be the basis for promoting change in health-related behaviours among students through positively changing and managing the very meaning of student.

Rich, Mavor and Webb (Chapter 19) challenge the reader to move beyond a social identity analysis to consider other discursive ways of understanding identity construction. They seek to bridge real and apparent theoretical chasms through an analysis of the construction of teachers' identities. In doing so, they identify common (or at least similar) principles and parameters between the social identity approach and post-structuralist analyses of self and identity. As Rich *et al.* point out, both approaches emphasise the importance and influence of the social context in constructing self and self-processes, the nature of social power and intergroup relations within these contexts, and the complete rejection of a reified individual self. By illustrating their argument through an analysis of the dynamic nature of teacher identity, they demonstrate how change is, essentially, inherent in self, a constituent part that is inseparable from the concept. Indeed, they emphasise this point even further by noting that self is understood more as a verb than a noun in post-structuralist analyses. Their analysis is powerful not only in its conceptual rigour but also in the tools it provides practitioners seeking change both within teachers and within students. It normalises change and it identifies causal social-structural variables that affect this change while broadening our conceptual arsenal through integrating these two often divergent approaches.

Finally, Thomas, McGarty, Stuart, Lala and Pedersen (Chapter 8) remind us that the very contexts in which students learn can be the crucibles of broader social change. Like the two previous chapters examining change promotion, Thomas *et al.* begin by focusing on processes that can change self and social identity. In their analysis, they consider the development of civic identities in both formal (e.g., the classroom) *and* informal (e.g., extracurricular) learning contexts. They then demonstrate how the normative content of these civic identities can yield behaviours oriented toward broader social change. As an example, one of the lines of research they review employs particular practices within classroom settings to develop a civic identity that is imbued with an anti-prejudice norm. The practice is complex and is fraught with potential stumbling blocks. However, in addition to this single classroom practice, Thomas *et al.* offer at least two other major sets of practices that allow students to develop a new social identity and to *learn* a specific normative content to that identity.

Conclusion

In some ways, this book represents the completion of a historical cycle in the analysis of learning and education. Self was, of course, a psychological concept with which John Dewey (1916/2005) had to contend in his analysis of education and democracy precisely 100 years prior to the completion of the current volume. He grappled with the notion of the self in the construction of beliefs and knowledge – not just a personal self, but a larger self based upon relations with others. And although, as we noted from the outset, self and identity have maintained a presence in the education literature over the years, a contemporary and detailed psychological deconstruction and subsequent reconstruction of these concepts *applied to the context of education* has been sorely missed. Indeed, psychology had a long period in which it turned its back on analyses of the self at all. When the analyses did return, they either failed to be applied to learning and education (e.g., Kashima, Foddy and Platow, 2002) or they remained highly individualistic in nature, focusing primarily on a personal self without recognition of – or, indeed, explicitly arguing against (e.g., Gaertner, Sedikides and Graetz, 1999) – an equally valid social self defined by valued group memberships.

This book, then, brings us back to Dewey's grappling, hopefully this time with a deeper understanding of the nature of both personal and social identities and of the roles they play in learning and education. As we have seen in the brief review of chapters above, at times, personal and social identities play important *moderating* roles by placing qualifications or limiting factors on otherwise simple processes (e.g., specific behaviour may emerge for those with higher rather than lower social identifications). At other times, personal and social identities play important *mediating* roles by serving, effectively, as the conduit through which specific inputs (e.g., learning approaches) produce specific outcomes (e.g., relative academic success). At the same time, of course, we do not offer this book as the definitive statement on self and identity in educational contexts. It is offered, instead, and should be taken as being informative with the goal of opening and expanding novel integrations between psychology and education for the mutual benefit of both. It is both a review of contemporary work in the area and a treatise of sorts, outlining a set of conceptual and empirical tools for practice and research. We truly hope that educators as well as psychologists, students and teachers will find value, insight and guidance in the chapters that follow.

References

Abouserie, R. (1995). Self-esteem and achievement motivation as determinants of students' approaches to studying. *Studies in Higher Education, 20*(1), 19–26.

Berndsen, M., McGarty, C., Van der Pligt, J. and Spears, R. (2001). Meaning-seeking in the illusory correlation paradigm: The active role of participants in the categorization process. *British Journal of Social Psychology, 40*(2), 209–33.

Biggs, J. B. (1987). *Student approaches to learning and studying.* Melbourne: Australian Council for Educational Research.

Billington, T. and Williams, T. (2015). Education and psychology: Change at last? In I. Parker (Ed.), *Handbook of critical psychology* (pp. 231–9). London: Routledge.

Bird, L. (1999). Towards a more critical educational psychology. *Annual Review of Critical Psychology, 1,* 21–33.

Bredo, E. (1997). The social construction of learning. In G. D. Phye (Ed.), *Handbook of academic learning: Construction of knowledge* (pp. 3–45). San Diego, CA: Academic Press.

Bruner, J. S. (1957). On perceptual readiness. *Psychological Review, 64*(2), 123–52.

Bruner, J. S. (1966). *Toward a theory of instruction.* New York: Norton.

Bruner, J. S. (1990). *Acts of meaning.* Cambridge, MA: Harvard University Press.

Bruner, J. S., Goodnow, J. J. and Austin, G. A. (1956). *A study of thinking.* New York: Chapman and Hall.

Dewey, J. (1916/2005). *Democracy and education.* Stilwell, KS: Digireads.com.

Doise, W. (1978). *Groups and individuals: Explanations in social psychology.* (D. Graham, Trans.). Cambridge: Cambridge University Press (original work published 1976).

Entwistle, N. (1997). Contrasting perspectives on learning. In F. Marton, D. Hounsell and N. Entwistle (Eds), *The experience of learning: Implications for teaching and studying in higher education* (2nd ed., pp. 3–22). Edinburgh: Scottish Academic Press.

Fiske, S. T. and Taylor, S. E. (1984). *Social cognition.* Reading, MA: Addison-Wesley.

Gaertner, L., Sedikides, C. and Graetz, K. (1999). In search of self-definition: Motivational primacy of the individual self, motivational primacy of the collective self, or contextual primacy? *Journal of Personality and Social Psychology, 76*(1), 5–18.

Grace, D. M., David, B. J. and Ryan, M. K. (2008). Investigating preschoolers' categorical thinking about gender through imitation, attention, and the use of self-categories. *Child Development, 79*(6), 1928–41.

Greenwald, A. G., Banaji, M. R., Rudman, L. A., Farnham, S. D., Nosek, B. A. and Mellott, D. S. (2002). A unified theory of implicit attitudes, stereotypes, self-esteem, and self-concept. *Psychological Review, 109*(1), 3–25.

Haslam, S. A. (2004). *Psychology in organizations: The social identity approach* (2nd ed.). London: Sage.

Haslam, S. A., Postmes, T. and Ellemers, N. (2003). More than a metaphor: Organizational identity makes organizational life possible. *British Journal of Management, 14*(4), 357–69.

Haslam, S. A., Powell, C. and Turner, J. C. (2000). Social identity, self-categorization, and work motivation: Rethinking the contribution of the group to positive and sustainable organisational outcomes. *Applied Psychology, 49*(3), 319–39.

Haslam, S. A., Reicher, S. and Platow, M. J. (2011). *The new psychology of leadership: Identity, influence and power.* London: Psychology Press.

Haslam, S. A., van Knippenberg, D., Platow, M. J. and Ellemers, N. (Eds). (2003). *Social identity at work: Developing theory for organisational practice.* New York: Psychology Press.

Hogg, M. A., Hardie, E. A. and Reynolds, K. J. (1995). Prototypical similarity, self-categorization, and depersonalized attraction: A perspective on group cohesiveness. *European Journal of Social Psychology, 25*(2), 159–77.

Jetten, J., Branscombe, N. R., Schmitt, M. T. and Spears, R. (2001). Rebels with a cause: Group identification as a response to perceived discrimination from the mainstream. *Personality and Social Psychology Bulletin, 27*(9), 1204–13.

Jetten, J., Haslam, C. and Haslam, S. A. (Eds). (2012). *The social cure: Identity, health and well-being.* New York: Psychology Press.

Kashima, Y., Foddy, M. and Platow, M. J. (Eds). (2002). *Self and identity: Personal, social and symbolic.* Mahwah, NJ: Laurence Erlbaum Associates.

Kuznetsov, A. and Kuznetsova, O. (2011). Looking for ways to increase student motivation: Internationalisation and value innovation. *Higher Education Quarterly, 65*(4), 353–67.

Kwan, A. (2009). Problem-based learning. In M. Tight, K. H. Mok, J. Huisman and C. Morphew (Eds), *The Routledge international handbook of higher education* (pp. 91–108). New York: Routledge.

McGarty, C. (1999). *Categorization and social psychology.* London: Sage.

McGarty, C., Haslam, S. A., Hutchinson, K. J. and Turner, J. C. (1994). The effects of salient group memberships on persuasion. *Small Group Research, 25*(2), 267–93.

Oakes, P. J. (1987). The salience of social categories. In J. C. Turner, M. A. Hogg, P. J. Oakes, S. D. Reicher and M. S. Wetherell (Eds), *Rediscovering the social group: A self-categorization theory* (pp. 117–41). Oxford: Blackwell.

Oakes, P. J. and Haslam, S. A. (2001). Distortion v. meaning: Categorization on trial for inciting intergroup hatred. In M. Augoustinos and K. J. Reynolds (Eds), *Understanding prejudice, racism and social conflict* (pp. 179–94). London: Sage.

Oakes, P. J., Haslam, S. A. and Turner, J. C. (1994). *Stereotyping and social reality.* Oxford: Blackwell.

Onorato, R. S. and Turner, J. C. (2004). Fluidity in the self-concept: The shift from personal to social identity. *European Journal of Social Psychology, 34*(3), 257–78.

Pajares, F. and Schunk, D. H. (2002). Self and self-belief in psychology and education: A historical perspective. In J. Aronson (Ed.), *Improving academic achievement: Impact of psychological factors on education* (pp. 3–21). San Diego, CA: Academic Press.

Platow, M. J. (2007). On the social psychology of social influence and persuasion: Thinking and identity. *Alternative Dispute Resolution Bulletin, 9*(10), 188–92.

Platow, M. J., Hunter, J. A., Haslam, S. A. and Reicher, S. D. (2015). Reflections on Muzafer Sherif's legacy in social identity and self-categorization theories. In A. Dost-Gözkan and D. S. Keith (Eds), *Norms, groups, conflict, and social change: Rediscovering Muzafer Sherif's psychology* (pp. 275–305). London: Transaction Publications.

Platow, M. J., Mavor, K. I. and Grace, D. M. (2013). On the role of discipline-related self-concept in deep and surface approaches to learning among university students. *Instructional Science*, 41(2), 271–85.

Platow, M. J., Voudouris, N. J., Gilbert, N., Jamieson, R., Najdovski, L., Papaleo, N., Pollard, C. and Terry, L. (2007). In-group reassurance in a pain setting produces lower levels of physiological arousal: Direct support for a self-categorization analysis of social influence. *European Journal of Social Psychology*, 37(4), 649–60.

Prosser, M. and Trigwell, K. (1999). *Understanding learning and teaching: The experience of higher education*. Buckingham: Society for Research into Higher Education and Open University Press.

Ramsden, P. (2003). *Learning to teach in higher education* (2nd ed.). London: RoutledgeFalmer.

Reicher, S., Haslam, S. A. and Hopkins, N. (2005). Social identity and the dynamics of leadership: Leaders and followers as collaborative agents in the transformation of social reality. *The Leadership Quarterly*, 16(4), 547–68.

Robinson, W. P. (Ed.). (1996). *Social groups and identities: Developing the legacy of Henri Tajfel*. Oxford: Butterworth Heinemann.

Rodicio, H. G., Sánchez, E. and Acuña, S. R. (2013). Support for self-regulation in learning complex topics from multimedia explanations: Do learners need extensive or minimal support? *Instructional Science*, 41(3), 539–53.

Schmeck, R. R., Geisler-Brenstein, E. and Cercy, S. P. (1991). Self-concept and learning: The revised inventory of learning processes. *Educational Psychology: An International Journal of Experimental Educational Psychology*, 11(3–4), 343–62.

Soltis, J. F. (1984). On the nature of educational research. *Educational Researcher*, 13(10), 5–10.

Songer, N. B. and Linn, M. C. (2006). How do students' views of science influence knowledge integration? *Journal of Research in Science Teaching*, 28(9), 761–84.

Tajfel, H. and Turner, J. C. (1986). The social identity theory of intergroup behaviour. In S. Worchel and W. G. Austin (Eds), *Psychology of intergroup relations* (pp. 7–24). Chicago, IL: Nelson-Hall.

Tang, K.-S., Delgado, C. and Moje, E. B. (2014). An integrative framework for the analysis of multiple and multimodal representations for meaning-making in science education. *Issues in Science Education*, 98(2), 305–26.

Terry, D. J., Hogg, M. A. and White, K. M. (1999). The theory of planned behaviour: Self-identity, social identity and group norms. *British Journal of Social Psychology*, 38(3), 225–44.

Thomas, C. R. and Gadbois, S. A. (2007). Academic self-handicapping: The role of self-concept clarity and students' learning strategies. *British Journal of Educational Psychology*, 77(1), 101–19.

Trautwein, U., Lüdtke, O., Köller, O. and Baumert, J. (2006). Self-esteem, academic self-concept, and achievement: How the learning environment moderates the dynamics of self-concept. *Journal of Personality and Social Psychology*, 90(2), 334–49.

Turner, J. C., Hogg, M. A., Oakes, P. J., Reicher, S. D. and Wetherell, M. S. (1987). *Rediscovering the social group: A self-categorization theory*. Oxford: Blackwell.

Wintre, M. G., Dilouya, B., Pancer, S. M., Pratt, M. W., Birnie-Lefcovitch, S., Polivy, J. and Adams, G. (2011). Academic achievement in first-year university: Who maintains their high school average? *Higher Education*, 62(4), 467–81.

Zimmerman, B. J. (2000). Self-efficacy: An essential motive to learn. *Contemporary Educational Psychology*, 25(1), 82–91.

2

THE SOCIAL IDENTITY APPROACH TO EDUCATION AND LEARNING

Identification, ideation, interaction, influence and ideology

S. Alexander Haslam

> With the renewal of physical existence goes, in the case of human beings,
> the re-creation of beliefs, ideals, hopes, happiness, misery, and practices. The
> continuity of any experience, through renewing of the social group, is a
> literal fact. Education, in its broadest sense, is the means of this continuity of
> life. . . . Each individual, each unit who is the carrier of the life-experience
> of his group, in time passes away. Yet the life of the group goes on.
>
> (Dewey, 1916, p. 3)

Introduction

As John Dewey's well-known treatise makes clear, education and learning are not
just central processes in group life – they are *the* central processes through which
group life endures. Accordingly, it makes sense that any psychological analysis of
group life should have a concern with education at its core. And yet, in the face
of these two statements, two startling facts stand out. First, the body of contemporary psychological theory which is most clearly associated with clarifying the
psychological reality and significance of the social group – namely, the large
corpus of work informed by social identity theorising (after Tajfel and Turner,
1979) – has hitherto had relatively little to say about education. Second, as a
result, the field of education has not been able to profit from social identity theorising in ways that Dewey's observation might lead us to expect it could. In line
with the goals of this volume as a whole, these are omissions that the present
chapter sets out to rectify, showing not only why education and learning are
essential topics for social identity theorists but also why social identity theorising
is an essential resource for educationalists.

Education-based learning is a fundamentally collaborative endeavour that
centres on the capacity for individuals to participate in self-development through

more or less constructive engagement with instructors and instructional systems. From the outset, it is important to acknowledge that this collaboration is no mean feat. Indeed, given the manifest dissimilarities (e.g., in power, status, expertise, age, experience) that routinely exist between teachers and learners, one might well wonder how it is that knowledge and skills – and, more particularly, the motivation to use them as a basis for *agentic self-expansion* – are ever passed on from one to the other. Consequently, as Vygotsky (1978) recognises (e.g., in his writings on the importance of the *zone of proximal development*; Chaiklin, 2003), understanding the psychological underpinnings of this accomplishment stands as something of a master problem for the field of educational psychology – if not psychology as a whole.

At the heart of our analysis is a claim that this capacity for knowledge co-production is grounded in the dynamic apprehension of shared group membership – such that the success (or otherwise) of the educational process is contingent upon educational participants seeing themselves as sharing social identity (a sense of 'us'). In the face of what would otherwise be insurmountable dissimilarity, we argue that it is this internalised (but often taken for granted) theory of the group that serves to structure the experience of key parties in the educational process in ways that ensure their interests are psychologically aligned. On the one hand, it means that instructors impart training in ways that are tailored to the goals of the groups with which they identify. On the other hand, individual learners engage with learning as a consequence of their understanding that instructors – and the systems in which they are embedded – embody identity-related developmental goals that they seek to attain. Moreover, to the extent that the social identities of diverse parties are constructively aligned in this way (Biggs, 1996), this promotes forms of collective self-continuity that ensure the sustainability of the group as a whole.

Yet before we can flesh out these claims in detail, or have a reasonable chance of convincing readers of their utility, we first need to sketch out the key tenets of the social identity theorising that underpins them. These speak to the capacity for groups to inform individuals' sense of self and for this to provide the psychological substrates for all forms of group behaviour – of which education is one. We then expand upon this analysis by showing – with the help of evidence presented elsewhere in this volume – how social identity processes bear in essential ways upon key aspects of the educational process. Here, we see, first, that social *identification* is a basis for learners to engage with instructors and instructional systems and vice versa; second, that social identity *ideation* informs the ways in which they do this; third, that these understandings are consolidated through identity-based educational *interaction*; fourth, that social identity provides a basis for teachers and learners to engage in mutual *influence*; and fifth, that their activities as a whole are structured by identity-related *ideology* that defines key parameters of intra- and inter-group relations.

By this means, a key goal of this contribution is to show how social identity serves to make education – and the learning this entails – meaningful, purposeful and successful. Yet following J. C. Turner (1982), a more radical goal is to pursue the case that it is social identity that makes education both *necessary* and *possible*. At the same time, once we acknowledge this, we see that education is not 'just another' domain in which social identity rears its head. Rather it is a (perhaps *the*) key arena in which public notions of 'who we are' and 'what we want to be' are both tested and contested and thereby the key site for the construction of community-relevant social identities (McLeod and Yates, 2006). And it is as a result of this that education constitutes the primary forge in which the material structures of society are produced and reproduced, formed and reformed.

The social identity approach

The claims that we want to make about the relevance of social identity for matters of education and learning are clearly quite ambitious. Accordingly, it makes sense to set about the task of developing these by summarising some of the key tenets of the two theories which together comprise the social identity approach: *social identity theory* (Tajfel and Turner, 1979) and *self-categorisation theory* (J. C. Turner, Hogg, Oakes, Reicher and Wetherell, 1987; J. C. Turner, Oakes, Haslam and McGarty, 1994; for relevant source material, see Postmes and Branscombe, 2010).

Social identity theory

Social identity theory's starting point is to assert that in a range of social contexts, people's sense of self – who they think they are and, hence, how they act – is determined not so much by their individuality (their *personal identity*) as by the groups to which they belong and by the internalised sense of *social identity* that they derive from those group memberships. It also suggests that when people's sense of self is defined by a given social identity (e.g., as 'us Australians' or 'us Princeton students'; or as 'Ann, the Australian' or 'Paul, the Princeton student'), this leads to behaviour that is qualitatively distinct from behaviour that is informed by personal identity. In particular, this is because when people define themselves in terms of social identity, they strive to achieve or maintain a positive view of themselves by positively differentiating their ingroup from comparison outgroups on valued dimensions. This quest for *positive group distinctiveness* means that when people think of themselves in terms of 'we' and 'us' rather than 'I' and 'me', they want to see 'us' as different from and better than 'them' in order to feel good about who they are and what they do.

However, achieving positive distinctiveness is not always easy. This is especially true for members of low-status groups in a world that seems to affirm their inferiority. For example, if you are a student at a community college with a bad reputation or in the bottom class at school, it may be hard to construe that group membership as positive – especially in a system that rewards, affirms and valorises the achievements of elite groups (e.g., the Ivy League, Oxbridge, top classes). Social identity theory asserts that in the face of such challenges, people can pursue a range of strategies in order to achieve a positive identity and that the specific strategy they pursue will vary as a function of their understanding of the prevailing *social structure*. Here the theory focuses on the importance of three structural elements: the perceived *permeability* of group boundaries and the perceived *stability* and *legitimacy* of the ingroup's position in relation to other groups (Tajfel and Turner, 1979; see also Ellemers, 1993; Ellemers and Haslam, 2012).

If members of low-status groups believe that group boundaries are *permeable*, such that it is possible to leave the group and join a better one, then this is what they will try to do – through a strategy of *individual mobility*. For example, if students in a low form think they may be able to join a higher one by studying harder, then they will be inclined to put in the effort to try to make this happen. If parents believe that they can improve their child's educational (and life) prospects by moving to a house in the catchment area of a better school, then this is something they may do (Noreisch, 2007).

However, if group boundaries are impermeable, it makes no sense to try to escape the negative implications of membership of a low-status group by investing energy in strategies of individual mobility. So, for example, in rural areas where catchment areas of better schools are less accessible than is the case in inner cities, family relocation may not be a realistic option (Parsons Chalkley and Jones, 2000). Under these conditions, it makes more sense for members of the low-status group to band together and act collectively in terms of their shared social identity with a view to improving the conditions of their ingroup as a whole. If status relations appear to be both stable and legitimate (i.e., *secure*), it is predicted that low-status group members will try to redefine the meaning of the comparative context through a process of *social creativity*. They might do this, for example, by endorsing the view that 'we may not be as smart as them, but we have more fun' or 'they may be more academic, but we are more in touch with the real world'. Indeed, it can lead to devaluation of and disengagement from formal education more generally. This can be seen, for example, in Willis' (1977) influential ethnographic study of working-class schoolboys in 'Hammertown' (a town in the British Midlands) who differentiated themselves, as down-to-earth 'lads', from the higher-achieving middle-class 'earoles' in the process of turning away from the world view that their school embodied. Likewise, educational institutions that find themselves performing poorly on league tables will be motivated to re-engineer those tables in ways that present them in a better light (e.g., by redefining inclusion criteria or dimensions of comparison; Elsbach and Kramer, 1996; for an example in the sporting arena, see Platow, Hunter, Branscombe and Grace, 2014).

Yet if status relations are impermeable but *in*secure – either because they are seen as illegitimate or as liable to change (or both) – members of low-status groups are more likely to engage in *social competition* with the high-status outgroup. This will involve acting collectively in a manner designed to bring about change to the status quo (in ways that individual and social creativity do not). This is what happened, for example, when women who were denied access to universities (or to exclusive university societies) banded together to protest for equal educational rights at the turn of the twentieth century (Solomon, 1985) and when black students and their supporters lobbied for equal educational rights and for an end to educational segregation in the United States another half-century later (Kluger, 2011).

A large body of research has tested these various predictions and clarified their implications for a range of social phenomena (e.g., Ellemers, 1993; Jetten, Haslam, Cruwys and Branscombe, in press). Much of this work has direct relevance for educational issues and contexts. For example, experimental work by Wright and his colleagues has shown that in a student hierarchy comprising high–status 'sophisticated decision-makers' and low–status 'unsophisticated decision-makers', members of low–status groups are far more likely to pursue strategies of conflict when access to the high–status group is impossible and the behaviour of that group appears illegitimate. Yet when the high–status group makes it possible for low–status group members to be promoted, members of the low–status group are far less likely to challenge the status quo – even if only a few token individuals are thus elevated – because the slightest possibility of promotion implies that group boundaries are permeable (Wright, 1997; Wright, Taylor and Moghaddam, 1990; see also Reicher and Haslam, 2006).

Amongst other things, such work underlines the point that the social identities that underpin group behaviour are *psychological* rather than sociological or biological and that they reflect people's *subjective beliefs* about their own group membership and the social structure within which it is embedded rather than objective demographic realities (Platow, Haslam, Reicher and Steffens, 2015; Platow, Hunter, Haslam and Reicher, 2015). Thus, whether one behaves as a woman, say, is not simply a matter of *being* a woman but, rather, depends critically upon whether this social identity is subjectively meaningful in the context at hand.

Self-categorisation theory

Yet while social identity theory speaks to the importance of social identity for social behaviour in intergroup contexts, the theory presents no general hypotheses either about *when* people will define themselves as members of a specific group or about the *consequences* of self-definition in group-based terms. These, though, are central concerns for self-categorisation theory, which builds upon social identity theory through three key insights. The first of these, to which we have already alluded, is that it is social identity that makes group behaviour *possible* (J. C. Turner, 1982). For example, it is only when, and to the extent that, people at a given educational institution define themselves in terms of a shared group membership (as 'us members of College X') that they are able to work together as a group in order to advance their collective interests (e.g., by supporting the college football team, organising reunions, making charitable donations; Mael and Ashforth, 1992).

A second core insight is that the self system reflects the operation of a *context-sensitive (self-)categorisation process* in which, within a given social setting, people see themselves as sharing category membership with others to a greater or lesser extent (J. C. Turner, 1982). Whether, and which, social identities become an operative basis for self-definition – such that they are psychologically *salient* – is argued to be an interactive product of the *fit* of a specific categorisation and a person's *readiness* to use it (Oakes, Haslam and Turner, 1994). For example, a group of people are more likely to define themselves as Arts students (sharing category membership with other Arts students and behaving like them) if this self-categorisation is consistent with patterns of perceived similarity and difference between Arts students and other groups in the context at hand (e.g., in their Arts-related behaviour) and if they have used this group as a basis for self-definition in the past (e.g., when participating in Arts events; Oakes, Turner and Haslam, 1991).

Following up on these ideas, a third insight is that shared social identity is the basis for *mutual social influence* (J. C. Turner, 1991). This means that when people perceive themselves as sharing group membership with others in a given context, they are motivated to strive actively to reach agreement with them and to coordinate their behaviour through activity that promotes their shared identity-relevant interests. They do this because, here, they recognise those 'others' as 'self' and, hence, see them as qualified to inform both their own perceptions and their actions. For example, if a young schoolgirl defines herself primarily as a girl, then her behaviour will be shaped primarily by the views and actions of other members of that ingroup (i.e., other girls) because they, unlike members of other groups, are in a position to speak to who she is and what she wants to be; however, if she defines herself as a student, then she will be more open to the influence of both girls and boys (Grace, David and Ryan, 2008; Platow *et al.*, 2007; see also Platow, Mills and Morrison, 2000; for discussion related to school cliques, see Adler and Adler, 1995; Kandel, 1978).

For this reason, shared social identity can be seen as the basis for all forms of productive social interaction between people – including leadership, motivation, communication, cooperation, helping, trust and organisation (Ellemers, De Gilder and Haslam, 2004; Foddy, Platow and Yamagishi, 2009; S. A. Haslam, 2001; S. A. Haslam, Postmes and Ellemers, 2003; J. C. Turner and Haslam, 2001). Clearly, too, all of these processes are relevant to the social dynamics of education and learning, in ways that we elaborate on more fully below. If one reflects, for example, on interactions between teachers and students, then self-categorisation theory leads us to expect that these should be more productive to the extent that these interactions are informed by a sense of shared group member-ship (e.g., as members of the same school community). Amongst other things, this helps to explain why educational activities that attempt to span chronic self-categorical fault lines (e.g., involving highly salient differences in ethnicity, culture, place and class) often prove less effective and less satisfactory than those that do not (e.g., along the lines of Burford and Rosenthal-Stott's discussion of doctor–patient communication, Chapter 16, this volume; see Fine *et al.*, 2004; Fleer, 2006; Krause, 2009; Sidanius, Van Laar, Levin and Sinclair, 2004). At the same time, it is important to stress that self-categorisation theory argues that the form and content of self-categories (i.e., the boundaries of 'us' and 'them') are not fixed but, rather, can be renegotiated in response to changes in social context (S. A. Haslam and Turner, 1992; J. C. Turner *et al.*, 1994). Accordingly, there is no sense in which suboptimal outcomes are an inevitable consequence of people's internalisation of particular subjective understandings of self and other.

Unpacking the significance of social identity for education and learning: the five 'I's

Over the last four decades, the above ideas have been subjected to rigorous and extensive scrutiny – mainly by experimental social psychologists who have been interested in testing and elaborating the various hypotheses at the core of the social identity approach. As some indication of the scale of this endeavour, according to Google Scholar, to date, Tajfel and Turner's (1979) original statement of social identity theory has been cited over 13,000 times, and the book in which self-categorisation theory was first outlined – *Rediscovering the Social Group* (J. C. Turner *et al.*, 1987) – has been cited over 10,000 times. Increasingly, too, it is apparent that researchers and practitioners have been interested in the applied relevance of the approach for disciplines and fields well beyond psychology (Haslam, 2014). Indeed, the findings of a survey by Postmes and Branscombe (2010) suggest that around half of the citations to the above publications are found in non-social-psychological outlets.

Nevertheless, the impact of social identity theorising has primarily been felt in organisational, clinical and political fields (e.g., see S. A. Haslam, 2004; Jetten, Haslam and Haslam, 2012; Reicher, 2004), and as we noted at the start of this chapter, it is apparent that only a small fraction of applied social identity research has been conducted in the domain of education. For example, according to Web of Science, less than 2 per cent of the citations to Tajfel and Turner's work have been made in educational outlets. Nevertheless, as the various contributions to this volume attest, there is growing interest in exploring social identity principles at work in educational spheres. Accordingly, having sketched out the theoretical underpinnings of this approach, it is instructive to reflect more directly on its relevance to processes of education and learning.

Identification

One of the fundamental principles of social identity theorising is that group membership will only have an impact upon individuals' behaviour to the extent that it is internalised into their sense of self as part of their social identity – so that 'we' becomes part of 'me'. Indeed, Tajfel's definition of social identity as 'the individual's knowledge that he [or she] belongs to certain social groups together with some emotional and value significance to him [or her] of this group membership' (1972, p. 292) makes it clear that a group membership needs to be psychologically significant for a person in order for it to have psychological (and behavioural) impact on them.

This point was confirmed in some of the original laboratory studies out of which social identity theory developed. These *minimal group studies* involved schoolboys being asked to assign points (signifying small sums of money) to members of two different groups – one to which they apparently belonged and one to which they did not (Tajfel, Flament, Billig and Bundy, 1971). The groups had no prior meaning (being based on things such as liking for abstract paintings that the boys did not know), and yet the boys used them as a basis for their behaviour – generally giving more points to boys who were in their own group (the ingroup) than they did to those who were in the other group (the outgroup). Importantly, though, subsequent studies demonstrated that this pattern of ingroup favouritism was only shown by participants who *identified* with the minimal groups to which they had been assigned. Those who did not were 'left cold' by the minimal group procedure and it had little impact on their behaviour (Gagnon and Bourhis, 1996; see Spears and Otten, 2012).

This same point also holds in the world of groups outside the laboratory, where social identification proves to be a more or less universal moderator of group-based social behaviour. For example, while people tend generally to like and trust ingroups more than outgroups, to feel more connected to their members, and to communicate and work better with them, these effects are more marked for high identifiers than for low identifiers (for reviews, see Haslam, 2001; Ellemers, Spears and Doosje, 1999).

Turning to the field of education, it makes sense that social identification should also be an important determinant of group-based behaviour in this domain. In particular, whether or not people engage with a given educational entity and with the activities that this entails should be contingent upon them identifying with that entity such that it comes to define their sense of self.

In the case of students, this is a point that is borne out by much of the research covered in various contributions to this volume. For example, longitudinal research by Reynolds and colleagues shows that students' identification with their school is a very good predictor of their engagement with the school and that increases in identification also predict increases in engagement (Reynolds, Subasic, Lee and Bromhead, Chapter 3, this volume). Likewise, in a study that examines students transitioning to university, Iyer and colleagues observe that coming to identify with university is a key predictor of the extent to which students engage with and enjoy university life (Jetten, Iyer and Zhang, Chapter 6, this volume; Iyer, Jetten, Tsivrikos, Postmes and Haslam, 2009). Importantly, too, institutional identification is shown to have significant consequences for key educational indicators – not least, high school grades and degree programme continuation.

Social identification is also an important determinant of how students treat others and how they feel as a result. Thus I. Turner and colleagues show that high school students are far less likely to bully each other if they have (or develop) a sense of shared social identity (I.Turner, Reynolds, Lee, Subasic and Bromhead, 2014). In ways anticipated by 'social cure' research (e.g., S. A. Haslam, Jetten, Postmes and Haslam, 2009; Jetten *et al.*, 2012), this also feeds into positive psychological health such that institutional identification predicts lower levels of anxiety and depression in both high school and university samples (Bizumic, Reynolds, Turner, Bromhead and Subasic, 2009; Iyer *et al.*, 2009). Such benefits also appear more pronounced to the extent that students identify with multiple sources of social identity in an educational context (Jetten *et al.*, 2015).

What is true for students is also true for those who instruct them. Support for this claim emerges from programmatic work with German schoolteachers conducted by van Dick, Wagner and colleagues (Christ, van Dick, Wagner and Stellmacher, 2003; van Dick and Wagner, 2001). First, this found that the teachers' identification with relevant collectives (e.g., those in their profession, school or department) was the key predictor of their willingness to support the activities of that collective and to 'go the extra mile' through relevant acts of organisational citizenship that underpinned collective success (e.g., attending conferences, helping colleagues in need; Christ *et al.*, 2003). Second, this work found that social identification predicted how teachers felt about their work as well as their well-being and health more generally. Thus, occupational and team identification were both good predictors of psychological health (e.g., stress and strain; van Dick and Wagner, 2001) and self-reported physical health (e.g., complaints of head-aches, neck and shoulder pain, weariness; van Dick and Wagner, 2002).

Perhaps most importantly, however, it is apparent that social identification is implicated in the process of learning that lies at the heart of education. This is seen clearly in the aligned research of Bliuc and colleagues (Bliuc, Goodyear and Ellis, Chapter 12, this volume; Bliuc, Ellis, Goodyear and Muntele Hendres, 2011a, 2011b) and Smyth, Platow and colleagues (Smyth, Mavor and Platow and Grace, Chapter 13, this volume; Platow, Mavor and Grace, 2013). This shows that social identification is often a key predictor of students' willingness to embrace a deep rather than a surface approach to learning tasks – itself a key predictor of long-term academic success (McCune and Entwistle, 2011). Along related lines, programmatic work by Bjerregaard and colleagues found that when professional care workers acquired qualifications to improve their on-the-job skills, the primary reason why this served to improve their work motivation (and their well-being) was that it helped to build a sense of shared social identity among co-workers (both as members of the same team and as members of the same organisation; Bjerregaard, Haslam, Morton and Ryan, 2015). Moreover, this research examined trainees' *motivation to transfer* training into their everyday work (Noe, 1986) and found that this motivation was only apparent when training tapped into, and helped build, a sense of shared social identity among trainees. In this case, this occurred when training was delivered face-to-face but not when it was delivered remotely via video link (Bjerregaraard, Haslam and Morton, 2016).

There are two interrelated reasons why social identification is so important for learning. First, when students' identity is defined by their educational group membership, the motivation to advance that group membership through learning is *intrinsic* rather than *extrinsic* (Platow *et al.*, 2013). As a result, the motivation to learn becomes internalised, and the pursuit of learning is driven by internal agency rather than external expectancy. Second, under conditions of shared identification, the motivation to engage deeply with a prescribed process of self-development follows from the learners' sense that the instructor (and the collective they represent) is qualified to inform them about the self (Ellemers *et al.*, 2004; Haslam, Adarves-Yorno, Postmes and Jans, 2013). In this respect, seeing an instructor as part of the projected self – rather than as 'other' – is the best qualification going. Here, then, social identification serves to structure learners' goals and aspirations in ways that are seen to provide a viable framework for future expansion of the self.

As well as showing that identification is important for learning, other contributions to this volume serve to flag some of the different *pathways* to identification that educators and educational environments can provide. In particular, Greenaway, Amiot, Louis and Bentley (Chapter 10, this volume) show that relevant forms of social identification can be promoted by institutional features that increase students' sense of self-determination (after Deci and Ryan, 2000); Cruwys, Gaffney and Skipper (Chapter 11, this volume) show that it can be promoted by a desire to resolve particular forms of uncertainty (after Hogg, 2000); while Monaghan and Bizumic (Chapter 14, this volume) show that certain individual differences (e.g., conscientiousness; after McCrae and Costa, 1997) may also play a role. It also seems likely that just as these various elements can facilitate social identification, so too they can be some of its important consequences. That is, social identification should have the capacity to encourage conscientiousness, to create (not just resolve) productive forms of uncertainty (e.g., a sense of 'needing to know more') and to promote a sense of self-determination and control (e.g., as shown by Greenaway *et al.*, 2015). Without necessarily wanting to privilege any of these elements – all of which speak in different ways to the importance of fit (Oakes *et al.*, 1994; see Burford and Rosenthal-Stott, this volume; Peters, Ryan and Haslam, 2013, 2014; Peters, Ryan, Haslam and Fernandes, 2012) – two key points made by these various lines of research are: (a) that social identification can clearly be cultivated in educational contexts (just as it can be crushed) and (b) that this has important consequences for the educational process as a whole.

Ideation

While mutual identification is critical for education, equally important is the question of what exactly teachers and students are identifying *with*. That is, what is the *ideational content* of their social identity in terms of its values, norms, morals and goals? When students think of themselves as students (e.g., at a particular institution or on a particular course), what specific meaning does this group membership have for them?

The importance of this question for learning is highlighted by research with medical students addressed in various chapters in the present volume. In the first instance, the work of McNeill, Smyth and Mavor (Chapter 18, this volume) observes that greater identification may not be associated with a deeper approach to learning among medical students, despite this being the case for other groups of tertiary students (e.g., Bliuc *et al.*, 2011a, 2011b; Platow *et al.*, 2013). This is because in medical training, discipline-specific norms encourage surface-level engagement with learning material (e.g., involving learning by rote and cramming). Accordingly, the more they identify with their ingroup, the more likely medical students are to strive to live out that identity by engaging in superficial learning practices. Likewise, work by Monrouxe and Rees (Chapter 17, this volume) shows that it is the specific moral content of medical identities that provides medical students with the framework for resolving the various ethical and professional dilemmas that they are exposed to in the course of their training. How exactly medical students behave is thus a consequence of who and what they think they are (for related evidence on this point, see Cruwys, Haslam, Fox and McMahon, 2015; Livingstone, Haslam, Postmes and Jetten, 2011; Millward and Haslam, 2013; Van Rijswijk, Haslam and Ellemers, 2006).

Essentially the same point is confirmed by studies of students more generally that examine the role of group norms in shaping motivations to engage in behaviour that is either consistent or inconsistent with (and possibly harmful for) positive educational outcomes. This is seen in the work of Cruwys *et al.* (this volume) where, as well as manipulating features of the educational context designed to promote group identification, the researchers also manipulated the content of relevant ingroup norms by suggesting to incoming university students that the ingroup they were led to identify with was primarily concerned either with education (e.g., studying and learning) or with entertainment (enjoying oneself and partying). As predicted, the more students were encouraged to identify with a group whose norms were aligned with education, the more they expressed intentions to engage in education-focused activity; but the more they were encouraged to identify with a group whose norms were aligned with entertainment, the more they expressed intentions to engage in entertainment-focused activity.

Work by Smith, Louis and Tarrant (Chapter 9, this volume; see also Tarrant, Hagger and Farrow, 2012) speaks to nuances surrounding such effects that arise from the fact that norms can be both descriptive (i.e., relating to 'what we do') and injunctive ('what we should do'). As these researchers note, people's behaviour is most likely to be in line with norms where these descriptive and normative elements are aligned. However, where they are in conflict, the descriptive norm will often trump the injunctive one. Thus, while a group may espouse an aspirational injunctive norm (e.g., 'we should party less and study more'), if identified group members sense that, in reality, their fellow group members do the opposite, it will often (but not always) be what they see (e.g., partying not studying) that determines what they do. This is a pattern that Smith and colleagues document specifically in relation to a range of health-related student behaviours (e.g., poor diet, excessive alcohol consumption; see also Howell *et al.*, 2014; Staunton, Louis, Smith, Terry and McDonald, 2014), but there is no reason to believe that it does not generalise to all realms of student behaviour, including those that bear directly upon academic performance.

This is a point that several chapters in this volume touch upon in their discussion of the way that performance on academic tests is affected by *stereotype threat* (Boucher and Murphy, Chapter 5; Burford and Rosenthal-Stott, chapter 16). Classic work on this phenomenon observes that students' performance on intellectual tasks is likely to be significantly worse than it might otherwise have been if they are made aware of stereotypes about poor performance associated with groups to which they belong. For example, Steele and Aronson (1995) found that high-achieving African-American students at Stanford University performed much worse on the graduate record exam (GRE) when they were led to believe that the exam was measuring intelligence rather than that it was not a test of ability at all. Along related lines, Beilock, Rydell and McConnell (2007) found that if female students were made aware of a stereotype that men have greater mathematical ability than women, then they tended to do worse on complex mathematical tasks than when they were not alerted to this stereotype. Similarly, work by Croizet and colleagues (e.g., Croizet and Claire, 1998; Croizet *et al.*, 2004) showed that students from working-class backgrounds performed less well in testing contexts which cue beliefs that they are intellectually inferior to their middle-class counterparts.

The standard explanation for such effects is that the performance of students from groups that stereotypically underperform in a particular domain is impeded when they become aware of the fact that their own performance may serve to confirm negative ingroup stereotypes. Amongst other things, this is because awareness of the stereotypes is seen to induce self-doubt and self-consciousness (Cadinu, Maass, Rosabianca and Kiesner, 2005). On the other hand, evidence that students from groups that stereotypically do well in a given domain perform better when they become aware of positive ingroup stereotypes is explained in terms of the capacity for awareness of ingroup stereotypes to boost performance. This is the phenomenon of *stereotype lift* (Walton and Cohen, 2003) in which awareness of the stereotypes is seen to increase confidence and 'flow'.

It is also possible, however, to explain these effects directly through the lens of self-categorisation theory – seeing academic performance as an interactive product of social identification and identity ideation (S. A. Haslam, Salvatore, Kessler and Reicher, 2008). This analysis has the advantage not only of being more parsimonious but also of connecting understanding in this area to a broader literature on the context-dependent functioning of the self process. It suggests that when, and to the extent that, people are led to define themselves in terms of a particular social identity, their behaviour will be structured by beliefs and norms pertaining to the perceived content of that identity (J. C. Turner, 1991). This explains, for example, not only why female Asian students do better on a maths test when they are led to think of themselves as Asian rather than as female (because maths performance is normative for Asians but not for women), but also why threat and lift effects are contingent upon ingroup identification (Shih, Pittinsky and Ambady, 1999; Schmader, 2002).

As Boucher and Murphy's thorough review in this volume affirms, self-categorisation principles are highly pertinent to an array of complex patterns that surround women's experience in STEM (Science, Technology, Engineering and Mathematics) subjects at school and university. Experimental research by C. Haslam and colleagues (2012) has also provided direct support for these principles among older adults. This found that participants performed much less well on generalised tests of cognitive functioning (of the form usually employed to access dementia) when they were led to self-categorise as older (rather than younger) and to believe that aging was associated with general cognitive deficits (rather than only poor memory). Moreover, this was shown to have profound practical implications insofar as 70 per cent of participants who were led to self-categorise as older and who believed being older was associated with generalised deficit subsequently performed in ways that met diagnostic criteria for dementia compared to an average of just 14 per cent in other conditions.

It is also clear that as well as having implications for 'us', identity ideation will also often have implications for 'them'. This is because, as well as regulating behaviour that is focused inwardly on the ingroup, norms and beliefs typically also have a bearing on the treatment meted out to members of relevant outgroups. At one level, these beliefs may determine who one interacts with and how much (e.g., as seen in medical students' norms for socialising more or less exclusively with other medical students; Blakey, Blanshard, Cole, Leslie and Sen, 2008; McNeill *et al.*, this volume). At another level, they determine the form and content of that interaction (Livingstone and Haslam, 2008). This is seen clearly in work on bullying of the form reviewed by Jones, Livingstone and Manstead (Chapter 4, this volume). As these researchers observe, one fundamental reason why students bully others is that they believe this behaviour to be normative for their ingroup – a point confirmed empirically in a large programme of work by Nesdale and colleagues (e.g., Nesdale, Durkin, Maass, Kiesner and Griffiths, 2008; Ojala and Nesdale, 2004). More generally, group norms also clarify what counts as bullying as well as which (and when) particular forms of bullying are legitimate (Reicher and Haslam, 2006). Accordingly, two potent ways in which interventions can help to reduce bullying (and other forms of violence and aggression towards others) involve (a) reducing students' identification with groups that condone bullying of others (Reynolds *et al.*, this volume) and/or (b) changing the content of ingroup norms in ways that serve to make various forms of bullying unacceptable (Hawkins, Farrington and Catalano, 1998; Paluck and Shepherd, 2012).

Interaction

Although social identities are psychological constructs derived from internalised group memberships, it is important to recognise that they do not relate only to the internal workings of individual minds. A key reason for this is that just as social identity allows group behaviour to occur, so too it is formed and galvanised through group behaviour (Postmes, Haslam and Swaab, 2005). Social identities are made for, and by, social interaction. As a result, learning and education are structured not only by the ideational content of social identities but also (a) by the way those identities are lived out as well as (b) by the way in which particular environments *allow* them to be lived out (or not) as a consequence of their *identity affordance*.

A large body of social identity research speaks to the ways in which group-based interaction shapes social identity and, through this, the nature of collective behaviour. In particular, work informed by the elaborated social identity model of collective action (Drury and Reicher, 1999, 2000) shows that when an authority treats a diverse group of individuals in an undifferentiated way, this can be a basis for those individuals to define themselves in terms of a shared social identity and to act together in ways that attack the perceived illegitimacy of that authority's actions (Stott and Drury, 2000). In these terms, a reason why 'blanket punishments' generally fail is that they lead those who have committed no offence to resent and challenge authorities rather than to work with them to deal with offenders. In contrast, actions that serve to position authorities and those for whom they have responsibility (e.g., teachers and students) as sharing identity tend to promote positive forms of interaction between them. These not only lead to more positive educational outcomes (e.g., see Reynolds *et al.*, this volume) but also prove more effective in tackling problem behaviour (e.g., bullying; Rigby and Griffiths, 2011).

More generally, it is apparent that because social identity is developed and galvanised through social interaction, it is often social interaction that is key to the capacity for social identities to have their impact. This is seen in work by Thomas, McGarty, Stuart, Lala and Pedersen (Chapter 8, this volume), which shows that specific educational programmes can help to promote civic responsibility and civic engagement by facilitating interaction that serves to build and consensualise identity content related to particular civic activities. More specifically, their research shows that students become much more committed to enacting particular civic policies (e.g., tackling prejudice and behaving in environmentally responsible ways) under conditions in which they are encouraged to come together in groups and interact (e.g., discuss, argue, plan) around issues of mutual normative concern (Thomas and McGarty, 2009).

Other work also shows that where individuals are encouraged to interact in ways that enhance and embed their sense of shared social identity, this serves generally to increase their social engagement and to have flow-on consequences for both their well-being and their intellectual performance (e.g., in ways suggested by Robinson, 2011). For example, in a series of three minimal group studies, Master and Walton (2013) found that very young children performed better on a cognitive task when they were encouraged to see themselves as members of a common group (a 'puzzles group') rather than as individuals ('a puzzles child') and when cognitive performance was relevant to that group membership. Likewise, in a care home setting where older adults were brought together to make decisions about the redecoration of communal living space (rather than having these decisions made for them), this led them to develop a stronger sense of shared identity and, subsequently, to use that space more and show elevated performance on measures of cognitive functioning (C. Haslam, Haslam, Knight, Gleibs, Ysseldyk and McCloskey, 2014; see also Knight, Haslam and Haslam, 2010). Significantly, too, experimental and epidemiological evidence indicates that such benefits materialise only to the extent that social interaction helps to build, maintain and advance group identities – with contact and experience that does not achieve this end having limited benefit (Cruwys *et al.*, 2014; C. Haslam, Cruwys and Haslam, 2014; C. Haslam, Cruwys, Milne, Chi-Hsin and Haslam, 2016; Sani, Herrera, Wakefield, Boroch and Gulyas, 2012).

Three key processes seem to account for these patterns and to be relevant to education more generally. First, a sense of shared social identity provides a motivation for people to see others as relevant to self and as having the capacity to enrich their lives. Second, it provides a basis to extend and stretch the self by reaching out beyond one's 'comfort zone' (in a way that interpersonal ties typically do not). Third, it provides people with the confidence to extend themselves in what might otherwise be a very threatening environment – one where opportunities for failure, ridicule and even humiliation abound (Fransen *et al.*, 2015).

Yet just as institutions and educators can allow for the enactment of positive identities, so too they can thwart that enactment or else facilitate the enactment of negative identities. In this regard, it is apparent that most educational experiences and environments contain cues as to which social identities are institutionally valorised and which are demonised. As Salmon (2003, p. 311) puts it:

> 'Knowledge' is never neutral; it carries the interests and concerns of particular sociocultural groupings. For school learners, the knowledge offered in their classrooms appears at first sight to 'belong' to the teachers who convey it. As such, it may seem attractive to some pupils for the very reasons that it seems alien to others.

Laboratory posters, for example, may communicate a sense that this is a space for enacting male identity and thereby undermine women's sense of belonging (Boucher and Murphy, Chapter 5, this volume; Cheryan, Plaut, Davies and Steele, 2009); Christmas decorations can reinforce Christian identity and thus make students of other faiths (and no faith) feel unwelcome (Schmitt, Davies, Hung and Wright, 2010); a curriculum that celebrates the culture and history of one group will tend to marginalise those who belong to another (Grace and Platow, Chapter 7, this volume); and middle-class cultural values and iconography – which are, amongst other things, implicit in the esoteric language, logic and machinery of intelligence testing (Croizet and Dutrévis, 2004) – can make those from disadvantaged backgrounds feel like outsiders in a range of educational settings (Bourdieu and Passeron, 1990; Burford and Rosenthal-Stott, this volume; Jetten *et al.*, this volume).

Again, evidence suggests that when individuals feel that they are 'in the wrong place', this will tend to undermine not only their sense of comfort and well-being but also, partly through this, their cognitive performance (Morton, van der Bles and Haslam, 2015; Reynolds *et al.*, this volume). Moreover, there is evidence that these processes are consolidated through group-based interactions in which those groups that feel at home and valorised in a given environment increasingly take control of it, while those that feel out of place steadily withdraw (Courneya and Carron, 2010; Finn, 1989; Hurtado and Carter, 1997; see also Bernstein, 2000; Greenaway, Haslam, Thai and Murphy, 2016; Iyer *et al.*, 2009). In short, feeling like 'we belong' is a good basis for coming to feel that 'we own the place' and then for interacting with others in ways that turn these perceptions into material reality.

Influence

> What we have loved, others will love. And we will teach them how.
>
> (*The Prelude,* Wordsworth, 1851, p. 548)

In reflecting on the importance of identification, ideation and interaction for education and learning, it is sometimes easy to imagine that these things 'just happen'. One reason for this is that when presenting the experimental evidence that confirms the importance of these elements, researchers rarely reflect directly on their own role in the process – for example, in promoting identification, in making certain identity content appear normative or in constructing environ-ments with particular identity affordances. Nevertheless, the fact that, as experi-menters, they are able to do this – often to considerable effect – speaks to the capacity for people to shape educational and learning outcomes through processes of *social influence*. More particularly, it speaks to the power of these outcomes to be structured by processes of *leadership* in which people are influenced in ways that motivate and enable them to contribute to the achievement of collective goals (again, with education clearly being one of the most important of these; Dewey, 1916).

Importantly, though, a large body of research confirms that leadership is only made possible by perceptions of shared identity between leaders (e.g., teachers) and followers (e.g., students; S. A. Haslam, Reicher and Platow, 2011; Hogg, 2001; J. C. Turner and Haslam, 2001). For example, experimental work shows that followers are more likely to do the bidding of leaders and respond creatively to their instructions when the ingroup-affirming behaviour of those leaders shows that they share social identity with the followers (S. A. Haslam and Platow, 2001). Other work also shows that leaders' *charisma* is something that flows from their being seen to be representative of a social identity that they share with followers (Platow, van Knippenberg, Haslam, van Knippenberg and Spears, 2006) and that this sense of shared identity is a basis for followers to feel a personal bond with leaders and then to respond enthusiastically to their guidance (Steffens, Haslam and Reicher, 2014). Critically, too, this body of work shows that a sense of shared identity induces followers to follow because they *want to* rather than because they feel they *have to* (S. A. Haslam *et al.*, 2011).

As evidence that bears upon this point, it is instructive to reflect on a large body of recent research that has explored findings from one of psychology's most influential studies. In this, two people come into a laboratory and one is assigned the role of 'teacher' and the other the role of 'learner'. The study is supposedly part of an important scientific programme designed to examine factors that assist memory and learning, and as an experimenter (who is male) explains, the teacher's role is to administer shocks of increasing magnitude to the learner (also male) to see if this punishment helps him to perform better on a word memory task. It turns out that the learner performs rather poorly, and in the face of his apparent inability to learn, the teacher is required to give him shocks of up to 450 volts – a potentially lethal punishment. In the most well-known variant of the study, a majority of teachers do.

This, of course, is hardly a typical learning study. Rather, it describes the paradigm in Milgram's famous 'obedience to authority' studies (1963, 1974; see Reicher and Haslam, 2012) in which the learner is a confederate of the experimenter and the shocks that he receives are not real. Moreover, rather than being interested in learning, the key question that Milgram was interested in exploring was how willing participants would be to obey the destructive instructions they were given. Debate about the psychology of evil need not concern us here (but see S. A. Haslam and Reicher, 2007, 2012a). Nevertheless, the underlying processes that Milgram explored can be seen as highly pertinent to matters of education. At one level (in Milgram's own terms), we can ask whether it is really the case that people are programmed to obey authority. At another (in our own terms), we can ask what it is that leads followers (in this case, participants cast in the role of teachers) to engage closely with the instructions of authorities and to do their bidding no matter how challenging this proves to be.

Upon close inspection, it turns out that the answers to these questions handed down from Milgram's research are unsatisfactory (Reicher, Haslam and Miller, 2014). First, it is apparent that rather than conform blindly, Milgram's participants struggled with the task of following instructions, with the result that across around 30 variants of the study, a majority actually end up *disobeying* the experimenter (Reicher, Haslam and Smith, 2012). This, we suspect, is a result that chimes more with the experience of teachers (and parents) than the idea that students tend 'naturally' to obey authority.

Second, it seems that whether or not participants follow instructions depends largely on whether or not they identify with the experimenter and with the project he is leading. Rather than the experimenter's status – and hence influence – being 'given', this is thus something that is contingent on perceptions that he is representative of a valued identity (Oldmeadow, Platow, Foddy and Anderson, 2003; J. C. Turner, 1991). Thus, on the one hand, factors that serve to increase identification with the experimenter (e.g., being in the same room, conducting the study at Yale) tend to increase obedience. On the other hand, factors that reduce this identification (e.g., having a non-scientist as the experimenter, conducting the study in a shopping mall) or increase identification with the learner (having him in the same room or him being a friend or relative) tend to reduce obedience. This is a point that has been confirmed empirically by observing in Milgram's original studies a very tight correlation between factors that promote identification with the experimenter and levels of observed obedience (Reicher *et al.*, 2012) as well as by new studies which systematically manipulate social identification in ethical analogues of the paradigm and show that that this has a direct impact on obedience (e.g., S. A. Haslam, Reicher and Millard, 2015). For example, if the experimenter *orders* the participant to obey instructions (e.g., by saying 'you have no other choice, you must continue'), this tends to undermine shared identification and hence obedience (S. A. Haslam, Reicher and Birney, 2014); however, if the study is described as furthering neuroscience rather than social science, it tends to increase identification (because it is seen to be more worthwhile) and hence to encourage obedience (Reicher, Birney and Haslam, 2015).

Third, the behaviour displayed by Milgram's participants (and those in related paradigms; e.g., the Stanford Prison Experiment; Haney, Banks and Zimbardo, 1973) is actually poorly captured by notions of 'obedience' or 'conformity' (S. A. Haslam and Reicher, 2012a). Instead, where participants prove willing to go along with the experimenter, their behaviour is better characterised as a form of *engaged followership* in which they respond actively and creatively to leadership. Moreover, while the process of following instructions is highly stressful, the sense that they have contributed to a worthy collective enterprise ultimately allows them to feel good about what they have done and to express enthusiasm for doing it anew (S. A. Haslam, Reicher, Millard and MacDonald, 2015).

This analysis, and more particularly, the social identity approach to leadership from which it emerges, has broad relevance for contexts of education and learning. The key reason for this is that these typically involve students being asked to respond to the instruction of others in ways that are demanding and often uncomfortable. Certainly, this will not typically involve inflicting pain on others (although where the leader is a bully, it might; see Jones *et al.*, this volume), but it will often involve putting oneself under a certain amount – sometimes an intense amount – of strain. As Aristotle observed, 'the roots of education are bitter, but the fruit is sweet' (cited in Maisuria, 2005, p. 150). Here again, though, a large corpus of social identity research suggests that people's willingness to endure this bitterness is contingent upon a leader's ability to create, advance, represent and embed a sense of shared identity that explains why the effort is meaningful and worthwhile (Haslam *et al.*, 2011; Steffens, Haslam, Reicher, Platow *et al.*, 2014). It is thus shared identity that is the engine house of education rather than rewards and punishment (in line with the Chinese philosopher Lao-Tzu's observation that the latter are 'the lowest form of education', as cited in Pritchard, 2013, p. 17; see also Angrist, Oreopoulos and Williams, 2014).

Along related lines, work by Adarves-Yorno and colleagues also shows that students are willing to engage in various forms of *creativity* – specifically, those that go with or against group norms – to the extent that they are encouraged to identify or not with the group that is the source of those norms (Adarves-Yorno, Postmes and Haslam, 2007). Interestingly, too, other work in this research programme also shows that *responses* to creativity are structured by social identity such that evaluators tend generally to be more appreciative of the creative efforts of those in their ingroup than those in outgroups (Adarves-Yorno, Haslam and Postmes, 2008). In this way, leaders who embody the meaning of shared identity play a key role both in *stimulating* forms of creativity that are aligned with ingroup interests and in *shaping* emergent acts of creativity to maintain that alignment (S. A. Haslam *et al.*, 2013).

Moreover, to the extent that they are able to promote a sense of shared identity, it is clear that leaders can help take the pain out of group-oriented labour and turn otherwise stressful tasks into enjoyable ones (Steffens, Haslam, Kerschreiter, Schuh and van Dick, 2014). In educational contexts, this point is confirmed by the work of Bizumic, Reynolds and colleagues, which shows that teachers' cultivation of shared identification with and among students increases not only those students' educational engagement and learning outcomes but also their well-being (Bizumic *et al.*, 2009; Reynolds *et al.*, this volume; see also Burford and Rosenthal-Stott, this volume; S. A. Haslam, Jetten and Waghorn, 2009; S. A. Haslam, Wegge and Postmes, 2009). To extend the metaphor of Yeats – who famously remarked that education is not the filling of a pail but the lighting of a fire – it is thus only when educators mobilise and harness a sense of shared identity that they give students a sense that the furnace of learning they are being exposed to is safe to draw close to and worth keeping alight.

Ideology

It is all very well to talk romantically about education as a fire that is lit by teachers in the hearts and minds of students, but it is clear that educational contexts are rarely characterised by the presence of just one fire. Instead, educational experience is generally framed by multiple identity-relevant concerns between which the participants – or those who formulate policy on their behalf – have to choose. These choices are essentially ideological in nature, and contributions to this volume reveal two to be particularly important.

First, at an overarching level, choices are made about the identities that participants in the educational process are encouraged to use to frame their interaction. As Sonnenberg makes clear in her contribution to this volume (Chapter 15), in contemporary higher education, one critical choice concerns whether educational participants engage with each other as teachers and students or else as service providers and consumers. Likewise, in the context of contemporary secondary education, policymakers debate whether students should be construed as employees-in-waiting (who therefore need to be given concrete skills for work) or as embryonic citizens (who therefore need to be given creative skills for citizenship; Maisuria, 2005). More generally, debate – and the *entrepreneurs of identity* who lead it (Reicher and Hopkins, 2001) – asks whether it is the student who is the 'customer' or the society in which they live and, even more fundamentally, whether educational activity should be framed by the mercantile language of economic exchange at all (Barnett, 2013; Collini, 2012; Molesworth, Scullion and Nixon, 2011). As Sonnenberg shows compellingly, these are choices that have profound implications not just for educational participants but also for the systems in which they are embedded. For example, if students are encouraged to see themselves as consumers rather than learners, and educators to see themselves as service providers rather than teachers, then this will tend to structure the content of the social identities that define their relationship in ways that undermine educational goals (e.g., by being focused more on satisfaction with service delivery than on self-extension). This, in turn, may have the effect of promoting discontent among students as well as discouraging them from feeling responsible for or being interested in their own intellectual development. Ironically, then, while the mindset associated with consumer identity is intended to empower students, it may ultimately mean that it undermines their capacity to take ownership of their own education and learning.

A second key set of choices relates to the question of whether students are led to identify with their educators and the institutions they represent or with alternative sources of social identification. In much of the above discussion, we have tended to imply that the only teachers and educators in a given institution are those who are formally employed for this purpose. But this is not the case. As in the Milgram paradigm, participants almost always have a choice between multiple sources of influence – not just the authority but also those who would resist and oppose it (S. A. Haslam and Reicher, 2012b). Thus in Willis' Hammertown, the 'lads' decided collectively to differentiate themselves from the studious 'earoles' and from the system that they had bought into (Willis, 1977). More generally, too, it is not that delinquent students fail to learn or to seek to improve themselves; rather, it is that what they learn and the ways in which they cultivate their self-esteem and reputation entails living out oppositional *identities of resistance* (Emler and Reicher, 1995; Finn, 1989). And again, this has profound implications – not just for individuals' experience within the educational system but also for their lives thereafter. As Willis (1997) observes, amongst other things, it helps to explain the key conundrum of how it is that working-class boys typically end up with working-class jobs.

It is for this reason that issues addressed by Reynolds and Jetten and their respective colleagues (this volume) are among the most important in the educational sphere – because these concern the question of how *identity relations* are construed and configured within the educational landscape (see also Rich, Mavor and Webb, Chapter 19, this volume). Here, the research of Jetten and colleagues shows that educational advancement may prove particularly problematic for students from disadvantaged backgrounds because their social identities turn out to be incompatible with those that are valorised in formal educational contexts. In British universities, this arises from the fact that while it is relatively easy for middle-class students to achieve *identity continuity* between school and university (due to the possibility of maintaining valued group memberships and associated social capital; e.g., ties with family and school friends), this is far less true for their working-class counterparts (Iyer *et al.*, 2009). In Chinese schools, incompatibility arises from the fact that, traditionally, high-status urban schools have simply not allowed those who were born elsewhere (e.g., in rural areas) to enroll as students. Nevertheless, the research of Jetten and colleagues shows that as these barriers to mobility were removed – so that prospects for educational advancement became more realistic – Chinese students proved willing to engage more constructively with the education system (in ways predicted by social identity theory). This engagement in turn is shown to have a positive impact not just on students' sense of self-efficacy but also on their school performance (Iyer, Zhang, Jetten, Cui and Hao, 2014; for an analogous demonstration of the reverse process, see Reicher and Haslam, 2006).

In a similar vein, long-term work by Reynolds and colleagues shows that interventions that are targeted at transforming identity relations – both between teachers and students and between subgroups of students – can have a profound impact on school climate and, through this, on educational experiences and outcomes. Here, the authors argue for the benefits of *organic pluralism* in which an overarching sense of superordinate identity (e.g., 'us members of School X') also accommodates and respects meaningful subgroup differences (e.g., between 'us teachers' and 'us students'; as recommended by S. A. Haslam, Eggins and Reynolds, 2003 and outlined in their model for Actualizing Social and Personal Identity Resources, ASPIRe; see also S. A. Haslam, 2004; Hornsey and Hogg, 2000). They note that the advantage of this model compared to others (e.g., simple pluralism between 'us' and 'them') is that, because they are understood to share identity, teachers and students are much more likely to be able to engage in mutual influence. In ways anticipated by the elaborated social identity model (Drury and Reicher, 1999), it also means that the teachers and students who are most representative of the group – and hence best placed to exert leadership – are those who embody, rather than undermine, shared educational goals.

Significantly, too, Reynolds and colleagues also identify ways in which organic social identities can be promoted in schools. Aligned with the ASPIRe model and the 'three 'R's' of identity leadership (Haslam, Eggins and Reynolds, 2003; S. A. Haslam *et al.*, 2011), these involve *reflecting* on the nature of diverse group identities within the school, then *representing* these in ways that respect group-based similarities and differences and, finally, *realising* the emergent organic identity through activities that serve to embed it in practice.

Evidence on a range of measures of performance and well-being – for teachers as well as students – speaks to the efficacy of this approach relative to a range of alternatives. Nevertheless, it needs to be recognised that, like all other identity management strategies, the approach adopted by Reynolds and colleagues is ideological. In the world of education (as in all other applied fields; S. A. Haslam, 2014) there is no escaping this (Lingard and Mills, 2007; see also Grace and Platow, this volume). Ultimately, then, the value of the approach must be judged with regard to one key question: Is the model of education it seeks to promote aligned with the model of society that one wants that education to sustain?

Using Berry's (1974) influential framework as a guide, there would appear to be four key models one might champion here: *individualism* (in which group memberships are denied altogether, leading to the marginalisation of low-status group members; Berry, 2011), *separatism* (in which the subordinate group remains out of contact with the larger society, resulting in diverse groups being opposed to each other), *assimilationism* (in which low-status groups are encouraged to abandon their identities and are subjugated to those of high-status groups), and *integrationism* (in which all groups are engaged with both their own group and the larger society and all are recognised and respected as equals in the context of a shared superordinate identity – as in the ASPIRe model). In the educational debate, it is clearly possible to find passionate advocates of all these models. For example, those who approach education from the neoliberal perspective of free market economics tend to promote the philosophy and policy of individualism (Lingard, Hayes, Mills and Christie, 2003; Sonnenberg, this volume). Nevertheless, surveying the massive body of evidence that Berry and his colleagues have amassed over nearly 50 years of research (e.g., see Berry, 2011), it is clear that this speaks with minimal equivocation for the benefits of societal integrationism, or what we would call organic pluralism (S. A. Haslam, 2004). Accordingly, it is on this basis that we recommend it – and the strategies that advance it – as a model for education.

Conclusion

> My school days! The silent gliding on of my existence – the unseen, unfelt progress of my life.
>
> (*David Copperfield*, Dickens, 1849/2001, p. 132)

At their best, much like David Copperfield's school days, our experiences of education and learning are largely unproblematic. Indeed, where the identities of teachers and learners are aligned, the experience is one of *flow* in which much can be taken for granted and the identities themselves become invisible. So although there are undoubtedly many stressors to be tackled, these are largely of the eustressing variety, in which they are construed by all parties as opportunities for growth, rather than as fundamentally self-threatening. Certainly, those of us who self-categorise as members of groups that are not generally disadvantaged (e.g., white, middle class, male, able-bodied) never had to stress excessively about these identities in the course of our advancement – and had anyone had the temerity to suggest these were the *cause* of that advancement, we would in all likelihood have pointed them, like the privileged schoolboys in Michael Apted's *28 Up*, to all the immensely hard work we had been doing along the way, turning this into a narrative about individual differences (Duneier, 2009). Nevertheless, they *were* the cause of it – primarily because they made that hard work not only purposeful, fulfilling and enjoyable, but also *possible*.

Precisely because the role of social identity in this 'silent gliding on' is invisible, the truth of this analysis is something that can only be seen clearly when things go wrong. It is therefore instructive to examine what happens when social identities are problematised in various ways within the educational system – for example, through marginalisation, exclusion, stigma and prejudice. As various contributions to this volume attest, when we do, we find that education and learning are often anything but smooth.

One of the key challenges for practitioners and policymakers is thus to recognise the importance of identity for education, but not to make such a song and dance about it that self-consciousness gets in the way of processes that operate best when, as part of habitus (Harker, 1984), they are largely unseen and unfelt. As we have outlined, the solution here is not so much a matter of educational policy as of societal practice. For it is precisely when diverse identities are embraced within the models of culture and society that we live out in our daily lives that they stand the best chance of being naturally respected in the educational institutions and practices we rely upon to take that society forward.

More generally, too, if we take Dewey's (1916) analysis seriously and understand education and learning to be *all about* the renewal of the group, then it is clear that the key questions for us all are not so much 'What is the best educational policy?' and 'What should be in the curriculum?' as 'What is the nature of our group?' and 'What type of group do we want to become?' In these terms, the principal value of the social identity approach advanced in this chapter – and in this book as a whole – is not that it gives us definitive answers to such questions. Psychological analysis alone can never do this. Instead, its value is that it allows us to understand why, of all the questions we can ask in the educational sphere, these can lay claim to being among the most important. Perhaps *the* most important.

Acknowledgements

Work on this chapter was supported by a Laureate Fellowship from the Australian Research Council (FL110100199) and a Fellowship from the Canadian Institute for Advanced Research (Social Interactions, Identity, and Well-being programme). It was also supported by input from a large number of colleagues and, in reality, should have multiple co-authors. In the first instance, the chapter was initiated and, ultimately, completed after extensive discussions with Michael Platow. Ongoing conversations with Sarah Bentley and Katie Greenaway were also essential to the overall structure of the chapter. Clearly, too, the chapter presents the fruits of ongoing research collaboration with, amongst others, Inma Adarves-Yorno, Kirstien Bjerregaard, Catherine Haslam, Thomas Morton, Tom Postmes, Steve Reicher and Kate Reynolds. Finally, the content of the chapter was greatly improved by specific feedback from John Berry, Martin Mills and Phil Oreopoulos.

References

Adarves-Yorno, I., Haslam, S. A. and Postmes, T. (2008). And now for something completely different? The impact of group membership on perceptions of creativity. *Social Influence, 3*(4), 248–66.

Adarves-Yorno, I., Postmes, T. and Haslam, S. A. (2007). Creative innovation or crazy irrelevance? The contribution of group norms and social identity to creative behavior. *Journal of Experimental Social Psychology, 43*(3), 410–16.

Adler, P. A. and Adler, P. (1995). Dynamics of inclusion and exclusion in preadolescent cliques. *Social Psychology Quarterly, 58*(3), 145–62.

Angrist, J., Oreopoulos, P. and Williams, T. (2014). When opportunity knocks, who answers? New evidence on college achievement awards. *Journal of Human Resources, 49*(3), 572–610.

Apted, M. (Dir.). (1984). *28 Up* [documentary film]. Manchester: Granada.

Barnett, R. (2013). *Imagining the university*. London: Routledge.

Beilock, S. L., Rydell, R. J. and McConnell, A. R. (2007). Stereotype threat and working memory: Mechanisms, alleviation, and spillover. *Journal of Experimental Psychology: General, 136*(2), 256–76.

Bernstein, B. B. (2000). *Pedagogy, symbolic control, and identity: Theory, research, critique.* Lanham, MD: Rowman & Littlefield.

Berry, J. W. (1974). Psychological aspects of cultural pluralism: Unity and identity reconsidered. *Topics in Culture Learning, 2,* 17–22.

Berry, J. W. (2011). Integration and multiculturalism: Ways towards social solidarity. *Papers on Social Representations, 20*(1), 1–20.

Biggs, J. (1996). Enhancing teaching through constructive alignment. *Higher Education, 32*(3), 347–64.

Bizumic, B., Reynolds, K. J., Turner, J. C., Bromhead, D. and Subasic, E. (2009). The role of the group in individual functioning: School identification and the psychological well-being of staff and students. *Applied Psychology: An International Review, 58*(1), 171–92.

Bjerregaard, K., Haslam, S. A. and Morton, T. A. (2016). How identification facilitates effective learning: The evaluation of generic versus localised professionalization training. *International Journal of Training and Development, 20*(1), 17–37.

Bjerregaard, K., Haslam, S. A., Morton, T. A. and Ryan, M. K. (2015). Social and relational identification as determinants of care workers' motivation and wellbeing. *Frontiers in Psychology, 6,* 1460.

Blakey, H., Blanshard, E., Cole, H., Leslie, F. and Sen, R. (2008). Are medical students socially exclusive? A comparison with economics students. *Medical Education, 42*(11), 1088–91.

Bliuc, A.-M., Ellis, R. A., Goodyear, P. and Muntele Hendres, D. (2011a). The role of social identification as a university student in learning: Relationships between students' social identity, approaches to learning, and academic achievement. *Educational Psychology, 31*(5), 559–75.

Bliuc, A.-M., Ellis, R. A., Goodyear, P. and Muntele Hendres, D. (2011b). Understanding student learning in context: Relationships between social identity, perceptions of the learning community, approaches to learning and academic performance. *European Journal of Psychology of Education, 26*(3), 417–33.

Bourdieu, P. and Passeron, J.-C. (1990). *Reproduction in education, society and culture* (2nd ed.). London: Sage.

Cadinu, M., Maass, A., Rosabianca, A. and Kiesner, J. (2005). Why do women underperform under stereotype threat? Evidence for the role of negative thinking. *Psychological Science, 16*(7), 572–8.

Chaiklin, S. (2003). The zone of proximal development in Vygotsky's analysis of learning and instruction. In A. Kozulin, B. Gindis, V. S. Ageyev and S. M. Miller (Eds), *Vygotsky's educational theory in cultural context* (pp. 39–64). Cambridge: Cambridge University Press.

Cheryan, S., Plaut, V. C., Davies, P. and Steele, C. M. (2009). Ambient belonging: How stereotypical environments impact gender participation in computer science. *Journal of Personality and Social Psychology, 97*(6), 1045–60.

Christ, O., Van Dick, R., Wagner, U. and Stellmacher, J. (2003). When teachers go the extra mile: Foci of organisational identification as determinants of different forms of organisational citizenship behaviour among schoolteachers. *British Journal of Educational Psychology, 73*(3), 329–42.

Collini, S. (2012). *What are universities for?* London: Penguin.

Courneya, K. S. and Carron, A. V. (2010). The home advantage in sport competitions: A literature review. *Journal of Sport and Exercise Psychology, 14*(1), 13–27.

Croizet, J. C. and Claire, T. (1998). Extending the concept of stereotype threat to social class: The intellectual underperformance of students from low socioeconomic backgrounds. *Personality and Social Psychology Bulletin, 24*(6), 588–94.

Croizet, J. C. and Dutrévis, M. (2004). Socioeconomic status and intelligence: Why test scores do not equal merit. *Journal of Poverty, 8*(3), 91–107.

Croizet, J. C., Després, G., Gauzins, M. E., Huguet, P., Leyens, J. P. and Méot, A. (2004). Stereotype threat undermines intellectual performance by triggering a disruptive mental load. *Personality and Social Psychology Bulletin, 30*(6), 721–31.

Cruwys, T., Haslam, S. A., Dingle, G. A., Jetten, J., Hornsey, M. J., Chonga, E. M. D. and Oei, T. P. S. (2014). Feeling connected again: Interventions that increase social identification reduce depression symptoms in community and clinical settings. *Journal of Affective Disorders, 159*, 139–46.

Cruwys, T., Haslam, S. A., Fox, N. and McMahon, H. (2015). 'That's not what we do': Evidence that normative change is a mechanism of action in group interventions. *Behaviour Research and Therapy, 65*, 11–17.

Deci, E. L. and Ryan, R. M. (2000). The 'what' and 'why' of goal pursuits: Human needs and the self-determination of behavior. *Psychological Inquiry, 11*(4), 227–68.

Dewey, J. (1916). *Democracy and education: An introduction to the philosophy of education.* New York: Macmillan.

Dickens, C. (1849/2001). *David Copperfield.* Peterborough, Ontario: Broadview Press.

Drury, J. and Reicher, S. (1999). The intergroup dynamics of collective empowerment: Substantiating the social identity model of crowd behavior. *Group Processes and Intergroup Relations, 2*(4), 381–402.

Drury, J. and Reicher, S. (2000). Collective action and psychological change: The emergence of new social identities. *British Journal of Social Psychology, 39*(4), 579–604.

Duneier, M. (2009). Michael Apted's *Up!* series: Public sociology or folk psychology through film? *Ethnography, 10*(3), 341–5.

Ellemers, N. (1993). The influence of socio-structural variables on identity enhancement strategies. *European Review of Social Psychology, 4*(1), 27–57.

Ellemers, N., De Gilder, D. and Haslam, S. A. (2004). Motivating individuals and groups at work: A social identity perspective on leadership and group performance. *Academy of Management Review, 29*(3), 459–78.

Ellemers, N. and Haslam, S. A. (2012). Social identity theory. In P. Van Lange, A. Kruglanski and T. Higgins (Eds), *Handbook of theories of social psychology* (pp. 379–98). London: Sage.

Ellemers, N., Spears, R. and Doosje, B. (1999). *Social identity: Context, content and commitment.* Oxford: Blackwell.

Elsbach, K. D. and Kramer, R. D. (1996). Members' responses to organizational identity threats: Encountering and countering the Business Week rankings. *Administrative Science Quarterly, 41*(3), 442–76.

Emler, N. and Reicher, S. (1995). *Adolescence and delinquency: The collective management of reputation.* Oxford: Blackwell.

Fine, M., Bloom, J., Burns, A., Chajet, L., Guishard, M. and Perkins-Munn, T. (2004). *Echoes of Brown: The faultlines of racial justice and public education.* New York: The Graduate Center, City University of New York.

Finn, J. D. (1989). Withdrawing from school. *Review of Educational Research, 59*(2), 117–42.

Fleer, M. (2006). Troubling cultural fault lines: Some indigenous Australian families' perspectives on the landscape of early childhood education. *Mind, Culture, and Activity, 13*(3), 191–204.

Foddy, M., Platow, M. J. and Yamagishi, T. (2009). Group-based trust in strangers: The role of stereotypes and expectations. *Psychological Science, 20*(4), 419–22.

Fransen, K., Haslam, S. A., Steffens, N. K., Vanbeselaere, N., De Cuyper, B. and Boen, F. (2015). Believing in 'us': Exploring leaders' capacity to enhance team confidence and performance by building a sense of shared social identity. *Journal of Experimental Psychology: Applied, 12*(1), 89–100.

Gagnon, A. and Bourhis, R. Y. (1996). Discrimination in the minimal group paradigm: Social identity or self-interest? *Personality and Social Psychology Bulletin, 22*(12), 1289–301.

Grace, D. M., David, B. J. and Ryan, M. K. (2008). Investigating preschoolers' categorical thinking about gender through imitation, attention, and the use of self-categories. *Child Development, 79*(6), 1928–41.

Greenaway, K., Haslam, S. A., Branscombe, N. R., Cruwys, T., Ysseldyk, R. and Heldreth, C. (2015). From 'we' to 'me': Group identification enhances perceived personal control with consequences for health and well-being. *Journal of Personality and Social Psychology, 109*(1), 53–74.

Greenaway, K., Thai, H., Haslam, S. A. and Murphy, S. (2016). Spaces that signal identity improve workplace productivity. *Journal of Personnel Psychology, 15*(1), 35–43.

Haney, C., Banks, C. and Zimbardo, P. (1973). A study of prisoners and guards in a simulated prison. *Naval Research Reviews*, September, 1–17. Washington, DC: Office of Naval Research.

Harker, R. K. (1984). On reproduction, habitus and education. *British Journal of Sociology of Education, 5*(2), 117–27.

Haslam, C., Cruwys, T. and Haslam, S. A. (2014). 'The we's have it': Evidence for the distinctive benefits of group engagement in enhancing cognitive health in ageing. *Social Science and Medicine, 120*, 57–66.

Haslam, C., Cruwys, T., Milne, M., Chi-Hsin, K. and Haslam, S. A. (2016). Group ties protect cognitive health by promoting social identification and social support. *Journal of Aging and Health*, *28*(2), 244–66.

Haslam, C., Haslam, S. A., Knight, C., Gleibs, I., Ysseldyk, R. and McCloskey, L.-G. (2014). We can work it out: Group decision-making builds social identity and enhances the cognitive performance of care home residents. *British Journal of Psychology*, *105*(1), 17–34.

Haslam, C., Morton, T. A., Haslam, S. A., Varnes, L., Graham, R. and Gamaz, L. (2012). 'When the age is in, the wit is out': Age-related self-categorization and deficit expectations reduce performance on clinical tests used in dementia assessment. *Psychology and Aging*, *27*(3), 778–84.

Haslam, S. A. (2001). *Psychology in organizations*. London: Sage.

Haslam, S. A. (2004). *Psychology in organizations: The social identity approach* (2nd ed.). London: Sage.

Haslam, S. A. (2014). Making good theory practical: Five lessons for an Applied Social Identity Approach to challenges of organizational, health, and clinical psychology. *British Journal of Social Psychology*, *53*(1), 1–20.

Haslam, S. A., Adarves-Yorno, I., Postmes, T. and Jans, L. (2013). The collective origins of valued originality: A social identity approach to creativity. *Personality and Social Psychology Review*, *17*(4), 384–401.

Haslam, S. A., Eggins, R. A. and Reynolds, K. J. (2003). The ASPIRe model: Actualizing Social and Personal Identity Resources to enhance organizational outcomes. *Journal of Occupational and Organizational Psychology*, *76*(1), 83–113.

Haslam, S. A., Jetten, J., Postmes, T. and Haslam, C. (2009). Social identity, health and well-being: An emerging agenda for applied psychology. *Applied Psychology: An International Review*, *58*(1), 1–23.

Haslam, S. A., Jetten, J. and Waghorn, C. (2009). Social identification, stress, and citizenship in teams: A five-phase longitudinal study. *Stress and Health*, *25*(1), 21–30. doi: 10.1002/smi.1221

Haslam, S. A. and Platow, M. J. (2001). The link between leadership and followership: How affirming social identity translates vision into action. *Personality and Social Psychology Bulletin*, *27*(11), 1469–79.

Haslam, S. A., Postmes, T. and Ellemers, N. (2003). More than a metaphor: Organizational identity makes organizational life possible. *British Journal of Management*, *14*(4), 357–69.

Haslam, S. A. and Reicher, S. D. (2007). Beyond the banality of evil: Three dynamics of an interactionist social psychology of tyranny. *Personality and Social Psychology Bulletin*, *33*(5), 615–22.

Haslam, S. A. and Reicher, S. D. (2012a). Contesting the 'nature' of conformity: What Milgram and Zimbardo's studies really show. *PLoS Biology*, *10*(11), e1001426.

Haslam, S. A. and Reicher, S. D. (2012b). When prisoners take over the prison: A social psychology of resistance. *Personality and Social Psychology Review*, *16*, 152–79.

Haslam, S. A., Reicher, S. D. and Birney, M. (2014). Nothing by mere authority: Evidence that in an experimental analogue of the Milgram paradigm participants are motivated not by orders but by appeals to science. *Journal of Social Issues*, *70*(3), 473–88.

Haslam, S. A., Reicher, S. D. and Millard, K. (2015). Shock treatment: Using immersive digital realism to restage and re-examine Milgram's 'Obedience to Authority' research. *PLoS ONE*, *10*(3), e109015.

Haslam, S. A., Reicher, S. D., Millard, K. and McDonald, R. (2015). 'Happy to have been of service': The Yale archive as a window into the engaged followership of participants in Milgram's 'obedience' experiments. *British Journal of Social Psychology*, *54*(1), 55–83.

Haslam, S. A., Reicher, S. D. and Platow, M. J. (2011). *The new psychology of leadership: Identity, influence and power*. New York: Psychology Press.

Haslam, S. A., Salvatore, J., Kessler, T. and Reicher, S. D. (2008). The social psychology of success. *Scientific American Mind*, *19*(2), 24–31.

Haslam, S. A. and Turner, J. C. (1992). Context-dependent variation in social stereotyping 2: The relationship between frame of reference, self-categorization and accentuation. *European Journal of Social Psychology*, *22*(3), 251–77.

Haslam, S. A., Wegge, J. and Postmes, T. (2009). Are we on a learning curve or a treadmill? The benefits of participative group goal setting become apparent as tasks become increasingly challenging over time. *European Journal of Social Psychology*, *39*(3), 430–46.

Hawkins, I. D., Farrington, D. P. and Catalano, R. F. (1998). Reducing violence through the schools. In D. S. Elliott, B. A. Hamburg and K. R. Williams (Eds), *Violence in American schools: A new perspective* (pp. 188–216). Cambridge: Cambridge University Press.

Hogg, M. A. (2000). Subjective uncertainty reduction through self-categorization: A motivational theory of social identity processes. *European Review of Social Psychology*, *11*(1), 223–55.

Hogg, M. A. (2001). A social identity theory of leadership. *Personality and Social Psychology Review*, *5*(3), 184–200.

Hornsey, M. J. and Hogg, M. A. (2000). Assimilation and diversity: An integrative model of subgroup relations. *Personality and Social Psychology Review*, *4*(2), 143–56.

Howell, J., Koudenburg, N., Loschelder, D., Weston, D., Fransen, K., De Dominicis, S., Gallagher, S. and Haslam, S. A. (2014). Happy but unhealthy: The relationship between social ties and health in an emerging network. *European Journal of Social Psychology*, *44*(6), 602–11.

Hurtado, S. and Carter, D. F. (1997). Effects of college transition and perceptions of the campus racial climate on Latino college students' sense of belonging. *Sociology of Education*, *70*(4), 324–345.

Iyer, A., Jetten, J., Tsivrikos, D., Postmes, T. and Haslam, S. A. (2009). The more (and the more compatible) the merrier: Multiple group memberships and identity compatibility as predictors of adjustment after life transitions. *British Journal of Social Psychology*, *48*(4), 707–33.

Iyer, A., Zhang, A., Jetten, J., Cui, L. and Hao, Z. (2014). Yes, I can: Cognitive alternatives improve self-efficacy among disadvantaged school children. University of Queensland, unpublished manuscript.

Jetten, J., Branscombe, N. R., Haslam, S. A., Haslam, C., Cruwys, T., Jones, J. M., Cui, L., Dingle, G., Liu, J., Murphy, S. C., Thai, A., Walter, Z. and Zhang, A. (2015). Having a lot of a good thing: Multiple important group memberships as a source of self-esteem. *PLoS ONE*, *10*(6), e0131035.

Jetten, J., Haslam, C. and Haslam, S. A. (Eds). (2012). *The social cure: Identity, health and well-being*. Hove, UK: Psychology Press.

Jetten, J., Haslam, S. A., Cruwys, T. and Branscombe, N. R. (in press). Social identity, stigma and health. In B. Major, J. F. Dovidio and B. G. Link (Eds), *The handbook of stigma, discrimination and health*. Oxford: Oxford University Press.

Kandel, D. B. (1978). Homophily, selection, and socialization in adolescent friendships. *American Journal of Sociology*, *84*(2), 427–36.

Kluger, R. (2011). *Simple justice: The history of Brown v. Board of Education and Black America's struggle for equality*. Chicago, IL: Vintage Books.

Knight, C., Haslam, S. A. and Haslam, C. (2010). In home or at home? Evidence that collective decision making enhances older adults' social identification, well-being, and use of communal space when moving into a new care facility. *Ageing and Society, 30*(8), 1393–418.

Krause, K. (2009). Interpreting changing academic roles and identities in higher education. In M. Tight, K. H. Mok, J. Huisman and C. Morphew (Eds), *The Routledge international handbook of higher education* (pp. 413–26). New York: Routledge.

Lingard, B., Hayes, D., Mills, M. and Christe, P. (2003). *Leading learning: Making hope practical in schools.* Maidenhead, UK: McGraw-Hill Education.

Lingard, B. and Mills, M. (2007). Pedagogies making a difference: Issues of social justice and inclusion. *International Journal of Inclusive Education, 11*(3), 233–44.

Livingstone, A. and Haslam, S. A. (2008). The importance of social identity content in a setting of chronic social conflict: The case of intergroup relations in Northern Ireland. *British Journal of Social Psychology, 47*(1), 1–21.

Livingstone, A., Haslam, S. A., Postmes, T. and Jetten, J. (2011). 'We are, therefore we should': Evidence that ingroup identification mediates the acquisition of ingroup norms. *Journal of Applied Social Psychology, 41*(8), 1857–76.

McCrae, R. R. and Costa, P. T., Jr. (1997). Personality trait structure as a human universal. *American Psychologist, 52*(5), 509–16.

McCune, V. and Entwistle, N. (2011). Cultivating the disposition to understand in 21st century university education. *Learning and Individual Differences, 21*(3), 303–10.

McLeod, J. and Yates, L. (2006). *Making modern lives: Subjectivity, schooling, and social change.* Albany, NY: SUNY Press.

Mael, F. A. and Ashforth, B. E. (1992). Alumni and their alma mater: A partial test of the reformulated model of organizational identification. *Journal of Organizational Behavior, 13*(2), 103–23.

Maisuria, A. (2005). The turbulent times of creativity in the National Curriculum. *Policy Futures in Education, 3*(2), 141–52.

Master, A. and Walton, G. M. (2013). Minimal groups increase young children's motivation and learning on group-relevant tasks. *Child Development, 84*(2), 737–51.

Milgram, S. (1963). Behavioral study of obedience. *Journal of Abnormal and Social Psychology, 67*(4), 371–8.

Milgram, S. (1974). *Obedience to authority.* London: Tavistock.

Millward, L. J. and Haslam, S. A. (2013). Who are we made to think we are? Contextual variation in organizational, workgroup and career foci of identification. *Journal of Occupational and Organizational Psychology, 86*(1), 50–66.

Molesworth, M., Scullion, R. and Nixon, E. (Eds). (2011). *The marketisation of higher education and the student as consumer.* London: Routledge.

Morton, T. A., van der Bles, A.-M. and Haslam, S. A. (2015). Seeing our self reflected in the world around us: The role of identity in making (natural) environments restorative. Manuscript under review.

Nesdale, D., Durkin, K., Maass, A., Kiesner, J. and Griffiths, J. (2008). Effects of group norms on children's intentions to bully. *Social Development, 17*(4), 889–907.

Noe, R. A. (1986). Trainees' attributes and attitudes: Neglected influences on training effectiveness. *Academy of Management Review, 11*(4), 736–49.

Noreisch, K. (2007). School catchment area evasion: The case of Berlin, Germany. *Journal of Education Policy, 22*(1), 69–90.

Oakes, P. J., Haslam, S. A. and Turner, J. C. (1994). *Stereotyping and social reality.* Oxford: Blackwell.

Oakes, P. J., Turner, J. C. and Haslam, S. A. (1991). Perceiving people as group members: The role of fit in the salience of social categorizations. *British Journal of Social Psychology*, *30*(2), 125–44.

Ojala, K. and Nesdale, D. (2004). Bullying and social identity: The effects of group norms and distinctiveness threat on attitudes towards bullying. *British Journal of Developmental Psychology*, *22*(1), 19–35.

Oldmeadow, J. A., Platow, M. J., Foddy, M. and Anderson, D. (2003). Self-categorization, status, and social influence. *Social Psychology Quarterly*, *66*(2), 138–52.

Paluck, E. L. and Shepherd, H. (2012). The salience of social referents: A field experiment on collective norms and harassment behavior in a school social network. *Journal of Personality and Social Psychology*, *103*(6), 899–915.

Parsons, E., Chalkley, B. and Jones, A. (2000). School catchments and pupil movements: A case study in parental choice. *Educational Studies*, *26*(1), 33–48.

Peters, K. O., Ryan, M. and Haslam, S. A. (2013). Women's occupational motivation: The impact of being a woman in a man's world. In S. Vinnicombe, R. J. Burke, S. Blake-Beard and L. L. Moore (Eds), *Handbook of research on promoting women's careers* (pp. 162–77). Cheltenham, UK: Edward Elgar.

Peters, K. O., Ryan, M. K. and Haslam, S. A. (2014). Marines, medics and machismo: A lack of fit with masculine occupational stereotypes discourages men's participation. *British Journal of Psychology*, *106*(4), 635–55.

Peters, K. O., Ryan, M. K., Haslam, S. A. and Fernandes, H. (2012). To belong or not to belong: Evidence that women's occupational disidentification is promoted by lack of fit with masculine occupational prototypes. *Journal of Personnel Psychology*, *11*(3), 148–58.

Platow, M. J., Haslam, S. A., Reicher, S. D. and Steffens, N. K. (2015). There is no leadership if no-one follows: Why leadership is necessarily a group process. *International Coaching Psychology Review*, *10*(1), 20–37.

Platow, M. J., Hunter, J. A., Branscombe, N. R. and Grace, D. M. (2014). Social creativity in Olympic medal counts: Observing the expression of ethnocentric fairness. *Social Justice Research*, *27*(3), 283–304.

Platow, M. J., Hunter, J. A., Haslam, S. A. and Reicher, S. D. (2015). Reflections on Muzafer Sherif's legacy in social identity and self-categorization theories. In A. Dost-Gözkan and D. Sönmez-Keith (Eds), *Norms, groups, conflict, and social change: Rediscovering Muzafer Sherif's psychology* (pp. 275–305). London: Transaction Publications.

Platow, M. J., Mavor, K. I. and Grace, D. M. (2013). On the role of discipline-related self-concept in deep and surface approaches to learning among university students. *Instructional Science*, *41*(2), 271–85.

Platow, M. J., Mills, D. and Morrison, D. (2000). The effects of social context, source fairness, and perceived self-source similarity on social influence: A self-categorisation analysis. *European Journal of Social Psychology*, *30*(1), 69–81.

Platow, M. J., van Knippenberg, D., Haslam, S. A., van Knippenberg, B. and Spears, R. (2006). A special gift we bestow on you for being representative of us: Considering leadership from a self-categorization perspective. *British Journal of Social Psychology*, *45*(2), 303–20.

Platow, M. J., Voudouris, N. J., Gilbert, N., Jamieson, R., Najdovski, L., Papaleo, N., Pollard, C. and Terry, L. (2007). In-group reassurance in a pain setting produces lower levels of physiological arousal: Direct support for a self-categorization analysis of social influence. *European Journal of Social Psychology*, *37*(4), 649–60.

Postmes, T. and Branscombe, N. (Eds). (2010). *Rediscovering social identity: Core sources*. New York: Psychology Press.

Postmes, T., Haslam, S. A. and Swaab, R. (2005). Social influence in small groups: An interactive model of identity formation. *European Review of Social Psychology*, *16*(1), 1–42.

Pritchard, A. (2013). *Ways of learning: Learning theories and learning styles in the classroom.* London: Routledge.

Reicher, S. (2004). The context of social identity: Domination, resistance, and change. *Political Psychology*, *25*(6), 921–45.

Reicher, S. D., Birney, M. and Haslam, S. A. (2015). 'The progress paradox': When people do harm in the name of science. University of St Andrews, unpublished manuscript.

Reicher, S. D. and Haslam, S. A. (2006). Rethinking the psychology of tyranny: The BBC Prison Study. *British Journal of Social Psychology*, *45*(1), 1–40.

Reicher, S. D. and Haslam. S. A. (2012). Obedience: Revisiting Milgram's obedience studies. In J. R. Smith and S. A. Haslam (Eds), *Social psychology: Revisiting the classic studies* (pp. 106–25). London: Sage.

Reicher, S. D., Haslam, S. A. and Miller, A. G. (2014). What makes a person a perpetrator? The intellectual, moral, and methodological arguments for revisiting Milgram's research on the influence of authority. *Journal of Social Issues*, *70*(3), 393–408.

Reicher, S. D., Haslam, S. A. and Smith, J. R. (2012). Working towards the experimenter: Reconceptualizing obedience within the Milgram paradigm as identification-based followership. *Perspectives on Psychological Science*, *7*(4), 315–24.

Reicher, S. D. and Hopkins, N. (2001). *Self and nation: Categorization, contestation and mobilisation.* London: Sage.

Rigby, K. and Griffiths, C. (2011). Addressing cases of bullying through the Method of Shared Concern. *School Psychology International*, *32*(3), 345–57.

Robinson, K. (2011). *Out of our minds: Learning to be creative.* Chichester, UK: Wiley.

Salmon, P. (2003). A psychology for teachers. In F. Fransella (Ed.), *International handbook of personal construct psychology* (pp. 311–18). Chichester, UK: Wiley.

Sani, F., Herrera, M., Wakefield, J. R., Boroch, O. and Gulyas, C. (2012). Comparing social contact and group identification as predictors of mental health. *British Journal of Social Psychology*, *51*(1), 781–90.

Schmader, T. (2002). Gender identification moderates stereotype threat effects on women's math performance. *Journal of Experimental Social Psychology*, *38*(2), 194–201.

Schmitt, M. T., Davies, K., Hung, M. and Wright, S. C. (2010). Identity moderates the effects of Christmas displays on mood, self-esteem, and inclusion. *Journal of Experimental Social Psychology*, *46*(6), 1017–22.

Shih, M., Pittinsky, T. L. and Ambady, N. (1999). Stereotype susceptibility: Identity salience and shifts in quantitative performance. *Psychological Science*, *10*(1), 80–3.

Sidanius, J., Van Laar, C., Levin, S. and Sinclair, S. (2004). Ethnic enclaves and the dynamics of social identity on the college campus: The good, the bad, and the ugly. *Journal of Personality and Social Psychology*, *87*(1), 96–110.

Solomon, B. M. (1985). *In the company of educated women: A history of women and higher education in America.* New Haven, CT: Yale University Press.

Spears, R. and Otten, S. (2012). Revisiting Tajfel's minimal group studies. In J. R. Smith and S. A. Haslam (Eds), *Social psychology: Revisiting the classic studies* (pp. 160–77). London: Sage.

Staunton, M., Louis, W. R., Smith, J. R., Terry, D. J. and McDonald, R. I. (2014). How negative descriptive norms for healthy eating undermine the effects of positive injunctive norms. *Journal of Applied Social Psychology*, *44*(4), 319–30.

Steele, C. M. and Aronson, J. (1995). Stereotype threat and the intellectual test performance of African Americans. *Journal of Personality and Social Psychology*, *69*(5), 797–811.

Steffens, N. K., Haslam, S. A., Kerschreiter, R., Schuh, S. C. and van Dick, R. (2014). Leaders enhance group members' work engagement and reduce their burnout by crafting social identity. *German Journal of Research in Human Resource Management*, *28*(1–2), 183–204.

Steffens, N., Haslam, S. A. and Reicher, S. D. (2014). Up close and personal: Evidence that shared social identity is a basis for the 'special' relationship that binds followers to leaders. *Leadership Quarterly*, *25*(2), 296–313.

Steffens, N., Haslam, S. A., Reicher, S. D., Platow, M. J., Fransen, K., Yang, J., Ryan, M. K., Jetten, J., Peters, K. O. and Boen, F. (2014). Leadership as social identity management: Introducing the Identity Leadership Inventory (ILI) to assess and validate a four-dimensional model. *Leadership Quarterly*, *25*(5), 1001–24.

Stott, C. and Drury, J. (2000). Crowds, context and identity: Dynamic categorization processes in the 'poll tax riot'. *Human Relations*, *53*(2), 247–73.

Tajfel, H. (1972). Social categorisation. English translation of 'La categorisation sociale'. In S. Moscovici (Ed.), *Introduction à la Psychologie Sociale* (Vol. 1, pp. 272–302). Paris: Larosse.

Tajfel, H., Flament, C., Billig, M. G. and Bundy, R. F. (1971). Social categorization and intergroup behaviour. *European Journal of Social Psychology*, *1*(2), 149–77.

Tajfel, H. and Turner, J. C. (1979). An integrative theory of intergroup conflict. In W. G. Austin and S. Worchel (Eds), *The social psychology of intergroup relations* (pp. 33–47). Monterey, CA: Brooks/Cole.

Tarrant, M., Hagger, M. S. and Farrow, C. V. (2012). Promoting positive orientation towards health through social identity. In J. Jetten, C. Haslam and S. A. Haslam (Eds), *The social cure: Identity, health, and well-being* (pp. 39–54). New York: Psychology Press.

Thomas, E. F. and McGarty, C. A. (2009). The role of efficacy and moral outrage norms in creating the potential for international development activism through group–based interaction. *British Journal of Social Psychology*, *48*(1), 115–34.

Turner, I., Reynolds, K. J., Lee, E., Subasic, E. and Bromhead, D. (2014). Well-being, school climate, and the social identity process: A latent growth model study of bullying perpetration and peer victimization. *School Psychology Quarterly*, *29*(3), 320–35.

Turner, J. C. (1982). Towards a cognitive redefinition of the social group. In H. Tajfel (Ed.), *Social identity and intergroup relations* (pp. 15–40). Cambridge: Cambridge University Press.

Turner, J. C. (1991). *Social influence.* Milton Keynes: Open University Press.

Turner, J. C. and Haslam, S. A. (2001). Social identity, organizations and leadership. In M. E. Turner (Ed.), *Groups at work: Advances in theory and research* (pp. 25–65). Hillsdale, NJ: Erlbaum.

Turner, J. C., Hogg, M. A., Oakes, P. J., Reicher, S. D. and Wetherell, M. S. (1987). *Rediscovering the social group: A self-categorization theory.* Oxford: Blackwell.

Turner, J. C., Oakes, P. J., Haslam, S. A. and McGarty, C. A. (1994). Self and collective: Cognition and social context. *Personality and Social Psychology Bulletin*, *20*(5), 454–63.

van Dick, R. and Wagner, U. (2001). Stress and strain in teaching: A structural equation approach. *British Journal of Educational Psychology*, *71*(2), 243–59.

van Dick, R. and Wagner, U. (2002). Social identification among school teachers: Dimensions, foci, and correlates. *European Journal of Work and Organizational Psychology*, *11*(2), 129–49.

Van Rijswijk, W., Haslam, S. A. and Ellemers, N. (2006). Who do we think we are? The effects of social context and social identification on ingroup stereotyping. *British Journal of Social Psychology*, *45*(1), 161–74.

Vygotsky, L. S. (1978). *Mind in society: The development of higher mental process*. Cambridge, MA: Harvard University Press.

Walton, G. M. and Cohen, G. L. (2003). Stereotype lift. *Journal of Experimental Social Psychology, 39*(5), 456–67.

Willis, P. E. (1977). *Learning to labor: How working class kids get working class jobs*. New York: Columbia University Press.

Wordsworth, W. (1951). *The complete poetical works of William Wordsworth*. Philadelphia, PA: Troutman and Hayes.

Wright, S. C. (1997). Ambiguity, social influence, and collective action: Generating collective protest in response to tokenism. *Personality and Social Psychology Bulletin, 23*(12), 1277–90.

Wright, S. C., Taylor, D. M. and Moghaddam, F. M. (1990). Responding to membership in a disadvantaged group: From acceptance to collective protest. *Journal of Personality and Social Psychology, 58*(6), 994–1003.

PART II

Social identity in the classroom and playground

3

SCHOOL CLIMATE, SOCIAL IDENTITY PROCESSES AND SCHOOL OUTCOMES

Making the case for a group-level approach to understanding schools

Katherine J. Reynolds, Emina Subasic, Eunro Lee and David Bromhead

An important area of inquiry within the educational domain concerns *school climate* and related concepts such as school connectedness and school belonging (e.g., Thapa, Cohen, Higgins-D'Alessandro and Guffey, 2013). School climate is defined in different ways, but in essence, it focuses on student perceptions of academic emphasis, the way groups within a school (e.g., teachers, students, parents) relate to one another, and the higher-order norms, values, and practices (shared mission) that define the school as a whole (Thapa et al., 2013). In this chapter, we argue that incorporating a social-psychological analysis of the group within the school climate domain can advance understanding of school life. To date, most emphasis is placed on the psychology of individuals-as-individuals and interpersonal relationships. What is missing is an analysis of the group.

Much of the focus on school reform concerns developing effective and efficient interventions to enrich schools so they are engaging and safe contexts for learning and development. The message of this chapter is that such tasks are made harder through a lack of engagement with the social-psychological analysis of the group. If one considers only people's psychology as individuals and their interpersonal relationships, it may, indeed, be difficult to fully understand behaviours observed in schools or to achieve change in individual behaviours and functioning. As J. C. Turner stated, 'If you try to change the behaviour of an individual as if their behaviour is just the product of that individual, you're going to find that very difficult, if not impossible' (2006, p. 139).

Within the *group* or social identity approach, it is expected that school-level activities, processes and norms will come to shape individual behaviour most when individuals define themselves as group members – when there is a fusion of their individual and social selves as 'members of the school community'. When students come to experience the school in terms of a psychological group membership that shapes their self-definition (i.e., the school is an important reference group), school life should impact more on student engagement, well-being and behaviour (Bizumic, Reynolds, Turner, Bromhead and Subasic, 2009; I. Turner, Reynolds, Lee, Subasic and Bromhead, 2014). It can also be argued that these same group processes underpin learning. In this chapter, our analysis of these links is outlined in more detail. Our starting point is to consider the existing work on school climate, both its insights and its limitations.

The importance of school climate

It is recognised that a school, like any other kind of organisation, can have a unique 'personality' or set of shared norms, values and beliefs that define the group and coordinate action (e.g., who 'we' are). 'School climate' is a term used to describe such features of the school environment (Thapa et al., 2013). It is a complex, multidimensional construct that can be reliably measured through factors such as staff support for the goals and objectives of the school; fairness and clarity of rules and consistency in rule implementation; participatory decision-making; academic emphasis; cooperative and respectful relationships amongst staff, between staff and students, and amongst students; and parental involvement and school–community relations.

School climate has been identified in a large (mainly US) literature to be a significant explanatory factor in a range of critical school outcomes (Lehr and Christenson, 2002; MacNeil, Prater and Busch, 2009). For example, 'whole school' reform interventions (e.g., the Yale Child Study Center's School Development Program; Comer and Emmons, 2006) have shown that school climate is related to a range of outcomes including: (a) learning and achievement of students (e.g., numeracy and literacy), (b) attendance and dropout rates, (c) students' disruptive behaviours (e.g., aggression, class disruption, challenging authority), (d) students' global and academic self-esteem, and (e) students' and parents' satisfaction with the school.

Another example of such work indicated that school climate explained a significant percentage of delinquent behaviours (e.g., damaging or stealing school property, physical violence or threats of violence towards staff and/or students) after controlling for those factors largely outside of the school's control, such as community characteristics (poverty, community crime, crowding) and student composition within a school (racial heterogeneity, percentage of males; Gottfredson, Gottfredson, Payne and Gottfredson, 2005). Also a growing body of evidence suggests that schools with a positive climate may provide a 'protective factor' buffering the risk factors associated with problem behaviours, alcohol and drug use, and crime (e.g., Kuperminc, Leadbeater and Blatt, 2001). This buffering effect is believed to be particularly important in the middle school years of education (grades 6–8) where the development of positive self-perceptions and adult relationships as well as a sense of belonging are crucial to negotiating more successfully the transition to adulthood.

Despite the emerging consensus that school climate is important in improving students' academic and social functioning, there are unresolved issues. The first is that there is an overlap between different school climate constructs and measures, which leads to fragmentation and confusion about the real strength of the school climate–school outcomes relationship. The second issue is that it is unclear *how* school climate comes to impact on school outcomes, which means it is difficult to develop efficient and effective interventions. The third issue, as highlighted above, is that in understanding school climate and its impacts, there has been limited engagement with social identity processes.

Overlap between constructs

In relation to the first issue, there is an overlap between concepts such as school connectedness, student engagement, school bonding, emotional engagement and school climate. School connectedness has been defined as 'the belief by students that adults in the school care about their learning as well as about them as individuals' (*Wingspread Declaration on School Connections*, 2004, p. 233), and it is assessed using items such as: 'I am happy to be at this school', 'The teachers at this school treat me fairly', 'I feel safe at this school' and 'I feel like I am part of this school'. The importance of school connectedness is highlighted by the US Centers for Disease Control and Protection (CDC), which is part of the US Department of Health and Human Services. Based on research by Resnick *et al.* (1997), the CDC's 2009 report claimed school connectedness was a critical protective factor for adolescent health and educational outcomes (e.g., decreased substance use, school absenteeism, emotional distress, and risk of unintentional injury such as drink driving or not wearing seat belts). The impact of school connectedness exceeded the impact of family context and demographic factors such as poverty, ethnicity and family structure.

Another overlapping concept is student engagement, comprising cognitive, emotional and behavioural features including emotional reactions to the school and teachers as well as feelings of belonging and being important to the school (Finn, 1989; see Fredricks, Blumenfeld and Paris, 2004, for a review). Finn (1989) recognises that student success at school is related to an internalised sense of belongingness (described under such rubrics as 'affiliation', 'involvement', 'attachment', 'commitment' and 'bonding' or when absent 'alienation' and 'withdrawal') and a valuing of school-relevant goals (see also Goodenow, 1992; Osterman, 2000). Blum (2005) argues that all these terms are used to capture the sense of care and respect students feel in relation to their learning and as individuals. Such work highlights that psychological connection to the school is important in any analysis of school climate. As is explained in more detail below, incorporating an analysis of the psychological group provides a clear rationale for further distinguishing concepts like school climate from school connectedness and student engagement.

Explaining the school climate–school outcomes relationship

The second unresolved issue with the construct of school climate is that there have been limited systematic investigations of the mechanisms that explain the relationship between school climate and school outcomes (e.g., Borman, Hewes, Overman and Brown, 2003). There has been some emphasis on attachment theory (e.g., Comer and Emmons, 2006) and motivational theories (e.g., Ryan and Deci, 2000). With attachment theory, many authors speak about variables such as caretaker–child interactions where there is an emotional attachment and bond. Comer and Emmons draw on work in developmental psychology and describe a 'social learning' model where a child models and imitates, identifies with and internalises the attitudes and values of caretakers such as teachers (2006, p. 356). According to attachment theory, 'warm and supportive relationships, characterised by open communication, trust, involvement, and responsiveness influence social and emotional development through internalised models of accessibility and support' (Murray and Greenberg, 2000, p. 425; see also Bowlby, 1969). Such relationships between students and teachers are likely to result in better learning (e.g., engagement, intrinsic motivation) and behavioural (e.g., less challenging behaviour) outcomes.

With respect to motivational approaches, it is argued that there are three basic human needs – autonomy, competence and relatedness/belongingness – that are the basis of self-motivation (Baumeister and Leary, 1995; Ryan and Deci, 2000; see also Greenaway, Amiot, Louis and Bentley, Chapter 10, this volume). When students' basic psychological needs for human growth and development are met, they are more likely to engage in learning (Skinner and Belmont, 1993). Autonomy refers to acting in line with one's interest and values and voluntarily engaging in activities that satisfy curiosity and interest. Competence relates to being successful in meeting one's goals (Deci and Ryan, 1985) and is important in developing beliefs of self-efficacy (i.e., that one can successfully organise and perform tasks; J. C. Turner, Christensen, Kackar-Cam, Trucano and Fulmer, 2014). Relatedness or belongingness are terms that capture the need to feel securely connected with others and to experience oneself as worthy of love and respect. A body of literature exists showing a relationship between the satisfaction of these psychological needs and various school outcomes (Deci and Ryan, 2012; Jang, Kim and Reeve, 2012; Milyavskaya and Koestner, 2011). In this work, however, there is limited engagement with social identity processes. It is psychological group membership and feeling part of a group that may best provide a context in which relatedness (e.g., feeling connected to others), autonomy (e.g., defining one's interest) and competence (e.g., being motivated to achieve goals and achieve them in the same way as others 'like me') emerge and can flourish.

Schools and social identity processes

The third limitation is that work on school climate, school connectedness, and relatedness has largely developed without explicit connection to an analysis of the psychological group. There are pockets of work within the education literature where the importance of connection to, and being accepted within, a larger cohesive entity (e.g., the school as a community) are recognised (e.g., Finn, 1989; Goodenow, 1992; Osterman, 2000; Solomon, Battistich, Watson, Schaps and Lewis, 2000). When these ideas concerning connection to the group are inte-grated explicitly with theory and research on psychological group membership, they take on new importance (e.g., Bizumic *et al.*, 2009; I. Turner *et al.*, 2014) in explaining school outcomes.

A central insight of the social identity approach is that people can define them-selves as individuals ('I' and 'me') and as group members ('we' and 'us'). The terms 'personal identity' and the 'personal self' are used to describe when indi-viduals perceive themselves as being distinct and different from others; in contrast, social identity and the social self refer to an individual's 'knowledge that he [or she] belongs to certain groups together with some emotional and value signific-ance to him [or her] of the group membership' (Tajfel, 1972, p. 292). Within the social identity approach, then, the term 'group' does not refer to demographic, sociological or role groups (e.g., women, those with low socio-economic status or teachers; Platow, Haslam, Reicher and Steffens, 2015; Platow, Hunter, Haslam and Reicher, 2015). The term refers to *psychological* groups, wherein people define themselves as being members because the group is self-relevant and self-defining.

When people identify with a particular group (i.e., when they self-categorise as a group member), the norms, values and beliefs that define the group are inter-nalised (i.e., there is self-stereotyping in relation to this 'meaning' or 'content') and come to influence the attitudes and behaviour of group members (see Smyth, Mavor, Platow and Grace, Chapter 13, this volume). The stronger one's identi-fication with a particular group (and its salience in the context of interest), the more likely it is that one will behave in line with the norms, values and beliefs that define the group (e.g., engaging in deep learning behaviours, following school rules). There is now much evidence from the organisational field, for example, that shows that the more citizens identify with institutional authorities (e.g., government departments, courts, police), the more likely they are to perceive the authority as legitimate and to abide willingly to the authority's decisions (Tyler and Blader, 2000). Other consequences of a shared social identity include being motivated to achieve group goals, acting in ways that ensure the ingroup is positively distinct from other groups, and mutual influence and persua-sion within the group (e.g., Haslam, 2004). When there is a shared social identity, other ingroup members are considered to be similar to oneself and are considered a valid source of information about social reality (e.g., J. C. Turner, 1991).

This social identity approach has three direct implications for practice in schools. The first implication is that group psychology (and ingroup–outgroup relations) can give added insight into understanding behaviour in schools. Students' perceptions of their psychological connection to the school provides information about how important the school is to their self-definition – to their social identification. Stronger psychological connection means the features that characterise the school are likely to be internalised and to lead to consistent behaviours (J. C. Turner, 1991). The same analysis is relevant to other meaningful groups within the school such as classroom and peer groups. The group that becomes salient at a given time will impact on behaviour.

The second implication is that just as a group-based analysis can help better understand behaviour in schools, it can be used to shape behaviour. As the definitions of who 'we' are as a group vary and change and are internalised by members, there should be associated shifts in behaviour. For example, changes in higher-level organisational norms and values (systemic or school level) will produce change in the relations between different subgroups within a system (e.g., respectful relations between students and teachers). In turn, changes at the subgroup level will affect change in individual group members' attitudes and behaviour. Group (school) leadership plays an important role in defining, maintaining and enhancing certain definitions of who 'we' are and, through this process, affects behaviour in more sustainable ways (e.g., Haslam, Reicher and Platow, 2011; J. C. Turner, Reynolds and Subasic, 2008).

The third implication relates to learning itself. Under certain conditions, teachers may be perceived as representatives of the group (legitimate authority figures), and as a result, their influence within the school context should increase. The (re)positioning of teachers in this way should strengthen the learning enterprise. Teachers as (ingroup) leaders will have a greater ability to influence followers (students) to engage in tasks that will enhance learning. Ingroup relationships where 'we' are all in this together also create an environment of mutual respect and influence where teachers are likely to be open to student suggestions and input (J. C. Turner, 1991; J. C. Turner and Reynolds, 2011).

Extending the social identity analysis to the learning domain offers a promising direction for future research. There is already evidence that messages from ingroup members are more persuasive and better recalled than those of outgroup members (McGarty, Haslam, Hutchinson and Turner, 1994). Greenaway and colleagues (2015) have shown that instructions from a fellow ingroup member, compared to those from an outgroup member, can have very different outcomes on achievement (Greenaway, Wright, Willingham, Reynolds and Haslam, 2015; see also Morton, Wright, Reynolds and Haslam, 2012). In their study, the completeness and accuracy of a created product (a lego car model) was greater when the source of the instructional message was believed to originate from an ingroup compared to an outgroup source (even though the actual message was identical in both conditions). Thinking about the context of the school environment, these findings suggest that those teachers who are characterised as being 'one of us', under certain conditions (such as high expectations and an academic emphasis), are likely to have more learning-relevant influence, which should produce better learning outcomes.

Many of the arguments offered above emerge from that translation of theoretical ideas embedded in the social identity approach to the educational domain. It is also necessary to demonstrate support for these claims through research evidence. The details of a longitudinal research programme and the key findings are outlined in the next section of this chapter. The work to date has investigated school (social) identification as: (a) a predictor of school outcomes (academic achievement, well-being) within a context where a range of other predictors are also controlled and (b) a mediator of the relationship between school climate and school outcomes. Where possible, these relationships have been investigated using longitudinal designs, allowing us to be more confident in the directions of these relationships.

The importance of social identity processes in schools: research evidence

Researchers at the Australian National University have been involved in a longitudinal research project in partnership with the local government education department. The project is designed to integrate understandings of the psychological group within the educational context and has two main research aims. The first aim is to systematically investigate the relationship between school climate, school identification and school outcomes, including the role of school identification as a mediator in explaining the relationship between school climate and school outcomes (e.g., Bizumic *et al.*, 2009; Reynolds *et al.*, 2007; Reynolds, Subasic, Lee, Bromhead and Tindall, 2015). A second aim of the project is to assess the relationship between these variables over time using a longitudinal design. Figure 3.1 outlines the theoretical model in which key school outcomes are well-being, student engagement, challenging behaviour and academic achievement.

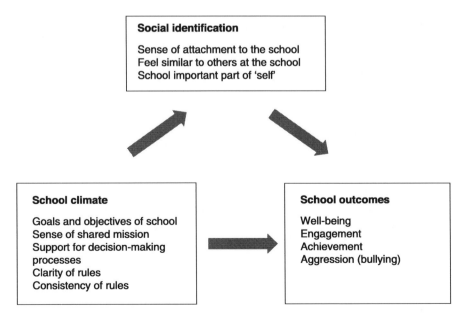

FIGURE 3.1 Theoretical model with school identification as mediator

More specifically, the research involves students completing a school climate and school identification measurement inventory on an annual basis (Lee, Reynolds, Subasic, Bromhead, Lin, Marinov and Smithsom, 2016). School climate is assessed using items measuring perceptions of a shared mission, fairness of decision-making processes, social relations between staff and students, and academic expectations. School identification is assessed with statements such as: 'I identify with this school'; 'Being part of this school is important to me'. The outcome variables of interest are student engagement (emotional and behavioural engagement), academic achievement (performance on the Australian National Assessment Program – Literacy and Numeracy (NAPLAN) standardised national test that assesses reading, writing and numeracy), well-being (feeling anxious, depressed and emotionally positive during the past month), and challenging behaviour (bullying and victimisation).

It is only possible to summarise the key findings in this chapter, but details are provided elsewhere (e.g., Bizumic et al., 2009; Reynolds, Subasic et al., 2015; I. Turner et al., 2014). Initial research by Bizumic et al. (2009) found that for students (grades 7–10), school identification was a significant predictor of student engagement, well-being and aggression (bullying) over and above gender and years at school and school climate. Furthermore, consistent with the model presented in Figure 3.1, school identification partially mediated the relationship between school climate and student engagement and positive well-being indicators. Full mediation was evident for aggression and negative well-being indicators.

An important extension of these findings is to explore whether these same patterns are evident using a longitudinal design where the same student is assessed across multiple time points. Using data collected in three phases, Lee, Reynolds, Subasic and Bromhead (2015) conducted latent growth models in order to examine the relationship between school climate, school identification and student engagement ('I try to complete my school work on time and to the best of my ability', 'I work hard on my school work') across time. In line with predictions, controlling for a range of other variables, there was evidence in support of the model that school identification mediated the relationship between school climate and student engagement *across time*. Increases in perceptions of positive school climate were related to greater school identification which were related to higher student engagement. These results are important because student engagement is a central predictor of academic achievement. Furthermore, these findings indicate that school identification is not static but can change over time and that such changes can lead to increases (and decreases) in school outcomes.

I. Turner et al. (2014) also used a longitudinal design with three waves of data to examine the predictors of bullying and victimisation over time in models where school climate (separated into the subfactors of group support (e.g., 'I believe that people at this school are accepting of one another's differences' and 'I believe people at this school help one another'), academic support (e.g., 'I believe the school is focused on helping me learn' and 'I believe the school sets high standards for work'), age, gender and student mental health (anxiety and depression) were also assessed. Key findings indicated that school climate, school identification and mental health were all significant predictors of bullying ('I pushed or shoved someone', ' I tried to make someone angry'; Orpinas, Horne and Staniszewski, 2003) across time. School identification was a predictor of bullying of similar strength to that of school climate and of greater strength than prior mental health. In subsequent research, the role of school social identification as a significant, albeit partial, mediator between school climate (group support) and bullying behaviour was investigated and confirmed (I. Turner, Reynolds, Lee, Subasic and Bromhead, 2015).

It has also been possible to investigate these relationships using behavioural rather than self-report measures. A standardised measure of academic achievement was used; the Australian National Assessment Program – Literacy and Numeracy (NAPLAN). Student scores from the three domains of writing, numeracy and reading were assessed while controlling for additional predictors of achievement such as socio-economic status and parental education. These additional controls provide a more robust model to investigate the contributions of school climate and school identification. The findings indicated that the variables most significantly and consistently associated with NAPLAN achievement were parental education and socio-economic status. However, for writing and numeracy, but not reading, school identification also was a significant predictor of NAPLAN achievement. Furthermore, there was evidence that school identification significantly mediated the relationship between school climate and NAPLAN achievement in these two learning areas (Reynolds, Subasic et al. in press).

Overall, then, what this research shows is that social identification is a significant predictor of school outcomes (e.g., academic achievement, well-being) even when alternative competing constructs are also taken into consideration. Furthermore, school identification often acts as a mediator in the school climate–school outcomes relationship. In this way, school identification helps explain *how* one's experiences of the climate of the school can affect individual behaviour and functioning.

From theory and research to practice: how to build school identity

A critical issue to emerge from this growing evidence concerning the importance of school identification is *how* to strengthen it. As part of this process, it is necessary to understand the norms, values and beliefs that define the school from the perspective of the various subgroups that comprise the school community. Identification with a school that is perceived by its members as having a negative school climate, a poor reputation and low status is likely to shape staff and student behaviour in detrimental ways. A social identity analysis places a dual focus on the school (group) norms and members' psychological connection to that group. Two ways forward in strengthening social identification are: (1) to remove obstacles to feelings of being included and accepted (much of this work concerns ethnic and gender group stereotypes related to learning) and (2) to strengthen school identification through building consensus regarding who 'we' are, what 'we' do and why 'we' do it. Both have implications for practice.

Removal of barriers to school identification

Recently, Reynolds, Subasic *et al.* (2015) highlighted the connections between social identity processes and fixed and incremental mindsets, and stereotype threat. Mindsets and stereotype threat have been extensively researched in the educational domain. It is argued that when students face setbacks and difficulties, it is the holding of fixed mindsets (i.e., a belief that ability is predetermined and unchangeable) and/or negative stereotypes of their group in relation to academic achievement (e.g., women perform worse in maths) that can be especially detrimental. Attributions to one's lack of mental ability or 'disadvantaged' group memberships (e.g., gender, ethnicity or class) can erode one's fundamental sense of place and belonging ('people like me do not really belong here').

An important but simple example of this point is provided by Walton and Cohen (2011) who introduced a programme designed specifically to remove threats to belonging among university students. In workshop sessions, they explained to the student body that experiencing setbacks and difficulties is common but is also something that can be addressed. African-American students who completed the programme had higher achievement and reported better health compared to controls. One explanation is that students' feelings of being a member of the relevant academic community were maintained (Walton and Cohen, 2011; 'I feel I belong to the community X', 'I feel like I am part of community X', 'I feel connected to the community X').

Along these same lines, Good, Rattan and Dweck (2012) have shown that in a maths community with gender stereotyping (e.g., a belief that women perform worse at maths than men) or a fixed ability view of performance (e.g., either one has got what it takes or not), women had a lower sense of belonging. Within such maths communities, a mindset where maths was perceived as something that could be improved with effort (incremental theory) allowed women 'to maintain a high sense of belonging in math and the intention to pursue math in the future' (Good *et al.*, 2012, p. 700). These research examples highlight that removing stereotype threat and fixed mindsets in educational domains is important in ensuring ongoing belonging and identification (see also Boucher and Murphy, Chapter 5, this volume).

Strengthening school identification

It is also possible to strengthen school identification by building a shared sense of who 'we' are as a group. Reynolds *et al.* (2015) outline steps that can be taken to clarify and consensualise school members' sense of shared mission (based on

Haslam, Eggins and Reynolds, 2003). Briefly, these researchers identified the meaningful subgroups in the school (year groups, teaching staff, parents/carers). In these groups, members were then asked to answer a series of questions designed to provide insight into the purpose, aspiration and behaviours typical within schools. Group members were asked to explain: 'What is the true purpose of the school?'; 'What is your vision for the "perfect" school?'; 'What are the desirable behaviours to be exhibited by staff, students and community members?'; and 'What are the key characteristics students should develop while at the school (know-how, knowledge, character)?'. The information from each group was collated, and the most important elements were agreed upon within the group and by each of the other groups. The outcome of this process was a shared under-standing of 'who we are', 'what we do' and 'why you would want to belong', using a process that was procedurally fair and respectful as all groups were repres-ented and had a 'voice' (Haslam, McGarty, Oakes and Turner 1993; Tyler and Blader, 2000). A whole range of school activities were designed to embed these emergent values and beliefs into the day-to-day life of the school, including displaying posters around the school and in classrooms and using school values framing at school assemblies when celebrating achievements and championing individuals.

More recently Lee *et al.* (2015) have considered the relationship between staff and students, in particular, as being important in building connection to the school as a whole and school identification. They have shown not only that student–teacher relations are correlated with the core school outcomes of student engagement and well-being, but also that these relationships are, at least in part, explained by school identification. Warm and respectful socio-emotional rela-tionships between students and teachers impact on student outcomes because they serve to build students' psychological connection to the school as a group. Such relations have impact beyond the immediate learning context of the classroom and connect students psychologically to the school as a whole.

There is more work to be done developing, implementing and evaluating interventions that build a positive school climate and school identification. The research findings across a number of studies to date reinforce the value of such efforts. Further integration of a group-based analysis incorporating social identity processes and concepts like belonging (and relatedness) but understood through the lens of group psychology does offer critical advance.

Conclusions

Can social psychology add value in understanding school improvement? A case has been made that bringing school values to life in a way that forges a strong sense of psychological connection for students is central to understanding and explaining school outcomes. Wedding their individual and social selves to being a member of the school community has been shown to help explain engagement, aggression, achievement and well-being. It has also been argued that the social identity approach generates new ways to understand learning itself. It can be interpreted as involving an influence process that depends on a shared sense of 'us' as students and teachers, as members of a learning enterprise.

Most importantly, though, this chapter provides a bridge between social-psychological concepts and educational domains, and it opens up new directions for research and practice. It is hoped that the theory and research outlined in this chapter enhances the toolkit available to policymakers and school leaders to improve school outcomes. Behaviour is not just the product of individual factors – psychological group memberships also matters in explaining what 'we' do and why 'we' do it.

Acknowledgements

This project was funded by the Australian Research Council Linkage Project with the Australian Capital Territory Directorate of Education and Training as linkage partner. We would like to thank research assistants Elle McIntosh, Stefano Portaluri and Corie Lin, staff at the Directorate of Education and Training, and the staff and students at the participating schools for help with data collection.

References

Baumeister, R. F. and Leary, M. R. (1995). The need to belong: Desire for interpersonal attachments as a fundamental human motivation. *Psychological Bulletin, 117*(3), 497–529. doi: 10.1037/0033-2909.117.3.497

Bizumic, B., Reynolds, K. J., Turner, J. C., Bromhead, D. and Subasic, E. (2009). The role of the group in individual functioning: School identification and the psychological well-being of staff and students. *Applied Psychology: An International Review, 58*(1), 171–92. doi: 10.1111/j.1464-0597.2008.00387.x

Blum, R. W. (2005). A case for school connectedness. *The Adolescent Learner, 62*(7), 16–20.

Borman, G. D., Hewes, G. M., Overman, L. T. and Brown, S. (2003). Comprehensive school reform and achievement: A meta-analysis. *Review of Educational Research, 73*(2), 125–230. doi: 10.3102/00346543073002125

Bowlby, J. (1969). Attachment and loss: Retrospect and prospect. *American Journal of Orthopsychiatry, 52*(4), 664–78.

Comer, J. P. and Emmons, C. (2006). The research program of the Yale Child Study Centre School Development Program. *The Journal of Negro Education, 75*(1), 353–72.

Deci, E. L. and Ryan, R. M. (1985). *Intrinsic motivation and self-determination in human behavior.* New York: Plenum.

Deci, E. L. and Ryan, R. M. (2012). Motivation, personality, and development within embedded social contexts: An overview of self-determination theory. In R. M. Ryan (Ed.), *Oxford handbook of human motivation* (pp. 85–107). Oxford: Oxford University Press. doi: 10.1093/oxfordhb/9780195399820.001.0001

Finn, J. D. (1989). Withdrawing from school. *Review of Educational Research, 59*(2), 117–42. doi: 10.3102/00346543059002117

Fredricks, J. A., Blumenfeld, P. C. and Paris, A. H. (2004). School engagement: Potential of the concept, state of the evidence. *Review of Educational Research, 74*(1), 59–109. doi: 10.3102/00346543074001059

Good, C., Rattan, A. and Dweck, C. S. (2012). Why do women opt out? Sense of belonging and women's representation in mathematics. *Journal of Personality and Social Psychology*, *102*(4), 700–17. doi: 10.1037/a0026659

Goodenow, C. (1992). Strengthening the links between educational psychology and the study of social contexts. *Educational Psychologist*, *27*(2), 177–96. doi: 10.1207/s15326985ep2702_4

Gottfredson, G. D., Gottfredson, D. C., Payne, A. A. and Gottfredson, N. C. (2005). School climate predictors of school disorder: Results from the National Study of Delinquency Prevention in Schools. *Journal of Research in Crime and Delinquency*, *42*(4), 412–44. doi: 10.1177/0022427804271931

Greenaway, K. H., Wright, R., Willingham, J., Reynolds, K. J. and Haslam, S. A. (2015). Shared identity is key to effective communication. *Personality and Social Psychology Bulletin*, *41*(2), 171–82. doi: 10.1177/0146167214559709

Haslam, S. A. (2004). *Psychology in organsiations: The social identity approach*. London: Sage.

Haslam, S. A., Eggins, R. A. and Reynolds, K. J. (2003). The ASPIRe model: Actualizing Social and Personal Identity Resources to enhance organizational outcomes. *Journal of Occupational and Organizational Psychology*, *76*(1), 83–113. doi: 10.1348/096317903321208907

Haslam, S. A., McGarty, C., Oakes, P. J. and Turner, J. C. (1993). Social comparative context and illusory correlation: Testing between ingroup bias and social identity models of stereotype formation. *Australian Journal of Psychology*, *45*(2), 97–101. doi: 10.1080/00049539308259125

Haslam, S. A., Reicher, S. D. and Platow, M. J. (2011). *The new psychology of leadership: Identity, influence and power*. London and New York: Psychology Press.

Jang, H., Kim, E. J. and Reeve, J. (2012). Longitudinal test of self-determination theory's motivation mediation model in a naturally occurring classroom context. *Journal of Educational Psychology*, *104*(4), 1175–88. doi: 10.1037/a0028089

Kuperminc, G. P., Leadbeater, B. J. and Blatt, S. J. (2001). School social climate and individual differences in vulnerability to psychopathology among middle school students. *Journal of School Psychology*, *39*(2), 141–59. doi: 10.1016/S0022-4405(01)00059-0

Lee, E., Reynolds, K. J., Subasic, E. and Bromhead, D. (2015). From the classroom to the school as an ingroup: Explaining how the teacher-student relationship impacts on student engagement and well-being. In submission.

Lee, E., Reynolds, K.J., Subasic, E., Bromhead, D., Lin, H., Marinov, V. and Smithsom, M. (2016). *Development of a dual School Climate and School Identification Measure–Student (SCASIM-St)*. Submitted manuscript.

Lehr, C. A. and Christenson, S. L. (2002). Best practices in promoting a positive school climate. In A. Thomas and J. Grimes (Eds), *Best practices in school psychology*, Vol. IV (pp. 929–47). Bethesda, MD: National Association of School Psychologists.

McGarty, C., Haslam, S. A., Hutchinson, K. J. and Turner, J. C. (1994). The effects of salient group membership on persuasion. *Small Group Research*, *25*(2), 267–93. doi: 10.1177/1046496494252007

MacNeil, A. J., Prater, D. L. and Busch, S. (2009). The effect of school culture and climate on student achievement. *International Journal of Leadership in Education: Theory and Practice*, *12*(1), 73–84.

Milyavskaya, M. and Koestner, R. (2011). Psychological needs, motivation, and well-being: A test of self-determination theory across multiple domains. *Personality and Individual Differences*, *50*(3), 387–91. doi: 10.1016/j.paid.2010.10.029

Morton, T., Wright, R., Peters, K. O., Reynolds, K. J. and Haslam, S. A. (2012). Social identity and the dynamics of organizational communication. In H. Giles (Ed.), *Handbook of intergroup communication* (pp. 319–30). New York: Routledge.

Murray, C. and Greenberg, M. T. (2000). Children's relationship with teachers and bonds with school: An investigation of patterns and correlates in middle childhood. *Journal of School Psychology*, *38*(5), 423–45. doi: 10.1016/S0022-4405(00)00034-0

National School Climate Centre (2007). School climate [online], *National School Climate Centre*. Retrieved from: www.schoolclimate.org/climate/ (accessed 1 September 2016).

Orpinas, P., Horne, A. M. and Staniszewski, D. (2003). School bullying: Changing the problem by changing the school. *School Psychology Review*, *32*(3), 431–44. Retrieved from: https://www.publichealth.uga.edu/hpb/sites/default/files/2003-Orpinas-SchoolBullying.pdf (accessed 1 September 2016).

Osterman, K. F. (2000). Students' need for belonging in the school community. *Review of Educational Research*, *70*(3), 323–67. doi: 10.3102/00346543070003323

Platow, M. J., Haslam, S. A., Reicher, S. D. and Steffens, N. K. (2015). There is no leadership if no one follows: Why leadership is necessarily a group process. *International Coaching Psychology Review*, *10*(1), 20–37.

Platow, M. J., Hunter, J. A., Haslam, S. A. and Reicher, S. D. (2015). Reflections on Muzafer Sherif's legacy in social identity and self-categorization theories. In A. Dost-Gözkan and D. Sönmez-Keith (Eds), *Norms, groups, conflict, and social change: Rediscovering Muzafer Sherif's psychology* (pp. 275–305). London: Transaction Publications.

Resnick, M. D., Bearman, P. S., Blum, R. W., Bauman, K. E., Harris, K. M., Jones, J., . . . Udry, J. R. (1997). Protecting adolescents from harm: Findings from the National Longitudinal Study on Adolescent Health. *Journal of the American Medical Association*, *278*(10), 823–32. doi: 10.1001/jama.1997.03550100090045

Reynolds, K. J., Lee, E., Turner, I., Subasic, E. and Bromhead. D. (in press). How does school climate impact on academic achievement? An examination of social identity processes. *School Psychology International*.

Reynolds, K. J., Subasic, E., Lee, E., Bromhead, D. and Tindall, K. (2015). Does education really transform us? The impact of school-based social processes on the person. In K. J. Reynolds and N. R. Branscombe (Eds), *The psychology of change: Life contexts, experiences and identities* (pp. 170–86). New York: Psychology Press.

Reynolds, K. J., Turner, J., Haslam, S. A., Ryan, M. K., Bizumic, B. and Subasic, E. (2007). Does personality explain in-group identification and discrimination? Evidence from the minimal group paradigm. *British Journal of Social Psychology*, *46*(3), 517–39. doi: 10.1348/014466606X153080

Ryan, R. M. and Deci, E. L. (2000). Self-determination theory and the facilitation of intrinsic motivation, social development, and well-being. *American Psychologist*, *55*(1), 68–78. doi: 10.1037/0003-066X.55.1.68

Skinner, E. A. and Belmont, M. J. (1993). Motivation in the classroom: Reciprocal effects of teacher behavior and student engagement across the school year. *Journal of Educational Psychology*, *85*(4), 571–81. doi: 10.1037/0022-0663.85.4.571

Solomon, D., Battistich, V., Watson, M., Schaps, E. and Lewis, C. (2000). A six-district study of educational change: Direct and mediated effects of the child development project. *Social Psychology of Education*, *4*(1), 3–51. doi: 10.1023/A:1009609606692

Tajfel, H. (1972). La catégorization sociale [Social categorization]. In S. Moscovici (Ed.), *Introduction à la psychologie sociale, Vol. 1* [*Introduction to social psychology, Vol. 1*] (pp. 272–302). Paris: Larousse.

Thapa, A., Cohen, J., Higgins-D'Alessandro, A. and Guffey, S. (2013). A review of school climate research. *Review of Educational Research*, *83*(3), 357–85. doi: 10.3102/0034654313483907

Turner, I., Reynolds, K. J., Lee, E., Subasic, E. and Bromhead, D. (2014). Well-being, school climate and the social identity process: A latent growth model study of bullying perpetration and peer victimization. *School Psychology Quarterly, 29*(3), 320–35. doi: 10.1037/spq0000074

Turner, I., Reynolds, K. J., Lee, E., Subasic, E. and Bromhead, D. (2015). Physical and verbal bullying behavior: A mediation study of two school climate sub-factors, school identification and student well-being. In submission.

Turner, J. C. (1991). *Social influence.* Pacific Grove, CA: Thomson Brooks/Cole Publishing Co.

Turner, J. C. (2006) Mind in the organized social environment. In P. A. M. Van Lange (Ed.), *Bridging social psychology: Benefits of transdisciplinary approaches* (pp. 139–44). Mahwah, NJ: Erlbaum.

Turner, J. C., Christensen, A., Kackar-Cam, H., Trucano, M. and Fulmer, S. M. (2014). Enhancing students' engagement: Report of a three-year intervention with middle school teachers. *American Educational Research Journal, 51*(6), 1195–226. doi: 10.3102/0002831214532515

Turner, J. C. and Reynolds, K. J. (2011). Self-categorization theory. In P. A. M. Van Lange, A. W. Kruglanski and E. T. Higgins (Eds), *Handbook of theories of social psychology* (pp. 399–417). London: Sage Publications.

Turner, J. C., Reynolds, K. J. and Subasic, E. (2008). Identity confers power: The new view of leadership in social psychology. In P. t'Hart and J. Uhr (Eds), *Public leadership: Perspectives and practices* (pp. 57–72). Canberra: ANU ePress.

Tyler, T. R. and Blader, S. L. (2000). *Cooperation in groups: Procedural justice, social identity and behavioral engagement.* Philadelphia, PA: Psychology Press.

Walton, G. M. and Cohen, G. L. (2011). A brief social-belonging intervention improves academic and health outcomes of minority students. *Science, 331*(6023), 1447–51. doi: 10.1126/science.1198364

Wingspread Declaration on School Connections. (2004). *Journal of School Health, 74*(7), 233–4.

4

BULLYING AND BELONGING

Social identity on the playground

*Siân E. Jones, Andrew G. Livingstone and
Antony S. R. Manstead*

> *The group involved consisted of two girls and four boys, from different classes. They
> knew each other but were not close friends. The bullying took place in the school play-
> ground and on the way to and from school. It was in the form of physical attacks as
> well as name calling and had been taking place for three weeks. As school counsellor,
> the bullying incident was reported to me by the Head of Year. He had found out about
> the bullying from the target, who had bruising.*

The quote above comes from a participant in one of our studies (Jones, Manstead
and Livingstone, 2014); it describes a case of bullying between 14-year-olds in
the 1970s. It was not until the 1970s that it was realised that the bullying which
was apparently built into the brickwork of some schools should be considered as
problematic rather than 'character-building', or part of the curriculum, and that
something should be done to stop it. Olweus' (1991) work in Scandinavia, and
Smith and Sharp's (1994) Sheffield Anti-Bullying Project in the UK began to
address what could be done to prevent bullying in schools. The present chapter
briefly reviews key approaches to tackling bullying that have emerged since
Olweus' (1978) seminal work was published before exploring the way in which
adopting a social identity approach to this phenomenon has helped to advance
thinking even further. The challenges for further research in this field are also
considered.

Individual-level approaches

The first psychological research in this area sought to examine the extent of
bullying in schools before and after anti-bullying work had been done with
children. It was public outrage at bullying-related suicides in 1982 that led the
Norwegian Ministry of Education to institute the world's first anti-bullying

programme, covering every primary and junior high school in the country. The programme employed a set of techniques that have since become established as the Olweus Bullying Prevention Program. This includes an assessment of the frequency and nature of bullying using the Olweus Bullying Questionnaire (Olweus, 1986); awareness raising, educating and problem-solving activities and meetings for staff, parents and pupils; higher levels of supervision during unstructured periods of the school day; class/pupil-developed rules about behaviours; and meetings with perpetrators and targets of bullying and other peripherally involved children and their parents. Ongoing mentoring was provided to the school by a team of specialists. After 20 months, the number of students bullying others had reduced by 35 per cent for boys and 75 per cent for girls. It also seemed that communities around schools benefited from a general reduction in antisocial behaviour.

Other programmes broadly following the Norwegian model were established in Europe and the USA with promising results. In the UK, specialist children's charities like the Anti-Bullying Campaign and Kidscape put the government under pressure to tackle bullying. In response, the Sheffield Bullying Project ran from 1991 to 1994 in 23 schools (16 primary schools and 7 secondary schools), surveying 6,500 students aged 8–16 years. Like the Olweus Program, it emphasised 'whole school' policy development. Lessons drawn from the project formed the basis of a guidance pack for all schools – *Don't Suffer in Silence* was first issued by the UK Department for Education and Skills in 1994, at which time it was requested by over 19,000 schools. Revised editions were published in 2000, 2002 and 2007.

Alongside these interventions, theories emerged that explained bullying in terms of *individual psychopathology*, suggesting that certain personality characteristics make some people more likely to be targets of bullying. For example, Carney and Merrell (2001) contended that targets have an exploitable weakness and are submissive. Researchers also suggested that those who bully tend to be unfriendly and emotionally unstable (Tani *et al.*, 2003), to have little or no empathy for their targets (Carney and Merrell, 2001) and to display negative attitudes towards them (Rigby, 2005). Other studies suggested that family dynamics lie at the root of the problem in that those who bully may learn maladaptive coping skills from their parents (Carney and Merrell, 2001) or come from families that are fraught with conflict (Schwartz *et al.*, 1997). Still other studies suggested that bullying behaviour is not psychologically abnormal or deficient, but is, in fact, a product of the superior social skills of a person who bullies (e.g., Sutton *et al.*, 1999). Also in this vein, experimental studies have shown that those who engage in bullying have a better understanding of emotional cues than other people, suggesting that bullying may be a tool that allows them to manipulate others more effectively (Sutton *et al.*, 1999).

At the same time, research on the pervasiveness of bullying was startling, revealing that as many as 30 per cent of children may be a target of bullying at any one time. Moreover, its effects can be devastating. We now know that bullying impacts negatively upon young people's mental well-being (Dempsey *et al.*, 2011; Hawker and Boulton, 2000; Reijntjes *et al.*, 2010; Schwartz *et al.*, 2005), physical health (Biebl *et al.*, 2011; Gini and Pozzoli, 2009) and academic outcomes (Nakamoto and Schwartz, 2010) regardless of whether the individual is a perpetrator, target or bystander. There are further implications for social development, with involvement in bullying as target or as perpetrator linked to low popularity (Ahn *et al.*, 2010; Hanish and Guerra, 2002) and low social acceptance (Kochel, Ladd and Rudolph, 2012; Woodhouse, Dykas and Cassidy, 2012) as well as lower levels of prosocial behaviour (Woodhouse *et al.*, 2012) and social skills (Fox and Boulton, 2006). It continues to be a problem for schools despite the efforts of anti-bullying work: rates of bullying remain high in schools worldwide. In the UK, Rigby and Smith (2011) reported that typically 5 per cent of children might be seen as perpetrators of bullying and 10 per cent as targets. These authors also state that since the 1970s, the incidence of traditional bullying seems to be declining but, on the other hand, rates of cyberbullying have increased.

Perspectives on bullying as a group phenomenon

The sheer pervasiveness of bullying suggests that something beyond the dyadic interplay between target and perpetrator must underlie it. The participant-role approach developed by Salmivalli *et al.* (1996) invited researchers to examine bystanders' behaviour in the playground. According to this approach, bullying in schools should be considered a whole–class problem in which every child – with differing levels of involvement – plays a role. Salmivalli *et al.* (1996) identified six participant roles that children may take on: victim, bully, bully reinforcer, bully's assistant, defender of the victim, and outsider. These researchers also observed that children who play similar roles in bullying tend to form networks with each other and that the behaviour of an individual child is strongly influenced by the behaviour of other children in his or her network. As Salmivalli's research high-lights, withdrawing friendships and forming alliances with those who bully others is a very effective method of (a) bullying and (b) ensuring one is not oneself bullied. In other words, other children can either help to maintain or resist bullying. These dynamics indicate that bullying is a *social relationship* that can neither be straightforwardly reduced to the characteristics of those involved nor be understood solely in those terms.

When it comes to resistance, it is defenders who seem to have the largest part to play. Defenders are those children who 'take sides with the victims, comforting and supporting them' (Salmivalli, 2010, p. 114). Children nominated as defenders by their classmates tend to be emotionally stable (Tani *et al.*, 2003) and cognitively skilled (Caravita *et al.*, 2009), are empathic (e.g., Caravita *et al.*, 2009; Gini *et al.*, 2007) and have a strong belief in their defending ability (Thornberg and Jungert, 2013). Defenders are well liked (Salmivalli *et al.*, 1996) and popular among their peers (Caravita *et al.*, 2009). In other words, children who are defenders are highly socially skilled. Salmivalli *et al.* (1998) found that defending behaviour was linked to high social acceptance. Salmivalli *et al.* (2011) also showed that defending a victim was negatively associated with the overall amount of bullying in a classroom. This research provided further evidence that children other than the perpetrator and target are involved in bullying reduction.

Other evidence has emerged regarding the protective role of other children, not only defenders but also friends. For example, it has been shown that children value the protection afforded by friendships and that friendships can protect children against peer victimisation (Fox and Boulton, 2006). It is not only the number of friends that is important but also their identity. Fox and Boulton (2006) found that children who had a friend with high peer acceptance were less likely to be bullied over time. The notion that friends' identities are important paved the way for a social identity analysis of bullying. That is, until this point, 'social' research had emphasised social dynamics but had, nevertheless, retained an analysis of bullying as essentially an interpersonal phenomenon. By contrast, research within the social identity approach suggests that group phenomena involve acting in terms of a social identity. This profoundly shapes our perceptions and orientations towards others because it involves seeing them – and us – in terms of group memberships. It is also possible that adopting a social identity approach could help to explain the ways in which bullying is maintained in some schools.

A social identity approach

A social identity approach to understanding bullying is one in which all parties directly involved – perpetrators, victims and bystanders – are treated as, and perceive themselves to be, members of social groups. Such an approach also suggests that strength of identification with these groups is likely to vary from one person to another. Group membership in this psychological sense implies that children define themselves in particular contexts in terms of these memberships; these self-definitions constitute their social identities in the contexts in which bullying takes place. The content of a given social identity is specified in terms of *group norms* – a set of characteristics which prescribe attitudes and behaviours that epitomise a social group and differentiate it from other groups (Turner, 1999). On this account, bullying may occur because it is normative for the group to which an individual belongs and with which he or she identifies (Haslam and Reicher, 2007; Reicher and Haslam, 2006). In other words, children bully other children because the groups to which they belong have the attitude that bullying is a normal thing for members of this group to do.

Ojala and Nesdale (2004) directly investigated the role of social identity principles in bullying by examining reactions to a story about a popular ingroup and an unpopular outgroup. Their study incorporated different versions of the story, allowing the researchers to manipulate the norms of the ingroup (either to bully or to be fair to other children), the similarity of the ingroup to the outgroup (representing a threat to the ingroup or not) and the behaviour of a particular member of the ingroup (either bullying or being helpful). As hypothesised, it was found that these variables moderated the acceptability of bullying behaviour. More specifically, the ingroup character (a boy) was more likely to be retained as a group member when he behaved in accordance with group norms, even if this involved bullying. Bullying was also judged to be more acceptable where the outgroup represented a threat to the ingroup.

Although this research goes some way to demonstrating that children's bullying can be understood in terms of social identity concerns, Ojala and Nesdale (2004) acknowledged that their study was limited because it neither manipulated nor measured the extent to which participants identified with the characters in the stories. Later work has involved assigning children to *minimal* (arbitrary, *ad hoc*, laboratory-created) groups (see Tajfel *et al.*, 1971) to manipulate their social identity concerns when it comes to bullying. In research by Jones and colleagues (e.g., Jones, Manstead and Livingstone, 2011), we employed these minimal groups, randomly allocating participants to one of the three group membership conditions using a dot estimation task. For this task, each child was shown five slides, each displaying between 20 and 100 yellow dots on a blue background. Each slide was presented for three seconds. Participants were asked to record the number of dots they estimated to be on each slide. Participants were then instructed that their responses to the dot estimation task would be used to place them into one of three groups. The researcher exchanged each participant's response sheet for one assigning them (in reality, at random) to a particular (same gender) group. The sheet also contained information about that group. Membership of each group was indicated by the statement:

> Your guesses tended to be too small. Most children in [Perpetrator/Target name's group] also tend to make guesses that are too small. [Perpetrator/Target name's group] are an [active/fun-loving/bright] group of [girls/boys], who [enjoy listening to music together/watching DVDs together/playing games together].

The descriptions were devised so as to encourage participants to identify with their group, and they were instructed to keep this information private until they completed a questionnaire booklet. Our research, like that of others, has focused on how social identity concerns influence the ways in which children appraise and understand bullying incidents and the ways in which they experience and respond to bullying. In the remainder of this chapter, we review some of our own work on these issues in which we used the paradigm described above.

Appraising bullying incidents

The role of group norms

If social identities imply the relevance of group norms, how do these norms shape appraisals of bullying incidents? We know from multiple studies (e.g., Brown,

Birch and Kancherla, 2005) that children, when asked, report that bullying is wrong. Why should their perceptions be any different when they respond as members of a group? Part of the answer is that it has been shown that even young children have an understanding of group norms (e.g., Sani and Bennett, 2003) and that they act in accordance with such norms when they are made aware of them. Sani, Bennett, Agostini, Malucchi and Ferguson (2000) told 8-, 10- and 12-year-olds about 'People of the Mountains', including their physical and psychological characteristics and their socially shared beliefs. They were also told about a social conflict with 'People of the Valley'. Mountain people invaded the village where Valley people lived. Explanations for the invasion provided by 12-year-olds relied on socially shared (normative) beliefs of group members. Those provided by 8- to 10-year-olds relied on psychological characteristics of group members. A second study moved beyond this to research how children and adults represented the identities of groups. Young children's conceptions were concerned with personal and behavioural attributes, whereas older children and adults recognised the role of shared beliefs. Five-year-olds made no reference to group members' beliefs, whereas the other age groups did do so. Importantly, this research shows that from the age of 7 years, children make reference to group norms and understand that members of a group have some beliefs and attributes in common.

The notion that children are sensitive to group norms is further supported by the work of Nesdale and colleagues (Nesdale and Brown, 2004; Nesdale and Flesser, 2001; Nesdale, Durkin, Maass and Griffiths, 2004; Nesdale, Griffiths, Durkin and Maass, 2005; Nesdale, Maass, Griffiths and Durkin, 2003). These studies were all conducted in minimal group settings in which group member-ships were arbitrarily assigned and had no meaning outside the experimental situation. For example, Nesdale, Durkin, Maass, Kiesner and Griffiths (2008) showed that children's intentions to aggress were enhanced by an outgroup-disliking norm relative to an outgroup-liking norm. The findings show that children: (a) understand the importance of behaving in accordance with group norms and (b) modify their own behaviour as a function of such norms. Collectively, these studies show that children are sensitive to norms of exclusion and inclusion.

Moving out of the laboratory and into the classroom has also shown that chil-dren's responses to bullying vary according to what is normatively acceptable (e.g., Henry et al., 2000). Moreover, it has been shown that among children who belong to a group with a pro-bullying norm, those who bully others gain status and power within that group (Roland and Idsøe, 2001). Thus, children are more likely to bully others if they belong to a group with a culture of bullying. Indeed, the effect of group norms on aggression has been demonstrated with school-age children. Researchers have shown that children's beliefs about the acceptability of aggression, whether such beliefs are shared at the classroom or peer group level, influence the amount of aggression they display (Henry et al., 2000; Nesdale et al., 2008; Stormshak, Bierman, Bruschi, Dodge and Coie, 1999). Sentse,

Scholte, Salmivalli and Voeten (2007) showed that children who bullied were more likely to be rejected by their peers in a class where bullying was counter-normative, but less likely to be rejected by their peers where bullying was a class norm. It is possible, then, that normative effects on aggression extend to peer group bullying behaviours. Peer groups are likely to have norms concerning bullying, and group members are likely to be rewarded for adherence to such norms or rejected by the group when they fail to adhere to them (Morrison, 2006).

The above research shows the influence of children's perceptions of and beliefs about group behaviour. However, no research with children in this area had yet looked at their emotional reactions to group-relevant events. As research with adults has shown, there is considerable value in assessing specific, differentiated emotional reactions to group-relevant events rather than simply assessing the positivity or negativity of reactions *per se* (Smith, 1993; see Iyer and Leach, 2008 for a review of group-based emotion research). Part of this value lies in the fact that specific emotional reactions – such as anger or pride – have been found to predict tendencies towards quite different behavioural responses (see Frijda, 1986). We elaborate on the nature and consequences of such emotional reactions later. For now, we focus on how we have examined the influence of norms and group membership on emotional reactions in our own research.

In one of our studies (Jones et al., 2011), 10- and 11-year-olds were randomly assigned to one of three group conditions: being in the same group as someone later described as engaging in bullying (the perpetrator's group); being in the same group as someone later described as being the target of that bullying (the target's group); or being in a third-party group. Children then read one of four scenarios that varied with respect to the norm of the perpetrator's group. In the scenario, a perpetrator, supported by his or her group, acted unkindly towards a target who belonged to a different group by sending the target an unpleasant text message on behalf of the group whilst walking home from school. There were parallel versions of the scenario for females and males, with protagonists always being of the same gender as the participants. The norm of the perpetrator's group (to be kind or unkind towards others) was manipulated (see Box 4.1). Responses to the scenario were measured in terms of emotions pertinent to bullying (pride, shame, guilt and anger). It was predicted that group membership would affect the group-based emotions experienced by participants and that these effects would be moderated by the norm of the perpetrator's group. To a large extent, this was borne out by the findings. Those in the same group as the target reported greater group-based anger than did those in other groups. For those in the same group as the perpetrator, group norms did affect responding such that normative (but not counter-normative) behaviour led to greater group-based pride. Thus, information regarding the norm consistency of the perpetrator's behaviour determined whether group-based pride would be reported by participants.

BOX 4.1 RESEARCHING BULLYING AND SOCIAL IDENTITY: VIGNETTE-BASED PARADIGM

Children in our own studies described in this chapter were asked to read a vignette similar to the one below (from Jones *et al.*, 2009) and to answer questions about it.

"Here, kitty", Debbie called to the cat on the wall ahead of her. The cat turned and looked at her before disappearing over the other side of the wall. Debbie shrugged and carried on walking home.

Debbie went to Lingley Primary School, a big school in Wales with two classes in each year group. Most children who went to the school lived nearby, and older children usually walked home from school together with their friends.

Debbie looked ahead and saw two of her friends; Melanie was one of them. She ran ahead to catch up with them. They turned round and stopped for her. Melanie had her MP3 player with her, and they were taking it in turns to listen to music. They offered the earphones to Debbie. She smiled: it was fun being in Melanie's group.

Bess's group was walking home, too, on the other side of the road. They were swapping cards as they walked along and didn't see Melanie's group at all.

Debbie turned round suddenly. Melanie turned off the music and looked behind her, too: Jenny's group. They were the cool group in the school but occasionally teased others. "It's OK, Debbie, they won't hurt us, they're miles away", said Melanie.

"Yes, you're right", decided Debbie, and they put the music back on again. Jenny's group were looking at something together over Jenny's shoulder as they walked; all three of them. They all laughed.

Debbie's 'phone beeped: a text message. She fished it out of her bag and read the message:

> **How r u, Debbie? Who cares?**
> **U r such a loser!**

It was from Jenny and her group. Debbie wiped away a tear and put her phone away quickly. She had hoped things would be alright tonight. Shakily, she said goodbye to the others, pushed open her garden gate, and let herself into the empty house. She started to cry to herself.

It has been argued that children's beliefs about what they might do in response to a situation like this may bear little relation to what they would actually do (Finch, 1987); actual behaviour has not been measured. However, there is evidence that the ways in which people respond to emotion-arousing vignettes does correspond to the ways in which they react to 'real-life' events. Robinson and Clore (2001) found high convergence between participants' reactions to pictorial anxiety-provoking stimuli and written descriptions of those same stimuli. This convergence was seen not only in reported emotions but also in the appraisals accompanying these emotions. Indeed, participants who read only written descriptions reported slightly more anxiety than those who saw the pictorial stimuli. Furthermore, in a meta-analysis, van Zomeren *et al.* (2008) found that there is good correspondence between intentions and behaviour in the context of collective action research. Thus, it seems that there is a good basis, at least among adults, for assuming that responses to vignettes do relate to real-life emotional experience and behaviour.

What about broader normative influences? In another study reported by Jones, Bombieri, Livingstone and Manstead (2012), the role of normative context on responses to bullying was explored. As described above, 10- to 13-year-olds were randomly assigned to a minimal group in one of three conditions. Children then read a gender-matched scenario in which a perpetrator acted unkindly towards a target who belonged to a different group. Normative context (competitive, cooperative or neutral) was manipulated by varying a game that participants played immediately before reading this scenario. A competitive norm was established via a game in which a fish-shaped piece of paper was given to each participant, and they were then asked to race it against other ingroup members along a corridor using only a sheet of [newspaper. A cooperative] in a game in which participants [were asked to stand, the] each of their ingroup members i[n] backwards onto other group mem[bers. Those in the] asked to sit in a circle and take [turn to point to an] while doing so, to say their own [name. The child who] choose another child to continu[e the game. Those who] group *and* who played a competi[tive game before] more likely to report group-bas[ed pride than were those] the cooperative game or the con[trol game. By contrast,] rator's group who played the co[operative game before] were more likely to express ang[er about the bullying] competitive or control games. R[elative to those in other] of group-based anger were als[o reported by participants] group as the target and who pla[yed the cooperative game.]

Social identification

Despite evidence that social identity concerns are relevant to children in the context of bullying and that appraisals of bullying have ramifications at the group level, it is possible that children may not think of themselves as members of a particular group. Merely placing oneself in a category is not equivalent to having a social identity (Sani and Bennett, 2003). Instead, social identity concerns – and the influence of group norms – are likely to be stronger to the extent that people subjectively *identify* with their group (e.g., Ellemers, Spears and Doosje, 1997). Indeed, we have consistently found that identification shapes children's reactions to bullying scenarios and group norms. As noted above in relation to the results of Jones *et al.*'s (2011) study, identification had a moderating role in the reporting of group-based pride. The more children identified with their group, the more group-based pride was reported. As we discuss in more detail below, bullying is a domain in which concerns for the positivity of one's ingroup are likely to be particularly acute, meaning that ingroup identification can also be an *outcome* of bullying, For example, Nesdale, Milliner, Duffy and Griffiths (2009) showed that liking of the ingroup varied depending on whether the ingroup did or did not have a norm of aggression. Thus, the implications of bullying for the intensity of one's social identification with an ingroup are shaped by whether or not bullying is consistent with ingroup norms because the degree to which ingroup members' behaviour is norm consistent also has implications for one's level of social identitification. For example, Nesdale, Durkin, Maass and Griffiths (2005) found that children's ethnic prejudice (understood here as a form of bullying) was positively related to strength of identification with their ethnic ingroup.

Responding to bullying incidents

Emotional responses

Doosje, Branscombe, Spears and Manstead (1998) argued that one consequence of belonging to a social group is that the actions of others who share that group membership can have emotional consequences for oneself (e.g., the guilt experienced by young Germans in the years since World War II regardless of their lack of personal involvement in wartime events). Emotion can, therefore, be experienced on the basis of shared group membership; for example, one may be 'guilty by association' (Doosje *et al.*, 1998, p. 872). The way in which adults respond emotionally to intergroup contexts has been the subject of a burgeoning literature since the publication of Smith's (1993) first statement of intergroup emotion theory. This theory proposes that group-based emotions are those which take groups rather than individuals as the subject and object of the emotion (Parkinson, Fisher and Manstead, 2005). Theories of group-based emotion propose that the degree to which we define ourselves and others as group members rather than as individuals and the extent to which we identify with a group play a role in determining: (a) whether we experience group-based emotion and (b) the intensity of that emotion. There is now a plethora of evidence that group-based emotions, including anger, fear, contempt, happiness, sadness and schadenfreude, are experienced by adults in intergroup contexts (see Iyer and Leach, 2008, for a review).

   In order to examine children's capacity to experience emotion on behalf of another group member, Bennett, Yuill, Banerjee and Thomson (1998) studied whether children were affected by the wrongdoings of ingroup members. Hypothetical scenarios were read to 5-, 7- and 9-year-olds in which they themselves were responsible for a negative, potentially embarrassing action or in which a member of their own group committed the same action. In an individual condition, all age groups indicated that they would want to apologise. In a social condition, however, only 7- and 9-year-olds wanted to apologise. Sani and Bennett (2003) argued that it is debatable whether younger children's references to group memberships have the same meaning as those of older children, suggesting that affect-based responding is unlikely to be seen in children younger than 7 years of age. This study was one of the earliest to examine social emotions in children and provided a basis for further research on the role of emotions in children's responses to intergroup contexts, at least among children aged 8 years or over.

Although many studies have examined group-based emotions in adults, few have researched intergroup emotions in children, especially in the context of bullying. Turner, Hewstone and Voci (2007) studied the role played by intergroup anxiety in the context of White children's friendships with Asian children and found that the anxiety mediated the link between time spent in cross-group friendships and positive attitudes towards the outgroup. This research shows that children experience emotions in relation to outgroups – but it is not clear whether anxiety resulted from children's identity as a group member or their identity as an individual (in other words, children might not have experienced *intergroup* anxiety *per se*). Further work by De Amicis (2009) studied interracial bullying, looking at the extent to which children *as group members* experienced emotions about group-relevant events. She introduced White children to an interethnic bullying scenario in which the race of the perpetrator and the race of the target (in each case White or Black) were independently manipulated. Among older children (aged 10–11 years), increased group-based anger resulted from a situation in which the target was White. Younger children (aged 8–9 years) felt more group-based sadness when the target was Black. This shows that children's group-based emotions are dependent upon the group identity (ingroup or outgroup) of those who have a perpetrator or target role in a bullying scenario. However, it is important to note that ethnic ingroup or outgroup identity was confounded with the minority versus majority status of that identity in these studies. Thus, group-based sadness might have resulted from the minority status of the target rather than from their position as an outgroup member.

The role of emotions in shaping reactions to bullying is also evidenced in our own work. For example, in Jones, Manstead and Livingstone's (2009) study, 9- to 11-year-olds were randomly assigned to the same group as story characters who were described as engaging in bullying, as being bullied, or as neither engaging in bullying nor being bullied. Participants read a story in which a perpetrator, supported by his or her group, was described as acting unkindly towards a child in a different group. The perpetrator's group norm (to be kind or unkind to other children) was varied. Children's group membership predicted the group-based emotions they reported in that perpetrator group members reported more pride and target group members reported more anger – effects that were, in turn, moderated by participants' ingroup identification. There was also an effect of group norm: the behaviour elicited more anger when the group acted counter-normatively.

Changing identification

As indicated earlier, our research (Jones *et al.*, 2009, 2011) also highlights that children's group identification is relevant to how they respond to group-level bullying. In these studies, children's group membership predicted the group-based emotions they reported, along with increasing ingroup identification; in other words, ingroup identification shaped the group-based emotions that were reported. Research with adults has shown that group-relevant events also *affect* ingroup identification and that the influence of such events is shaped by prior levels of identification (Ellemers *et al.*, 1997). To find out whether children respond similarly to group-relevant events (namely, a bullying incident), in the study reported by Jones, Manstead and Livingstone (2012), children were randomly assigned to either a perpetrator's group or a target's group. They then read a scenario which described an incident in which a member of the perpetrator's group bullied a target group member. The incident was either consistent or inconsistent with the norms of the perpetrator's group. How strongly perpetrator group members identified with that group after learning about the bullying incident was determined by their initial level of identification in interaction with the perpetrator's group norm: when initial identification with the group was high, counter-normative bullying behaviour (i.e., when the group norm was to be kind) resulted in higher subsequent identification compared to when the bullying behaviour was norm consistent (i.e., when the group norm was to be unkind). A trend in the opposite direction emerged when initial identification was low. One interpretation of this pattern is that children are *strategic* in their group-based responses to bullying: they report higher identification with a group whose member perpetrated an act of bullying when that act can be seen as counter-normative compared to when it is normative, but only when initial levels of identification are high (found in other research to predict a concern for the group's image; e.g., Spears *et al.*, 1997).

Action tendencies

As members of social groups, children may appraise and react emotionally to an intergroup bullying scenario in multiple ways. When it comes to anti-bullying policies and interventions aimed at tackling bullying, what is crucial is how children think they would intervene in light of their thoughts and feelings concerning the bullying incident. It is important to know what children think and feel in response to a bullying incident precisely because different appraisals and group-based emotions lead to different action tendencies. Pride leads to a tendency to seek out others and to talk about one's achievements (Tracy and Robins, 2004), whereas anger leads to tendencies to act against a harming party (e.g., Mackie, Devos and Smith, 2000). Action tendencies also serve as a basis for distinguishing shame from guilt (Tangney and Dearing, 2002). Shame typically leads to a tendency to distance oneself from the source of one's shame, whereas guilt typically leads to a tendency to make reparations for the wrongdoing. Jones *et al.* (2009) showed that pride following a bullying incident was associated with affiliation with a bullying group, whereas guilt was associated with a tendency to apologise to the target, and anger with a tendency to tell an adult. Relatedly, Jones *et al.* (2011) showed that the degree to which children identified with a group membership, in combination with the group norm, affected their emotional responses to a cyberbullying incident. In turn, emotional responses to bullying were linked to the actions children said they would undertake after witnessing bullying.

What next for a social identity approach to studying bullying?

Over the past few years, considerable support has been found for the hypothesis that bullying can be meaningfully conceptualised as intergroup behaviour that is influenced by social identity processes (Ojala and Nesdale, 2004), which, in turn, have implications for social identities (e.g., Nesdale and Pelyhe, 2009). This extends to the domain of group-based emotions. Given that the studies described above are among the first to examine group-based emotions in children, it is worth considering how research on group-based emotion and bullying is likely to develop.

One potential limitation of the research to date is that it has relied very heavily on variations on the minimal group paradigm (cf. Tajfel *et al.*, 1971). This has certainly produced striking effects in that large differences are found between children's responses to bullying simply as a result of assigning them to different groups in this paradigm. Using this method also affords a high level of control over the group-level factors in the research. Nevertheless, the fact remains that the groups in these studies were artificial ones, thereby limiting the ecological validity of the findings. Because of this, we cannot yet draw firm conclusions about the ways in which children's actual friendship groups are likely to respond to a genuine intergroup bullying incident. Children's social networks and friendship groups are likely to be much more complicated and fluid over time than the intergroup settings to which children have been exposed thus far in our research: children belong to multiple groups, some of which may be nested within each other and which may extend beyond classroom or school boundaries.

Investigating bullying *within* children's actual friendship groups is another important challenge for future work. Different lines of social identity research with adult participants have highlighted some of the intra-group processes that may be relevant for such future work. Important observations here include that members of a group can vary in terms of the prototypicality (or representativeness) of the group (Spears *et al.*, 1997), the extent to which they adhere to ingroup norms (Hornsey and Jetten, 2004) and the extent to which they are peripheral/ marginal in the group (e.g., Jetten, Branscombe, Spears and McKimmie, 2003). On the one hand, some research suggests that hostility towards members of other groups may serve strategic intra-group purposes for relatively new or peripheral members of a group, providing a way of ingratiating oneself to the rest of the group (Noel, Wann and Branscombe, 1995). On the other hand, research (e.g., on the 'black sheep' effect, Marques, Yzerbyt and Leyens, 1988; on 'subjective group dynamics', Marques, Abrams and Serôdio, 2001) highlights how deviation from ingroup norms can lead group members to be derogated by their fellow ingroup members. Recent research has begun to examine such processes amongst children (e.g., Abrams, Rutland, Ferrell and Pelletier, 2008; Hitti, Mulvey, Rutland, Abrams and Killen, 2013), suggesting that principles from social identity and self-categorisation theories may be fruitfully applied to understanding bullying within as well as between groups.

Indeed, in line with a social identity account, research has begun to look at intra-group dynamics in terms of children's different evaluations of ingroup members who deviate from or adhere to group norms (e.g., Abrams and Rutland, 2008) and whether the importance of adhering to group norms is considered reason enough by children to exclude members who challenge group norms. Research by Hitti *et al.* (2013) has shown that children do judge the social exclusion of a group member from the group as legitimate when group norms have been transgressed. In other words, children have the capacity to judge individual ingroup members in line with social identity concerns. Finally, in the intra-group domain among adults, it has been shown that shared emotion with other ingroup members concerning group-relevant events predicts future collaboration among group members (Livingstone, Shepherd, Spears and Manstead, 2016). The time is now ripe to extend this research to child participants in terms of shared emotional responses with ingroup members.

Because it is hard to manipulate the norms of pre-existing groups, researchers have tended to assign children to *ad hoc* groups. However, it is possible that the children who took part in these studies were responsive to group norms precisely because the groups involved were new to them and they were keen to fit in as soon as possible. It is, therefore, not clear from this research whether children are more sensitive to group norms in: (a) *ad hoc* groups or (b) groups with which they already identify. This is another issue that will be important for future research to disentangle in order to better predict children's responses to bullying.

For reasons of experimental control, the situations depicted in the studies deliberately avoided specifying any overt status or power relations between or within groups. However, children's friendship groups are highly unlikely to be devoid of these factors, and investigating group-based emotional responses to bullying between groups with different power and status is an important task for future research given that social identity theory (Tajfel and Turner, 1979) makes specific predictions concerning group members' behaviour as a function of these relations, particularly regarding the legitimacy and stability of group status relations (i.e., whether status differences are seen as fair or unfair and as fixed or changeable).

Another criticism that can be levelled at the research reviewed above is the use of scenarios to elicit responses about bullying. The use of a vignette methodology necessarily constrains the type of bullying that is described. However, the bullying actually experienced by children is often multifaceted. It may involve different numbers of children, may escalate over time and is likely to involve more than one 'method'. It would, nonetheless, be worth studying the extent to which group processes are pertinent to other forms of bullying and (retrospectively) the extent to which they are pertinent to actual bullying episodes.

The extant literature generates broader research questions concerning children's socio-emotional development in the context of bullying. It would be particularly interesting to extend our knowledge of children's abilities to process others' emotions at the group level. Thus far, a first-person perspective on bullying has been taken: children have been told that they are members of a group that engaged in or was on the receiving end of bullying and then asked about the group-based emotions they imagined they would feel as a result of that situation. Social appraisal theory argues that one's own emotional reaction to an event can change as a function of what one believes others are feeling (Bruder, Fischer and Manstead, 2014; Manstead and Fischer, 2001). Applying this to a bullying context, it would be interesting to examine not only what group-based emotions children are experiencing as group members in response to bullying but also what group-based emotions they imagine their fellow group members are experiencing and to investigate whether their own emotional reactions converge with those of other children. If it were to be discovered that children, like adults, are influenced by others' emotions in this way, this would add a further dimension to anti-bullying interventions.

Summary

This chapter has charted the development of bullying research since the 1970s, shifting from an initial focus on individual psychopathology towards a more social-psychological and, then, an explicitly social identity-based approach. Research using the social identity approach shows that children are sensitive to the nuances of intergroup relations. In their responses to bullying, children take account of the norms of a perpetrating group as well as the wider normative context. They also consider different possible appraisals of bullying in light of group norms and adjust their levels of ingroup identification in response to intergroup bullying. Further research now needs to account for the group-level nature of bullying in *real-life* bullying incidents, for the involvement of group member bystanders, and for the group processes by which children (a) come to be involved in bullying in the first place and (b) are motivated or empowered to resist it.

References

Abrams, D. and Rutland, A. (2008). The development of subjective group dynamics. In S. R. Levy and M. Killen (Eds), Intergroup relations and attitudes in childhood through adulthood (pp. 47–65). Oxford: Oxford University Press.

Abrams, D., Rutland, A., Ferrell, J. and Pelletier, J. (2008). Children's judgments of disloyal and immoral peer behaviour: Subjective group dynamics in minimal intergroup contexts. *Child Development, 79*(2), 444–61.

Ahn, H-J., Garandeau, C. F. and Rodkin, P. C. (2010). Effects of classroom embeddedness and density on the social status of aggressive and victimized children. *Journal of Adolescence, 30*(1), 76–101.

Bennett, M., Yuill, N., Banerjee, R. and Thompson, S. (1998). Children's understanding of extended identity. *Developmental Psychology, 34*(2), 322–31. doi: 10.1037/0012-1649.34.2.322

Biebl, S. J., DiLalla, L. F., Davis, E. K., Lynch, K. A. and Shinn, S. O. (2011). Longitudinal associations among peer victimization and physical and mental health problems. *Journal of Pediatric Psychology, 36*(8), 868–77.

Brown, S., Birch, D. and Kancherla, V. (2005). Bullying perspectives: Experiences, attitudes, and recommendations of 9- to 13-year-olds attending health education centers in the United States. *Journal of School Health, 75*(10), 384–92. doi: 10.1111/j.1746-1561.2005.00053.x

Bruder, M., Fischer, A. and Manstead, A. S. R. (2014). Social appraisal as a cause of collective emotions. In C. von Scheve and M. Salmela (Eds), *Collective emotions* (pp. 141–55). Oxford: Oxford University Press.

Caravita, S., Di Blasio, P. and Salmivalli, C. (2009). Unique and interactive effects of empathy and social status on involvement in bullying. *Social Development, 18*(1), 140–63.

Carney, A. G. and Merrell, K. W. (2001). Bullying in schools: Perspectives on understanding and preventing an international problem. *School Psychology International, 22*(3), 364–82. doi: 10.1177/0143034301223011

De Amicis, L. (2009). The role of emotions in children's responses to intergroup contexts. University of Sussex, unpublished thesis.

Dempsey, A. G., Haden., S. C., Goldman, J., Sivinski, J. and Wiens, B. A. (2011). Relational and overt victimization in middle and high schools: Associations with self-reported suicidality. *Journal of School Violence, 10*(4), 374–92.

Doosje, B., Branscombe, N. R., Spears, R. and Manstead, A. S. R. (1998). Guilty by association: When one's group has a negative history. *Journal of Personality and Social Psychology, 75*(4), 872–86. doi: 10.1037/0022-3514.75.4.872

Ellemers, N., Spears, R. and Doosje, B. (1997). Sticking together or falling apart: Ingroup identification as a psychological determinant of group commitment versus individual mobility. *Journal of Personality and Social Psychology, 72*(3), 617–26. doi: 10.1037/0022-3514.72.3.617

Finch, J. (1987). The vignette technique in survey research. *Sociology, 21*(1), 105–14. doi: 10.1177/0038038587021001008

Fox, C. L. and Boulton, M. J. (2006). Longitudinal associations between social skills problems and different types of peer victimisation. *Violence and Victims, 21*(3), 387–404.

Frijda, N. H. (1986). *The emotions.* Cambridge: Cambridge University Press.

Gini, G., Albiero, P., Benelli, B. and Altoe, G. (2007). Does empathy predict adolescents' bullying and defending behavior? *Aggressive Behavior, 33*(5), 467–76.

Gini, G. and Pozzoli, T. (2009). Associations between bullying and psychosomatic problems: A meta-analysis. *Pediatrics, 123*(3), 1059–65. doi: 10.1542/peds. 2008-1215

Hanish, L. D. and Guerra, N. G. (2002). A longitudinal analysis of patterns of adjustment following peer victimization. *Development and Psychopathology, 14*(1), 69–89.

Haslam, S. A. and Reicher, S. D. (2007). Beyond the banality of evil: Three dynamics of an interactionist social psychology of tyranny. *Personality and Social Psychology Bulletin, 33*(5), 615–22.

Hawker, D. S. J. and Boulton, M. J. (2000). Twenty years' research on peer victimization and psychosocial maladjustment: A meta-analytic review of cross-sectional studies. *Journal of Child Psychology and Psychiatry, 41*(4), 441–55.

Henry, D., Guerra, N., Huesmann, R., Tolan, P., VanAcker, R. and Eron, L. (2000). Normative influences on aggression in urban elementary school classrooms. *American Journal of Community Psychology, 28*(1), 59–81. doi: 10.1023/A:1005142429725

Hitti, A., Mulvey, K. L., Rutland, A., Abrams, D. and Killen, M. (2013). When is it okay to exclude a member of the ingroup? Children's and adolescents' social reasoning. *Social Development, 23*(3), 451–69. doi: 10.1111/sode.12047

Hornsey, M. J. and Jetten, J. (2004). The individual within the group: Balancing the need to belong with the need to be different. *Personality and Social Psychology Review, 8*(3), 248–64.

Iyer, A. and Leach, C. W. (2008). Emotion in intergroup relations. *European Review of Social Psychology, 19*(1), 86–125. doi: 10.1080/10463280802079738

Jetten, J., Branscombe, N. R., Spears, R. and McKimmie, B. M. (2003). Predicting the paths of peripherals: The interaction of identification and future possibilities. *Personality and Social Psychology Bulletin, 29*(1), 130–40.

Jones, S. E., Bombieri, L., Livingstone, A. G. and Manstead, A. S. R. (2012). The influence of norms and social identities on children's responses to bullying. *British Journal of Educational Psychology, 82*(2), 241–56.

Jones, S. E., Manstead, A. S. R. and Livingstone, A. (2009). Birds of a feather bully together: Group processes and children's responses to bullying. *British Journal of Developmental Psychology, 27*(4), 853–73. doi: 10.1348/02615 1008X390267

Jones, S. E., Manstead, A. S. R. and Livingstone, A. G. (2011). Ganging up or sticking together: Group processes and children's responses to bullying. *British Journal of Psychology, 102*(1), 71–96.

Jones, S. E., Manstead, A. S. R. and Livingstone, A. G. (2012). Fair-weather or foul-weather friends? Group identification and children's responses to bullying. *Social Psychology and Personality Science, 3*(4), 414–20.

Jones, S. E., Manstead, A. S. R. and Livingstone, A. G. (2014). Bullying and belonging: Teachers' reports of school aggression. *Frontline Learning Research, 2*(1), 64–77.

Kochel, K. P., Ladd, G. W. and Rudolph, K. D. (2012). Longitudinal associations among youth depressive symptoms, peer victimization, and low peer acceptance: An interpersonal process perspective. *Child Development, 83*(2), 637–50.

Livingstone, A. G., Shepherd, L., Spears, R. and Manstead, A. S. R. (2016). 'Fury, us': Anger as a basis for new group self-categories. *Cognition and Emotion, 30*(1), 183–92.

Mackie, D. M., Devos, T. and Smith, E. R. (2000). Intergroup emotions: Explaining offensive action tendencies in an intergroup context. *Journal of Personality and Social Psychology, 79*(4), 602–16. doi: 10.1037/0022-3514.79.4.602

Manstead, A. S. R. and Fischer, A. H. (2001). Social appraisal: The social world as object of and influence on appraisal processes. In K. R. Scherer and A. Schorr (Eds), *Appraisal processes in emotion: Theory, methods, research* (pp. 221–32). New York: Oxford University Press.

Marques, J. M., Abrams, D. and Serôdio, R. G. (2001). Being better by being right: Subjective group dynamics and derogation of ingroup deviants when generic norms are undermined. *Journal of Personality and Social Psychology, 82*(3), 436–47.

Marques, J. M., Yzerbyt, V. Y. and Leyens, J.-P. (1988). The black sheep effect: Judgmental extremity towards ingroup members as a function of group identification. *European Journal of Social Psychology, 18*(1), 1–16.

Morrison, B. (2006). School bullying and restorative justice: Toward a theoretical understanding of the role of respect, pride and shame. *Journal of Social Issues, 62*(2), 371–92. doi: 10.1111/j.1540-4560.2006.00455.x

Nakamoto, J. and Schwartz, D. (2010). Is peer victimization associated with academic achievement? A meta-analytic review. *Social Development, 19*(2), 221–42.

Nesdale, D. and Brown, K. (2004). Children's attitudes towards an atypical member of an ethnic ingroup. *International Journal of Behavioral Development, 28*(4), 328–35. doi: 10.1080/01650250444000018

Nesdale, D., Durkin, K., Maass, A. and Griffiths, J. (2004). Group status, outgroup ethnicity and children's ethnic attitudes. *Applied Developmental Psychology, 25*(2), 237–51. doi: 10.1016/j.appdev.2004.02.005

Nesdale, D., Durkin, K., Maass, A. and Griffiths, J. (2005). Threat, group identification, and children's ethnic prejudice. *Social Development, 14*(2), 189–205. doi: 10.1111/j.1467-9507.2005.00298.x

Nesdale, D., Durkin, K., Maass, A., Kiesner, J. and Griffiths, J. (2008). Effects of group norms on children's intentions to bully. *Social Development, 17*(4), 889–907. doi: 10.1111/j.1467-9507.2008.00475.x

Nesdale, D. and Flesser, D. (2001). Social identity and the development of children's group attitudes. *Child Development, 72*(2), 506–17. doi: 10.1111/1467-8624.00293

Nesdale, D., Griffiths, J., Durkin, K. and Maass, A. (2005). Empathy, group norms and children's ethnic attitudes. *Journal of Applied Developmental Psychology, Special Issue: Children's and Adolescents' Intergroup Attitudes About Race and Ethnicity, 26*(6), 623–37. doi: 10.1016/j.appdev.2005.08.003

Nesdale, D., Maass, A., Griffiths, J. and Durkin, K. (2003). Effects of ingroup and outgroup ethnicity on children's attitudes towards members of the ingroup and outgroup. *British Journal of Developmental Psychology, 21*(2), 177–92. doi: 10.1348/026151003765264039

Nesdale, D., Milliner, E., Duffy, A. and Griffiths, J. A. (2009). Group membership, group norms, empathy, and young children's intentions to aggress. *Aggressive Behavior, 35*(3), 244–58. doi: 10.1002/ab.20303

Nesdale, D. and Pelyhe, H. (2009). Effects of experimentally induced peer-group rejection and out-group ethnicity on children's anxiety, self-esteem, and in-group and out-group attitudes. *European Journal of Developmental Psychology, 6*(3), 294–317. doi: 10.1080/17405620601112436

Noel, J. G., Wann, D. and Branscombe, N. (1995). Peripheral ingroup membership status and public negativity toward out-groups. *Journal of Personality and Social Psychology, 68*(1), 127–37.

Ojala, K. and Nesdale, D. (2004). Bullying and social identity: The effects of group norms and distinctiveness threat on attitudes towards bullying. *British Journal of Developmental Psychology, 22*(1), 19–35. doi: 10.1348/0261510047 72901096

Olweus, D. (1978). *Aggression in the schools. Bullies and whipping boys.* London: John Wiley and Sons.

Olweus, D. (1986). *The Olweus Bully/Victim Questionnaire* [mimeo]. Bergen, Norway: Research Center for Health Promotion, University of Bergen.

Olweus, D. (1991). Bully/victim problems among schoolchildren: Basic facts and effects of a school based intervention program. In D. Pepler and K. Rubin (Eds), *The development and treatment of childhood aggression* (pp. 411–48). Hillsdale, NJ: Lawrence Erlbaum.

Parkinson, B., Fischer, A. and Manstead, A. S. R. (2005). *Emotion in social relations: Cultural, group and interpersonal processes.* Hove, UK: Psychology Press.

Reicher, S. D. and Haslam, S. A. (2006). Rethinking the psychology of tyranny: The BBC Prison Study. *British Journal of Social Psychology, 45*(1), 1–40.

Reijntjes, A., Kamphius, J. H., Prinzie, P. and Telch, M. J. (2010). Peer victimization and internalizing problems in children: A meta-analysis of longitudinal studies. *Child Abuse and Neglect, 34*(4), 244–52.

Rigby, K. (2005). Why do some children bully at school? The contributions of negative attitudes towards victims and the perceived expectations of friends, parents and teachers. *School Psychology International, 26*(2), 147–61.

Rigby, K. and Smith, P. K. (2011). Is school bullying really on the rise? *Social Psychology of Education, 14*(4), 441–55.

Robinson, M. D. and Clore, G. L. (2001). Simulation, scenarios, and emotional appraisal: Testing the convergence of real and imagined reactions to emotional stimuli. *Personality and Social Psychology Bulletin, 27*(11), 1520–32. doi: 10.1177/01461672012711012

Roland, E. and Idsøe, T. (2001). Aggression and bullying. *Aggressive Behavior, 27*(6), 446–62. doi: 10.1002/ab.1029

Salmivalli, C. (2010). Bullying and the peer group: A review. *Aggression and Violent Behavior, 15*(2), 112–20.

Salmivalli, C., Lagerspetz, K. M. J., Björkqvist, K., Österman, K. and Kaukiainen, A. (1996). Bullying as a group process: Participant roles and their relations to social status within the class. *Aggressive Behavior, 22*(1), 1–15. doi: 10.1002/(SICI)1098-2337(1996)22:1<1::AID-AB1>3.0.CO;2-T

Salmivalli, C., Lappalainen, M. and Lagerspetz, K. (1998). Stability and change of behavior in connection with bullying in schools: A two-year follow-up. *Aggressive Behavior, 24*(3), 205–18.

Salmavalli, C., Voeten, M. and Poskiparta, E. (2011). Bystanders matter: Associations between reinforcing, defending, and the frequency of bullying behaviour in classrooms. *Journal of Clinical Child and Adolescent Psychology, 40*(5), 668–76.

Sani, F. and Bennett, M. (2003). Developmental aspects of social identity. In M. Bennett and F. Sani (Eds), *The development of the social self* (pp. 77–102). Hove, UK: Psychology Press.

Sani, F., Bennett, M., Agostini, L., Malucchi, L. and Ferguson, N. (2000). Children's conception of characteristic features of category members. *Journal of Social Psychology, 140*(2), 227–39.

Schwartz, D., Dodge, K. A., Petit, G. S. and Bates, J. E. (1997). The early socialization and adjustment of aggressive victims of bullying. *Child Development, 68*(4), 665–7.

Schwartz, D., Gorman, A. H., Nakamoto, J. and Toblin, R. L. (2005). Victimization in the peer group and children's academic functioning. *Journal of Educational Psychology, 97*(3), 425–35.

Sentse, M., Scholte, R., Salmivalli, C. and Voeten, M. (2007). Person–group dissimilarity in involvement in bullying and its relation with social status. *Journal of Abnormal Child Psychology, 35*(6), 1009–19. doi: 10.1007/s108 02-007-9150-3

Smith, E. R. (1993). Social identity and social emotions: Toward new conceptualizations of prejudice. In D. M. Mackie and D. L. Hamilton (Eds), *Affect, cognition, and stereotyping: Interactive processes in group perception* (pp. 297–315). San Diego, CA: Academic Press.

Smith, P. K. and Sharp, S. (1994). *School bullying: Insights and perspectives*. London: Routledge.

Spears, R., Doosje, B. and Ellemers, N. (1997). Self-stereotyping in the face of threats to group status and distinctiveness: The role of group identification. *Personality and Social Psychology Bulletin*, 23(5), 538–53.

Stormshak, E. A., Bierman, K. L., Bruschi, C., Dodge, K. A. and Coie, J. D. (1999). The relation between behavior problems and peer preference in different classroom contexts. *Child Development*, 70(1), 169–82. doi: 10.1111/1467-8624.00013

Sutton, J., Smith, P. K. and Swettenham, J. (1999). Bullying 'theory of mind': A critique of the 'social skills deficit' view of anti-social behaviour. *Social Development*, 8(1), 117–27.

Tajfel, H., Billig, M. G., Bundy, R. P. and Flament, C. (1971). Social categorization and intergroup behavior. *European Journal of Social Psychology*, 1(2), 149–77. doi: 10.1002/ejsp.2420010202

Tajfel, H. and Turner, J. (1979). An integrative theory of intergroup conflict. In W. G. Austin and S. Worchel (Eds), *The social psychology of intergroup relations* (pp. 7–24). Monterey, CA: Brooks Cole.

Tangney, J. P. and Dearing, R. (2002). *Shame and guilt*. New York: Guilford.

Tani, F., Greenman, P. S., Schneider, B. H. and Fregoso, M. (2003). Bullying and the Big Five: A study of childhood personality and participant roles in bullying incidents. *School Psychology International*, 24(2), 131–46.

Thornberg, R. and Jungert, T. (2013). Bystander behavior in bullying situations: Basic moral sensitivity, moral disengagement and defender self-efficacy. *Journal of Adolescence*, 36(3), 475–83.

Tracy, J. L. and Robins, R. W. (2004). Putting the self into self-conscious emotions: A theoretical model. *Psychological Inquiry*, 15(2), 103–25. doi: 10.1207/s15327965pli1 502_01

Turner, J. C. (1999). Some current issues in research on social identity and self-categorization theories. In N. Ellemers, R. Spears and B. Doosje (Eds), *Social identity: Context, commitment, content* (pp. 6–34). Oxford: Blackwell.

Turner, R., Hewstone, M. and Voci, A. (2007). Reducing explicit and implicit prejudice via direct and extended contact: The mediating role of self-disclosure and intergroup anxiety. *Journal of Personality and Social Psychology*, 93(3), 369–88. doi: 10.1037/0022-3514.93.3.369

Woodhouse, S. S., Dykas, M. J. and Cassidy, J. (2012). Loneliness and peer relations in adolescence. *Social Development*, 21(2), 274–93.

PART III
Social identities between the classroom and beyond

5

WHY SO FEW?

The role of social identity and situational cues in understanding the underrepresentation of women in STEM fields

Kathryn L. Boucher and Mary C. Murphy

Consider this scenario. Sarah is in her first year of college/university and is excited to be an engineering major. Sarah feels prepared for her coursework as she got great grades in her past advanced maths and science courses and received high scores on her college entrance exams. Although there were slightly more male students than female students in her past maths and science classes, Sarah felt like she belonged and was accepted there. However, when she arrives at her first college classes, she is surprised to find that the vast majority of her classmates in maths and science classes are male and most of her instructors are also male.

She has rarely considered her gender and the stereotypic expectations tied to this social identity before college; now these are unwelcome but constant thoughts as she sits in her maths and science classes. Several professors make comments as to how their courses delineate who the promising students and poor performers are, the people who *should* and *should not* be in a science or maths major. These messages, coupled with there being few other women present in class, prompt Sarah to worry that she may not have what it takes to excel in maths and science and, by extension, as an engineer. Moreover, even if she does well, it is unclear to her whether other people will believe that she belongs in engineering.

Despite her concerns about fitting in and measuring up to others' expectations, her existing knowledge and the numerous hours she spends studying in her maths and science classes results in early success; however, when the course material gets more difficult, her performance starts to suffer. Sarah's double concern of performing well for herself and on behalf of her gender, in spite of gender stereo-types, makes class difficulties a greater blow to her sense of belonging in these classes. These difficulties lead her to consider dropping these courses and changing her major. Sarah wants to ask for help but is afraid she will be seen as confirming stereotypes if she reaches out to her predominately male professors and classmates. Instead of dreading class and spending countless hours struggling to understand the material in the maths and science courses she once loved, Sarah decides to change her major to a field where she feels she has a better chance of excelling, one that is free from the identity concerns that arose in maths and science.

Gender representation in science, technology, engineering and maths

Unfortunately, this hypothetical scenario echoes the real-life experiences of many women who enter science, technology, engineering and maths (STEM) classrooms, majors and careers (Ceci and Williams, 2007; Margolis and Fisher, 2003). Women who have the necessary skills and interest in this area disproportionally drop out of STEM courses and majors (Hill, Corbett and St. Rose, 2010; National Center for Science and Engineering Statistics [NCSES], 2013). Among women with STEM degrees, a smaller number enter STEM careers (United Nations Educational, Scientific and Cultural Organization [UNESCO], 2007; US Department of Labor, Bureau of Labor Statistics, 2009). Women in STEM careers advance to higher positions at a slower pace and leave STEM fields at higher rates than their male counterparts (Hill *et al.*, 2010; UNESCO, 2007). At every critical transition point, fewer and fewer women remain in STEM.

Women's underrepresentation is not solely due to women who are highly STEM-identified, like Sarah, leaving these fields. There is also a gender gap in students' early interest in STEM (Hill *et al.*, 2010; UNESCO, 2007). Although middle and high school girls and boys in the United States now take nearly equal numbers of STEM courses and receive similar grades (Brainard and Carlin, 1998; Huang, Taddese, and Walter, 2000), girls remain less interested in pursuing STEM majors in college than their male classmates. It is imperative to understand why such a large portion of the population does not appear interested or becomes disinterested in pursuing the knowledge and skills that lead to STEM careers.

The possibility that a female student's choice of whether to pursue and stay in STEM is constrained by societal stereotypes about who excels and belongs in STEM has spurred many questions: How are these stereotypes communicated? How are women impacted by them? How can we mitigate their influence for women? In this chapter, we review existing empirical social-psychological evidence that addresses these central questions. We focus on how individuals' social identities and the environment interact to influence their experiences in STEM contexts and, in turn, their decisions to enter and stay in STEM. Additionally, we introduce new questions that arise from applying a person-by-situation, social-contextual approach to the problem of women's underrepresentation in STEM.

Explanations for women's underrepresentation in STEM

Multiple explanations have been posited for why women are underrepresented in STEM (Ceci and Williams, 2007; Halpern *et al.*, 2007). The view that biological differences between women and men drive this underrepresentation has been supplanted by evidence revealing the importance of socialisation and gender bias (Eccles, 1994; Moss-Racusin, Dovidio, Brescoll, Graham and Handelsman, 2012). Cultural expectations about what interests and occupations women and men should hold as well as prejudice towards women who are successful in traditionally male-dominated fields are, indeed, influential factors in women's underrepresentation in STEM.

However, these explanations cannot fully explain the issue of underrepresentation as the percentage of women in many historically male-dominated disciplines (e.g., medicine, law) has greatly increased over the last few decades. Yet, most STEM fields have not enjoyed similar increases in women's representation (NCSES, 2013; Snyder and Dillow, 2013). So what factors explain this pattern? Although social norms and prejudice undoubtedly sway women's recruitment and retention within STEM fields, we argue that how one's social identity is perceived and valued in STEM classrooms and careers plays a powerful role in whether women seek and remain in these environments.

Experience of social identity threat

People are members of multiple social groups (e.g., relating to gender, occupation). The social identities associated with these groups can be viewed positively (e.g., non-stigmatised group memberships) or negatively (e.g., stigmatised group memberships), and how one's group membership is valued in a particular context greatly impacts experiences within it (Tajfel and Turner, 1979). Negative social identities, associated with groups devalued through negative stereotypes or a history of bias or exclusion, are likely to be of particular concern to people (e.g., the 'women are bad at maths' stereotype; gender bias in evaluation and treatment of students in STEM classrooms; Major and O'Brien, 2005).

When an identity is perceived to be devalued, people can experience social identity threat: the worry and uncertainty that they will be viewed and evaluated through the lens of their group's negative stereotypes (Steele, Spencer and Aronson, 2002). Even if individuals do not personally espouse negative views of their social identity, knowing that others, and society more broadly, devalue this identity in a particular context is enough to evoke social identity threat when considering that context (Kiefer and Sekaquaptewa, 2007; McKown and Weinstein, 2003; Nosek *et al.*, 2009; see Burford and Rosenthal-Stott, Chapter 16, this volume). It is in this way that many women experience social identity threat when considering joining or remaining in STEM settings (Schmader, 2010; C. M. Steele *et al.*, 2002).

Who is most vulnerable to social identity threat?

Although anyone who is a member of a negatively stereotyped or devalued social group can experience social identity threat, not all members of the group are equally likely to experience this or to experience it with the same intensity. People differ in the extent to which they identify with a group (Tajfel and Turner, 1979; Turner, Hogg, Oakes, Reicher and Wetherell, 1987). Individuals can view a group membership as an important part of how they see themselves, as an identity they care about and highly value and from which they draw some of their sense of self-worth or self-esteem (i.e., higher identification). Conversely, individuals can perceive a group membership to be less important to their self-concept (i.e., lower identification).

As social identification with a group increases, vulnerability to social identity threat also increases. For example, female students who highly identify with their gender or with STEM fields are more likely to experience and are more greatly impacted by social identity threat in STEM environments than women who do not highly identify with their gender or STEM fields (Cadinu, Maass, Frigerio, Impagliazzo and Latinotti, 2003; Schmader, 2002; Spencer, Steele and Quinn, 1999). Moreover, female students who are highly identified with *both* their gender and STEM fields are the most vulnerable to social identity threat. This is the case because those who are more highly identified with certain groups are likely to have these identities more chronically salient and, thus, are more sensitive to application of negative stereotypes to them (Brown and Pinel, 2003; Murphy, Steele and Gross, 2007). Given that individuals who are highly identified with an educational domain have usually experienced some level of success in it, the likely targets of social identity threat in STEM are, ironically, those who may have the strongest skills and the greatest motivation to excel in STEM classes (Good, Aronson and Harder, 2008).

Many forms of social identity threat

Knowing what concerns are evoked by social identity threat is as important as understanding who is most impacted by it. When people perceive that they will be negatively viewed in terms of a group membership, they can experience a wide range of concerns that are linked to this group membership: stereotype threat concerns, belonging concerns, social exclusion concerns and trust and fairness concerns (Murphy and Taylor, 2012). For instance, members of stigmatised groups can worry about confirming negative stereotypes that exist for their group, a specific form of social identity threat called stereotype threat (Steele, 1997; Steele and Aronson, 1995). The explicit mention that male students usually perform better on STEM tasks than female students or that gender differences are likely to occur on STEM tasks reliably elicits stereotype threat concerns (Beilock, Rydell and McConnell, 2007; Keller, 2002).

Even less explicit cues, such as viewing particular stereotypical depictions of women in the media and interacting with subtly biased individuals, can lead to stereotype threat concerns (Adams, Garcia, Purdie-Vaughns and Steele, 2006; Davies, Spencer, Quinn and Gerhardstein, 2002; Logel et al., 2009). For example, almost exclusively calling on male students to answer questions or asking female students if they need help in STEM classes can communicate instructors' expectations and, thus, prompt concerns about gender stereotypes and one's academic performance. Female instructors' personal levels of maths anxiety can also communicate gendered expectations in STEM classes as students construe their anxiety as weaker maths ability (Beilock, Gunderson, Ramirez and Levine, 2010).

Aspects of STEM tasks can give rise to stereotype threat concerns. Just being asked to identify one's group membership in a stigmatised group (e.g., indicating one's gender or race on a form) prior to completing an academic task invokes stereotype threat (Danaher and Crandall, 2008; Schmader and Johns, 2003). Moreover, evaluation in and of itself can elicit stereotype threat concerns, especially when the task is difficult and the stakes for success are high (e.g., getting into college or getting a good job; Jamieson and Harkins, 2010; O'Brien and Crandall, 2003; Schmader, Forbes, Zhang and Mendes, 2009).

Stigmatised group members are additionally concerned as to how comfortable they will feel within a setting and to what extent they will fit in interpersonally (Cheryan, Plaut, Davies and Steele, 2009; Murphy, Steele and Garcia, 2015; Walton and Cohen, 2007). These belonging concerns can be triggered by many types of situational cues, such as numerical underrepresentation. For instance, being one of few female students in a STEM class or student group can lead to belonging concerns (Inzlicht and Ben-Zeev, 2000). Cues in classroom environments, like posters of famous scientists and mathematicians that only include men or stereotypically male activities, can also signify to female students that they may not fit in these environments (Cheryan et al., 2009; Murphy et al., 2007).

Relatedly, educational contexts can communicate the extent to which members of stigmatised groups can be themselves as unique individuals – free from representing their larger social group (C. M. Steele et al., 2002). Stigmatised group members look for cues that suggest whether their behaviour will be taken as representative of their group or whether they will be viewed as individuals (London, Downey, Romero-Canyas, Rattan and Tyson, 2012). As one of few in a STEM class, women can become concerned that they will be expected to provide 'the female perspective' on course topics and feel the need to present the image of a woman who does not struggle with course material – proving their group's worthiness and standing in the class. Moreover, in contexts like these, choices that are usually trivial – such as what to wear – can become important decisions as they signal one's identity (Pronin, Steele and Ross, 2004; Seymour and Hewitt, 1997).

Although stereotype threat and belonging concerns have received the most attention empirically, members of stigmatised groups are vigilant for evidence in the environment as to how they will be treated by others (Kaiser and Miller, 2001; Major, Quinton and McCoy, 2002). Social exclusion and discrimination concerns arise when physical and social segregation occurs along group lines. When female students are assigned to work groups with only other female students or when leadership roles in the classroom are predominately held by male classmates, female students likely experience concerns about social exclusion and discrimination.

Stigmatised group members do not just wish to be included numerically; they are also vigilant for cues that, once accepted into an environment, they can trust the current environment and be treated fairly and with respect (Bergsieker, Shelton and Richeson, 2010; Emerson and Murphy, 2014, 2015; Purdie-Vaughns, Steele, Davies, Ditlmann and Crosby, 2008). Trust and fairness concerns can arise when there are only a few women in esteemed authority positions (e.g., principals, deans) or when authority figures show inaction to instances of sexism and unwillingness to discuss gender or cultural issues. Specifically, members of stigmatised groups worry as to whether they will be afforded the same opportunities as members of non-stigmatised groups and whether they will be targets of disrespect and harassment. When it is uncertain whether fair treatment will be afforded, interpersonal and institutional trust (e.g., trust in the instructor and in the education system more generally) is diminished.

Environments can vary in terms of the number of the social identity concerns they trigger. While some situational cues may prompt a single type of social identity concern, many cues – such as numerical representation – likely spark multiple concerns at once as they raise many questions about why the cue is present in the environment. For instance, taking a STEM course with few other female classmates can lead women to have stereotype threat and belonging concerns and could possibly elicit other types of concerns. Moreover, having multiple concerns could result in greater social identity threat than having few concerns, and different concerns may be more strongly linked to certain consequences of social identity threat (e.g., underperformance, dis-identification or leaving the field) than others.

Consequences of social identity threat

Social identity concerns have a deleterious impact on important psychological and behavioural outcomes, which have been especially well documented for women in STEM (Nguyen and Ryan, 2008). Worrying can usurp cognitive resources needed for STEM tasks: women experiencing stereotype threat are less able to suppress their concerns and perform the cognitive operations necessary to solve difficult problems (Cadinu, Maass, Rosabianca and Kiesner, 2005; Schmader and Beilock, 2012). In turn, reduced cognitive resources lead to poorer learning and performance (Beilock et al., 2007; Schmader and Johns, 2003; Schmader, Johns and Forbes, 2008). Learning of novel STEM tasks, the transfer of what is learned to similar tasks, and performance on a wide range of STEM tests are impaired under stereotype threat (Nguyen and Ryan, 2008; Rydell, Rydell and Boucher, 2010; Taylor and Walton, 2011).

Additionally, social identity threat influences the way women think about themselves in relation to STEM fields. After performing poorly on a STEM task, women experiencing threat cope with this negative event by psychologically or physically distancing themselves from STEM activities (Steele, 1997). To pre-emptively deflect the impact of threat on future performance in STEM, women can view these domains as ones in which they, personally, just do not perform well (Koch, Müller and Sieverding, 2008); this can, in turn, result in reduced interest, motivation and persistence during future STEM activities (Davies *et al.*, 2002; Good, Rattan and Dweck, 2012; Murphy *et al.*, 2007; Steele, James and Barnett, 2002; Wang, Eccles and Kenny, 2013). Over time, the chronic experience of social identity threat can lead women to dis-identify with STEM domains – to avoid these domains and no longer link one's self-esteem with performance in them – and alter their career aspirations to no longer include STEM careers.

Importantly, evidence of threat's pernicious impact on these important educational outcomes is found in laboratory experiments as well as in real-world examinations of academic experiences, performance (e.g., grades, standardised test scores) and interests (Danaher and Crandall, 2008; Good *et al.*, 2008, 2012; Keller, 2007; Stout, Dasgupta, Hunsinger and McManus, 2011; Walton and Spencer, 2009). Furthermore, when women are not thinking of themselves primarily in terms of their gender or when their gender is not devalued in the current STEM context, women's experiences in STEM are positive and similar to men's (Spencer *et al.*, 1999; C. M. Steele *et al.*, 2002). *The negative outcomes described above, thus, occur in actual STEM contexts and result mainly from situational differences, not stable gender differences.* For these reasons, social identity threat is argued to be one of several critical factors that independently, or in concert with other factors, contribute to women's hesitancy to enter or stay in STEM fields.

Social-contextual approach to social identity threat

The types of concerns discussed above and the situational cues that prompt them are common to many STEM settings encountered by female students. Whether in lectures, visiting office hours or studying for exams, women in STEM are exposed to situational cues that subtly question whether their gender has what it takes to succeed, whether they belong and how others will view them and their efforts. However, do women always notice these cues and perceive them as psychologically threatening?

The same situational cue can be present in different classrooms but only noticed and perceived as threatening in those where one's gender identity becomes salient (i.e., in contexts in which women have been traditionally stigmatised). For instance, a female student who is one of a few women in her engineering class is more likely to notice and be concerned about this numerical underrepresentation than if she is one of a few women in her English class – a domain in which women tend to be positively viewed. The same cue can have a different meaning for one's salient social identity based on the particular context (Oakes and Turner, 1986; Oakes, Turner and Haslam, 1991). Therefore, one's group membership interacts with the local situation to determine whether a situational cue is perceived as threatening and, thus, likely to lead to social identity threat (Murphy and Taylor, 2012; Murphy *et al.*, 2007).

In this social-contextual approach, we propose that aspects of a local context can indicate the value or importance of one's group memberships within it. There are numerous situational cues in every context. Which situational cues influence our psychological and behavioural outcomes is determined by how relevant they are to one's group memberships. Situational cues that are relevant to one's social identities and indicate the value of one's social groups will be especially noticed, considered and remembered. These group memberships then become the primary identities through which one experiences the setting (Branscombe, Ellemers, Spears and Doosje, 1999; Tajfel and Turner, 1979; Turner *et al.*, 1987).

For example, female students can have several social identities that are relevant in a STEM classroom (e.g., being female, being a student, being a budding scientist or mathematician). However, a situational cue in the classroom, such as gender segregation or pictures of exclusively male scientists adorning the walls, can call to mind stereotypes pertaining to women in STEM, making the female identity particularly central to how female students view themselves and/or think they will be viewed by others (Ambady, Paik, Steele, Owen-Smith and Mitchell, 2004). Such cues serve as antecedents to social identity threat as they make the devalued aspects of social identities more accessible, which can prompt worries and concerns indicative of social identity threat.

Male students in STEM classrooms are less likely to have their gender made salient in these environments because situational cues that are found within them do not imply that their gender will be negatively implicated in these contexts (Murphy *et al.*, 2007, 2015). If male students' gender identity is not particularly salient, it is possible that they will be less likely to notice situational cues that pose identity threat to female students (Boucher, 2013). Even if male students become aware of situational cues that their male identity may be relevant in STEM contexts, they are less likely to experience social identity threat in this setting because these cues do not suggest that their male identity is devalued – and may even imply that their identity is valued – in STEM (Murphy *et al.*, 2015; Walton and Cohen, 2003).

Strong situational cues, such as statements that women perform worse or do not fit in as well in STEM as men, are unambiguous indications that a social identity is devalued and, in turn, elicit social identity threat (Nguyen and Ryan, 2008). However, as reviewed above, situational cues need not be explicit or blatant in order to evoke social identity threat. If a situational cue's meaning and influence in the current situation is unclear or uncertain, people seek additional evidence to determine whether a social identity, such as one's gender, is valued or, instead, may be a liability in the situation (Cohen and Garcia, 2008; Schmader *et al.*, 2008). Vigilance subsides when appraisals of additional situational cues signal identity safety (e.g., that women will not be judged in terms of their gender in the local setting). Conversely, vigilance increases when appraisals of additional situational cues confirm the possibility of experiencing social identity threat. As a consequence of this vigilance process, seemingly innocuous cues (e.g., instructor's sex or race) may initiate social identity threat.

Situational cues that signal identity safety

Social identity threat research clearly demonstrates that situational cues have a significant impact on the appraisals of educational environments and people's experiences within them. However, some settings may not be perceived as identity-threatening because they offer few situational cues that point to the devaluation of important social identities. Some environments may even be 'identity-safe' as they convey that one's group membership will be affirmatively accepted and respected and will not pose a barrier to success. From its inception, social identity threat research has explored not only the situational cues that lead to identity threat but also the cues that communicate identity safety (C. M. Steele *et al.*, 2002). This work has examined the efficacy of strategies that aim to reduce the influence of identity-threatening cues or add identity-safe cues in important settings, such as classrooms and other evaluative situations (Cohen, Purdie-Vaughns and Garcia, 2012; Yeager and Walton, 2011).

Situational cues that signal identity safety include those which suggest stereotypes have no bearing on people's outcomes in the current environment. For instance, telling women taking STEM tests that gender differences do not exist on this particular exam or that the test is unbiased (i.e., 'gender-fair') buffers women from experiencing stereotype threat and the impaired learning and performance that stem from it (Boucher, Rydell, Van Loo and Rydell, 2012; Spencer *et al.*, 1999). Explicitly refuting the link between negative group stereotypes and students' performance leads to the greatest reduction in stereotype threat for women in STEM because it sends a strong and clear message that one's group membership is valued (Nguyen and Ryan, 2008; Walton and Cohen, 2003). Stereotype threat concerns are also allayed by more subtle situational cues that reduce evaluation apprehension present in high-stakes testing situations. Simply relabelling a test as a problem-solving exercise or a puzzle places students' focus on the assignment instead of social identity concerns, thereby leading to better performance (Brown and Day, 2006).

Additionally, situational cues that reframe the meaning of difficulty are cues to identity safety; these cues communicate that experiencing difficulty during a test or assignment is not inherently bad or identity-relevant and that difficulties can be overcome. When instructors pair critical feedback with an emphasis on high standards and assurance that students can meet these high standards, students from stigmatised groups are more likely to accept and learn from this feedback (Cohen, Steele and Ross, 1999). Feedback given in this manner increases motivation and identification within stereotyped domains like STEM fields.

Another way to reframe the experience of difficulty is to promote a growth mindset (Dweck, 2006; Dweck and Leggett, 1988; see also Reynolds, Subasic, Lee and Bromhead, Chapter 3, this volume). Instructors can convey that intelligence is malleable and can be expanded by hard work and effort. This message can be imparted to students by explicitly stating in course objectives and assignments that the goal of classwork is to facilitate learning and development. Instructors who ask students to focus on their improvement and growth, not grades, communicate that the value is on learning – not proving whether you, or your group, is capable and intelligent. Furthermore, teachers can provide feedback that praises effort instead of inherent abilities. By eliminating the pressure students feel to prove their (and their group's) intelligence, these identity-safe cues increase the enjoyment and value of education and lead to better learning outcomes and higher grades (Blackwell, Trzesniewski and Dweck, 2007; Good, Aronson and Inzlicht, 2003). Given that STEM lessons and assignments are perceived to be relatively difficult, these identity-safe cues that reframe appraisals of difficulty are particularly important for mitigating threat's impact in STEM classrooms.

Identity-safe cues likely mitigate more than just concerns about confirming negative group stereotypes. Although much of the research examining identity-safe cues has focused on these stereotype threat concerns, identity-safe cues should also reduce or eliminate concerns related to belonging, trust and being valued and treated fairly. Numerical representation and role models are potent cues to identity safety that alleviate multiple identity-relevant concerns (e.g., stereotype threat, belonging, fairness). Having a critical mass of individuals who share one's social identity lowers the possibility of experiencing social identity threat in the setting (Inzlicht and Ben-Zeev, 2000; Murphy et al., 2007). For women in STEM classrooms, majors and careers, being in an evaluative setting (e.g., assessment, presentation or interview situations) with other women lessens their concerns about representing their entire gender group.

Moreover, sharing group membership with successful role models (e.g., instructors, advanced students) in potentially threatening environments can buffer students of negatively stereotyped groups from stereotype threat and belonging concerns. Seeing and interacting with female STEM instructors and more senior students leads younger female students to have enhanced identification and interest in STEM fields (Dasgupta, 2011; McIntyre et al., 2005; McIntyre, Paulson and Lord, 2003; Marx and Roman, 2002; Stout et al., 2011). Interestingly, belonging concerns can be reduced for members of underrepresented groups by also considering the common experiences all students share (Walton and Cohen, 2007; Wilson and Linville, 1985). When students learn that the social and academic hardships that accompany the first year of college/university are experienced by most students and lessen with time, stigmatised students experience fewer belonging concerns and better academic performance. Taken together, pointing to other successful group members and emphasising commonalities across groups can contribute to the identity safety of educational settings (Rosenthal and Crisp, 2006).

These established cues hold great promise for transforming identity-threatening environments into identity-safe ones. Many of these identity-safe cues can be easily and inexpensively incorporated into educational settings. Indeed, research suggests that even a single identity-safe cue may be sufficient in changing the whole meaning of the situation. However, before the introduction of, or change in, any situational cue, it is imperative to have a solid understanding of the situational cues already at play in the environment. As one situational cue can shape the interpretation of others (Purdie-Vaughns *et al.*, 2008), it is critical to know how new and established situational cues may interact and which types of cues are most impactful under different circumstances. Future research of this nature is needed in both controlled laboratory settings and the actual educational contexts we hope to transform.

Future directions for social identity threat research

Social identity threat research has drawn heavily from the broader social identity theory approach (C. M. Steele *et al.*, 2002; Tajfel and Turner, 1979). As such, a more intensive focus on the strength and types of social identities suggests exciting new directions for the social-contextual approach to social identity threat we have detailed in this chapter. Group memberships and the importance people place on them interact with situational cues to determine the meaning of these cues and, thus, individuals' vulnerability to social identity threat. Research from this person-by-situation approach has only begun examining how the situational cue detection and appraisal process may differ when people identify with different social groups and do so with different levels of importance or strength in stereo-typed domains like STEM fields.

Women who highly identify with STEM fields may notice different and a greater number of situational cues that question their ability and acceptance in STEM than women who are less identified. When the same situational cue is detected by both high and low identifiers, highly STEM-identified women may infer different meanings from the cues and have lower thresholds for perceiving STEM contexts as threatening to their STEM identity than less STEM-identified women. For example, the situational cue of instructor's gender may not mean the same thing for female students who are turned off by STEM and are just taking the class as a requirement (i.e., likely low domain identifiers) and female students who have chosen to pursue a STEM major (i.e., likely high domain identifiers). Indeed, research shows that male and female role models can actually be equally effective for recruiting women into STEM, while female role models may be most beneficial for retaining women in this area (Akcinar, Carr and Walton, 2011; Drury, Siy and Cheryan, 2011).

In addition to the strength of identification, new questions arise when considering how different types of available social identities influence the detection and appraisal of situational cues. One particularly interesting question involves the experiences of members of positively viewed or non-stigmatised groups. Given that past research has almost exclusively focused on the situational cues that make members of stigmatised groups aware of their group's devalued status, future research is needed to assess the consequences of activating the identities of members of non-stigmatised groups.

In STEM classrooms, men may not think of themselves in terms of their gender identity. If they do, it will be important to determine what situational cues lead them to think of their group membership and what the effects of these cues, if any, are on their educational outcomes. Experiments show that male students in STEM who are aware of their gender's positive stereotypes in this domain can experience performance boosts, an effect called stereotype lift (Walton and Cohen, 2003); although if the pressure to confirm positive group stereotypes is too high, men can also show impairment or 'choking' under pressure (Beilock, Kulp, Holt and Carr, 2004). This focus on positively stereotyped group memberships is particularly necessary when trying to mitigate the influence of social identity threat for one group, such as women in STEM, without making another group, such as men in STEM, more vulnerable to it.

In this chapter, we have discussed the experience of social identity threat in terms of a single social identity being especially salient (i.e., being female). People, however, have multiple social identities; therefore, it is possible to have several social identities that are relevant and accessible in a setting. When multiple group memberships are negatively stereotyped (e.g., Black women or Latinas in STEM), individuals are much more likely to experience social identity threat (Gonzalez, Blanton and Williams, 2002). People who consider multiple stigmatised identities to be important to their sense of self (i.e., high identifiers) are especially likely to experience concerns about how they will be viewed by others.

However, when one of the social identities is negatively stereotyped and another social identity is positively stereotyped (e.g., being female and being Asian), social identity threat is often eliminated. Reminding female college students who are concerned about negative gender–maths stereotypes about the positive stereotype pertaining to college students' maths abilities, relative to non-college students, eliminates the experience of stereotype threat and its usual impairment of maths performance (Rydell, McConnell and Beilock, 2009; Shih, Pittinsky and Ambady, 1999). Similarly, being able to affirm other valued social identities that are not relevant to STEM (e.g., in relation to family or sports) has the positive impact of increasing overall self-esteem and buffering students from stereotype threat and belonging concerns (Cohen, Garcia, Apfel and Master, 2006; Martens, Johns, Greenberg and Schimel, 2006; Miyake et al., 2010). These self-affirmation techniques put students' lives in a broader context by asking students to reflect upon the most important aspects of their life outside of the classroom.

Exploring the effects of multiple social identities in specific contexts can highlight the situational cues that lead to experiences of double stigma as well as those where one social identity has a protective influence. In the case of two devalued social identities, the same cues in a stereotyped context may make both more accessible. For example, numerical representation in the classroom could signify that one's gender *and* one's ethnicity are both lenses through which one may be judged. Under these circumstances, situational cues, even subtle ones, could be perceived earlier on, and the threshold for threat could be lower when individuals experience double stigma. When negatively and positively stereotyped social identities are both relevant in an environment such as a STEM classroom, the cue detection and appraisal process could differ. Because people have a tendency to give more weight to negative attributes than positive attributes (Baumeister, Bratslavsky, Finkenauer and Vohs, 2001), more explicit cues (e.g., a critical mass or statements referring to specific positive identities) may be necessary for a positively stereotyped social identity to seem relevant. Furthermore, identification with this positive social identity may need to be relatively strong to mitigate the social identity concerns stemming from the negatively stereotyped social identity.

Lastly, a social-contextual approach to social identity threat that illuminates the situational cues that communicate identity threat (or safety) can help explain an intriguing pattern in women's underrepresentation in STEM. More women have been entering and staying in STEM over the last few decades; however, the magnitude of this increase varies greatly across STEM fields (NCSES, 2013; Snyder and Dillow, 2013). Women are now well represented in the life sciences (e.g., biology, chemistry), but they continue to be grossly underrepresented in STEM fields such as physics, engineering and computer science.

This pattern points to the possibility that STEM fields may differ in terms of the situational cues they contain and, thus, could differ as to the extent to which these fields elicit social identity threat. Alternatively, life science contexts may have similar cues to social identity threat as traditional STEM fields, but they may also have more identity-affirming cues that mitigate this threat. Perceptions of the life sciences as being more people-oriented and geared towards helping others could blunt the negative impact of threatening situational cues by aligning the goals of the disciplines with the female gender role (Diekman and Steinberg, 2013; Woodcock *et al.*, 2013); these disciplines may even call to mind other positive social identities (e.g., team member, difference maker).

Conclusion

We presented evidence of social identity threat's role in the underrepresentation of women in STEM. While women in STEM was our primary focus, the reviewed research also illuminates how belonging to social groups that are viewed negatively can, in general, lead to deleterious consequences for how individuals view themselves, the situation and their place within it. Indeed, much research supports the idea that stigmatised ethnic and racial groups are vulnerable to similar cues, processes and outcomes (C. M. Steele *et al.*, 2002). By focusing on the situational cues in environments, the social-contextual approach described here pinpoints the cues that trigger or diffuse social identity threat. This knowledge can be used to create or transform academic settings that are welcoming to all social groups and provide opportunities to excel without the burden of negative group-based expectations.

References

Adams, G., Garcia, G. M., Purdie-Vaughns, V. and Steele, C. M. (2006). The detrimental effects of a suggestion of sexism in an instruction situation. *Journal of Experimental Social Psychology*, *42*(5), 602–15.

Akcinar, E. N., Carr, P. B. and Walton, G. M. (2011). Interactions with men and whites matter too. *Psychological Inquiry*, *22*(4), 247–51.

Ambady, N., Paik, S. K., Steele, J., Owen-Smith, A. and Mitchell, J. P. (2004). Deflecting negative self-relevant stereotype activation: The effects of individuation. *Journal of Experimental Social Psychology*, *40*(3), 401–08.

Baumeister, R. F., Bratslavsky, E., Finkenauer, C. and Vohs, K. D. (2001). Bad is stronger than good. *Review of General Psychology*, *5*(4), 323–70.

Beilock, S. L., Gunderson, E. A., Ramirez, G. and Levine, S. C. (2010). Female teachers' math anxiety affects girls' math achievement. *Proceedings of the National Academy of Sciences, USA*, *107*(5), 1060–63.

Beilock, S. L., Kulp, C. A., Holt, L. E. and Carr, T. H. (2004). More on the fragility of performance: Choking under pressure in mathematical problem solving. *Journal of Experimental Psychology: General*, *133*(4), 584–600.

Beilock, S. L., Rydell, R. J. and McConnell, A. R. (2007). Stereotype threat and working memory: Mechanisms, alleviation, and spill-over. *Journal of Experimental Psychology: General*, *136*(2), 256–76.

Bergsieker, H. B., Shelton, J. N. and Richeson, J. A. (2010). To be liked versus respected: Divergent goals in interracial interactions. *Journal of Personality and Social Psychology*, *99*(2), 248–64.

Blackwell, L. S., Trzesniewski, K. H. and Dweck, C. S. (2007). Implicit theories of intelligence predict achievement across an adolescent transition: A longitudinal study and an intervention. *Child Development*, *78*(1), 246–63.

Boucher, K. L. (2013). *Forecasting stereotype threat: Role of perspective and gender salience on the perception of stereotype threat*. Indiana University, unpublished dissertation.

Boucher, K. L., Rydell, R. J., Van Loo, K. J. and Rydell, M. T. (2012). Reducing stereotype threat to facilitate learning. *European Journal of Social Psychology*, *42*(2), 174–9.

Brainard, S. G. and Carlin, L. (1998). A six-year longitudinal study of undergraduate women in engineering and science. *Journal of Engineering Education*, *87*(4), 369–75.

Branscombe, N. R., Ellemers, N., Spears, R. and Doosje, B. (1999). The context and content of social identity threat. In N. Ellemers, R. Spears and B. Doosje (Eds), *Social identity: Context, commitment, content* (pp. 35–58). Oxford: Blackwell Science.

Brown, R. P. and Day, E. A. (2006). The difference isn't black and white: Stereotype threat and the race gap on Raven's Advanced Progressive matrices. *Journal of Applied Psychology*, *91*(4), 979–85.

Brown, R. P. and Pinel, E. C. (2003). Stigma on my mind: Individual differences in the experience of stereotype threat. *Journal of Experimental Social Psychology*, *39*(6), 626–33.

Cadinu, M., Maass, A., Frigerio, S., Impagliazzo, L. and Latinotti, S. (2003). Stereotype threat: The effect of expectancy on performance. *European Journal of Social Psychology*, *33*(2), 267–85.

Cadinu, M., Maass, A., Rosabianca, A. and Kiesner, J. (2005). Why do women underperform under stereotype threat? Evidence for the role of negative thinking. *Psychological Science*, *16*(7), 572–8.

Ceci, S. J. and Williams, W. M. (2007). *Why aren't more women in science? Top researchers debate the evidence*. Washington, DC: American Psychological Association.

Cheryan, S., Plaut, V. C., Davies, P. G. and Steele, C. M. (2009). Ambient belonging: How stereotypical cues impact gender participation in computer science. *Journal of Personality and Social Psychology, 97*(6), 1045–60.

Cohen, G. L. and Garcia, J. (2008). Identity, belonging, and achievement: A model, interventions, implications. *Current Directions in Psychological Science, 17*(6), 365–9.

Cohen, G. L., Garcia, J., Apfel, N. and Master, A. (2006). Reducing the racial achievement gap: A social-psychological intervention. *Science, 313*(5791), 1307–10.

Cohen, G. L., Purdie-Vaughns, V. and Garcia, J. (2012). An identity threat perspective on intervention. In M. Inzlicht and T. Schmader (Eds), *Stereotype threat: Theory, process, and application* (pp. 280–98). New York: Oxford University Press.

Cohen, G. L., Steele, C. M. and Ross, L. D. (1999). The mentor's dilemma: Providing critical feedback across the racial divide. *Personality and Social Psychology Bulletin, 25*(10), 1302–18.

Danaher, K. and Crandall, C. S. (2008). Stereotype threat in applied settings re-examined. *Journal of Applied Social Psychology, 38*(6), 1639–55.

Dasgupta, N. (2011). Ingroup experts and peers as social vaccines who inoculate the self-concept: The stereotype inoculation model. *Psychological Inquiry, 22*(4), 231–46.

Davies, P. G., Spencer, S. J., Quinn, D. M. and Gerhardstein, R. (2002). Consuming images: How television commercials that elicit stereotype threat can restrain women academically and professionally. *Personality and Social Psychology Bulletin, 28*(12), 1615–28.

Diekman, A. B. and Steinberg, M. (2013). Navigating social roles in pursuit of important goals: A communal goal congruity account of STEM pursuits. *Social and Personality Psychology Compass, 7*(7), 487–501.

Drury, B. J., Siy, J. O. and Cheryan, S. (2011). When do female role models benefit women? The importance of differentiating recruitment from retention in STEM. *Psychological Inquiry, 22*(4), 265–9.

Dweck, C. (2006). *Mindset: The new psychology of success.* New York: Random House.

Dweck, C. S. and Leggett, E. (1988). A social-cognitive approach to motivation and personality. *Psychological Review, 95*(2), 256–73.

Eccles, J. S. (1994). Understanding women's educational and occupational choices: Applying the Eccles et al. model of achievement-related choices. *Psychology of Women Quarterly, 18*(4), 585–609.

Emerson, K. T. U. and Murphy, M. C. (2014). Identity threat at work: How social identity threat and situational cues contribute to racial and ethnic disparities in the workplace. *Cultural Diversity and Ethnic Minority Psychology, 20*(4), 508–20.

Emerson, K. T. U. and Murphy, M. C. (2015). A company I can trust? Organizational lay theories moderate stereotype threat for women. *Personality and Social Psychology Bulletin, 41*(2), 295–307.

Gonzales, P. M., Blanton, H. and Williams, K. J. (2002). The effects of stereotype threat and double-minority status on the test performance of Latino women. *Personality and Social Psychology Bulletin, 28*(5), 659–70.

Good, C., Aronson, J. and Harder, J. A. (2008). Problems in the pipeline: Stereotype threat and women's achievement in high-level math courses. *Journal of Applied Developmental Psychology, 29*(1), 17–28.

Good, C., Aronson, J. and Inzlicht, M. (2003). Improving adolescents' standardized test performance: An intervention to reduce the effects of stereotype threat. *Journal of Applied Developmental Psychology, 24*(6), 645–62.

Good, C., Rattan, A. and Dweck, C. S. (2012). Why do women opt out? Sense of belonging and women's representation in mathematics. *Journal of Personality and Social Psychology, 102(4)*, 700–17.

Halpern, D. F., Benbow, C. P., Geary, D. C., Gur, R., Hyde, J. S. and Gernsbacher, M. A. (2007). The science of sex differences in science and mathematics. *Psychological Science in the Public Interest*, 8(1), 1–51.

Hill, C., Corbett, C. and St. Rose, A. (2010). *Why so few? Women in science, technology, engineering, and mathematics*. Washington, DC: American Association of University Women.

Huang, G., Taddese, N. and Walter, E. (2000). *Entry and persistence of women and minorities in college science and engineering education*, NCES 2000-601. Washington, DC: US Department of Education, National Center for Education Statistics.

Inzlicht, M. and Ben-Zeev, T. (2000). A threatening intellectual environment: Why females are susceptible to experiencing problem-solving deficits in the presence of males. *Psychological Science*, 11(5), 365–71.

Jamieson, J. P. and Harkins, S. G. (2010). Evaluation is necessary to produce stereotype threat performance effects. *Social Influence*, 5(2), 75–86.

Kaiser, C. R. and Miller, C. T. (2001). Stop complaining! The social costs of making attributions to discrimination. *Personality and Social Psychology Bulletin*, 27(2), 254–63.

Keller, J. (2002). Blatant stereotype threat and women's math performance: Self-handicapping as a strategic means to cope with obtrusive negative performance expectations. *Sex Roles*, 47(3–4), 193–8.

Keller, J. (2007). When negative stereotypic expectancies turn into challenge or threat: The moderating role of regulatory focus. *Swiss Journal of Psychology*, 66(3), 163–8.

Kiefer, A. K. and Sekaquaptewa, D. (2007). Implicit stereotypes and women's math performance: How implicit gender–math stereotypes influence women's susceptibility to stereotype threat. *Journal of Experimental Social Psychology*, 43(5), 825–32.

Koch, S. C., Müller, S. M. and Sieverding, M. (2008). Women and computers: Effects of stereotype threat on attribution of failure. *Computers and Education*, 51(4), 1795–803.

Logel, C., Walton, G. M., Spencer, S. J., Iserman, E. C., Von Hippel, W. and Bell, A. E. (2009). Interacting with sexist men triggers social identity threat among female engineers. *Journal of Personality and Social Psychology*, 96(6), 1089–103.

London, B., Downey, G., Romero-Canyas, R., Rattan, A. and Tyson, D. (2012). Gender-based rejection sensitivity and academic self-silencing in women. *Journal of Personality and Social Psychology*, 102(5), 961–79.

McIntyre, R. B., Lord, C. G., Gresky, D. M., Ten Eyck, L. L., Frye, G. D. J. and Bond, C. F. (2005). A social impact trend in the effects of role models on alleviating women's mathematics stereotype threat. *Current Research in Social Psychology*, 10(9), 116–36.

McIntyre, R. B., Paulson, R. and Lord, C. (2003). Alleviating women's mathematics stereotype threat through salience of group achievements. *Journal of Experimental Social Psychology*, 39(1), 83–90.

McKown, C. and Weinstein, R. S. (2003). The development and consequences of stereotype consciousness in middle childhood. *Child Development*, 74(2), 498–515.

Major, B. and O'Brien, L. T. (2005). The social psychology of stigma. *Annual Review of Psychology*, 56, 393–421.

Major, B., Quinton, W. J. and McCoy, S. K. (2002). Antecedents and consequences of attributions to discrimination: Theoretical and empirical advances. In M. P. Zanna (Ed.), *Advances in experimental social psychology*, Vol. 34. (pp. 251–330). San Diego, CA: Academic Press.

Margolis, J. and Fisher, A. (2003). *Unlocking the clubhouse: Women in computing*. Cambridge, MA: MIT Press.

Martens, A., Johns, M., Greenberg, J. and Schimel, J. (2006). Combating stereotype threat: The effect of self-affirmation on women's intellectual performance. *Journal of Experimental Social Psychology*, 42(2), 236–43.

Marx, D. M. and Roman, J. S. (2002). Female role models: Protecting women's math test performance. *Personality and Social Psychology Bulletin, 28*(9), 1183–93.

Miyake, A., Kost-Smith, L. E., Finkelstein, N. D., Pollock, S. J., Cohen, G. L. and Ito, T. A. (2010). Reducing the gender achievement gap in college science: A classroom study of values affirmation. *Science, 330*(6008), 1234–7.

Moss-Racusin, C. A., Dovidio, J. F., Brescoll, V. L., Graham, M. J. and Handelsman, J. (2012). Science faculty's subtle gender biases favor male students. *PNAS: Proceedings of the National Academy of Sciences of the United States of America, 109*(41), 16474–9.

Murphy, M. C., Steele, C. M. and Garcia, J. A. (2015). The fragility of fit: Cues affect the concerns, belonging, and performance of women and men in STEM settings. Manuscript submitted for review.

Murphy, M. C., Steele, C. M. and Gross, J. J. (2007). Signaling threat: How situational cues affect women in math, science, and engineering settings. *Psychological Science, 18*(10), 879–85.

Murphy, M. C. and Taylor, V. J. (2012). The role of situational cues in signaling and maintaining stereotype threat. In M. Inzlicht and T. Schmader (Eds), *Stereotype threat: Theory, process, and application* (pp. 17–33). New York: Oxford University Press.

National Center for Science and Engineering Statistics. (2013). *Women, minorities, and persons with disabilities in science and engineering: 2013.* Special report NSF 13-304. Arlington, VA: National Science Foundation.

Nguyen, H. H. D. and Ryan, A. M. (2008). Does stereotype threat affect test perform-ance of minorities and women? A meta-analysis of experimental evidence. *Journal of Applied Psychology, 93*(6), 1314–34.

Nosek, B. A., Smyth, F. L., Sriram, N., Lindner, N. M., Devos, T., Ayala, A., . . . Greenwald, A. G. (2009). National differences in gender-science stereotypes predict national sex differences in science and math achievement. *PNAS: Proceedings of the National Academy of Sciences of the United States of America, 106*(26), 10593–7.

Oakes, P. J. and Turner, J. C. (1986). Distinctiveness and the salience of social category memberships: Is there an automatic perceptual bias towards novelty? *European Journal of Social Psychology, 16*(4), 325–44.

Oakes, P. J., Turner, J. C. and Haslam, S. A. (1991). Perceiving people as group members: The role of fit in the salience of social categorizations. *British Journal of Social Psychology, 30*(2), 125–44.

O'Brien, L. T. and Crandall, C. S. (2003). Stereotype threat and arousal: Effects on women's math performance. *Personality and Social Psychology Bulletin, 29*(6), 782–9.

Pronin, E., Steele, C. and Ross, L. (2004). Identity bifurcation in response to stereotype threat: Women and mathematics. *Journal of Experimental Social Psychology, 40*(2), 152–68.

Purdie-Vaughns, V., Steele, C. M., Davies, P. G., Ditlmann, R. and Crosby, J. R. (2008). Social identity contingencies: How diversity cues signal threat or safety for African Americans in mainstream institutions. *Journal of Personality and Social Psychology, 94*(4), 615–30.

Rosenthal, H. E. S. and Crisp, R. J. (2006). Reducing stereotype threat by blurring inter-group boundaries. *Personality and Social Psychology Bulletin, 32*(4), 501–11.

Rydell, R. J., McConnell, A. R. and Beilock, S. L. (2009). Multiple social identities and stereotype threat: Imbalance, accessibility, and working memory. *Journal of Personality and Social Psychology, 96*(5), 949–66.

Rydell, R. J., Rydell, M. T. and Boucher, K. L. (2010). The effect of negative performance stereotypes on learning. *Journal of Personality and Social Psychology, 99*(6), 883–96.

Schmader, T. (2002). Gender identification moderates stereotype threat effects on women's math performance. *Journal of Experimental Social Psychology, 38*(2), 194–201.

Schmader, T. (2010). Stereotype threat deconstructed. *Current Directions in Psychological Science, 19*(1), 14–18.

Schmader, T. and Beilock, S. L. (2012). An integration of processes that underlie stereotype threat. In M. Inzlicht and T. Schmader (Eds), *Stereotype threat: Theory, process, and application* (pp. 34–50). New York: Oxford University Press.

Schmader, T., Forbes, C. E., Zhang, S. and Mendes, W. B. (2009). A metacognitive perspective on the cognitive deficits experiences in intellectually threatening environments. *Personality and Social Psychology Bulletin, 35*(5), 584–96.

Schmader, T. and Johns, M. (2003). Converging evidence that stereotype threat reduces working memory capacity. *Journal of Personality and Social Psychology, 85*(3), 440–52.

Schmader, T., Johns, M. and Forbes, C. (2008). An integrated process model of stereotype threat on performance. *Psychological Review, 115*(2), 336–56.

Seymour, E. and Hewitt, N. M. (1997). *Talking about leaving: Why undergraduates leave the sciences.* Boulder, CO: Westview.

Shih, M., Pittinsky, T. L. and Ambady, N. (1999). Stereotype susceptibility: Identity salience and shifts in quantitative performance. *Psychological Science, 10*(1), 80–3.

Snyder, T. D. and Dillow, S. A. (2013). *Digest of Education Statistics 2012*, NCES 2014-015. Washington, DC: National Center for Education Statistics, Institute of Education Sciences, US Department of Education.

Spencer, S. J., Steele, C. M. and Quinn, D. M. (1999). Stereotype threat and women's math performance. *Journal of Experimental Social Psychology, 35*(1), 4–28.

Steele, C. M. (1997). A threat in the air: How stereotypes shape the intellectual identities and performance. *American Psychologist, 52*(6), 613–29.

Steele, C. M. and Aronson, J. (1995). Stereotype threat and the intellectual test performance of African Americans. *Journal of Personality and Social Psychology, 69*(5), 797–811.

Steele, C. M., Spencer, S. J. and Aronson, J. (2002). Contending with group image: The psychology of stereotype and social identity threat. In M. Zanna (Ed.), *Advances in experimental social psychology*, Vol. 34 (pp. 379–440). New York: Academic Press.

Steele, J., James, J. B. and Barnett, R. (2002). Learning in a man's world: Examining the perceptions of undergraduate women in male-dominated academic areas. *Psychology of Women Quarterly, 26*(1), 46–50.

Stout, J. G., Dasgupta, N., Hunsinger, M. and McManus, M. A. (2011). STEMing the tide: Using ingroup experts to inoculate women's self-concept in science, technology, engineering, and mathematics (STEM). *Journal of Personality and Social Psychology, 100*(2), 255–70.

Tajfel, H. and Turner, J. C. (1979). An integrative theory of intergroup conflict. In W. G. Austin and S. Worchel (Eds), *The social psychology of intergroup relations*. Monterey, CA: Brooks/Cole.

Taylor, V. J. and Walton, G. M. (2011). Stereotype threat undermines academic learning. *Personality and Social Psychology Bulletin, 37*(8), 1055–67.

Turner, J. C., Hogg, M. A., Oakes, P. J., Reicher, S. D. and Wetherell, M. S. (1987). *Rediscovering the social group: A self-categorization theory*. Cambridge, MA: Basil Blackwell.

United Nations Educational, Scientific, and Cultural Organization. (2007). *Science, technology, and gender: An international report*. Paris, France.

US Department of Labor, Bureau of Labor Statistics. (2009). *Women in the labor force: A databook*, Report 1018. Washington, DC.

Walton, G. M. and Cohen, G. L. (2003). Stereotype lift. *Journal of Experimental Social Psychology, 39*(5), 456–67.

Walton, G. M. and Cohen, G. L. (2007). A question of belonging: Race, social fit, and achievement. *Journal of Personality and Social Psychology, 92*(1), 82–96.

Walton, G. M. and Spencer, S. J. (2009). Latent ability: Grades and test scores systematically underestimate the intellectual ability of negatively stereotyped students. *Psychological Science, 20*(9), 1132–9.

Wang, M.-T., Eccles, J. S. and Kenny, S. (2013). Not lack of ability but more choice: Individual and gender differences in choice of careers in science, technology, engineering, and mathematics. *Psychological Science, 24*(5), 770–5.

Wilson, T. D. and Linville, P. W. (1985). Improving the performance of college freshman with attributional techniques. *Journal of Personality and Social Psychology, 49*(1), 287–93.

Woodcock, A., Graziano, W. G., Branch, S. E., Habashi, M. M., Ngambeki, I. and Evangelou, D. (2013). Person and thing orientations: Psychological correlates and predictive utility. *Social Psychological and Personality Science, 4*(1), 116–23.

Yeager, D. S. and Walton, G. M. (2011). Social psychological interventions in education: They're not magic. *Review of Educational Research, 81*(2), 267–301.

6

THE EDUCATIONAL EXPERIENCE OF STUDENTS FROM LOW SOCIO-ECONOMIC STATUS BACKGROUND

Jolanda Jetten, Aarti Iyer and Airong Zhang

Education is an important social mobility route; those with higher and better degrees enjoy greater occupational success and acquire greater wealth over the course of their lives. For example, research has shown that university graduates obtain a better salary (Hossler and Coopersmith, 1989) and have higher lifetime earnings compared to those without a university degree (Marmot, 2004). One would, therefore, suspect that (especially when education is accessible and open to all) those from lower socio-economic status (SES) backgrounds would be particularly motivated to pursue a good education because this constitutes the most straightforward way to improve individual status (Tajfel and Turner, 1979; Wright, Taylor and Moghaddam, 1990).

However, the statistics suggest otherwise: it is middle- and upper-class students who populate high-status universities, whereas students from lower SES backgrounds are underrepresented (Feinstein and Vignoles, 2008). Similarly, in high schools, it is students from lower SES backgrounds who are more likely to drop out, and it is these students who have poorer educational outcomes compared to their higher SES counterparts (Fiske and Markus, 2012).

We define SES background quite broadly. Consistent with reasoning by DiMaggio (2012), SES background can be determined by an individual's education, wealth or social class (we refer the reader to Argyle, 1994, DiMaggio, 2012, and Fiske and Markus, 2012, for a detailed discussion of these concepts in the British and North American contexts). However, our current analysis looks beyond such fine-grained distinctions; our argument considers all students who are generally categorised as lower in SES. Therefore, we use various terms – social class, social status and SES – interchangeably in the present contribution. These terms characterise SES background in terms of social class and economic wealth as well as membership in a disadvantaged group.

In this contribution, our aim is twofold. First, we focus on the trajectories of students of lower SES backgrounds and we examine the specific barriers they face. In particular, we review work showing that the path to a good educational outcome (i.e., attending university or other types of higher education) is more difficult for lower SES students than it is for students from higher SES backgrounds. Building on recent social identity research examining identity transitions (as developed in the social identity model of identity change [SIMIC]; Haslam *et al.*, 2008; Jetten, Haslam, Iyer and Haslam, 2009), we propose that students from lower (compared to higher) SES backgrounds face many barriers that make individual mobility through higher education particularly difficult.

Second, and after unpacking the barriers students of low SES backgrounds face in educational contexts, we discuss how the prospect of change to the broader socio-structural context can further affect the educational outcomes of those who are disadvantaged. Specifically, the appraisal of these barriers may change when societies are rapidly changing and when disadvantaged group members perceive that there will be fewer barriers for their group in the future. To illustrate our reasoning, we focus on recent changes that have been implemented in the Chinese education system allowing children of migrant country-workers – a severely disadvantaged group in large Chinese cities – to enrol, for the first time, in mainstream public primary schools. We review recent empirical work showing that for children of country-workers, cognitive alternatives to the status quo are important in changing views that 'education is not for people like us'. We propose that such cognitive alternatives are, therefore, important ways to overcome and tackle barriers to seek out education as a way to get ahead.

To understand how social identity is involved in the choice to enter higher education and how social identity processes affect the success of transitioning into university life, we start our contribution with a brief theoretical overview of key tenets of the social identity approach.

Entering higher education = social identity change

According to the social identity approach – consisting of social identity theory (Tajfel and Turner, 1979) and self-categorisation theory (Turner, Hogg, Oakes, Reicher and Wetherell, 1987) – there are different ways in which people can self-categorise. Individuals can either focus on the features that make them unique and different from others (i.e., their personal identity) or they can think of themselves in terms of their memberships in social groups (i.e., their social identity). Important life transitions often involve losing or changing group memberships and, thus, affect social and personal identities. For example, in the transition to university, high school graduates might lose their membership in groups that were central while they were in high school, but they may gain new group memberships as they enter university (e.g., becoming a psychology student). Because an individual's self-concept is partly defined by the groups to which he or she belongs (Tajfel and Turner, 1979), it is clear that when the person's relationship to groups changes, the self is affected in important ways. In other words, life transitions often involve social identity change and the social and personal self can be deeply affected in the process (Iyer, Jetten, Tsivrikos, Postmes and Haslam, 2009).

For many young people, the transition to higher education is the first and most dramatic social identity change they encounter because entering a university involves breaking with old groups (e.g., high school friends, local communities) and becoming a member of new groups (e.g., residence hall, extracurricular activities, programme of study). University life is more than the attainment of tertiary qualifications in a field of study: it involves being part of a new community, being socialised into a new group, and taking on new values, beliefs and norms (Iyer, Jetten and Tsivrikos, 2008; Moreland and Levine, 2003) – all of which require individuals to form new identities (Newcomb, 1943). There is a great deal of excitement and anticipation associated with the transition to university life, but these changes can also be overwhelming and challenging. There is evidence that well-being is, at least temporarily, negatively affected for those who enter university (Ethier and Deaux, 1994; Iyer *et al.*, 2008) or undergo similar types of significant social identity change (Jetten, O'Brien and Trindall, 2002).

In line with the SIMIC (Haslam *et al.*, 2008; Jetten *et al.*, 2009), changes to social identities are expected to be challenging for at least two reasons (see Figure 6.1). First, social identities strengthen psychological grounding and stability for individuals, as they provide self-definition, meaning, and a sense of belonging (Jetten, Haslam and Haslam, 2012). For many students, entering university

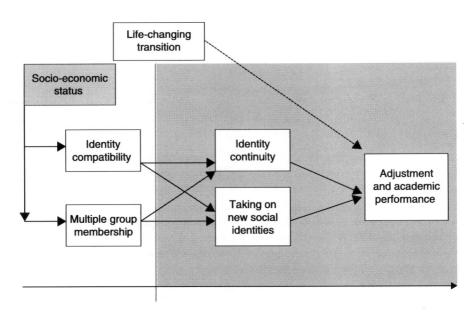

FIGURE 6.1 A social identity model of identity change (SIMIC) to explain adjustment and academic performance after the transition to university

involves leaving old groups behind (i.e., family, friends, school) that have been central to their lives (Hopkins and Reicher, 1997). The life transition, thus, means that the individual's relationship with these *old* identity resources changes. For many new university students, the old identities are no longer relevant or they are no longer available on a daily basis. These students may feel that they have lost identity when leaving their old lives behind to enter university. A growing body of work has demonstrated the negative well-being effects of social identity discontinuity (Haslam *et al.*, 2008; Iyer and Jetten, 2011; Jetten and Hutchison, 2011) and social identity loss more generally (Jetten *et al.*, 2002).

According to the SIMIC, social identity change that results from life transitions is challenging for a second reason: the individual has to join a new group and adopt a new identity, and this process may not be straightforward and easy. For example, it is quite common for individuals to resist identification with the new group if they have not yet relinquished their old identity (Ellemers, 2003) or if the old identity is not reconciled and represented in the new context (Haslam, Eggins and Reynolds, 2003; Hornsey and Hogg, 2000). It may be particularly difficult for some individuals to take on a new identity because members of the new group do not easily accept them, or may even discriminate against them (Postmes and Branscombe, 2002).

SES and higher education

While both these challenges are likely to affect *all* students who enter higher education, we would argue that they particularly affect those of lower SES backgrounds. There are two reasons in particular why lower SES students experience the transition to higher education as one of identity loss and discontinuity in which they will struggle to take on the new student identity (see Figure 6.1). First, lower SES students face institutional barriers because universities seem designed to meet the needs of students from higher SES backgrounds. As a result, higher education appears to be incompatible with the lower SES background. Second, students from lower (compared to higher) SES backgrounds have fewer social identity resources to facilitate a smooth transition to university (i.e., less social and cultural capital). We discuss these two barriers in more detail in the following sections.

1. Education is 'not for people like us'

Social identity relating to societal rank (e.g., in terms of social class, SES) is a particularly strong determinant of whether one will enrol at a higher education institution (Argyle, 1994). Whether entering higher education and being a student at university is compatible with one's background is an important determinant of whether people are able to adjust and successfully take on a new identity. If students come from family that is university educated, if many of their friends have entered university, and if university attendance is expected in their wider social background, perceptions of compatibility between being a university student and social background will be high. As a result, the transition to university involves a less dramatic life change for those for whom attending university is a logical and compatible extension of their high school identity. Such compatibility reinforces perceptions of continuity between the past and the present when undergoing social identity change. Because identity continuity allows individuals to maintain connection to their past and to use the old identity as a solid platform on which to build new identities, it is not surprising that there is a growing body of work showing that identity continuity can buffer against the negative consequences of change (Amiot, de la Soblonnière, Terry and Smith, 2007; Bluck and Alea, 2008; Chandler and Proulx, 2008; Haslam et al., 2008; Sani, 2008).

Conversely, if university students perceive that their friends and family have not had any experience with university life, expectations about attending university are very different. Reay (1996) asserts that young people acquire expectations that are adjusted to what is possible for people 'like us', leading to more negative attitudes towards higher education among those from lower SES backgrounds. If those of lower SES backgrounds make it, nevertheless, to university, they are less likely to make a smooth transition to university life compared to students for whom this life choice is more compatible. Hence, the psychological price of individual mobility could end up being high because the new identity does not sit well with the old identity. As a result, students may be reluctant to fully adopt this new identity.

Incompatibility perceptions may be further compounded by the fact that, in most Western countries, universities are not populated by working-class students but by middle- and upper-class students. For example, a British Department for Education and Skills (DFES) report concluded in 2003 that 'Students from families with professional and non-manual occupations continue to dominate higher education enrolments; students from families with skilled (manual), partly skilled or unskilled occupations are correspondingly underrepresented' (DFES, 2003). Douglas (2005) adds that the more selective the institution, the less representative it is of the population in general. In a similar vein, in the USA, only 9 per cent of lower SES students (i.e., who have two parents without college degrees) went to high-status universities compared to 62 per cent of students of higher SES backgrounds (i.e., two parents with a college degree; Astin and Oseguera, 2004).

Given the dominance of higher SES students at universities and other higher education institutions, it is not surprising that the educational system caters to their needs and demands (Bourdieu, 1984). As a result, lower SES background students feel unwelcome at high-status educational institutions, or worse, they encounter exclusion that can make it more likely for them to drop out. For students of lower SES background, this makes the transition to university particularly difficult because they are less able than their higher SES counterparts to fit in and take on the new university student identity (Iyer et al., 2009).[1]

2. Lack of identity resources among those lower in SES

Having a rich and diverse social network has been found to be an important predictor of health, well-being, and resilience (Cohen and Janicki-Deverts, 2009; Haslam et al., 2008; Jones and Jetten, 2011), and belonging to many groups facilitates taking on new group memberships (Jones et al., 2012). SES has been found to be an important predictor of whether individuals belong to many groups. It has been shown that those from higher SES backgrounds belong to more groups than do those from lower SES backgrounds (Iyer et al., 2009; Jetten et al., 2008; Jetten, Haslam and Barlow, 2013). More generally, high SES gives people access to more social and cultural capital (Putnam, 2000), which would help higher SES students approach higher education with more confidence than do students from lower SES backgrounds (Reay, 1996). In educational contexts, it is not just that those from higher SES backgrounds have more social capital, these students also appear to have the *right* social capital. That is, with many people in their family being university educated and with many of their peers enrolling in higher education institutions, students from higher SES backgrounds are optimally prepared for the transition to university. As a result, they will have many more effective sources of social, economic and financial support than students from lower SES backgrounds. Indeed, because lower SES students do not have access to the same social and cultural capital, identity change associated with entering and attending university is particularly difficult because they have fewer identity and support resources at their disposal that they can fall back on when facing stressors at university compared to their higher SES counterparts.

Evidence for SIMIC predictions in educational contexts

There is a growing body of work supporting predictions of the SIMIC (e.g., Haslam et al., 2008). Importantly for our argument, much of the support was obtained in educational contexts. For example, in a longitudinal study conducted in the UK, Iyer and colleagues (2009) and Jetten and colleagues (2008) surveyed new students at the University of Exeter[2] a few months before they made the transition to university and again after they had been at university for three or four months. Results revealed that students' well-being was higher before the transition than after the transition to university. It thus appeared that, even though new students were excited about the move to university, they also experienced the change as quite challenging and stressful. However, Iyer et al. (2009) also found that students who had taken on the new 'university student' identity more quickly and who identified with it more strongly after a few months at university were less negatively affected by the change. These students, thus, appeared to be better buffered against the negative effects of the transition on well-being.

Subsequent analyses were conducted to identify the best predictors of taking on the new university identity. In line with the SIMIC, Iyer and colleagues

(2009) found that identification as a university student was higher when students perceived more compatibility between old and new identities and when they belonged to multiple social groups before the transition to university. Importantly, too, students' SES background was an important predictor of incompatibility perceptions and the extent to which students belonged to many groups before their transition to university. Specifically, students from lower SES backgrounds reported that higher education was more incompatible with their social background and that they belonged to fewer groups than students from higher SES backgrounds. In turn, fewer group memberships and increased incompatibility perceptions reduced the likelihood that students took on the identity as university student after they had been at university for a couple of months.

It is also important to note that these relationships remained reliable when controlling for other factors that have been found to be relevant when entering university life. In particular, compatibility perceptions and belonging to many groups before the transition remained significant predictors of taking on the university identity after accounting for individuals' uncertainty about how the transition was going to affect their life, the support they had from family and friends to go to university, their perceived ability to achieve goals at university, and academic (e.g., perceived difficulty of keeping up with the coursework at university) and financial obstacles (e.g., the extent to which they struggled financially at university).

It thus appears that, because attending higher education does not represent a logical transition for lower SES students, the decision to enter higher education represents a clear break from the past. Attending university, thus, undermines identity continuity for students lower in SES, more so than for students higher in SES. There is evidence that, over time, this reduces the belief that education is a viable individual mobility route (Jetten et al., 2008). More specifically, Jetten and colleagues (2008, Study 2) found that lower SES was associated with higher perceptions that higher education is incompatible with one's social background. This belief reduced the likelihood that new students took on the identity as a university student, and had detrimental longitudinal effects: initial perceptions that a university education is incompatible with one's social background (measured before arriving at university) negatively predicted the belief that university education serves as a successful individual mobility strategy (measured after student had been at university for nine months). This finding is consistent with other work showing that members of minority groups withdraw psychologically or physically from education when they feel they do not belong. For example, there is evidence that minority status is associated with psychological disengagement, whereby members of minority groups detach their self-worth from academic achievement and success (Major and Schmader, 1998; Schmader, Major and Gramzow, 2001). Furthermore, stereotype threat research has shown that minority members' intellectual performance is hampered as soon as their minority status is made salient (Steele and Aronson, 1995; see also Boucher and Murphy, Chapter 5, this volume).

Cognitive alternatives: 'It does not have to be this way'

Due to the barriers outlined in Figure 6.1, it unfortunately appears that individual mobility through education can appear more costly and, therefore, least attractive, for those who stand to gain the most from such opportunities. As pessimistic as this conclusion may be, there is also some hope. Although the socio-structural context is an important barrier to seeing higher education as a viable individual mobility strategy, it is not an immutable one. In the second part of this contribution, we further unpack these processes. We argue that the prospects for lower SES students can change quite dramatically when the socio-structural context is perceived to be changing. Indeed, our research with country-workers' children in China has demonstrated that perceiving impending change in the socio-structural context can have a remarkable impact. These so-called perceived 'cognitive alternatives' to the status quo (Tajfel, 1978, p. 93) affected these children's outcomes. Before reviewing some of our findings on how change in the broader socio-structural context affects educational outcomes of students of lower SES background in greater detail, we provide a brief overview of the context.

School segregation in Chinese cities

In China, millions of country-workers have been moving to cities over the last two decades to seek better employment opportunities (China Labour Bulletin, 2012). Until recently, children of these country-workers were not allowed to attend the same schools as city children because of China's Household Registration (hukou) system. According to this system, citizens can only access services at their registered place of residence. Because registration cannot easily be changed when one moves, country-workers moving to the city are prevented from accessing basic services such as healthcare, social services, social security and education (Wong, Chang and He, 2009). To meet the need to provide education, separate schools were built for the children of these country-workers. However, these schools are typically of inferior quality: they are under-resourced and provide only basic schooling (Huang and Xu, 2006).

The segregation in schooling of city and country children was successfully challenged in 2011 and the central government passed legislation requiring urban governments to provide country-workers' children with access to mainstream public schools. Given the large number of country-workers' children in Chinese cities, the desegregation process has been rolled out in stages. At the time that we conducted our studies in Shanghai, some country children were already enrolled in integrated schools with city children, whereas others were still being educated in segregated schools. This meant that the socio-structural context for the former and the latter group of country-workers' children differed, allowing us to examine the effect of awareness of cognitive alternatives. That is, we asked whether the awareness that one's group status has improved or will improve in the future because socio-structural barriers have been removed affects these children's personal self-esteem, self-efficacy, and their performance on intellectual tasks.

Effects of cognitive alternatives on self-esteem, self-efficacy and performance

We started our examination with the question of how segregation affects children's self-esteem (Zhang, Jetten, Iyer and Cui, 2013). In a pilot study, we found that even though country-workers' children in integrated schools reported lower self-esteem than city children (i.e., the advantaged group), the self-esteem of country-workers' children in integrated schools was higher than that of country-workers' children in segregated schools. This suggests that the integrated context allows minority group members to become aware that the existing context is not the only possible reality, and that alternatives to the status quo are achievable and attainable. This awareness possibly opens paths to a better future for the minority group. This explanation was tested in two further studies where perceptions of cognitive alternatives were measured (Study 1) and manipulated (Study 2). Both studies showed that higher perceptions of cognitive alternatives were associated with higher self-esteem. We also found in both studies that identification with the minority group was higher when cognitive alternative perceptions were higher. This suggests that perceptions of cognitive alternatives to the status quo have an impact on group-level outcomes, and that they are thus akin to a collective mobility strategy, rather than an individual mobility strategy.

A further line of research revealed that cognitive alternatives not only positively affected the self-esteem of country-workers' children, but also enhanced perceived self-efficacy and performance on academic tasks (Iyer, Zhang, Jetten, Cui and Hao, 2014). Our explanation for these results extended the reasoning underlying the boundary conditions to stereotype threat effects. More specifically, several researchers have shown that the negative impact of stereotype threat on task performance is neutralised when minority group members perceive the cause of their disadvantage as malleable compared to fixed (e.g., Aronson, Fried and Good, 2002; Dar-Nimrod and Heine, 2006). Similarly, we reasoned that the perception of cognitive alternatives enhances the idea that the status quo is changeable and that minority group status can be improved, thus boosting performance on intellectual tasks.

We examined support for this prediction in three studies (Iyer *et al.*, 2016). A pilot study among country migrant workers' children in a large Chinese city showed that perceiving a better future for one's disadvantaged group was associated with higher self-efficacy. We then manipulated cognitive alternatives among country migrant workers' children (following procedures developed by Zhang *et al.*, 2013) and found increased self-efficacy in the high (compared to the low) cognitive alternatives condition. The final study examined the impact of manipulated cognitive alternatives on academic performance: country migrant workers' children in the high cognitive alternatives condition performed significantly better on a mathematics task and an attention task, compared to those in the low cognitive alternatives condition.

Taken together, these lines of research show that the socio-structural context might constrain the extent to which lower SES students can take advantage of education. However, membership in a lower status group does not bar students from academic success. We also show that being able to see alternatives to the current status quo enhances self-esteem and educational outcomes.

Final thoughts

Even though Akerlof and Kranton optimistically noted that 'individuals may – more or less consciously – choose who they want to be', they immediately qualified this statement, saying that 'Limits on this choice may also be the most important determinant of an individual's economic well-being' (2000, p. 717). Applying this reasoning to the educational context and SES, one can argue that if higher education is perceived only in terms of its potential to be an effective individual mobility route, we will miss the more complex issues that surround higher education choice and engagement for those of lower SES status. To understand students' continued engagement with higher education, and perhaps also the long-term relationship with higher education, we need to understand the specific barriers that students from lower SES backgrounds face.

In the first part of this chapter, we outlined two barriers that students from lower SES backgrounds face when transitioning into higher education. In the second section, we considered the process by which these barriers might be alleviated for students from lower SES backgrounds, focusing in particular on their perceptions that their group will have a better future. The time perspective to this notion of cognitive alternatives suggests that, despite the current disadvantaged status, the promise of future collective mobility powerfully affects minority members' present outcomes. In this way, dreams for a better group future might become concrete realities that affect individual outcomes in the present.

Having said this, it is perhaps not surprising that cognitive alternatives are particularly relevant when considering education: the full value of education for children becomes clear in the future (i.e., prospects for them as adults) rather than in the present. Education is concerned with beliefs and attitudes about 'becoming' (and is thus future-oriented) rather than 'being' – where the focus is on the present (Reicher, 2001). Put differently, education can be considered an investment in future identities.

We conclude that the social system must be brought back into the analysis of examining educational outcomes and experiences through the examination of socio-structural characteristics within educational systems. To understand whether young individuals see education as a viable and profitable strategy to get ahead, we need to understand the students' position in the broader system. It is this position in the system that motivates, but clearly also constrains, educational choices and shapes student experiences in higher education.

Author's Note

This research was supported by an Australian Research Council Future Fellowship (FT110100238) awarded to the first author.

Notes

1   On a more positive note, there is evidence that programmes to 'widen participation' have led to higher enrolment of lower SES students in higher education institutions. In Britain, the Department for Education and Skills estimates that, partly due to these widening participation programmes that were rolled out nationwide, the number of students from skilled (manual), partly skilled and unskilled backgrounds (often labelled as social classes I, II, and III) had increased from 10 per cent to 18 per cent of all higher education students in the period 1993 to 2003.

2   Note that the University of Exeter has a particular reputation within the UK educational context with respect to its students' ethnicity (i.e., white British) and SES background (i.e., middle and upper class). It is likely that this further contributes to incompatibility perceptions among lower SES background students.

References

Akerlof, G. A. and Kranton, R. E. (2000). Economics and identity. *Quarterly Journal of Economics, 115*(3), 715–53.

Amiot, C. E., de la Soblonnière, R., Terry, D. J. and Smith, J. R. (2007). Integration of social identities in the self: Toward a cognitive-developmental model. *Personality and Social Psychology Review, 11*(4), 364–88.

Argyle, M. (1994). *The psychology of social class.* London: Routledge.

Aronson, J., Fried, C. B. and Good, C. (2002). Reducing the effects of stereotype threat on African American college students by shaping theories of intelligence. *Journal of Experimental Social Psychology, 38*(2), 113–25.

Astin, A. W. and Oseguera, L. (2004). The declining equity of American higher education. *The Review of Higher Education, 27*(3), 321–41.

Bluck, S. and Alea, N. (2008). Remembering being me: The self-continuity function of autobiographical memory in younger and older adults. In F. Sani (Ed.), *Self-continuity: Individual and collective perspectives* (pp. 55–70). Mahwah, NJ: Erlbaum.

Bourdieu, P. (1984). *Distinction: A social critique of the judgment of taste.* Cambridge, MA: Harvard University Press.

Chandler, M. J. and Proulx, T. (2008). Personal persistence and persistent peoples: Continuities in the lives of individual and whole cultural communities. In F. Sani (Ed.), *Self-continuity: Individual and collective perspectives* (pp. 213–26). Mahwah, NJ: Erlbaum.

China Labour Bulletin. (2012). A decade of change: The workers' movement in China 2000–2012, *China Labour Bulletin.* Retrieved from: www.clb.org.hk/en/sites/default/files/File/research_reports/Decade%20of%20the%20Workers%20Movement%20final.pdf (accessed 21 May 2012).

Cohen, S. and Janicki-Deverts, D. (2009). Can we improve our physical health by altering our social networks? *Perspectives on Psychological Science, 4*(4), 375–8.

Dar-Nimrod, I. and Heine, S. J. (2006). Exposure to scientific theories affects women's math performance. *Science, 314*(5798), 435.

DiMaggio, P. (2012). Sociological perspectives on the face-to-face enactment of class distinction. In S.T. Fiske and H. R. Markus (Eds), *Facing social class: How societal rank influences interaction* (pp. 15–38). New York: Russell Sage Foundation.

Department for Education and Skills. (2003). *Widening participation in higher education.* London: HMSO.

Douglas, J. (2005). A comparative look at the challenges of access and equity: Changing patterns of policy making and authority in the UK and US higher education. *Higher Education Policy, 18*(2), 87–116.

Ellemers, N. (2003). Identity, culture, and change in organisations: A social identity analysis and three illustrative cases. In S. A. Haslam, D. van Knippenberg, M. J. Platow and N. Ellemers (Eds), *Social identity at work: Developing theory for organisational practice* (pp. 191–204). New York: Psychology Press.

Ethier, K. A. and Deaux, K. (1994). Negotiating social identity when contexts change: Maintaining identification and responding to threat. *Journal of Personality and Social Psychology, 67*(2), 243–51.

Feinstein, L. F. and Vignoles, A. (2008). Individual differences in the pathways into and beyond higher education in the UK: A life-course approach. *Journal of Social Issues, 64*(1), 115–33.

Fiske, S. T. and Markus, H. R. (2012). *Facing social class: How societal rank influences interaction.* New York: Russell Sage Foundation.

Haslam, C., Holme, A., Haslam, S. A., Iyer, A., Jetten, J. and Williams, W. H. (2008). Maintaining group membership: Identity continuity and well-being after stroke. *Neuropsychological Rehabilitation, 18*(5–6), 671–91.

Haslam, S. A., Eggins, R. A. and Reynolds, K. J. (2003). The ASPIRe model: Actualizing social and personal identity resources to enhance organizational outcomes. *Journal of Occupational and Organisational Psychology, 76*(1), 83–113.

Hopkins, N. and Reicher, S. D. (1997). The construction of social categories and processes of social change: Arguing about national identities. In G. Breakwell and E. Lyons (Eds), *Changing European identities* (pp. 69–93). Oxford: Butterworth-Heinemann.

Hornsey, M. J. and Hogg, M. A. (2000). Assimilation and diversity: An integrative model of subgroup relations. *Personality and Social Psychology Review, 4*(2), 143–56.

Hossler, D. B. J. and Coopersmith, G. (1989). Understanding student college choice. In J. Smart (Ed.), *Higher education: Handbook of theory and research*, Volume 5 (pp. 231–88). New York: Agathon Press.

Huang, Z. and Xu, K. (2006). Education of migrant workers and their children and its solutions. *Journal of Zhejiang University (Humanities and Social Sciences), 36*(4), 108–14.

Iyer, A. and Jetten, J. (2011). What's left behind: Identity continuity moderates the effect of nostalgia on well-being and life choices. *Journal of Personality and Social Psychology, 101*(1), 94–108.

Iyer, A., Jetten, J. and Tsivrikos, D. (2008). Torn between identities: Predictors of adjustment to identity change. In F. Sani (Ed.), *Self-continuity: Individual and collective perspectives* (pp. 187–97). New York: Psychology Press.

Iyer, A., Jetten, J., Tsivrikos, D., Postmes, T. and Haslam, S. A. (2009). The more (and the more compatible) the merrier: Multiple group memberships and identity compatibility as predictors of adjustment after life transitions. *British Journal of Social Psychology, 48*(4), 707–33.

Iyer, A., Zhang, A., Jetten, J., Cui, L. and Hao, Z. (2016). Yes, I can: Cognitive alternatives improve self-efficacy among disadvantaged school children. Manuscript submitted for publication.

Jetten, J., Haslam, S. A. and Barlow, F. K. (2013). Bringing back the system: One reason why conservatives are happier than liberals is that higher socioeconomic status gives them access to more group memberships. *Social Psychological and Personality Science*, *4*(1), 6–13.

Jetten, J., Haslam, C. and Haslam, S. A. (Eds). (2012). *The social cure: Identity, health and well-being*. Hove, UK: Psychology Press.

Jetten, J., Haslam, S. A., Iyer, A. and Haslam, C. (2009). Turning to others in times of change: Social identity and coping with stress. In S. Stürmer and M. Snyder (Eds), *The psychology of prosocial behavior: Group processes, intergroup relations, and helping* (pp. 139–56). Oxford: Blackwell.

Jetten, J. and Hutchison, P. (2011). When groups have a lot to lose: Historical continuity enhances resistance to a merger. *European Journal of Social Psychology*, *41*(3), 335–43.

Jetten, J., Iyer, A., Tsivrikos, D. and Young, B. M. (2008). When is individual mobility costly? The role of economic and social identity factors. *European Journal of Social Psychology*, *38*(5), 866–79.

Jetten, J., O'Brien, A. and Trindall, N. (2002). Changing identity: Predicting adjustment to organizational restructure as a function of subgroup and superordinate identification. *British Journal of Social Psychology*, *41*(2), 281–97.

Jones, M. J. and Jetten, J. (2011). Recovering from strain and enduring pain: Multiple group memberships promote resilience in the face of physical challenges. *Social Psychological and Personality Science*, *2*(3), 239–44.

Jones, J. M., Williams, W. H., Jetten, J., Haslam, S. A., Harris, A. and Gleibs, I. H. (2012). The role of psychological symptoms and social group memberships in the development of post-traumatic stress after traumatic injury. *British Journal of Health Psychology*, *17*(4), 798–811.

Major, B. and Schmader, T. (1998). Coping with stigma through psychological disengagement. In J. Swim and C. Stangor (Eds), *Prejudice: The target's perspective* (pp. 219–41). New York: Academic.

Marmot, M. (2004). *Status syndrome: How your social standing affects your health and life expectancy*. London: Bloomsbury Publishing.

Moreland, R. L. and Levine, J. M. (2003). Group composition: Explaining similarities and differences among group members. In M. A. Hogg and J. Cooper (Eds), *Sage handbook of social psychology* (pp. 367–80). London: Sage.

Newcomb, T. M. (1943). *Personality and social change*. New York: Dryden Press.

Postmes, T. and Branscombe, N. R. (2002). Influence of long-term racial environmental composition on subjective well-being in African Americans. *Journal of Personality and Social Psychology*, *83*(3), 735–51.

Putnam, R. D. (2000). *Bowling alone: The collapse and revival of American community*. New York: Simon & Schuster.

Reay, D. (1996). Contextualising choice: Social power and parental involvement. *British Educational Research Journal*, *22*(5), 581–96.

Reicher, S. D. (2001). Social identity definition and enactment; a broad SIDE against irrationalism and relativism. In T. Postmes, R. Spears, M. Lea and S. D. Reicher (Eds), *SIDE issues centre stage: Recent developments of de-individuation in groups* (pp. 175–90). Amsterdam: Proceedings of the Dutch Royal Academy of Arts and Sciences.

Sani, F. (2008). *Individual and collective self-continuity*. Mahwah, NJ: Erlbaum.

Schmader, T., Major, B. and Gramzow, R. (2001). Coping with ethnic stereotypes in the academic domain: Perceived injustice and psychological disengagement. *Journal of Social Issues*, *57*(1), 93–111.

Steele, C. M. and Aronson, J. (1995). Stereotype threat and the intellectual test performance of African Americans. *Journal of Personality and Social Psychology, 69*(5), 797–811.

Tajfel, H. (Ed.). (1978). *Differentiation between social groups: Studies in the social psychology of intergroup relations.* London: Academic Press.

Tajfel, H. and Turner, J. C. (1979). An interactive theory of intergroup conflict. In W. G. Austin and S. Worchel (Eds), *The social psychology of intergroup relations* (pp. 33–47). Monterey, CA: Brooks/Cole.

Turner, J. C., Hogg, M. A., Oakes, P. J., Reicher, S. D. and Wetherell, M. S. (1987). *Rediscovering the social group: A self-categorization theory.* Oxford: Blackwell.

Wong, F. K. D., Chang, Y. L. and He, X. S. (2009). Correlates of psychological wellbeing of children of migrant workers in Shanghai, China. *Social Psychiatry and Psychiatric Epidemiology, 44*(10), 815–24.

Wright, S. C., Taylor, D. M. and Moghaddam, F. M. (1990). Responding to membership in a disadvantaged group: From acceptance to collective protest. *Journal of Personality and Social Psychology, 58*(6), 994–1003.

Zhang, A., Jetten, J., Iyer, A. and Cui, L. (2013). 'It will not always be this way': Cognitive alternatives improve self-esteem in contexts of segregation. *Social Psychological and Personality Science, 4*(2), 159–66.

7

INDIGENOUS EDUCATION IN AUSTRALIA

A battle of identities

Diana M. Grace and Michael J. Platow

Preamble

Examining self and social identity processes in educational contexts can have one of two foci. The first involves examination of how self and identity processes affect educational outcomes; the second examines how specific educational processes affect self and identity. Although both processes are implicitly recognised in the current chapter, our precise focus is how educational contexts – and education more broadly – can serve as a battleground between identities in a world comprising groups that differ in power and status. Identities are not simply transported into educational contexts; nor are they passively and benignly formed within them. Rather, educational contexts, including formal schooling as practiced in many cultures, serve to construct specific identities. These identities are instilled into students, often with the explicit intent of denying, devaluing and destroying existing personal and social identities of these students. In doing so, schools can become instruments of hegemonic identity imposition.

With this recognition as background, our chapter focuses explicitly on the case of the Australian education system and its (historical) attempts to redefine, if not obliterate, Indigenous identities. We recognise that such attempts are not unique to Australia; however, a detailed description of all countries in which such practices have occurred would be a complete book in itself. Thus, despite our focus being of particular relevance to readers interested in the Australian context, our theoretical analysis is, of course, applicable to an understanding of education and educational systems in a wider variety of social contexts.

Introduction

In Australia, the term 'Indigenous education' has been variously used with regard to the education of Aboriginal and Torres Strait Islander people.[1] It refers both to the (largely within-groups) transmission of Indigenous knowledges and cultures and to the (between-groups) transfer of culturally dominant (white) educational practice to Indigenous people. Permeating all of this discourse has been a focus on deficits. Since white settlement, Indigenous Australians have been considered 'in need' of educating in 'white' ways; while even the treatment of within-cultural transmission of knowledge has been shrouded in mystery and commonly seen as something only relevant to 'them'. Together with the recent emphasis on 'closing the gap',[2] this has enabled and encouraged the focus to remain on Indigenous people 'catching up' to white people. An alternative view – and one espoused in this chapter – centres on the experiences, and context, of Indigenous Australians who, *in their own country*, have been 'locked out' of a (white) dominant education system. The chapter focuses on how the identities of Indigenous Australians, which have been formed through their individual and collective histories, experiences, and social and political contexts, have been subjected to ongoing challenges and contests. Our analysis draws on social-psychological and sociological analyses of intergroup processes and social justice frameworks. We conclude by making a call for adopting a *recognitive justice* view of social inclusion that, in this instance, places Aboriginal and Torres Strait Islander people firmly at the centre of Indigenous education by *recognising* the rights, obligations and contributions to be made, and how this can ultimately lead to benefits for all.

In this chapter, we begin with an historical account that outlines the many ways in which educational systems and educational discourse in Australia have reinforced the relative position of Aboriginal and Torres Strait Islander people. The account echoes analyses provided by social identity and self-categorisation theories that explain how intergroup actions serve to maintain the boundaries between, and the social positions of certain groups. We then draw on recent analyses of recognitive justice that incorporates a moral imperative for the recognition of certain groups (in this case Indigenous Australians). Our concluding arguments suggest that changes in educational systems and practice can benefit not only Aboriginal and Torres Strait Islander students, but the Australian population as a whole.

Indigenous education in Australia

Aboriginal and Torres Strait Islander people are among the longest-surviving cultures in the world (Macintyre, 1999) – estimated to be between 50,000 and 500,000 years old (Commonwealth of Australia, 1998). At the time of white settlement, Australia's population numbered from 300,000 to over 1,000,000 (Harris, 2003), comprising approximately 250 distinct language groups with several hundred dialects (Walsh, 1993). Each language, or nation, group was (is) connected to a specific land area – each with its own identity, culture, customs and laws. Complex kinship systems identified intra- and inter-group relationships and provided guidelines for behaviour, again both within and between language/nation groups. As hunting/gathering/fishing societies, these tight social structures had both individual and group benefits. Inclusive family structures provided a comprehensive social welfare system for people of all ages, while reciprocal obligations reduced intergroup conflict (Ranzijn, McConnochie and Nolan, 2009).

These hunter–gatherer groups were highly communal and often mobile, with many of the population involved in numerous activities. Education commonly involved taking part in those activities appropriate to one's age and gender. Education, thus, involved systematic learning processes that operated on spoken language and involved observation and experience (Cadzow, 2007). Ironically, this 'discovery learning' method has been 'rediscovered' in many guises throughout modern educational practice (through variously termed experiential learning methods; e.g., Kolb, Boyatzis and Mainemelis, 2001; Kraft, 1986; Montessori, 1975). Nonetheless, when white settlement began in 1788, Indigenous Australians were invariably regarded as uncivilised and backward (Said, 1978) and in need of education.

Colonisation and Indigenous education

Carrying the legal fiction of *terra nullius* (i.e., the view that the land that became Australia was empty of human settlement), the arrival of the First Fleet from Britain in 1788 marked the beginning of events that would change the world for Indigenous Australians (Langton, 2010). Despite some initial amity between the white settlers and the local people, the goal of the British was clear: they were to establish a British colony in Australia. Hence, as the competition for land developed into open conflict, attempts to eliminate the Aboriginal people intensified (Boyce, 2010). Despite large-scale massacres (Collins, 2002) and the spread of diseases (Kunitz, 1994; Mear, 2008) that amounted to open genocide (Harris, 2003; Moses, 2000), the Aboriginal people's refusal to surrender their lands was met with increasing efforts to contain them – efforts that were sanctioned by the British and Australian governments (Markus, 1994). Sadly, this proved to be the introduction of British and Australian legislation that would enable the removal of Aboriginal people from their lands onto reserves and missions, ultimately leading to the forced removal of children from their families (Human Rights and Equal Opportunity Commission [HREOC], 1997).

In 1814, Governor Macquarie opened the Native Institution – the first school specifically for Aboriginal children (Fletcher, 1989). Transcripts pertaining to its establishment emphasise its ostensible purpose – 'to render their habits more domesticated and industrious' (NSW Government, n.d., p. 11) – but also its underlying objectives. Educating these young people was to occur entirely within the confines of British/European practices. This would be achieved through a complete separation of the children from their families:

> no Child, after having been admitted to the Institution, shall be permitted to leave it, or be taken away by any Person whatever (whether Parents or other Relatives) until such Time as the Boys shall have attained the Age of Sixteen Years, and the Girls Fifteen Years.
>
> (Ma Rhea, 2015, p. 93)

There is little doubt that the purpose of the Native Institution was to remove children from their families – a practice that sometimes occurred by deceit (Kociumbas, 1997; Kyle, 1986). There is also little doubt that its purpose was the complete decimation of existing Indigenous identities, cultures, norms and customs, replacing them, instead, with those sanctioned by the more powerful British and Australian authorities. Tragically, this foreshadowed what was to become one of the saddest chapters of Aboriginal history in Australia; that is, the Stolen Generations (HREOC, 1997).

Endorsed by the House of Commons in England, the Australian government expanded its initiatives for Aboriginal (re)education (Reynolds, 2009). Aside from brief attempts at integrating Aboriginal students into existing schools, this largely involved the establishment of schools on Aboriginal reserves. However, attendance was intermittent, and with the onset of the gold rushes in the mid-eighteenth century, the governments – in both Australia and Britain – were beset with new priorities. Any instruction that did take place during this time was largely under the auspices of religious organisations – again with the alternative (or at least additional) motive of eliminating existing Indigenous identities and beliefs by converting them to Christianity (e.g., Rademaker, 2015).

Additional legislation was enacted in 1880 to make formal education compulsory in Australia (Campbell and Proctor, 2014). White children were to be educated until the age of 14 but Aboriginal children, only until 12. That this so-called education of Aboriginal children largely took place in separate schools had important implications for Aboriginal people who were increasingly coming under the legal control of the Chief Protector of Aboriginal People in each state. Each 'protector' had the legal guardianship of every Aboriginal and half-caste[3] under the age of 18 and was, thus, free to remove children from their families at will (HREOC, 1997).

Although some Aboriginal children attended public schools, it was possible for schools to refuse entry if non-Aboriginal parents objected (Australian Human Rights Commission, 2001). Following several of these incidents (e.g., Harris, 1978), more and more Aboriginal-only schools were established. By 1940, this number had risen to over 40 in the state of New South Wales alone. Unlike the experiences of white children, emphasis in Aboriginal schools was given to manual activities, and those employed in the role of teachers were usually untrained (Reynolds, 2009). Although basic instruction was provided in literacy and maths, all teaching was firmly grounded in Western knowledge, history and ideology (Brooks, 2007). The aim of this education was clearly to benefit white people as Aboriginal people were considered physically and mentally inferior (Johnston, 1937) and largely uneducable – especially those from the north and central Australia (Ford, 2013).

Dual system of education

With public schools holding the right to exclude Aboriginal children and the poor standard of the Aboriginal schools, there was a clear dual system of education operating in Australia. Although firmly based on a view of Aboriginal inferiority, such a system served to ensure that position. Through legal doctrine and (under) education, Indigenous Australians remained economically and politically powerless within white Australia, yet disconnected from and uneducated in their own cultures. Moreover, this occurred within a context of increasing legal control by the state. Parents were expected to send their children to school – schools that often bore no relevance to the students, their families or their culture and where the children were often treated poorly. Even the simple act of sending a child to school could place him/her at greater risk of being taken by the government and placed into institutional or other out-of-home care (Healy, 1998; Ivec, Braithwaite and Harris, 2009).

In contrast, the schooling of white children was largely undertaken in public schools where British history and values were espoused. Only extremely violent or neglectful white parents faced any risk of having their children removed, but this was extremely rare. Ironically, protecting (white) children from their parents was seen as interfering in the private family sphere (Australian Institute of Family Studies, 2014). Even in the case of extreme abuse, 'boarding out' to another family was the preferred option to institutional care (Liddell, 1993). Not until the 1960s was any real recognition given to the severity of child maltreatment (Kempe, Silverman, Steele, Droegemueller and Silver, 1962), ultimately leading to the development of child protection policies and practices.

By the 1950s, however, racial segregation was fully entrenched in Australia. During this so-called assimilationist period (Burridge and Chodkiewicz, 2012; Morgan, 2006), Aboriginal people's lives were strictly controlled. Many lived on clearly defined missions or reserves, often located near rubbish dumps or sanitation sites (Beresford, 2003), and Aboriginal people were subjected to legal restrictions pertaining to all aspects of their lives (Wright, 2001). Although Australia had become a Federation in 1901, the Constitution *denied* any citizenship rights to Aboriginal people. It was not until 1967 that Indigenous people were allowed to vote (although it was not compulsory as it was for non-Indigenous people, thereby contributing to their continued disenfranchisement); white parents retained veto over enrolment of Aboriginal children in public schools until 1972; and the forcible removal of children from their families continued until the 1970s (HREOC, 1997). Growing up in Australia throughout much of the twentieth century continued to be a vastly different experience for Indigenous and non-Indigenous people: education was both a cause and a consequence of this.

Educational policy and its impacts

British educational practices have dominated – and strongly influenced – Australian educational policy. Early policies were a 'direct export of ideas and models from Britain' (O'Donoghue, 2009, p. 788) in an attempt to model Australian society on that of the British. These ideas (and practices) were entirely consistent with those of populating a new British colony – one that was supposedly devoid of existing inhabitants.

Schools were initially (i.e., following white settlement) funded by the centralised colonial government, although such funding was minimal and resulted in poor facilities with often untrained teachers (Shinkfield, 1988). By the mid nineteenth century, involvement by churches grew, fuelled by a belief of the inseparable nature of education and moral training (O'Donoghue, 2009; Shinkfield, 1988). Using this argument, churches applied for – and received – government funding. However, antagonism – especially between the Church of England and the Catholic Church – prompted further interest in the establishment of non-denominational (government-run) schools. These schools had increasing responsibility for students' academic, moral and social development, again firmly in the mould of the British system (Freebody, 2014). Students thus received instruction that was intended to assist them to create *self-definitions* in the British mould.

At the same time, the population of Australia was increasing dramatically following the discovery of gold in 1851. It is claimed that the population tripled from 430,000 in 1851 to 1.7 million in 1871 (Australian Government, n.d.), although Aboriginal people were probably not included in these counts. This population boom placed further demand on an education system that was, itself, in the process of being devolved to the states (Campbell and Proctor, 2014). Not surprisingly, the result of this was an education system (or systems) that was fragmented and poorly resourced. Despite a belief by many that this new – and multi-ethnic – society was class-free (Denoon, 1983), the reality was that children from poor families often received no schooling at all (Austin, 1977).

The latter part of the nineteenth century thus saw legislation enacted to make school attendance compulsory – beginning with the New South Wales Public Instruction Act of 1880 – and a growing emphasis on secondary education (Campbell and Proctor, 2014). With an increasing population overall, the 'Aboriginal problem' (Ellinghaus, 2003; Reynolds, 2009) facing the Australian government became one of many concerns vying for official attention, which became increasingly divided between these competing matters. Existing legislation, however, remained in place well into the twentieth century; for example, school principals in New South Wales retained power to exclude Aboriginal children until 1972 (Burridge and Chodkiewicz, 2012).

Indigenous identity and intergroup relations

Since white settlement, Indigenous Australians have been subjected to a range of discriminatory policies and practices, beginning with open genocide (Harris, 2003; Moses, 2000) and continuing with systematic, systemic and often subtle forms of racism (de Plevitz, 2006, 2007). Few Aboriginal and Torres Strait Islander people today have not been the direct target of racism (Ferdinand, Paradies and Kelaher, 2013). Characterising these attacks and affronts has been – and continues to be – a disregard for Aboriginal people and their heritage, including their identities, norms, values, customs and knowledge.

Early government policies were explicitly focused on the elimination – or at least the 'ultimate absorption' – of the Aboriginal race (Johnston, 1937). 'Full-blood natives' were to be kept in 'inviolable reserves' (1937, p. 3) and efforts directed at the ultimate absorption of the 'half-castes' and 'quadroons'[4] into the white race. The tenor of the language used in this and other official documents clearly demonstrates how Aboriginal people were regarded. Not only were they considered 'an inferior race' (Anderson, 2003; McConnochie, Hollinsworth and Pettman, 1988), but their ongoing resistance to relinquish their lands for the purposes of 'civilised' farming and industry was seen as problematic. Reflected in this discourse is the prevailing view of Indigenous people: at best an inconvenience, at worst detestable.

Such explicit attempts to eradicate the 'Aboriginal race' differ little from those to exterminate rabbits and other common pests in Australia. Similar, too, is the language that has been applied. We use this analogy to emphasise the blatancy of the intergroup relations between Indigenous and non-Indigenous (mostly white) people, extending to the dehumanisation of Aboriginal people. As demonstrated in infrahumanisation research, this reflects the denial of a form of human essence to outgroups (Haslam, Bain, Douge, Lee and Bastian, 2005). In other words, Aboriginal people's identities – including that of being human – were denied.

Clear intergroup distinctions were also made between Aboriginal and non-Aboriginal people, and these are particularly evident in the language used in legal documents. Laws continually referred to 'natives', 'full-bloods' and 'half-castes', including 'quadroons', 'octoroons', etc. (e.g., Hollinsworth, 2006). Although the terminology was sometimes shrouded in benevolent intent, it nonetheless worked to distinguish between the two groups, to legitimise differences and to emphasise the impermeability between the group boundaries – an impermeability that, at best, could be overcome by simply 'breeding out' any Aboriginality.

Social identity theory and intergroup relations

This historical evidence of Indigenous education in post-white settlement Australia is clearly one characterised by conflictual – if not outright violent – intergroup relations. Intergroup relations are the core of social identity theory (Tajfel, 1978; Tajfel and Turner, 1979, 1986). Decades of theoretical and empirical research have explicated the mechanisms by which members of groups work to maintain, diminish or traverse intergroup boundaries. Central to this are three concepts outlined by Tajfel and Turner (1979) that, independently and in interaction, continue to explain a range of intergroup processes.

The first of these is the *stability* of the group differences. When differences between groups are perceived as stable, or unchanging, attempts to change group boundaries are seen as less viable. Similarly, the second concept, *legitimacy*, concerns the validity of group differences: the greater the legitimacy – including legally sanctioned ones – the less successful will be attempts to challenge these boundaries. The majority of research has focused on the combined effects of stability and legitimacy, with stability tending to accentuate the impact of legitimacy. For example, Turner and Brown (1978) found that members of high-status groups showed greater ingroup favouritism when group boundaries were perceived as legitimate and unstable. That is, when boundaries are seen as justifiable and appropriate, but when they could (potentially) be subject to change, high-status group members take the strongest measures to reinforce their position.

The third concept, *permeability*, refers to the range of possible movement between groups. The extent of group permeability impacts on both the likelihood of movement between groups and the strategies adopted (by the members of each group) to achieve a positive identity. For members of low-status groups, the permeability of boundaries has important consequences. In situations of high permeability, group members may decide to adopt a strategy of upward mobility and, individually, pursue entry into the high-status group (Ellemers, van Knippenberg, de Vries and Wilke, 1988; Ellemers, van Knippenberg and Wilke, 1990). In contrast, when the possibility of movement between groups is low, group members are more likely to adopt a collective strategy to achieve, among other things, a positive sense of identity (Ellemers *et al.*, 1988, 1990).

Again, we stress that these effects and the complex interaction effects of these variables have been the subject of numerous studies. What we emphasise here, however, is that these theoretical (and empirical) accounts also describe the historical treatment of Indigenous Australians. The intergroup boundaries and intergroup differences between Indigenous Australians and white settlers were continually emphasised as being stable (they were not going to change) and legitimate (as evidenced by law). That states retained legal 'guardianship' over Aboriginal people until the mid-twentieth century is testament to the continued attempts to legitimise these category boundaries. That similar laws remain in effect today (e.g., income management schemes in the Northern Territory) demonstrates the strength of this resolve.

In contrast, there has been much ambiguity surrounding boundary permeability. Again, legal documents are revealing. For example, within the transcript of the Aboriginal Welfare conference (Johnston, 1937), much consideration was given to the treatment and future of 'full-bloods' and 'half-castes'. Lamenting the futility of the future of the 'full-blood natives', who would be best 'kept under a benevolent supervision', the conference stated its explicit aim of 'ultimate absorption of the native race into *ordinary* community' (1937, p. 34, emphasis added). Education efforts were focused on those of 'less than full blood' with the aim of 'their taking their place in the white community on an equal footing with the whites' (1937, p. 21).

Momentarily leaving aside the racist nature of these remarks, this proposed social mobility implied, on the one hand, that ('mixed blood') Aboriginal people could, under the receipt of the 'proper' (re)education and (re)employment, become a member of the high-status (white) group. On the other hand, the definition of 'people of mixed blood' and their 'capabilities' were hotly debated. Hence, the boundary between being Indigenous or not was sometimes permeable but sometimes not.

This duality of simultaneous acceptance and rejection of category membership has been addressed recently under the concept of 'marginalising racism' (Platow, Grace and Smithson, 2014). Critical to the present analysis is that marginalising racism emphasises the flexibility of category definition (by others) as much as the flexibility of (potential) categories that can be invoked (e.g., Grace, Straiton, Hewett-Reeves and Platow, 2015). Laws imposed after white settlement placed increasing restrictions on Aboriginal people – by non-Aboriginal people – while simultaneously defining 'Aboriginal'. Indeed, white legislators decided on, and continually debated, the meaning of 'Aboriginal'.

In the education arena, category boundaries were made explicit first through the establishment of separate schools for Aboriginal children and then through laws that allowed non-Aboriginal parents to control who could and could not attend non-segregated schools. At one level, it was made clear that Aboriginal children were different from white children. At the same time, Aboriginal children were encouraged to become like white children. Indeed, they were considered (at least potentially) white when espousing the benefits of 'breeding out' Aboriginality, but considered black when warning of inherent deficiencies.

In essence, the history of Indigenous education in Australia clearly set up a demarcation between Indigenous and non-Indigenous students. Rules and curricula were set by non-Indigenous people (specifically, those who were white and British), and these same rules and curricula reflected non-Indigenous values and benefited non-Indigenous people. In this way, the education system supported and reinforced the belief in as well as the actual economic and political superiority of non-Indigenous Australians.

This preference for non-Indigenous identity, histories and values remains evident today. Despite some changes to national teaching curricula throughout Australia (Australian Curriculum, Assessment and Reporting Authority, 2012) to introduce Indigenous perspectives, their impact has not been great. Moreover, these efforts have been further attenuated through recent changes to the national curriculum framework (Australian Government, 2014) in which the teaching of Indigenous history and themes remains optional. Such policies often unwittingly contribute to the perpetuation of Indigenous histories, knowledges and people as 'others' (e.g., Carey, 2015; Carey and Prince, 2015). Hence, boundaries continue to be drawn between who is (and is not) Indigenous, what does (and does not) constitute Indigenous knowledge, and who has (and does not have) the authority to determine the answers to these questions. Far from being a historical issue, such debates highlight (and, unfortunately, perpetuate) questions of stability, legitimacy and permeability of category boundaries.

Contemporary Indigenous education experiences

As we emphasise throughout this chapter, Indigenous identities have been continually constructed and reconstructed – most noticeably by non-Indigenous people since white settlement. This has resulted in, and continues to contribute to, the deficit discourse surrounding Aboriginal and Torres Strait Islander students at all levels of education (Howlett, Seini, Matthews, Dillon and Hauser, 2008; Vass, 2013). Not only do Indigenous students compare poorly to their non-Indigenous peers on a range of achievement measures (e.g., Ford, 2013; Steering Committee for the Review of Government Service Provision, 2014), these same figures are used to support Indigenous deficits (Gray and Beresford, 2008; Harrison, 2007). In other words, Indigenous education is seen as a 'problem that needs fixing' (Vass, 2013, p. 85), and Indigenous people are seen as the source of that problem (Gorringe, 2011).

Although useful in both justifying and maintaining educational discrepancies, such views can also be seen as little more than contemporary versions of the policies and practices we document throughout this chapter – policies and practices that have served to inhibit Indigenous achievement while maintaining non-Indigenous privilege and power. Underlying this is the assumption that non-Indigenous identities, cultures, values and knowledge are superior. Even attempts at social justice and social inclusion are aimed at Indigenous people 'fitting in with' or 'catching up to' non-Indigenous Australians.

An alternative to this view is one in which Indigenous identities, cultures, values and knowledges take centre stage. This, recognitive justice, approach (Gale, 2000; Gale and Tranter, 2011) explicitly *recognises* the rights and obligations of all groups and the contributions to be made by them, which can ultimately lead to benefits for all. Indeed, it is only through exercising these rights and obligations that *all* groups can benefit.

In the context of education, a recognitive justice approach recognises and values the contributions to be made by the disadvantaged and the disenfranchised *as much as* those by people with advantage and franchise. In the context of *Australian* education, such an approach recognises the advantages to *all social groups* of valuing Indigenous knowledges by incorporating Indigenous values, cultures, norms and knowledges into *all* Australian educational curricula. It recognises that non-Indigenous Australians have much to learn *from* Indigenous Australians.

Conclusion

In this chapter, we have detailed how Indigenous education in Australia since white settlement has served to maintain clear boundaries between Indigenous and non-Indigenous Australians while denigrating the lives, histories and identities of Indigenous Australians. Not only have Indigenous identities been devalued, they have been openly attacked. Since white settlement, education in Australia has been shaped by British experiences and British expectations. What our analysis has shown are the systematic ways in which white Australians worked to remove Indigenous identities, cultures, knowledge – and even the people themselves – and supplant them with British identities, cultures, knowledge and people. Testament to the strength of Indigenous people – and their identities – is that these attempts have never fully been successful.

Notwithstanding the overtly genocidal and racist activities that pervade the history of Indigenous education in Australia, this state of affairs has left Indigenous Australians in a struggle for their identities. This struggle has meant they remain disadvantaged in the contemporary (white) Australian education system while, at the same, time they have been separated from their own histories, cultures, languages and identities.

To reverse these injustices requires a reversal of the ideologies that have underpinned education in Australia. It involves building an educational system and developing educational curricula that recognise not only the sovereignty of the First Australians, but also that non-Indigenous Australians have much to learn *from* Indigenous Australians. It involves building an educational system that, far from de-emphasising category boundaries, emphasises and values the (superior) status of Indigenous Australians. It recognises, too, that Indigenous Australians will not be the only ones to benefit from this.

Notes

1 Throughout the chapter, we use the terms 'Indigenous', 'Aboriginal' and 'Aboriginal and Torres Strait Islander' interchangeably. Aboriginal people were the first inhabitants of Australia, as were Torres Strait Islander people, whose islands were annexed by Queensland in 1879. The varying terminology also reflects its changing use over time.
2 'Closing the gap' is a government-led, Australia-wide campaign launched in 2007 to address the disparity between Indigenous and non-Indigenous life expectancies. Although initially focused on health issues, the initiative now incorporates education, employment and community safety.
3 'Half-caste' is one of many (primarily derogatory) terms used throughout the world to describe people of mixed racial descent.
4 Used in pejorative ways along with 'half-caste', the terms 'quadroon' and 'octoroon' were specifically used to define the extent of one's Aboriginality (i.e., one-quarter and one-eighth).

References

Anderson, W. (2003). *The cultivation of whiteness: Science, health and racial destiny in Australia.* New York: Basic Books.

Austin, A. G. (1977) *Australian education 1788–1900: Church, state and public education in Australia.* Carlton, VIC: Pitman.

Australian Curriculum, Assessment and Reporting Authority. (2012). *The shape of the Australian Curriculum, Version 4.0.* Sydney: ACARA. Retrieved from: www.acara.edu.au/verve/_resources/the_shape_of_the_australian_curriculum_v4.pdf (accessed 1 September 2016).

Australian Government. (2014). *Review of the Australian curriculum: Final report.* Canberra: Department of Education. Retrieved from: https://docs.education.gov.au/system/files/doc/other/review_of_the_national_curriculum_final_report.pdf (accessed 1 September 2016).

Australian Human Rights Commission. (2001). *Rural and remote education inquiry briefing paper: A history of Indigenous education.* Retrieved from: https://www.humanrights.gov.au/publications/rural-and-remote-education-inquiry-briefing-paper-26 (accessed 1 September 2016).

Australian Institute of Family Studies. (2014). History of child protection services [online], *Australian Institute of Family Studies*. Retrieved from: https://aifs.gov.au/cfca/publications/history-child-protection-services (accessed 1 September 2016).

Beresford, Q. (2003). The context of Aboriginal education. In Q. Beresford and G. Partington (Eds), *Reform and resistance in Aboriginal education: The Australian experience* (pp. 10–25). Perth: University of Western Australia Press.

Boyce, J. (2010). Towlangany: To tell lies. In R. Perkins and M. Langton (Eds), *First Australians* (pp. 1–42). Melbourne: The Miegunyah Press.

Brooks, M. C. (2007). Charting the 'false maps' of Australian Aboriginal education: Rethinking education policy from a general semantics perspective. *ETC: A review of General Semantics, 64*(2), 135–43.

Burridge, N. and Chodkiewicz, A. (2012). An historical overview of Aboriginal education policies in the Australian context. In N. Burridge, F. Whalan and K. Vaughan (Eds), *Indigenous education: A learning journey for teachers, schools and communities* (pp. 11–21). Rotterdam: Sense Publishers.

Cadzow, A. (2007). *A NSW Aboriginal education timeline 1788–2007*. Sydney: Board of Studies NSW.

Campbell, C. and Proctor, H. (2014). *A history of Australian schooling*. Sydney: Allen & Unwin.

Carey, M. (2015). The limits of cultural competence: An Indigenous studies perspective. *Higher Education Research and Development, 34*(5), 828–40.

Carey, M. and Prince, M. (2015). Designing an Indigenous studies curriculum for the twenty-first century: Nakata's 'cultural interface', standpoints and working beyond binaries. *Higher Education Research and Development, 34*(2), 270–83.

Collins, P. (2002). *Goodbye Bussamarai: The Mandandanji land war, Southern Queensland, 1842–1852*. St Lucia, QLD: University of Queensland Press.

Commonwealth of Australia. (1998). *As a matter of fact: Answering the myths and misconceptions about Indigenous Australians*. Canberra: Aboriginal and Torres Strait Islander Commission.

de Plevitz, L. (2006). Special schooling for Indigenous students: A new form of racial discrimination. *The Australian Journal of Indigenous Education, 35*, 44–53.

de Plevitz, L. (2007). Systemic racism: The hidden barrier to educational success for Indigenous school students. *Australian Journal of Education, 51*(1), 54–71.

Denoon, D. (1983). *Settler capitalism: The dynamics of dependent development in the southern hemisphere*. Oxford: Oxford University Press.

Ellemers, N., van Knippenberg, A., de Vries, N. and Wilke, H. (1988). Social identification and permeability of group boundaries. *European Journal of Social Psychology, 18*(6), 497–513.

Ellemers, N., van Knippenberg, A. and Wilke, H. (1990). The influence of permeability of group boundaries and stability of group status on strategies of individual mobility and social change. *British Journal of Social Psychology, 29*(3), 233–46.

Ellinghaus, K. (2003). Absorbing the 'Aboriginal problem': Controlling interracial marriage in Australia in the late 19th and early 20th centuries. *Aboriginal History, 27*, 183–207.

Ferdinand, A., Paradies, Y. and Kelaher, M. (2013). *Mental health impact of racial discrimination in Victorian Aboriginal communities: The localities embracing and accepting diversity (LEAD) experiences of racism survey*. Melbourne: The Lowitja Institute.

Fletcher, J. J. (1989). *Clean, clad and courteous: A history of Aboriginal education in New South Wales*. Sydney: Southwood Press.

Ford, M. (2013). Achievement gaps in Australia: What NAPLAN reveals about education inequality in Australia. *Race, Ethnicity and Education, 16*(1), 80–102.

Freebody, P. (2014). Geoffrey Sherington and the history of Australian education: 'Ideas of use to a needy world'. *Journal of Educational Administration and History, 46*(2), 125–33.

Gale, T. (2000). Rethinking social justice in schools: How will we recognise it when we see it? *International Journal of Inclusive Education, 4*(3), 253–69.

Gale, T. and Tranter, D. (2011). Social justice in Australian higher education policy: An historical and conceptual account of student participation. *Critical Studies in Education, 52*(1), 29–46.

Gorringe, S. (2011). Honouring our strengths – moving forward. *Education in Rural Australia, 21*(1), 21–37.

Grace, D. M., Straiton, M., Hewett-Reeves, W. and Platow, M. J. (2015). Insides and outsides: Investigating preschoolers' understanding of biological and environmental aspects of essentialism with novel categories. *Australasian Journal of Early Childhood, 40*(1), 33–41.

Gray, J. and Beresford, Q. (2008). A 'formidable challenge': Australia's quest for equity in Indigenous education. *Australian Journal of Educational Research, 52*(2), 197–223.

Harris, J. (2003). Hiding the bodies: The myth of the humane colonisation of Aboriginal Australia. *Aboriginal History, 27*, 79–104.

Harris, J. W. (1978). The education of Aboriginal children in New South Wales public schools since 1788. *Aboriginal Child at School, 6*(4), 22–35.

Harrison, N. (2007). Where do we look now? The future of research in Indigenous Australian education. *The Australian Journal of Indigenous Education, 36*, 1–5.

Haslam, N., Bain, P., Douge, L., Lee, M. and Bastian, B. (2005). More human than you: Attributing humanness to self and others. *Journal of Personality and Social Psychology, 89*(6), 937–50.

Healy, K. (1998). Participation and child protection: The importance of context. *British Journal of Social Work, 28*(6), 897–914.

Hollinsworth, D. (2006). *Race and racism in Australia* (3rd ed.). South Melbourne: Thomson Learning/Social Science Press.

Howlett, C., Seini, M., Matthews, C., Dillon, B. and Hauser, V. (2008). Retaining Indigenous students in tertiary education: Lessons from the Griffith School of Environment. *The Australian Journal of Indigenous Education, 37*(1), 18–27.

Human Rights and Equal Opportunity Commission. (1997). *Bringing them home: Report of the national inquiry into the separation of Aboriginal and Torres Strait Islander children from their families.* Sydney.

Ivec, M., Braithwaite, V. and Harris, N. (2009). *'Resetting the relationship' in Indigenous child protection: Public hope and private reality.* Canberra: Australian National University, Regulatory Institutions Network.

Johnston, L. F. (1937). *Aboriginal welfare: Initial conference of Commonwealth and State Aboriginal Authorities.* Canberra: Australian Government Printer.

Kempe, C. H., Silverman, F. N., Steele, B. F., Droegemueller, W. and Silver, H. K. (1962). The battered-child syndrome. *Journal of the American Medical Association, 181*(1), 17–24.

Kociumbas, J. (1997). *Australian childhood: A history.* Sydney: Allen and Unwin.

Kolb, D. A., Boyatzis, R. E. and Mainemelis, C. (2001). Experiential learning theory: Previous research and new directions. In R. J. Sternberg and L.-F. Zhang (Eds), *Perspectives on thinking, learning and cognitive styles* (pp. 227–48). New York and London: Routledge.

Kraft, R. J. (1986). Toward a theory of experiential education. In R. J. Kraft and M. S. Sakofs (Eds), *The theory of experiential education* (2nd ed., pp. 7–38). Boulder, CO: Association for Experiential Education.

Kunitz, S. (1994). *Disease and diversity: The European impact on the health of non-Europeans*. New York: Oxford University Press.

Kyle, N. (1986). *Her natural destiny: The education of women in New South Wales*. Sydney: New South Wales University Press.

Langton, M. (2010). Ngura barbagai: Country lost. In R. Perkins and M. Langton (Eds), *First Australians* (pp. 1–42). Melbourne: The Miegunyah Press.

Liddell, M. (1993). Child welfare and care in Australia: Understanding the past to influence the future. In C. R. Goddard and R. Carew (Eds), *Responding to children: Child welfare practice* (pp. 28–62). Melbourne: Longman Cheshire.

Ma Rhea, Z. (2015). Unthinking the 200-year-old colonial mind: Indigenist perspectives on leading and managing Indigenous education. *The International Education Journal: Comparative Perspectives, 14*(2), 90–100.

McConnochie, K., Hollinsworth, D. and Pettman, J. (1988). *Race and racism in Australia*. Wentworth Falls, NSW: Social Science Press.

Macintyre, S. (1999). *A concise history of Australia*. Cambridge: Cambridge University Press.

Markus, A. (1994). *Australian race relations, 1788–1993*. St Leonards, NSW: Allen & Unwin.

Mear, C. (2008). The origin of the smallpox outbreak in Sydney in 1789. *Journal of the Royal Australian Historical Society, 94*, 1–22.

Montessori, M. (1975). *The child in the family*. London: Pan.

Morgan, G. (2006). Memory and marginalisation: Aboriginality and education in the assimilation period. *Australian Journal of Education, 50*(1), 40–9.

Moses, A. D. (2000). An antipodean genocide? The origins of the genocidal moment in the colonisation of Australia. *Journal of Genocide Research, 2*(1), 89–106.

NSW Government. (n.d.). *Establishment of the Native Institution, 1814*. Retrieved from https://www.records.nsw.gov.au/state-archives/digital-gallery/lachlan-macquarie-visionary-and-builder/public-notices/full-transcript-establishment-of-the-native-institution-1814 (accessed 15 January 2016).

O'Donoghue, T. (2009). Colonialism, education and social change in the British Empire: The cases of Australia, Papua New Guinea and Ireland. *Paedagogica Historica, 45*(6), 787–800.

Platow, M. J., Grace, D. M. and Smithson, M. J. (2014). When immigrants and converts are not truly one of us: Examining the social psychology of marginalising racism. In F. Jenkins, M. Nolan and K. Rubenstein (Eds), *Allegiance and identity in a globalised world* (pp. 192–220). Cambridge: Cambridge University Press.

Rademaker, L. (2015). Missions and Aboriginal difference: Judith Stokes and Australian missionary linguistics. *Journal of Australian Studies, 39*(1), 66–78.

Ranzijn, R., McConnochie, K. and Nolan, W. (2009). *Psychology and Indigenous Australians: Foundations of cultural competence*. South Yarra, VIC: Palgrave Macmillan.

Reynolds, R. J. (2009). 'Clean, clad and courteous' revisited: A review history of 200 years of Aboriginal education in New South Wales. *The Journal of Negro Education, 78*(1), 83–94.

Said, E. W. (1978). *Orientalism*. New York: Vintage Books.

Shinkfield, A. J. (1988). Significant aspects of education in Australia. *Education, 108*(3), 310–14.

Steering Committee for the Review of Government Service Provision. (2014). *Overcoming Indigenous disadvantage: Key indicators 2014*. Canberra: Productivity Commission.

Tajfel, H. (1978). Social categorization, social identity and social comparison. In H. Tajfel (Ed.), *Differentiation between groups: Studies in the social psychology of intergroup relations* (pp. 61–76). London: Academic Press.

Tajfel, H. and Turner, J. C. (1979). An integrative theory of intergroup conflict. In W. G. Austin and S. Worschel (Eds), *The social psychology of intergroup relations* (pp. 33–47). Monterey, CA: Brooks/Cole.

Tajfel, H. and Turner, J. C. (1986). The social identity theory of intergroup behaviour. In S. Worschel and W. G. Austin (Eds), *Psychology of intergroup relations* (2nd ed., pp. 7–24). Chicago: Nelson-Hall.

Turner, J. C. and Brown, R. (1978). Social status, cognitive alternatives and intergroup relations. In H. Tajfel (Ed.), *Differentiation between social groups: Studies in the social psychology of intergroup relations* (pp. 202–34). New York: Academic Press.

Vass, G. (2013). So, what is wrong with Indigenous education? Perspective, position and power beyond a deficit discourse. *The Australian Journal of Indigenous Education, 41*(2), 85–96.

Walsh, M. (1993). Languages and their status in Aboriginal Australia. In M. Walsh and C. Yallop (Eds), *Language and culture in Aboriginal Australia* (pp. 1–13). Canberra: Aboriginal Studies Press.

Wright, B. (2001). Australia 1788–1988: An aboriginal perspective on the Centennial. *Education, 108*(3), 325–9.

8

EDUCATION AND SOCIAL PARTICIPATION

Civic identity and civic action in formal and informal education contexts

Emma F. Thomas, Craig McGarty, Avelie Stuart, Girish Lala and Anne Pedersen

Engaged electorates are central to the functioning of democracy, yet we know surprisingly little about how engaged orientations develop. Existing research points to the important role of formal education (Beaumont, Colby, Ehrlich and Torney-Purta, 2006; Galston, 2001; Torney-Purta, 2002; Youniss, 2011) and informal educational activities (Kahne and Sporte, 2008) in developing an orientation towards participation in civic life. The education literature also emphasises the important role of a developing sense of civic responsibility and civic identity (Youniss, McLellan and Yates, 1997) but says little about the ways in which these personal and social transformations are realised (Flanagan, 2003; Sherrod, Flanagan and Youniss, 2002).

Here, we bring together work on education and civic identity with insights from the social identity approach to answer questions that have long concerned education, developmental and political scholars: How do we encourage a sense of civic identity through the education process? What is the role of formal and informal education in encouraging the development of civic identity? While civic identity has primarily been considered from an Eriksonian identity perspective (e.g., Crocetti, Jahromi and Meeus, 2012; Yates and Youniss, 1998), the social identity approach has much to contribute to these questions. We describe these contributions in further detail below.

In this chapter, we argue that the development of civic identity through education is a social achievement. When opinions about how the world should be are experienced as social identity ('we') rather than as personal identity ('me'), then they gain increased power to bring about change (see McGarty, Lala and Thomas, 2012; Smith, Thomas and McGarty, 2015). We describe empirical work showing that people can come to a new understanding of themselves (identity) and the civic world that they live in (participation) through structured group interaction or discussion (Thomas and McGarty, 2009; Thomas, McGarty and Mavor, 2009; Thomas, Smith, McGarty and Postmes, 2010; see also Campbell, 2008). Other work shows social identity transformation through an intervention where university students learn to oppose everyday racism (Pedersen, Paradies, Hartley and Dunn, 2011). Finally, we discuss how providing support for people recovering from severe trauma (genocide survivors) precipitates identity change and promotes global civic engagement (McGarty *et al.*, 2012).

Promoting civic engagement through education: what do we know?

There is considerable educational and psychological research showing that civic engagement is fostered in formal and informal education. Flanagan argued that schools and universities are spaces where young people 'spend time, where they have politically relevant experiences including belonging to groups and exercising the rights and responsibilities associated with membership in those groups' (2013, p. 7). Research has consistently shown that duration of formal schooling – and attendance at university or college – predicts subsequent civic engagement (e.g., Finlay, Flanagan and Wray-Luke, 2011). Other research implicates specific educational curricula geared towards promoting civic engagement. Beaumont *et al.* (2006) showed, for example, that educational interventions with a focus on political engagement can significantly boost many dimensions of democratic participation, including expectations for future political activity, increased knowledge, and skills for effective participation. Informal contexts also help develop an orientation towards participation in civic life. An informal context can be defined as a setting where people gather together for an activity that may not necessarily follow a structured plan or where civic learning is an indirect outcome but not the primary aim of the exercise. For example, Finlay *et al.* (2011; also Flanagan and Levine, 2010) showed that a service and training programme provided beneficial civic learning opportunities, particularly for disadvantaged youth. Youniss *et al.* (1997) found that community service predicted both conventional (e.g., voting) and unconventional (e.g., boycotting/demonstrating) political involvement as well as subsequent involvement in community service projects. Elsewhere, one recent study suggests that formal (classroom-based) and more informal (service learning opportunities) education may promote different kinds of engagement in civic and political action (Kahne, Crow and Lee, 2013). Discussion of societal issues in the classroom promotes engagement with political issues and voting (so-called 'big P' politics), while service learning increases interest and participation in community-based actions (so-called 'little p' politics).

However, we know surprisingly little about how to foster these processes in specific interventions or classroom practices. That is, beyond pointing to the years of schooling, participation in voluntary activities or the important role of classroom discussion in promoting a sense of civic engagement (e.g., Campbell, 2008; Torney-Purta, 2002; Youniss, 2011), the literature does not explain how to harness these forces to bolster engagement in the classroom. Research that uses the social identity approach may help fill some of these gaps.

Civic identities are social identities

Civic engagement refers to interest, values, beliefs, skills, knowledge and action in matters within the community and the political system and beyond the immediate self, friends and family (Adler and Goggin, 2005; Crocetti *et al.*, 2012). Civic involvement extends beyond the immediate personal self and interpersonal relationships to doing things that benefit members of other groups and the broader community. Working within assumptions of both social identity theory and self-categorisation theory, these actions can be understood as being underpinned by identity at a *social* or group level of self-definition (a social identity) rather than individual or personal identity (Turner, Oakes, Haslam and McGarty, 1994): civic identities are inherently social identities. The social identity approach is, thus, especially relevant here as it offers a conceptual framework for understanding the relation between individual and society – and civic involvement is entirely about that relationship.

Arguably, the social identity approach to civic identity formation provides a complementary approach to the Eriksonian civic identity project (Youniss *et al.*, 1997). For example, research from the Eriksonian perspective has emphasised that adolescence is a critical period during which people explore different identities and – ideally – eventually commit to one ('identity achievement'; Marcia, 1966). Indeed, Crocetti *et al.* (2012) demonstrated that obtaining an 'achieved' identity enhances one's likelihood of becoming civically engaged. Much of this identity exploration is likely to occur in educational contexts, where adolescents spend much of their time (Flanagan, 2013). As with the Eriksonian approach, social identity theorists agree that individual and society are not separate entities but part of a single relationship (Youniss *et al.*, 1997, p. 626; see Turner and Oakes, 1986). We share a concern with the development of ideological clarification by which civic identity emerges from the effort of youth to find meaning by linking ideology with existing group memberships (Youniss *et al.*, 1997, p. 625). We agree that our understanding of civic identities is first and foremost an understanding of the formation of aspects of self that have ideology (understandings of how the world should be) at their core. However, our approach differs from the Eriksonian identity perspective in that – within the social identity approach – there is not just one (achieved or diffuse; Marcia, 1966) personal, individual self. Rather, self is comprised of a multitude of both personal and social identities (Turner *et al.*, 1994). As such, the social identity approach is well placed to complement the Eriksonian identity perspective by emphasising that identity is represented and constituted socially.

An extension of the social identity approach is the proposal that many forms of civic participation (e.g., letter writing, petition signing, consciousness raising with friends and family, joining grass-roots organisations, voting) rest on identities derived from opinions about 'the way the world should be' (Smith *et al.*, 2015; Thomas *et al.*, 2009). That is, civic identities can be opinion-based identities (McGarty *et al.*, 2012). Expanding on the arguments above, where opinions about the way the world should be are experienced as shared and as a defining feature of 'us' (a social identity or group membership) rather than as idiosyncratic features of 'me' (a personal identity; Bliuc, McGarty, Reynolds and Muntele, 2007; McGarty, Bliuc, Thomas and Bongiorno, 2009), they gain power to promote change. Put differently, in order to sustain efforts, these opinions need to be shared with others; it is difficult to coordinate social action unless other people agree with the cause. Consistent with these points, opinion-based groups have been shown to be excellent predictors of engagement in a range of civic actions including sociopolitical action (Bliuc *et al.*, 2007; Cameron and Nickerson, 2009; Thomas, Mavor and McGarty, 2012), solidarity-based action with sexual minority groups (Russell, 2011) and volunteerism (Thomas, 2005).

Where do such opinion-based group identities come from?

The interactive model of identity formation (Postmes, Haslam and Swaab, 2005) helps explain where opinion-based identities come from. The model distinguishes between identities that are formed 'top-down' from an awareness of shared characteristics (deductive identities) and those that are formed 'bottom-up' by combining characteristics of individuals in context (inductive identities). Whereas deductive identity formation occurs when people access shared existing social category membership ('what it means' to be a man, woman, young person, political opponent or supporter), inductive identity formation involves communication (social interaction, emotional displays) between potential group members. That is, individuals construct a shared sense of 'us' through processes of communication, negotiation and debate.

Recent work has extended this to consider the formation of opinion-based social identities that can promote civic action. Thomas *et al.*'s (2009) normative alignment model drew on collective action research (see van Zomeren, Postmes and Spears, 2008) to suggest that social interaction helps people to develop integrated understandings of themselves (identity), their feelings (emotions) and their beliefs about intended action. This integration of identity and norms for action, emotion and belief promotes the formation of identities that can be sustainable over time. More recently still, Smith *et al.* (2015; see especially Table 1) developed a broader process account of how individuals become aware of, and engaged in, various forms of civic action. According to Smith *et al.*, the formation of the 'identity-norm nexus' has its origins in an awareness that things *are* not as they *should* be (see Packer, 2008). However, as we argue above, isolated opinion is not sufficient to enable mobilisation. Rather, this awareness needs to be shared in order to provide the basis for the formation of groups that can seek to change the world. Moreover, and importantly for our current purposes, Smith *et al.* (2015) specify a crucial moderator of these identity formation processes; namely, that interaction must be experienced as validating and consensual in order for this shared world view to take force in the minds of individuals.

The implications of this theoretical framework are twofold: civic identities are dynamic and changeable (Turner *et al.*, 1987; also Drury and Reicher, 1999,

2000, 2005); and they can be constructed and negotiated through interaction and deliberation. Put differently, *civic identities are collective achievements* that are aired and validated in public spaces (Smith *et al.*, 2015; also McGarty, Thomas, Lala, Smith and Bliuc, 2014; McGarty *et al.*, 2012). In what follows, we consider three applications of this approach to promoting engagement with civic issues (international development, prejudice reduction, support for victims of genocide) in formal and informal education contexts. Note that in distinguishing between formal and informal education contexts, we are distinguishing between those settings where people gather for the explicit purpose of 'being educated' (formal contexts; e.g., classrooms, school systems, tertiary institutions) versus those settings where people may learn in a more indirect way through, for example, extracurricular activity participation (informal contexts; see Eccles, Barber, Stone and Hunt, 2003; Mahoney, Cairns and Farmer, 2003).

Civic social identity formation in practice: identity in the classroom

Fostering civic social identity formation in the classroom through social interaction

In this first section, we directly consider the role of social interaction in fostering civic social identity formation in the classroom. Building on the arguments above, Thomas *et al.* (2009) suggest that it is through structured small-group discussion that participants come to experience their opinions as social and shared. The opinion-based group interaction method (OBGIM; Thomas and McGarty, 2009; Thomas, McGarty and Louis, 2014; Thomas, McGarty and Mavor, 2016; also Bongiorno, McGarty, Kurz, Haslam and Sibley, 2016; Gee, Khalaf and McGarty, 2007) illustrates how these processes occur in practice. It comprises three steps. In the first step, participants are given basic information about a relevant cause; this information is intended to provide background for a subsequent discussion and to establish whether the participant nominally supports that cause. Much of our work to date has focused on global citizenship in relation to efforts to achieve safe drinking water for people in developing nations (United Nations, 2015); in this case, participants read information about the need for safe drinking water for people in developing countries. In the second step, participants are assigned to small groups of three to five and instructed to engage in 20 to 30 minutes of discussion. Participants are asked to generate practical ways to ensure access to safe drinking water for people in developing countries. The written instructions to participants signify the importance of consensus in the interaction:

> During your discussion a number of views and opinions are likely to be raised, but it is really important that you come to an agreement on what your position is on this issue and come to an agreement on strategies that you all believe will be effective.

In a final step, participants complete quantitative measures of their: (1) intended engagement with action; (2) civic opinion-based social identity ('I identify as someone who supports the goals of Water for Life'; following Cameron, 2004; Leach *et al.*, 2008); (3) consensus of opinion ('my group agreed on the importance of this issue'); and (4) action ('my group agreed on relevant strategies'), emotions and efficacy beliefs (see Thomas and McGarty, 2009; also Thomas *et al.*, 2016).

Thomas and McGarty (2009) found that group interaction among university students boosted opinion-based social identification, feelings of outrage, beliefs about the effectiveness of coordinated action (group efficacy; Bandura, 2000) and, significantly, commitment to engage in collective action to support access to safe drinking water for people in developing countries. They also found that these effects were pronounced where interacting groups had been primed with an injunctive outrage norm; specifically, participants were requested to think of ways to make community members outraged about injustice. Another study suggests that through social interaction, members of a community sample developed a sense of political engagement in opposition to battery farming of chickens, and that this translated to immediate concrete action (signing a letter to a government minister; Thomas *et al.*, 2014).

This evidence suggests that, through co-construction of meaning, group interaction in an informal context helped validate new world views, ways of being (identity) and intended actions. However, such group interactions can backfire (Finlay, Wray-Luke and Flanagan, 2010; Hardy, Lawrence and Grant, 2005). Smith *et al.* (2015; see also Festinger, 1950, 1954) explicitly describe the establishment of consensus and validation as boundary conditions for the subsequent emergence of positive effects. Thus, anything that blocks a group's ability to reach agreement or that inhibits a sense of enjoyment and validation from the task will mean that effects are attenuated or, worse, may promote backlash such that group members are even less engaged post interaction. These boundary conditions may be particularly significant in classrooms where students may have a shared (perhaps antagonistic) history with individuals in their small group; and they may see the activity as a mundane learning task rather than one with 'real-world' significance.

Although our previous evidence has demonstrated a positive effect on average, to consider the process and variation in the method in more detail and test effects in a formal education environment, we recently employed the OBGIM with high school students in their classrooms. To promote engagement with the task, students were given iPads to read the information. To investigate the process and *variability* associated with the emergence of positive effects, we measured the degree of consensus of opinion and action; the extent to which the activity had been internalised as effective and useful (following Ryan and Deci, 2000); and key outcomes relating to immediate and future civic action, identity, hope for the future (cf. Flanagan, 2013) and feelings of personal responsibility (cf. Yates and Youniss, 1998).

Consistent with the framework above, results showed that reaching agreement on opinion and action among students precipitated the formation of a new civic social identity, feelings of personal responsibility, hope for the future, and commitment to immediate and future action. These effects were mediated, however, by the extent to which students had internalised the activity as effective and useful (see also Watts and Flanagan, 2007). Put differently, failure to reach consensus or agreement blocked the internalisation of effective agency which, in turn, undermined the formation of civic identity and action.

The implications that can be drawn from these studies are that the classroom context can serve as a crucial environment for the emergence of civic social identity. However, just as there are processes that will facilitate identity formation, there are also processes that will undermine it. Educators need to be aware of the structural conditions that may produce engagement and disengagement – in particular, it is important when conducting similar classroom activities to highlight the task as requiring collaborative, not individual, effort.

Fostering civic social identity through educational interventions

The promotion of social harmony and inclusion are also important components of civic engagement, and in another line of research, we have been considering how these components can be fostered through educational interventions. Research identifies formal education as central to social attitudes (e.g., Finlay, Flanagan and Wray-Luke, 2011), but, again, relatively little is known about how this can be effectively executed in the classroom. One exception here is the work of Pedersen and colleagues. They report a promising educational intervention, finding a 9.4 per cent reduction in prejudice against Indigenous Australians in one study (Pedersen and Barlow, 2008) and a 17.2 per cent reduction in another (Pedersen, Paradies *et al.*, 2011; also Beaumont *et al.*'s, 2006, work on political competence).

The educational intervention is based on the anti-prejudice mechanisms described by Pedersen, Walker, Paradies and Guerin (2011). Specifically, there are 12 steps involved in facilitating this process: (1) providing accurate information about marginalised groups; (2) showing respect for the audience; (3) choosing emotions to target wisely (e.g., attempting to invoke empathy rather than guilt); (4) not only emphasising similarity between ingroups and outgroups, but also acknowledging differences; (5) taking local needs into account (i.e., context matters); (6) using cognitive dissonance with respect to egalitarian values but not prejudiced views (e.g., pointing out that their prejudiced views are incompatible with espoused egalitarian views); (7) invoking positive social norms (e.g., discussion of the research finding that people high in prejudice overestimate their community support); (8) arranging appropriate contact with the outgroup; (9) providing a space to examine the role of self and identity in prejudice (in particular, discussing the role of 'whiteness' and a more inclusive collective identity); (10) finding alternate talk (e.g., how to deal with prejudice when you come face-to-face with it); (11) taking into account the function of attitudes or why we think the way we do; and (12) using multiple voices from multiple disciplines.

The goals of this approach are to provide time and a (supportive) space that allow participants to consider fully what their views are and to interrogate the origins of those views. For many people, the only information they receive is from the media, and this is often inaccurate, dehumanising and inflammatory (e.g., Sulaiman-Hill, Thompson, Afsar and Hodliffe, 2011, with respect to asylum seekers). Participants are encouraged in Pedersen, Walker et al.'s (2011) procedures to freely but respectfully share their world views and to consider alternative viewpoints to those often heard in the community or in the media. Students are also asked to air and debate their views through an emphasis on active deliberation on these matters. In short, the pedagogical approach emphasises the need to air views collectively and deconstruct, renegotiate and reconstruct those views in a way that supports inclusion. Participants are also brought into contact with members of marginalised groups. For example, as outlined in Pedersen and Hartley (2015), these authors routinely bring in a young Tamil refugee who had originally arrived in Australia by boat to speak to their classes, and this has a dramatic and positive effect on the students (following, e.g., the work of Pettigrew and Tropp, 2006, on intergroup contact theory). Finally, it is important to know how to deal with prejudice and racism when exposed to it. Research shows the importance of 'being prepared' for prejudice (Dunn, Nelson and Pedersen, 2013; Plous, 2000). Without this preparation, it is likely that many opponents of prejudice will not able to respond effectively to everyday prejudice. Accordingly, classroom discussion focuses on 'finding words' to effectively and safely confront prejudice in everyday social interaction.

Given that this educational intervention has previously shown positive effects in boosting favourable attitudes towards many stigmatised or disadvantaged groups in contemporary Australian society (Muslim people, asylum seekers, Indigenous Australians), we have sought to consider the role of social identity in engendering these shifts. Consistent with our theoretical framework above, we focused on identities based on shared opinion about the ways that things should be (opinion-based groups) rather than, say, contestable superordinate national social identities (see Bliuc et al., 2012). Specifically, we considered an opinion-based identity with its basis in harmonious relations between Muslim and non-Muslim people. So far, our research has shown that, along with the increased positivity towards Muslim people, participants reported an increased sense of 'self' as someone who supports harmonious, inclusive social relations between Muslim and non-Muslim people. That is, participants reported that they were more likely to see themselves as part of a group supporting better relations between Muslim and non-Muslim Australians, demonstrating that identity may be an anchor for changing relevant self-understandings, attitudes, beliefs, norms and actions.

Consistent with the research on the dynamics of small interacting groups, this research in large-group teaching contexts suggests that providing spaces for people to contest and debate is central. If we are correct that identity is often about ideology (McGarty *et al.*, 2009; also Wright, 2009), then it is essential that those who seek to promote ideologies that oppose prejudice and injustice provide spaces for those ideologies to emerge as valid expressions of identities rather than seeking to impose them as orthodoxies.

Fostering civic social identity through online content creation

Beyond the formal classroom or educational setting *per se*, in a third line of research, we are investigating how participation in informal activities (specific-ally, creating online audiovisual messages) can promote civic engagement in rela-tion to support for victims of the 1994 Rwandan genocide. As described above, existing research implicates volunteerism and community work in fostering a subsequent sense of civic engagement into adulthood (Finlay *et al.*, 2011; Flanagan, 2003; Youniss *et al.*, 1997). Taking inspiration from this and from the prolifera-tion of online methods for disseminating support (i.e., beyond traditional notions of volunteerism and community participation), this line of research entails young Australians creating and disseminating audiovisual messages of support for the survivors of the Rwandan genocide.

Participation comprises three steps. In the first step, participants (who are adolescents or young adults under 25) watch audiovisual 'messages of hope' from survivors of the Rwandan genocide (see www.100messagesofhope.com). These messages do not focus on traumatic details and events surrounding the genocide; rather, they are intended to convey hope for the future and a sense of resilience in the face of adversity. In this way, survivors are making a statement of collective hope for their future and for themselves as Rwandans (see also Braithwaite, 2004).

In a second step, participants are asked to record their own messages of support for these survivors. These messages are intended to support and affirm survivors' efforts to heal and rebuild, but participants are allowed full control over the length and content of their own messages. Prior to the content creation activity, participants are told that their final messages would be shared online to an inter-national audience that could, potentially, include genocide survivors themselves. In generating these messages, participants begin to publicly air, communicate and share their perceptions and world views (Hardin and Higgins, 1996). Moreover, through this process, participants are explicitly placed in the role of 'supporter'. As with traditional forms of social or community work, doing so allows them to enact alternative versions of 'self' and to shift their focus from their personal or idiosyncratic self in order to identify with a broader group and its goals (see Flanagan, 2003). Indeed, Yates and Youniss (1998) have shown that young parti-cipants in traditional forms of community service often reflect on this service as having an ongoing influence that helped to define their sense of identity. Similarly, here, this creative exercise allows participants to form identities congruent with a hopeful orientation about how they want the world to be (see also Haslam, Adarves-Yorno, Postmes and Jans, 2013). We contend that these individual acts of creation – in our case, the creation and sharing of supportive messages – when undertaken in a context explicitly purposed towards emphasising social goodwill, similarly invoke and advance social identity characterised by a focus on positive social change.

In a third and final stage, messages are posted online (on a closed YouTube channel; see www.youtube.com/sppru). Participants then complete quantitative measures of key variables relating to their own personal well-being, feelings of hope and satisfaction, and their intention to engage in future action to support post-conflict reconciliation and global citizenship.

Consistent with our arguments above, pilot research showed that Australian high school and university students expressed a range of positive emotions (including hope, admiration and pride) in relation to participation. These students expressed belief in what Rwandan survivors had achieved and what they themselves were achieving through their support messages. They viewed creating and sharing hope and support messages as helping Rwandan survivors by raising awareness and support among others not directly affected by the genocide, and as a mechanism to cultivate social engagement and unity. Indeed, many of the messages themselves speak directly to processes of engagement and solidarity (cf. Reicher, Cassidy, Wolpert, Hopkins and Levine, 2006):

> You need to know that the world does support you and the world will stand at your back.
>
> As you continue to heal my own brothers and sisters, I want you to know that you are not alone in building a brighter future.
>
> Let us understand, acknowledge, and maybe accept, so one day we can unite as a community, share our stories of life, and build a world in which we never have to experience the hurt and pain that human beings can inflict.

Importantly, all of the students who took part in the pilot study genuinely engaged in the creation task, and every student found the processes of both viewing and creating hope and support messages rewarding and worthwhile. Through this process, participants are allowed and encouraged to imagine alternative ways of being and form identities congruent with a hopeful orientation about how they want the world to be.

While our ongoing programme is currently focused on students taking part independently of their formal classroom settings, one of our aims is to develop a framework for the production and exchange of hopeful and supportive messages that can be applied across broad contexts, including formal classroom settings. The broader programme of research also involves participants who are, themselves, recruited from vulnerable communities (e.g., cancer survivors, people with mental illnesses). The research follows the logic that the act of supporting vulnerable others can, itself, bestow benefits on those helping, not just on those being helped (Weinstein and Ryan, 2010). If this is the case, there may be particular benefits for people who are traditionally recipients of assistance (i.e., vulnerable young people) as they transform their self-perception from being passive recipients of support to active providers of support. More generally, our research suggests that implementing such a framework in and outside the classroom might also challenge students and other young people to develop cognitive alternatives (see also Jetten, Iyer and Zhang, Chapter 6, this volume) for and about themselves and others, and engender different, positively oriented, sets of social relations between groups and communities (see Gee and McGarty, 2013a, 2013b).

Concluding comments

We started this chapter by illustrating that, although it has long been recognised that the classroom is an important space for developing forms of civic engagement and consciousness, there is little research that speaks to the underlying psychological processes. In this chapter, we have considered the evidence in relation to: small-group learning exercises, large-group learning, evidence in relation to global citizenship of international development and post-conflict reconstruction, as well as domestic citizenship regarding standing up to prejudice and discrimination in everyday social interaction. Looking beyond 'formal' educational contexts, we have also considered the role of these processes in settings that harness the proliferation of online methods to provide messages of support for victims of genocide.

The body of research we have outlined seeks to highlight the opportunities for educational contexts (both formal and informal) to provide the building blocks for civic participation through social identity. Central to the current research are the ideas that civic identities are often underpinned by opinions about how the world should be (opinion-based identities) and that people can come to new understandings of themselves (i.e., identity) and the world that they live in through carefully structured small-group discussion and deliberation. Educators need to find ways of providing spaces that allow for people to 'become the change they want to see in the world' (paraphrasing words attributed to M. H. Ghandi) in order to foster these processes in the classroom.

Acknowledgments

This project is supported by the Young and Well Cooperative Research Centre, an Australian-based international research centre that unites young people with researchers, practitioners, innovators and policymakers from over 70 partner organisations. The Young and Well CRC is established under the Australian Government's Cooperative Research Centres Programme. It is also supported by grants from the Spencer Foundation's New Civics Initiative and the Australian Research Council (DE120101029).

References

Adler, R. P. and Goggin, J. (2005). What do we mean by 'civic engagement'? *Journal of Transformative Education*, 3(3), 236–53. doi: 10.1177/1541344605276792

Bandura, A. (2000). Exercise of human agency through collective efficacy. *Current Directions in Psychological Science, 9*(3), 75–8.

Beaumont, E., Colby, A., Ehrlich, T. and Torney-Purta, J. (2006). Promoting political competence and engagement in college students: An empirical study. *Journal of Political Science Education, 2*(3), 249–70.

Bliuc, A.-M., McGarty, C., Hartley, L. and Muntele Hendres, D. (2012). Manipulating national identity: The strategic use of rhetoric by supporters and opponents of the 'Cronulla riots' in Australia. *Ethnic and Racial Studies, 35*(12), 2174–94.

Bliuc, A.-M., McGarty, C., Reynolds, K. J. and Muntele, D. (2007). Opinion-based group membership as a predictor of commitment to political action. *European Journal of Social Psychology, 37*(1), 19–32.

Bongiorno, R., McGarty, C., Kurz, T., Haslam, S. A. and Sibley, C. G. (2016). Mobilizing cause supporters through group-based interaction. *Journal of Applied Social Psychology, 46*(4), 203–15.

Braithwaite, V. (2004). Collective hope. *The Annals of the American Society of Political and Social Science, 592*(1), 6–15.

Cameron, J. (2004). A three-factor model of social identity. *Self and Identity, 3*(3), 239–62.

Cameron, J. E. and Nickerson, S. L. (2009). Predictors of protest among anti-globalization demonstrators. *Journal of Applied Social Psychology, 39*(3), 734–61.

Campbell, D. E. (2008). Voice in the classroom: How an open classroom climate fosters political engagement among adolescents. *Political Behavior, 30*(4), 437–54.

Crocetti, E., Jahromi, P. and Meeus, W. (2012). Identity and civic engagement in adolescence. *Journal of Adolescence, 35*(3), 521–32.

Drury, J. and Reicher, S. (1999). The intergroup dynamics of collective empowerment: Substantiating the Social Identity Model of crowd behaviour. *Group Processes and Intergroup Relations, 2*(4), 381–2.

Drury, J. and Reicher, S. (2000). Collective action and psychological change: The emergence of new social identities. *British Journal of Social Psychology, 39*(4), 579–604.

Drury, J. and Reicher, S. (2005). Explaining enduring empowerment: A comparative study of collective action and pyschological outcomes. *European Journal of Social Psychology, 35*(1), 35–58.

Dunn, K., Nelson, J. and Pedersen, A. (2013). Educating young people for bystander anti-racism: Overcoming racism. Paper presented at the *13th International Conference on Diversity in Organisations, Communities and Nations*, Charles Darwin University, Darwin, Australia, 26–28 June.

Eccles, J. S., Barber, B. L., Stone, M. and Hunt, J. (2003). Extracurricular activities and adolescent development. *Journal of Social Issues, 59*(4), 865–89.

Festinger, L. (1950). Informal social communication. *Psychological Review, 57*(5), 271–82.

Festinger, L. (1954). A theory of social comparison processes. *Human Relations, 7*(2), 114–70.

Finlay, A. K., Flanagan, C. and Wray-Luke, L. (2011). Civic engagement patterns and transitions over 8 years: The AmeriCorps national study. *Developmental Psychology, 47*(6), 1728–43. doi: 0.1037/a0025360

Finlay, A., Wray-Luke, L. and Flanagan, C. (2010). Civic engagement during the transition to adulthood: Developmental opportunities and social policies at a critical juncture. In L. R. Sherrod, J. Torney-Purta and C. A. Flanagan (Eds), *Handbook of research on civic engagement in youth.* (pp. 277–305). Hoboken, NJ: John Wiley & Sons.

Flanagan, C. (2003). Developmental roots of political engagement. *PS: Political Science and Politics, 36*(2), 257–61.

Flanagan, C. (2013). *Teenage citizens. The political theories of the young.* Cambridge, MA: Harvard University Press.

Flanagan, C. and Levine, P. (2010). Civic engagement and the transition to adulthood. *The Future of Children, 20*(1), 159–78.

Galston, W. A. (2001). Political knowledge, political engagement and civic education. *Annual Review of Political Science, 4*, 217–34.

Gee, A., Khalaf, A. and McGarty, C. (2007). Using group-based interaction to change stereotypes about people with mental disorders. *Australian Psychologist, 42*(2), 98–105.

Gee, A. and McGarty, C. (2013a). Aspirations for a cooperative community and support for mental health advocacy: A shared orientation through opinion-based group membership. *Journal of Applied Social Psychology, 43*(S2), E426–E441.

Gee, A. and McGarty, C. (2013b). Developing cooperative communities to reduce stigma about mental disorders. *Analyses of Social Issues and Public Policy, 13*(1), 137–64.

Hardin, C. D. and Higgins, E. T. (1996). Shared reality: How social verification makes the subjective objective. In R. M. Sorrentino and E. T. Higgins (Eds), *Handbook of motivation and cognition,* Vol. 3 (pp. 28–84). New York: Guilford Press.

Hardy, C., Lawrence, T. B. and Grant, D. (2005). Discourse and collaboration: The role of conversations and collective identity. *Academy of Management Review, 30*(1), 58–77.

Haslam, S. A., Adarves-Yorno, I., Postmes, T. and Jans, L. (2013). The collective origins of valued originality: A social identity approach to creativity. *Personality and Social Psychology Review, 17*(4), 384–401.

Kahne, J., Crow, D. and Lee, N. (2013). Different pedagogy, different politics: High school learning opportunities and youth political engagement. *Political Psychology, 34*(3), 419–41.

Kahne, J. E. and Sporte, S. E. (2008). Developing citizens: The impact of civic learning opportunities on students' commitment to civic participation. *American Education Research Journal, 45*(3), 738–66.

Leach, C. W., van Zomeren, M., Zebel, S., Vliek, M. L. W., Pennekamp, S., Doosje, B., . . . Spears, R. (2008). Group-level self definition and self-investment: A hierarchical (multicomponent) model of in-group identification. *Journal of Personality and Social Psychology, 95*(1), 144–65.

McGarty, C., Bliuc, A.-M., Thomas, E. and Bongiorno, R. (2009). Collective action as the material expression of opinion-based group membership. *Journal of Social Issues, 65*(4), 839–57.

McGarty, C., Lala, G. and Thomas, E. F. (2012). Opinion-based groups and the restoration of civil society. In K. Jonas and T. Morton (Eds), *Restoring civil society* (pp. 250–64). Chichester, UK: Wiley-Blackwell.

McGarty, C., Thomas, E. F., Lala, G., Smith, L. G. E. and Bliuc, A.-M. (2014). New technologies, new identities and the growth of mass opposition in the 'Arab Spring'. *Political Psychology, 35*(6), 725–40.

Mahoney, J. L., Cairns, B. D. and Farmer, T. W. (2003). Promoting interpersonal competence and educational success through extracurricular activity participation. *Journal of Educational Psychology, 95*(2), 409–18.

Marcia, J. E. (1966). Development and validation of ego-identity status. *Journal of Personality and Social Psychology, 3*(5), 551–8.

Packer, D. (2008). On being both with us and against us: A normative conflict model of dissent in social groups. *Personality and Social Psychology Review, 12*(1), 50–72.

Pedersen, A. and Barlow, F. (2008). Theory to social action: A university-based strategy targeting prejudice against Aboriginal Australians. *The Australian Psychologist, 43*(3), 148–59.

Pedersen, A. and Hartley, L. K. (2015). Can we make a difference? Prejudice towards asylum seekers in Australia and the effectiveness of antiprejudice interventions. *Journal of Pacific Rim Psychology, 9*(1), 1–14. doi: 10.1017/prp.2015.1

Pedersen, A., Paradies, Y., Hartley, L. K. and Dunn (2011). Bystander antiprejudice: Cross-cultural education, links with positivity towards cultural 'outgroups' and preparedness to speak out. *Journal of Pacific Rim Psychology, 5*(1), 19–30.

Pedersen, A., Walker, I., Paradies, Y. and Guerin, B. (2011). How to cook rice: A review of ingredients for teaching anti-prejudice. *Australian Psychologist, 46*(1), 55–63.

Pettigrew, T. F. and Tropp, L. R. (2006). A meta-analytic test of intergroup contact theory. *Journal of Personality and Social Psychology, 90*(5), 751–83.

Plous, S. (2000). Responding to overt displays of prejudice: A role-playing exercise. *Teaching of Psychology, 27*(3), 198–200.

Postmes, T., Haslam, S. A. and Swaab, R. (2005). Social influence in small groups: An interactive model of social identity formation. *European Review of Social Psychology, 16*(1), 1–42.

Reicher, S., Cassidy, C., Wolpert, I., Hopkins, N. and Levine, M. (2006). Saving Bulgaria's Jews: An analysis of social identity and the mobilisation of social solidarity. *European Journal of Social Psychology, 36*(1), 49–72.

Russell, G. M. (2011). Motives of heterosexual allies in collective action for equality. *Journal of Social Issues, 67*(2), 376–93.

Ryan, R. M. and Deci, E. L. (2000). Intrinsic and extrinsic motivations: Classic definitions and new directions. *Contemporary Educational Psychology, 25*(1), 54–67.

Sherrod, L. R., Flanagan, C. and Youniss, J. (2002). Dimensions of citizenship and opportunities for youth development: The what, why, when, where and who of citizenship development. *Applied Developmental Science, 6*(4), 264–72.

Smith, L. G. E., Thomas, E. F. and McGarty, C. (2015). 'We must be the change we want to see in the world': Integrating norms and identities through social interaction. *Political Psychology, 36*(5), 543–57.

Sulaiman-Hill, C. M. R., Thompson, S. C., Afsar, R. and Hodliffe, T. L. (2011). Changing images of refugees: A comparative analysis of Australian and New Zealand print media 1998–2008. *Journal of Immigration and Refugee Studies, 9*(4), 345–66.

Thomas, E. F. (2005). The role of social identity in creating positive beliefs and emotions to motivate volunteerism. *The Australian Journal of Volunteering, 10*(2), 45–52.

Thomas, E. F. and McGarty, C. (2009). The role of efficacy and moral outrage norms in creating the potential for international development activism through group-based interaction. *British Journal of Social Psychology, 48*(1), 115–34.

Thomas, E. F., McGarty, C. and Louis, W. R. (2014). Social interaction and psychological pathways to political engagement and extremism. *European Journal of Social Psychology, 44*(1), 15–22.

Thomas, E. F., McGarty, C. and Mavor, K. I. (2009). Aligning identities, emotions and beliefs to create sustained support for social and political action. *Personality and Social Psychology Review, 13*(3), 194–218.

Thomas, E. F., McGarty, C. and Mavor, K. I. (2016). Group interaction as the crucible of social identity formation: A glimpse at the foundations of social identities for collective action. *Group Processes and Intergroup Relations, 19*(2), 137–51.

Thomas, E. F., Mavor, K. I. and McGarty, C. (2012). Social identities facilitate and encapsulate action-relevant constructs: A test of the social identity model of collective action. *Group Processes and Intergroup Relations, 15*(1), 75–88. doi: 10.1177/1368430211413619

Thomas, E. F., Smith, L. G. E., McGarty, C. and Postmes, T. (2010). Nice and nasty: The formation of prosocial and hostile social movements. *International Review of Social Psychology, 23*(2), 17–55.

Torney-Purta, J. (2002). The school's role in developing civic engagement: A study of adolescents in twenty-eight countries. *Applied Developmental Science, 6*(4), 203–12.

Turner, J. C., Hogg, M. A., Oakes, P. J., Reicher, S. D. and Wetherell, M. S. (1987). *Rediscovering the social group: A self-categorization theory.* Oxford: Blackwell.

Turner, J. C. and Oakes, P. J. (1986). The significance of the social identity concept for social psychology with reference to individualism, interactionism and social influence. *British Journal of Social Psychology, 25*(3), 237–52.

Turner, J. C., Oakes, P. J., Haslam, S. A. and McGarty, C. (1994). Self and collective: Cognition and social context. *Personality and Social Psychology Bulletin, 20*(5), 454–63.

United Nations. (2015). A 10 years story: The Water for Life decade 2005–2015 and beyond. Geneva: Author. Retrieved from: www.unwaterbestpractices.org/WaterforLifeENG.pdf (accessed 1 September 2016).

van Zomeren, M., Postmes, T. and Spears, R. (2008). Toward an integrative social identity model of collective action: A quantitative research synthesis of three socio-psychological perspectives. *Psychological Bulletin, 134*(4), 504–35.

Watts, R. J. and Flanagan, C. (2007). Pushing the envelope on youth civic engagement: A developmental and liberation psychology perspective. *Journal of Community Psychology, 35*(6), 779–92.

Weinstein, N. and Ryan, R. M. (2010). When helping helps: Autonomous motivation for prosocial behaviour and its influence on well-being for the helper and recipient. *Journal of Personality and Social Psychology, 98*(2), 222–44.

Wright, S. C. (2009). The next generation of collective action research. *Journal of Social Issues, 65*(4), 859–79.

Yates, M. and Youniss, J. (1998). Community service and political identity development in adolescence. *Journal of Social Issues, 54*(3), 495–512.

Youniss, J. (2011). Civic education: What schools can do to encourage civic identity and action. *Applied Developmental Science, 15*(2), 98–103.

Youniss, J., McLellan, J. A. and Yates, M. (1997). What we know about engendering civic identity. *The American Behavioral Scientist, 40*(5), 620–31.

PART IV
Becoming and influencing
The role of social identity in student life

9

UNIVERSITY STUDENTS' SOCIAL IDENTITY AND HEALTH BEHAVIOURS

Joanne R. Smith, Winnifred R. Louis and Mark Tarrant

Information on the actions required for a healthy lifestyle is abundant. We are informed by health professionals, government agencies, supermarkets and food producers and even by family and friends that, for example, we should consume at least five portions of fruit and vegetables daily, that we should limit our sugar intake, that we should engage in at least 150 minutes of moderate exercise each week, that we should limit our alcohol consumption and have alcohol-free days, and that we should practise safe sex. If there is one group that we might hope would not only possess but also act upon this knowledge, it would be university students. It is a reasonable assumption that the young people who enter university are not only intelligent but also have the ability to engage in the goal-directed actions required for a healthy lifestyle. Unfortunately, however, this does not appear to be the case. Indeed, Steptoe *et al.* (2002) found a lack of progress towards healthier behaviour among students over a period in which health information was more widely accessible (1990–2000) and a corresponding decline in the strength of beliefs about the importance of maintaining a healthy lifestyle. Other research has found that students' engagement in health behaviours actually declines over the course of their studies, with students in later years of university becoming more likely to engage in a range of harmful practices such as smoking, alcohol consumption, unsafe sex and drink driving (de Franco and Colares, 2008). Moreover, in the case of alcohol consumption, university students are more likely than their non-student peers to engage in excess and harmful alcohol consumption (e.g., in the UK context, Gill, 2002). Thus, we might wonder why, if students are so smart, they do so many dumb (health-related) things?

In recognition of the potential negative impact of students' unhealthy practices on both individuals and broader society, governments have called on universities to take a much more active role in promoting behaviour change in students (e.g., House of Commons Health Committee, 2010). Indeed, universities have attempted to address the negative health practices of university students with actions ranging from making healthy options easily available (e.g., providing a wide selection of fruits and vegetables at mealtimes in halls of residence and in campus food outlets) to providing health awareness opportunities for students (e.g., compelling them to attend alcohol awareness workshops or having health professionals visit campuses to distribute condoms or screening kits for sexually transmissible infections).

One problem with such approaches, however, is the assumption that health behaviour is solely an individual problem – if you want to increase healthy behaviour, then you need to change the individual. This might make intuitive sense; after all, it is the individual who chooses to engage (or not engage) in healthy and unhealthy behaviours, and it is the individual who, largely, bears the cost of their behaviour (i.e., ill health). However, such a view fails to take into account that seemingly individual behaviour occurs within a social (group) context that provides an important framework through which behaviour (and its consequences) is understood. Accordingly, social groups influence the type of behaviour in which an individual member engages. To the extent that a particular social group promotes engagement in health behaviour (i.e., has health-oriented norms and values), people for whom that group has psychological meaning (who identify with the group) will be more likely to engage in healthy behaviour. The reverse is true for groups with unhealthy norms.

In this chapter, we explore the role of social identity and group norms in students' health behaviours, focusing particularly on how these factors influence healthy eating and alcohol consumption. The student identity is an important one for students. Research has found that identification with one's university is meaningful for students, and a strong sense of university identification has a generally positive effect in terms of psychological and physical well-being (Cassidy, 2004). As a result, the norms of the student group are likely to play a central role in structuring health-related cognitions and behaviours. We explore four themes related to students' social identities and health behaviours: the impact of student social identities on health behaviours, how norms and student identities interact to influence health behaviours, the role of different types of norms on health behaviours, and the lessons we can learn from research on norms-based behaviour change campaigns.

The impact of 'healthy' and 'unhealthy' social identities on health behaviours

When people define themselves in terms of a social group membership, they internalise and seek to conform to the norms (i.e., typical and expected actions) of the group (Turner, 1991). As a result, whether or not individuals engage in behaviours that are beneficial to their health depends crucially on the meaning of those behaviours for the groups to which they belong. People engage in health behaviour to the extent that it is congruent with the norms of their social identities and allows them to express and affirm their identities (Oyserman, Fryberg and Yoder, 2007). This observation helps to explain the inconsistencies frequently seen in people's behaviour – why many of us personally claim commitment to pursuing a healthy lifestyle yet often find ourselves in (social) situations where our behaviour contradicts this goal (Tarrant, Hagger and Farrow, 2012). Such an observation may also explain the well-documented gap between people's stated intentions and their behaviours (e.g., Armitage and Conner, 2001): our personal intentions to pursue a healthy lifestyle can be undermined in contexts where unhealthy social identities are salient.

The identity-based motivation model (Oyserman *et al.*, 2007), which applies a social identity approach (Tajfel and Turner, 1979; Turner, Hogg, Oakes, Reicher and Wetherell, 1987) to health behaviour, argues that health-promotion activities are not simply personal choices made in the moment but, rather, reflect social identity-infused habits. When a behaviour becomes identity-infused, such that the behaviour is part of the way that *we* (as group members) do things, engaging in the behaviour allows people to express their identity and to affirm their membership within the group. Identity-infused behaviours can have positive or negative consequences depending on which behaviours become identity-infused. As an example, think of the central role in the national psyche of the full English breakfast, the meat-laden Australian BBQ or the fried food of the American South relative to the classic Mediterranean diet or the preponderance of fresh fish and vegetables in Japan. Making national identity salient in relation to food choices will, therefore, likely have very different health implications as a function of nation. Moreover, because unhealthy behaviours can be identity-defining, group members may be resistant to external attempts to change behaviour (e.g., Livingstone, Young and Manstead, 2011; Oyserman *et al.*, 2007) even if such change would improve their health.

The impact of identity-infused behaviours on the health orientation of minority groups was investigated by Oyserman and colleagues (2007). Across seven studies, they found that members of minority groups were more likely to perceive health promotion as a White and middle-class activity and less likely to perceive health-promotion behaviours as belonging to their ingroup. Minority group members were also more likely to see unhealthy behaviours, rather than healthy behaviours, as ingroup-defining. Moreover, experimentally making their social identity salient increased minority group members' fatalism about improving their health and reduced the accessibility of health knowledge. Thus, if healthy behaviours are not seen to be central to what it means to be a member of a particular group, then individuals are less likely to engage in those behaviours, particularly when that group membership is salient.

But is it the case that health behaviour is seen as incongruent with the university student identity? Unfortunately, the answer is likely to be 'yes'. Students often describe ill health behaviours such as excessive drinking as 'normal' within the university context (e.g., de Visser, Wheeler, Abraham and Smith, 2013), and many have expectations about such norms even before they go to university (Carpenter *et al.*, 2008). It seems reasonable to assume that the effects identified by Oyserman *et al.* (2007) might also be found in relation to the university student identity. Indeed, this is supported by Tarrant and Butler's (2011) examination of the role of the university student identity relative to national identity in students' intentions to engage in health-related behaviours (alcohol consumption and salt intake). Students reported weaker intentions to engage in health-promotion behaviours when their student identity was salient than when their national identity was salient. In addition, students saw the health-related behaviours as less congruent with their student identity than with their national identity, again suggesting that the norms of the student identity are generally not health-promoting.

In terms of implications for health promotion, efforts to change student behaviour that deliberately or inadvertently make that identity salient may be likely to fail or even backfire given that the university student identity does not promote health behaviour. However, by encouraging people to categorise in terms of an identity for which healthy behaviour is normative, or identity congruent (or by changing the content of the identity so that health becomes identity congruent), health-promotion campaigns may come to have a positive impact on people's efforts to lead a healthy lifestyle (Tarrant *et al.*, 2012).

The interplay of group norms and social identification on health behaviours

It is clear that social identities do influence health behaviours, but how does this influence arise? The work of Oyserman and colleagues (2007) and Tarrant and colleagues (2011, 2012) suggests strongly that it is not group membership *per se* that impacts on health but, rather, the *content* of people's social identities that determine the health-related decisions that they make. More formally, when a group membership is contextually or chronically salient, it is the norms of the group that influence the behaviour of group members.

The basic premise of the social identity approach is that belonging to a social group – such as being a university student – provides members with a definition of who they are and a description and prescription of what is involved in being a group member. Social identities are associated with distinctive group behaviours – behaviours that are regulated by group norms (e.g., see Abrams and Hogg, 2001). When individuals see themselves as belonging to a group and feel that being a group member is important to them, they will bring their behaviour into line with the perceived norms and standards of the group. Thus, according to the social identity approach, group norms will influence behaviour, especially for those who are strongly attached – or identified – with the reference group (Terry and Hogg, 1996; see Hogg and Smith, 2007, for a review).

Researchers have investigated the role of university student identity and norms in determining health-related choices. Johnston and White (2003) tested the interplay of group norms and identification in the context of university students' binge drinking behaviour and found that students who perceived this behaviour as normative for university students reported stronger intentions to engage in binge drinking, an effect that was particularly evident for those who identified strongly with the student identity. Similar effects were found by Louis, Davies, Smith and Terry (2007) in relation to healthy eating: students who identified weakly with the student group were unresponsive to perceived group norms, while those who identified more strongly conformed to perceived group norms, intending to eat more healthily when they perceived the group approved of healthy eating but intending to eat less healthily when they perceived the group did not approve of healthy eating.

It should be noted, however, that past research has often measured students' existing perceptions of group norms (e.g., Borsari and Carey, 2001; Johnston and White, 2003; Louis *et al.*, 2007; Perkins and Berkowitz, 1986; Perkins, Haines and Rice, 2005) rather than attempting to manipulate norms directly using experimental methods. Consequently, the research says little about how changes in those perceptions relate to subsequent behavioural decision-making. This is important because if it is possible to change people's beliefs about their group's norms, then the procedures by which change is motivated could be usefully employed in health interventions.

Experimental research within the social identity approach to students' behavioural decision-making is quite common (e.g., Smith *et al.*, 2012; Wellen, Hogg and Terry, 1998; White, Hogg and Terry, 2002) but somewhat rare in the specific domain of students' health behaviour. Nevertheless, some research has tested the impact of the framing of manipulated health-related norms. For example, Stok, de Ridder, de Vet and de Wit (2011) exposed students to information that the majority of Dutch university students did (termed a 'majority norm') or did not (termed a 'minority norm') consume sufficient fruit and examined the impact of this information on fruit consumption intentions (Study 1) or self-reported consumption behaviour (Study 2). In line with earlier research, it was found that exposure to a 'minority norm' led to lower intentions to consume sufficient fruits compared to exposure to a 'majority norm', but only for those who identified strongly with the group. Thus, as suggested by Cialdini (2003), although it may seem intuitively sound to inform people that the desired behaviour is performed by only a minority in the hope of motivating remedial action, such information can actually reduce engagement in the desired behaviour, particularly for those for whom the source of the norm represents an important group membership.

The idea that one can change perceptions of group norms through the provision of norm information is central to one of the most common forms of interventions on university campuses: the social norms approach (e.g., see Perkins, 2002). Based on a substantial body of evidence that students misperceive the extent to which their peers engage in and approve of alcohol consumption and evidence that these misperceptions promote alcohol consumption, social norms interventions attempt to correct these understandings through the provision of accurate information about the alcohol consumption of university students. Although there is some evidence to support the social norms approach (e.g., DeJong *et al.*, 2006; Perkins and Craig, 2002), other evidence suggests that such interventions are often ineffective or can even backfire (e.g., DeJong *et al.*, 2009; Moreira, Smith and Foxcroft, 2009; Wechsler *et al.*, 2003).

Livingstone, Young and Manstead (2011) investigated one possible identity-related reason for such negative effects: the role of threat to group image. When group members are aware of the identity relevance of a particular behaviour, like alcohol consumption at university, normative feedback about the prevalence of the behaviour can impact on members' subjective experience of the group – and prompt identity-protecting reactions. Indeed, Livingstone *et al.* found that strongly identified university students who had a positive attitude to drinking were more willing to place social pressures on non-drinkers to drink (as well as being more willing to drink in the future themselves), thereby maintaining the central role of alcohol in university culture. In fact, if normative feedback suggests that other group members are failing to conform to an ingroup-defining group norm, strongly identified group members (those most invested in protecting the group) take action to address the image threat that such failure presents.

In terms of implications for interventions, it is clear that because group members follow the norms of the group, changing group norms to become healthier should make positive behaviour change more likely. However, it is equally clear that behaviours seen as central to identity may be difficult to change: strong identifiers might resist such change attempts and seek to increase conformity to the norm across the group. When this happens (or when it can be anticipated as likely to happen), it might be more productive to try to disrupt the link between the university student identity and unhealthy practices or change the centrality of the unhealthy norm for group identity (see Smith, Terry, Crosier and Duck, 2005). For example, an intervention could seek to make more central other aspects of the student identity that are more conducive to health, such as being studious, so that students are normatively encouraged to make smarter choices about their health.

The role of congruent and conflicting descriptive and injunctive norms on health behaviours

Social norms, particularly the norms of groups that are important to the individual, shape behaviour. However, it is important to recognise that norms are not unitary constructs: norms consist of both descriptive and injunctive elements (Cialdini, Kallgren and Reno, 1991; Cialdini, Reno and Kallgren, 1990). Descriptive norms reflect what is commonly done by others, while injunctive norms reflect what is approved of by others. In the social identity approach, norms are seen to have both descriptive and injunctive properties: group norms provide information about how group members should and do behave (Turner, 1991). In practice, however, empirical research has often failed to distinguish and consider both descriptive and injunctive aspects. In correlational research, descriptive and injunctive aspects are often collapsed into a single measure (e.g., Johnston and White, 2003; Louis *et al.*, 2007). In experimental research, studies have typically manipulated either the injunctive (Terry, Hogg and McKimmie, 2000) or descriptive components (e.g., White *et al.*, 2002).

Injunctive and descriptive norms can both influence behaviour

Recent research on the impact of identities and norms on student health behaviour has tended to focus on the role of descriptive norms (Livingstone *et al.*, 2011; Stok *et al.*, 2011), perhaps because this type of norm has most commonly been targeted in norms-based interventions. However, relying on changing perceptions of the descriptive norm to change behaviour assumes that individuals follow such norms rather blindly without considering the impact of other types of normative influence (Rimal and Real, 2003). More specifically, individuals might consider both the descriptive *and* the injunctive norm when deciding whether or not to engage in actions to support a healthy lifestyle.

According to norm focus theorists (Cialdini *et al.*, 1990, 1991), descriptive and injunctive norms represent separate sources of motivation and should have separate influences on behaviour. However, in an effort to shed further light on the way in which descriptive and injunctive norms shape behaviour, recent research has begun to consider how these might interact to influence behaviour. At the most basic level, researchers have argued that a behaviour is more likely to occur if people believe that the behaviour is commonly done by others and if they believe it is approved by others (i.e., when the descriptive and injunctive norms align). Indeed, outside of the domain of health behaviour, correlational research has demonstrated that behaviour rates are highest when both types of norms are supportive of the behaviour (e.g., Gockeritz *et al.*, 2010).

It is not always the case, however, that descriptive and injunctive norms align. The issue of norm conflict is particularly important in the health domain because people are often aware of what they should be doing to protect their health (i.e., the injunctive norm is salient), yet fail to engage in those practices – perhaps because of the salience of a conflicting descriptive norm. To understand how group norms shape behaviour more fully, it is critical to understand how conflicting descriptive and injunctive norms influence behaviour. Indeed, recent research has begun to examine this question in the domain of student health behaviour.

Descriptive norms can change how influential injunctive norms are, and vice versa

Bodimeade and colleagues (2014) investigated how students' perceptions of a descriptive and injunctive norm interacted to influence sun-protection behaviour. In this correlational research, it was found that when students perceived that their fellow students engaged in sun-protection behaviour, high levels of action occurred regardless of perceptions of approval for this behaviour. However, when perceptions of the descriptive norm were less positive, action was more likely when students perceived strong approval for sun-protection behaviour.

Thus, perceptions of the descriptive norm determined whether injunctive norm perceptions influenced behaviour.

Using experimental methods, Staunton, Louis, Smith, Terry and McDonald (2014) manipulated the extent to which existing 'healthy' or 'unhealthy' injunctive and descriptive norms were made salient to university students in the context of healthy eating behaviour (i.e., following six guidelines recommended by the Australian Government for a healthy diet). More specifically, students were: reminded that the group injunctive norm supported healthy eating; reminded that the group descriptive norm did *not* support healthy eating; had both norms made salient (i.e., the norm conflict condition); or received no norm information at all. Results revealed that, again, there was a significant interaction between the two types of norms. When the negative descriptive norm was made salient, the effect of the positive injunctive norm was eliminated such that students actually reported *lower* intentions to eat healthily in this condition relative to the other experimental conditions. Thus, it seems that making salient the fact that other members of a group do not 'practise what they preach' is counterproductive in terms of attempts to promote health behaviour.

Do injunctive norms of approval versus disapproval have different impacts?

Healthy behaviour is not simply about engaging in behaviours such as using sunscreen or eating sufficient fruits and vegetables; it also involves avoiding unhealthy behaviours such as binge drinking or smoking. Research has shown that conflict between injunctive and descriptive norms also affects people's orientation towards these behaviours (Smith, Louis, Terry and Hobbs, 2014). In one experimental condition, Smith and colleagues exposed students to a 'healthy' injunctive group norm (i.e., that students approve of sun-protection behaviour [Experiment 1] or that students disapprove of binge drinking [Experiment 2]). Participants in a second condition were exposed to the 'healthy' injunctive norm paired with an 'unhealthy' descriptive group norm (i.e., that students do not engage in sun-protection behaviour or that students engage in binge drinking behaviour), and participants in a third condition received no norm information.

In both experiments, it was found that a 'healthy' injunctive group norm had a beneficial effect, increasing intentions to engage in healthy practices relative to the no norm control condition. However, adding information about the 'unhealthy' descriptive norm eliminated completely the beneficial effect of the injunctive norm. That is, it was not simply the case that the norm conflict condition dampened the effect of the injunctive norm; students in this condition reported intentions (and behaviour in Experiment 1) equivalent to the control condition. Thus, it is clear that health campaigners would be advised *not* to make salient any conflict between injunctive and descriptive norms as this strategy undermines any potential beneficial effect of the injunctive norm such that one might as well not use norms at all.

Understanding the mediators of descriptive and injunctive normative influence

In addition to mapping out the shape of descriptive and injunctive norm interactions, thereby identifying the negative effects of norm conflict, it is also critical to understand *why* conflict between the injunctive and descriptive group norms undermines the effectiveness of the injunctive norm. Outside of the health domain, researchers have suggested that conflict between injunctive and descriptive norms might undermine the effects of interventions because such conflict signals to individuals that it is acceptable for group members to behave in ways that are inconsistent with approved forms of action (e.g., Smith and Louis, 2008) or because such conflict weakens the goal to behave appropriately relative to other possible goals (e.g., to behave hedonically; Keizer, Lindenberg and Steg, 2008, 2011). However, one possibility that has been tested empirically is whether norm conflict impacts upon behaviour by altering individual-level variables known to be important in understanding behavioural decision-making. Smith, Louis, Terry and Hobbs (2014) found that the negative effects of norm conflict on students' intentions to binge drink were mediated by attitudes and perceived control such that exposure to norm conflict was associated with more positive attitudes to binge drinking and reduced perceptions of personal control.

Research on injunctive and descriptive norm interactions in health behaviour has found that although these norms interact to influence intentions and behaviour, these interactions do not always look the same across studies. In some studies, a conflicting descriptive norm stymies the effect of the injunctive norm on the desired behaviour (Smith, Louis, Terry and Hobbs, 2014; Staunton *et al.*, 2014; see also Keizer *et al.*, 2008, 2011; Smith and Louis, 2008, Study 2; Smith *et al.*, 2012), but in other cases, a supportive injunctive norm is influential even when the descriptive norm is unsupportive (Bodimeade *et al.*, 2014; see also Smith and Louis, 2008, Study 1). Given the importance of understanding the nature of descriptive/injunctive norm interactions in health behaviour, more research is needed in this area.

In particular, it is important to understand the conditions under which norm conflict might be motivating rather than demotivating for group members. For example, norm conflict might be motivating when such conflict threatens the image of the group (e.g., see Livingstone *et al.*, 2011) or when individuals are personally invested in the behaviour (e.g., see McDonald, Fielding and Louis, 2013, 2014). In addition, it is vital to focus more on the processes through which descriptive/injunctive norm interactions influence intentions and behaviours. It is clear that it is necessary to survey the identity landscape thoroughly to examine the range of individual and group-level factors that shape people's orientation towards health behaviour. It is only when change agents have all this information that they will be able to predict the effects of norms and norm conflict on behaviour and have more confidence in using norms in behaviour change interventions.

Social identities and behaviour change: what lessons can we learn?

Campaigners in the higher education sector have long recognised the potential for social norms, particularly descriptive norms, to be implemented in behaviour change campaigns. As noted earlier, social norms marketing campaigns aim to reduce alcohol consumption among university students by correcting students' misperceptions about the extent to which their peers consume alcohol. However, evidence of the effectiveness of such campaigns is mixed. Some research has shown that behaviour can be changed by providing descriptive norm information, but other research has found such campaigns to be ineffective or counterproductive (see DeJong et al., 2006, 2009; Perkins, 2003; Wechsler et al., 2003). Early failures of social norms campaigns might be attributed to what Cialdini (2003) has termed a 'backlash effect', in which an intervention inadvertently makes the problem behaviour salient by focusing on the prevalence of the undesired behaviour (e.g., 'heavy drinking is too common among students') rather than the prevalence of the desired behaviour (e.g., 'most students drink in moderation'). However, the failure of more recent interventions to reduce alcohol consumption on campus that avoid problematic framings of descriptive norm information (e.g., DeJong et al., 2009; Russell, Clapp and DeJong, 2005) cannot be explained in this way.

One possibility is that although campaigns are often effective in changing norm perceptions, more accurate perceptions do not translate into reduced alcohol consumption. For example, Stewart et al. (2002) found that students were aware of the campus norm around alcohol consumption, but that knowledge of the norm did not lead to behaviour change. Licciardone (2003) found that accurate perceptions of the campus norm were associated with *higher* levels of alcohol consumption. Clearly, other factors determine whether these changes in norm perception translate into behaviour change. As elaborated below, a key question is whether students identify with the source of the normative message.

More work is also required to ensure that the messages used in social norms campaigns are believable and credible to their targets. Although the content of such campaigns might be based on accurate information about student behaviour, students might not believe such messages (see Park et al., 2011). Indeed, Stewart et al. (2002) found that students questioned the credibility of the campaign message aimed at changing drinking behaviour, believing that alcohol norms were actually more in favour of alcohol consumption than those reported in the message. Polonec, Major and Atwood (2006) found that only one quarter of students believed the message that 'most students drink 0 to 4 drinks when they party', and they suggested that students' own experiences with alcohol on campus contributed to disbelief in the message.

Social norms campaigns might fail also because they are top-down rather than bottom-up, leading to students discounting campaigns as another attempt by university administrators to control student drinking behaviour. If this is the case, then it is possible that student-designed campaigns will be effective in tackling excessive drinking among university students. Co-designing health-related messages with members of the target population is also consistent with recent trends to employ patients in the delivery of health information (e.g., patient expert groups; Coulter and Collins, 2011).

It is important to examine whether student-designed campaigns do have a positive impact on students' health behaviour, however, before allowing students free rein to design health interventions. Smith, Louis and Abraham (2014) invest-igated the impact of a student-designed campaign on drinking intentions and whether the addition of injunctive and descriptive norm information enhanced any campaign effects. The campaign in question was produced by a students' associ-ation following the alcohol-related death of a student during an initiation event involving drinking games. The campaign aimed to reduce 'bolting' (aka 'skulling', 'chugging'); that is, drinking alcoholic drinks in a single draught, or without pausing. Bolting is part of many drinking games, which have been implicated in socialisation of first-year university students into heavy episodic alcohol consump-tion (e.g., Borsari, 2004) and which increase the likelihood of negative alcohol-related consequences (e.g., Adams and Nagoshi, 1999).

Across three experiments, Smith and colleagues (2014) found that the campaign designed and delivered by students was *in*effective in changing students' perceptions about the level of approval for bolting and the prevalence of bolting and in changing students' intentions in relation to bolting. In fact, there was some evidence that exposure to the campaign *increased* perceptions of the normative-ness of bolting among students. In relation to the role of injunctive and descriptive norms, some unexpected findings emerged. Specifically, it was found that the addition to the existing campaign of a message that the majority of students disapproved of bolting *increased* intentions to bolt. It appears that students exposed to the original campaign along with an injunctive norm message perceived that bolting was more common, and these negative descriptive norm perceptions led to stronger bolting intentions. The central role of the descriptive norm was confirmed in the final study: the addition of explicit information about the low prevalence of bolting among student information to the campaign was associated with reduced intentions to engage in bolting behaviour.

There are a number of lessons that can be learned from research that attempts to understand the (in)effectiveness of norms-based behaviour change campaigns for university students. (And although the majority of research that we review has concerned university students, we expect that these lessons would apply equally to educators in high school and earlier contexts. There is little reason to believe that high school or younger students are immune to these social and psycho-logical processes!) First, it is important to understand how students view messages featured in behaviour change campaigns, evaluating and refining such messages to ensure that the target audience finds them believable (e.g., Park, Smith, Klein and Martell, 2011; Polonec *et al.*, 2006) and that backlash effects do not emerge (e.g., Fishbein, Hall-Jamieson, Zimmer, Von Haeften and Nabi, 2002). Second, the answer to the failure of descriptive norms-based campaigns is not necessarily to switch to injunctive norms-based campaigns (cf. Blanton, Köblitz and McCaul, 2008; Mollen, Ruiter and Kok, 2010). The provision of injunctive norm information can increase health-related intentions (Smith *et al.*, 2014), but the influence of injunctive norm information may be more fragile and subject to interference than descriptive norm information (Jacobson, Mortensen and Cialdini, 2011; Staunton *et al.*, 2014). Thus, information about the levels of approval or disapproval for a behaviour should be used with caution, and it is important to understand the change processes induced by this kind of information before including it in campaigns. It is important to note, however, that campaigns should not include false or misleading normative information such that targets come to believe something that is not reality. Rather, change agents should work with the data that they have and frame both identities and norms in a way that maximises their potential to change behaviour in a societally desired direction. However, behaviour change agents should recognise that interventions are always political (see Haslam, 2014) in terms of who is seen to need to change, what needs to be changed and what are the best methods to achieve change. Finally, although it makes sense to involve the target of behaviour change efforts in the design of interventions, it is just as important to evaluate the impact of these campaigns.

It is worth stating explicitly that although we have addressed the issues of normative influence in the health domain in this chapter, in line with our brief from the editors, it is clear that group identities and norms are important for educators to consider in other contexts, such as in attempting to influence academic outcomes. University campaigns that target behaviour such as attending class or studying regularly would similarly benefit from care not to reinforce a negative descriptive norm and from consideration of the benefits of highlighting approval of a desired behaviour versus disapproval of an undesired behaviour. A well-meaning lecturer who starts to urge students to attend class regularly, for example, might inadvertently *decrease* their student's attendance by signalling that inattendance is common and thereby reinforcing a negative descriptive norm that students conform to! In short, we believe that careful attention to normative-influence processes is likely to be useful and important for educators across a range of contexts, not solely in the health domain. Within the present volume, interested readers may refer to chapters by Bliuc, Goodyear and Ellis (Chapter 12) and Smyth, Mavor, Platow and Grace (Chapter 13) that address identity and norm implications in approaches to learning in more detail, while Reynolds, Subasic, Lee and Bromhead (Chapter 3) address school culture more generally and Jones, Manstead and Livingstone (Chapter 4) address bullying specifically.

Concluding remarks

Social identities play a central role in shaping and guiding students' health behaviours. If healthy behaviours are not seen to be central to what it means to be a university student, then students are unlikely to take action to protect their health, particularly when that identity is salient. A key challenge is to make healthy actions central to the student identity so that following a healthy lifestyle comes to be seen as part of what it means to be a university student (i.e., to instil student norms that are health-promoting). But in focusing on the way in which student identity can be harnessed to promote health-related actions, it is important – in order to avoid potential reactance or backlash effects – to consider the extent to which that identity is salient and important to students and the way in which the descriptive and injunctive elements of student norms interact to determine behaviour. And if behaviour change agents wish to use norms to change behaviour, it is critical that appropriate evaluation occurs prior to campaign dissemination to ensure that norms-based messages are accepted by the group. Finally, it is important to recognise that although identity-related factors such as group memberships and group norms are increasingly being considered in the design of the content of interventions, these factors are not always considered in the way such interventions are implemented. That is, many norms-based interventions are delivered in ways that overlook the fact that many healthy or unhealthy behaviours occur in group settings, suggesting that group-based interventions might be more effective than individual-based interventions (e.g., see Haslam *et al.*, 2010). Bringing groups and identities into all elements of behaviour change interventions might allow researchers to unlock the full potential of social identities so that these become a positive force for students' health behaviour.

Acknowledgements

Some of the research discussed in this chapter was supported by awards from the Australian Research Council to the first two authors (DP0877146, DP1092490). Mark Tarrant is supported by the National Institute for Health Research (NIHR). The views expressed in this publication are those of the authors and not necessarily those of the NIHR, the National Health Service or the Department of Health.

References

Abrams, D. and Hogg, M. A. (2001). Collective identity: Group membership and self-conception. In M. A. Hogg and R. S. Tindale (Eds), *Blackwell Handbook of Social Psychology: Group Processes* (pp. 425–60). Oxford: Blackwell.

Adams, C. E. and Nagoshi, C. T. (1999). Changes over one semester in drinking game playing and alcohol use and problems in a college student sample. *Substance Abuse, 20*(2), 97–106.

Armitage, C. J. and Conner, M. (2001). Efficacy of the theory of planned behaviour: A meta-analytic review. *British Journal of Social Psychology, 40*(4), 471–99.

Blanton, H., Köblitz, A. and McCaul, K. D. (2008). Misperceptions about norm misperceptions: Descriptive, injunctive, and affective 'social norming' efforts to change health behaviors. *Social and Personality Psychology Compass, 2*(3), 1379–99.

Bodimeade, H., Anderson, E., La Macchia, S., Smith, J. R., Terry, D. J. and Louis, W. R. (2014). Testing the direct, indirect, and interactive roles of referent group injunctive and descriptive norms for sun protection in relation to the theory of planned behavior. *Journal of Applied Social Psychology, 44*(11), 739–50. doi: 10.1111/jasp.12264

Borsari, B. (2004). Drinking games in the college environment: A review. *Journal of Alcohol and Drug Education, 48*(2), 29–51.

Borsari, B. and Carey, K. B. (2001). Peer influences on college drinking: A review of the research. *Journal of Substance Abuse, 13*(4), 391–424.

Carpenter, R., Fishlock, A., Mulroy, A., Oxley, B., Russell, K., Salter, C., . . . Heffernan, C. (2008). After 'Unit 1421': An exploratory study into female students' attitudes and behaviours towards binge drinking at Leeds University. *Journal of Public Health, 30*(1), 8–13.

Cassidy, T. (2004). Mapping variables related to social identity, distress, and perceived health in an undergraduate student population. *Social Psychology of Education, 7*(3), 339–52.

Cialdini, R. B. (2003). Crafting normative messages to protect the environment. *Current Directions in Psychological Science, 12*(4), 105–9.

Cialdini, R. B., Kallgren, C. A. and Reno, R. R. (1991). A focus theory of normative conduct: A theoretical refinement and re-evaluation. *Advances in Experimental Social Psychology, 24*, 201–34.

Cialdini, R. B., Reno, R. R. and Kallgren, C. A. (1990). A focus theory of normative conduct: Recycling the concept of norms to reduce littering in public places. *Journal of Personality and Social Psychology, 58*(6), 1015–26.

Coulter, A. and Collins, A. (2011). *Making shared decision-making a reality: No decision about me, without me*. London: The King's Fund. Retrieved from: www.kingsfund.org.uk/publications/making-shared-decision-making-reality (accessed 1 September 2016).

de Franco, C. and Colares, V. (2008). Comparative study of health behaviour among college students at the start and end of their courses. *Revue Saude Publica, 42*(3), 1–7.

DeJong W., Schneider, S. K., Towvim, L. G., Murphy, M. J., Doerr, E. E., Simonsen, N. R., . . . Scribner, R. A. (2006). A multisite randomized trial of social norms marketing campaigns to reduce college student drinking. *Journal of Studies on Alcohol, 67*(6), 868–79.

DeJong, W., Schneider, S. K., Towvim, L. G., Murphy, M. J., Doerr, E. E., Simonsen, N. R., . . . Scribner, R. A. (2009). A multisite randomized trial of social norms marketing campaigns to reduce college student drinking: A replication failure. *Substance Abuse, 30*(2), 127–40.

De Visser, R. O., Wheeler, Z., Abraham, C. and Smith, J. A. (2013). 'Drinking is our modern way of bonding': Young people's beliefs about interventions to encourage moderate drinking. *Psychology and Health, 28*(12), 1460–80.

Fishbein, M., Hall-Jamieson, K., Zimmer, E., Von Haeften, I. and Nabi, R. (2002). Avoiding the boomerang: Testing the relative effectiveness of antidrug public service announcements before a national campaign. *American Journal of Public Health, 92*(2), 238–45.

Gill, J. (2002). Reported levels of alcohol consumption and binge drinking within the UK undergraduate student population over the last 25 years. *Alcohol and Alcoholism, 37*(2), 109–20.

Gockeritz, S., Schultz, P. W., Rendon, T., Cialdini, R. B., Goldstein, N. J. and Griskevicius, V. (2010). Descriptive normative beliefs and conservation behaviour: The moderating role of personal involvement and injunctive normative beliefs. *European Journal of Social Psychology, 40*(3), 514–23.

Haslam, C., Haslam, S. A., Jetten, J., Bevins, A., Ravenscroft, S. and Tonks, J. (2010). The social treatment: Benefits of group reminiscence and group activity for the cognitive performance and well-being of older adults in residential care. *Psychology and Aging, 25*(1), 157–67.

Haslam, S. A. (2014). Making good theory practical: Five lessons for an Applied Social Identity Approach to challenges of organizational, health, and clinical psychology. *British Journal of Social Psychology, 53*(1), 1–20. doi: 10.1111/bjso.12061

Hogg, M. A. and Smith, J. R. (2007). Attitudes in social context: A social identity perspective. *European Review of Social Psychology, 18*(1), 89–131.

House of Commons Health Committee. (2010). *First report: Alcohol.* London: House of Commons.

Jacobson, R. P., Mortensen, C. R. and Cialdini, R. B. (2011). Bodies obliged and unbound: Differentiated response tendencies for injunctive and descriptive social norms. *Journal of Personality and Social Psychology, 100*(3), 433–48.

Johnston, K. L. and White, K. M. (2003). Binge drinking: A test of the role of group norms in the theory of planned behaviour. *Health Psychology, 18*(1), 63–71.

Keizer, K., Lindenberg, S. and Steg, L. (2008). The spreading of disorder. *Science, 322*(5908), 1681–5.

Keizer, K., Lindenberg, S. and Steg, L. (2011). The reversal effect of prohibition signs. *Group Processes and Intergroup Relations, 14*(5), 681–8.

Licciardone, J. C. (2003). Perceptions of drinking and related findings from the nationwide campuses study. *Journal of American College Health, 51*(6), 238–45.

Livingstone, A. G., Young, H. and Manstead, A. S. R. (2011). 'We drink, therefore we are': The role of group identification and norms in sustaining and challenging heavy drinking 'culture'. *Group Processes and Intergroup Relations, 14*(5), 637–49.

Louis, W. R., Davies, S., Smith, J. R. and Terry, D. J. (2007). Pizza and pop and the student identity: The role of referent group norms in healthy and unhealthy eating. *Journal of Social Psychology, 147*(1), 57–74.

McDonald, R. I., Fielding, K. S. and Louis, W. R. (2013). Energizing and de-motivating effects of norm conflict. *Personality and Social Psychology Bulletin, 39*(1), 57–72.

McDonald, R. I., Fielding, K. S. and Louis, W. R. (2014). Conflicting norms highlight the need for action. *Environment and Behavior, 46*(2), 139–62.

Mollen, S., Ruiter, R. A. C. and Kok, G. (2010). Current issues and new directions in *Psychology and Health*: What are the oughts? The adverse effects of using social norms in health communication. *Psychology and Health, 25*(3), 265–70.

Moreira, M. T., Smith, L. and Foxcroft, D. (2009). Social norms interventions to reduce alcohol misuse in university or college students. *Cochrane Database Systematic Reviews,* 3. Art. No.: CD006748. doi: 10.1002/14651858.CD006748.pub2

Oyserman, D., Fryberg, S. A. and Yoder, N. (2007). Identity-based motivation and health. *Journal of Personality and Social Psychology, 93*(6), 1011–27.

Park, H. S., Smith, S. W., Klein, K. A. and Martell, D. (2011). College students' estimation and accuracy of other students' drinking and believability of advertisements featured in a social norms campaign. *Journal of Health Communication, 16*(5), 504–18.

Perkins, H. W. (2002). Social norms and the prevention of alcohol misuse in college contexts. *Journal of Studies on Alcohol,* Supplement 14, 164–72.

Perkins, H. W. (Ed.). (2003). *The social norms approach to preventing school and college age substance abuse: A handbook for educators, counselors, and clinicians.* San Francisco: Jossey-Bass.

Perkins, H. W. and Berkowitz, A. D. (1986). Perceiving the community norms of alcohol use among students: Some research implications for campus alcohol education programming. *International Journal of the Addictions, 21*(9–10), 961–76.

Perkins, H. W. and Craig, D. W. A. (2002). *Multifaceted social norms approach to reduce highrisk drinking: Lessons from Hobart and William Smith Colleges.* Newton, MA: Higher Education Center for Alcohol and Other Drug Prevention.

Perkins, H. W., Haines, M. P. and Rice, R. (2005). Misperceiving the college drinking norm and related problems: A nationwide study of exposure to prevention information, perceived norms and student alcohol misuse. *Journal of Studies on Alcohol*, *66*(4), 470–8.

Polonec, L. D., Major, A. M. and Atwood, L. E. (2006). Evaluating the believability and effectiveness of the social norms message 'Most students drink 0 to 4 drinks when they party'. *Health Communication*, *20*(1), 23–34.

Rimal, R. N. and Real, K. (2003). Understanding the influence of perceived norms on behaviors. *Communication Theory*, *13*(2), 184–203.

Russell, C. A., Clapp, J. D. and DeJong, W. (2005). Done 4: Analysis of a failed social norms marketing campaign. *Health Communication*, *17*(1), 57–65.

Smith, J. R. and Louis, W. R. (2008). Do as we say and as we do: The interplay of descriptive and injunctive group norms in the attitude–behaviour relationship. *British Journal of Social Psychology*, *47*(4), 647–66.

Smith, J. R., Louis, W. R. and Abraham, C. (2014). When and how does normative feedback reduce irresponsible drinking? An experimental investigation. Manuscript in preparation.

Smith, J. R., Louis, W. R., Terry, D. J., Greenaway, K. H., Clarke, M. R. and Cheng, X. (2012). Congruent or conflicted? The impact of injunctive and descriptive norms on pro-environmental intentions. *Journal of Environmental Psychology*, *32*(4), 353–63.

Smith, J. R., Louis, W. R., Terry, D. J. and Hobbs, L. (2014). When norms clash: The impact of conflicting injunctive and descriptive norms on health intentions. Manuscript in preparation.

Smith, J. R., Terry, D. J., Crosier, T. and Duck, J. M. (2005). The importance of the relevance of the issue to the group in voting intentions. *Basic and Applied Social Psychology*, *27*(2), 163–70.

Staunton, M., Louis, W. R., Smith, J. R., Terry, D. J. and McDonald, R. I. (2014). How negative descriptive norms for healthy eating undermine the effects of positive injunctive norms. *Journal of Applied Social Psychology*, *44*(4), 319–30. doi: 10.1111/jasp.12223

Steptoe, A., Wardle, J., Cui, W., Bellisle, F., Zotti, A., Baranyai, R. and Sanderman, R. (2002). Trends in smoking, diet, physical exercise, and attitudes towards health in European university students from 13 countries, 1990–2000. *Preventive Medicine*, *35*(2), 97–104.

Stewart, L. P., Lederman, L. C., Golubow, M., Cattafesta, J. L., Goodhart, F. W., Powell, R. L., . . . Laitman, L. (2002). Applying communication theories to prevent dangerous drinking among college students: The RU sure campaign. *Communication Studies*, *53*(4), 381–99.

Stok, F. M., de Ridder, D. T. D., de Vet, E. and de Wit, J. B. F. (2011). Minority talks: The influence of descriptive social norms on fruit intake. *Psychology and Health*, *27*(8), 956–70.

Tajfel, H. and Turner, J. C. (1979). An integrative theory of intergroup conflict. In W. G. Austin and S. Worchel (Eds), *The social psychology of intergroup relations* (pp. 33–47). Monterey, CA: Brooks/Cole.

Tarrant, M. and Butler, K. (2011). Effects of self-categorization on orientation towards health. *British Journal of Social Psychology*, *50*(1), 121–39.

Tarrant, M., Hagger, M. S. and Farrow, C. V. (2012). Promoting positive orientation towards health through social identity. In J. Jetten, C. Haslam and S. A. Haslam (Eds), *The social cure: Identity, health, and well-being* (pp. 39–54). New York: Psychology Press.

Terry, D. J. and Hogg, M. A. (1996). Group norms and the attitude-behaviour relation-ship: A role for group identification. *Personality and Social Psychology Bulletin, 22*(8), 776–93.

Terry, D. J., Hogg, M. A. and McKimmie, B. M. (2000). Attitude-behaviour relations: The role of ingroup norms and mode of behavioural decision-making. *British Journal of Social Psychology, 39*(3), 337–61.

Turner, J. C. (1991). *Social influence.* Milton Keynes, UK: Open University Press.

Turner, J. C., Hogg, M. A., Oakes, P. J., Reicher, S. D. and Wetherell, M. S. (1987). *Rediscovering the social group: A self-categorisation theory.* Oxford: Blackwell.

Wechsler, H., Nelson, T. F., Lee, J. E., Seibring, M., Lewis, C. and Keeling, R. P. (2003). Perception and reality: A national evaluation of social norms marketing interventions to reduce college students' heavy alcohol use. *Journal of Studies on Alcohol and Drugs, 64*(4), 484–94.

Wellen, J. M., Hogg, M. A. and Terry, D. J. (1998). Group norms and attitude-behaviour consistency: The role of group salience and mood. *Group Dynamics: Theory, Research, and Practice, 2*(1), 48–56.

White, K. M., Hogg, M. A. and Terry, D. J. (2002). Improving attitude-behaviour correspondence through exposure to normative support from a salient ingroup. *Basic and Applied Social Psychology, 24*(2), 91–103.

10

THE ROLE OF PSYCHOLOGICAL NEED SATISFACTION IN PROMOTING STUDENT IDENTIFICATION

Katharine Greenaway, Catherine E. Amiot,
Winnifred R. Louis and Sarah V. Bentley

The transition to university is a challenging period of adjustment and change (see also Cruwys, Gaffney and Skipper, Chapter 11, this volume). Students are expected to let go of a high school identity and embrace a new, more independent university identity. Individuals who manage this identity transition and develop ties with their new group membership have an advantage over those who do not. As is true in most domains of life, identifying with an educational group – such as a particular school or discipline or, more generally, as a student – confers decided benefits in terms of personal well-being and academic success.

As a result of these benefits, it is important to understand how educational identity can be fostered and nurtured, especially during times of academic transition that risk undermining the development of such an identity. As in other aspects of life, in the context of education, people are constantly transitioning (e.g., Antaki, Condor and Levine, 1996). Educational identities are necessarily transient as people progress through the educational system – from primary school to secondary school and possibly on to university. How do people navigate these identity transitions and come to adopt (or not) different educational social identities?

In this chapter, we explore the motivational factors that determine when and why people come to identify with educational groups. We adopt a theoretical framework outlined within *self-determination theory* – a theory of human motivation based on the satisfaction of three basic needs: autonomy, relatedness and competence. We employ this theory alongside the *social identity approach* and discuss how psychological need satisfaction underscores the development of educational social identity. We propose that individuals will be more likely to identify with educational groups when those groups satisfy members' motivational needs for autonomy, competence and relatedness.

The social identity approach to education

Education researchers have long considered identity as an important ingredient in the educational process (e.g., Gee, 2001). Students are more likely to engage with the academic process if they adopt identities of 'student' or 'learner' into their self-concept (Osbourne and Jones, 2011). This process of identification influences students' sense of belonging within the learning environment, which in turn affects their learning outcomes. Baumeister, Twenge and Nuss (2002) demonstrated the detrimental effect of lack of belonging on higher-order cognitive processes such as reasoning and comprehension. Similarly, Stephens, Fryberg, Markus, Johnson and Covarrubias (2012) revealed a reduction in academic performance for students whose social background did not match with the cultural norms of the educational context (see also Jetten, Iyer and Zhang, Chapter 6, this volume). From these findings, it is clear that a sense of connectedness and belonging is important for ensuring educational success.

The social identity approach can be, and has been, usefully applied to understand processes of social belonging and educational outcomes because it provides structure to the somewhat amorphous concept of 'identity' and outlines a range of concrete, testable hypotheses about the effects of social identification on educational outcomes (see Reynolds, Subasic, Lee and Bromhead, Chapter 3, this volume). As this volume demonstrates, there is emerging interest in the role of social identity and identification in educational systems, processes and outcomes. This interest is based on previous research showing the variety of positive outcomes that flow from possessing a strong educational identity, ranging from personal well-being to academic success (e.g., Cameron, 1999; Mavor, McNeill, Anderson, Kerr, O'Reilly and Platow, 2014; Oyserman, Bybee and Terry, 2006). It has also been observed within the education literature for some time that a process of dis-identification is a recognisable precurser to educational attrition (Finn, 1989).

In one application of social identity theorising to the educational context, Bizumic, Reynolds, Turner, Bromhead and Subasic (2009) surveyed staff and students at a high school. Students who identified strongly with the school showed a range of positive well-being outcomes, including higher self-esteem and positive affect, as well as lower rates of anxiety and depression. Highly identified students also tended to show better self-regulation abilities, reporting that they felt less aggressive than students who were not highly identified. School identification was associated with similar well-being benefits for teachers, predicting lower stress, anxiety and depression as well as greater job involvement.

Recent research has investigated the relationship between educational social identification and academic processes. Bluic, Ellis, Goodyear and Hendres (2011; and Bluic, Goodyear and Ellis, Chapter 12, this volume) found that psychology students who identified strongly with the discipline of psychology were more likely to adopt a deep learning approach (characterised by an intrinsic interest in learning material and improving one's understanding) compared to a surface learning approach (characterised by an aim to reproduce material rather than understand it). Adopting a deep learning approach has been reliably demonstrated to predict better academic performance (Richardson *et al.*, 2012). Research by Smyth, Mavor, Platow, Grace and Reynolds (2013; and Smyth, Mavor, Platow and Grace, Chapter 13, this volume) found that identification with one's academic discipline predicted endorsement of deep learning norms, and conformity to those norms among high identifiers was associated with deep learning practices. The reciprocal relationship of learning approach and educational social identification has, therefore, been shown to improve academic outcomes through a process of conformity to student norms.

This cross-sectional evidence reveals associations between identification and positive learning outcomes, but it cannot answer the question of whether identification *improves* learning outcomes (i.e., suggesting the causal direction of the relationship). In this sense, the literature is particularly in need of longitudinal research that tests whether changes in group identity and identification are associated with changes in well-being and educational outcomes (Bizumic *et al.*, 2009). Research by Platow, Mavor and Grace (2013) used a longitudinal approach to examine this question – surveying first-year psychology students across two semesters. The researchers found that adopting a deep learning approach in semester 1 (shown in previous work to be increased by high educational identification) predicted greater educational identification in semester 2. This relationship was mediated through actual learning assessed in terms of student grades.

Platow *et al.* (2013) concluded that as students develop an intrinsic interest in their field of study, they begin to adopt normative interests held by psychology students and so come to identify with the educational group. In this chapter, we build on this earlier work by developing and assessing a model of psychological need satisfaction in the educational domain – a precursor to intrinsic motivation (Deci and Ryan, 2000) – as aid to the development of educational social identity. We discuss the theory behind our argument and then present longitudinal evidence for our hypothesised model.

The self-determination approach to education

Self-determination theory (Deci and Ryan, 1985, 2000) is a theory of motivation based upon the notion that humans have a built-in propensity for autonomy, self-expression and self-determination. The theory outlines factors that allow individuals to meet their psychological needs. As noted above, individuals are assumed within self-determination theory to have three core needs: autonomy (freedom to choose), relatedness (closeness with others) and competence (demonstrated capability). When individuals' psychological needs are met, they are more likely to internalise the behaviours, attitudes or ideas that are reinforced in the supportive social environment. That is, behaviours that allow a person to be autonomous, related and competent will be engaged in out of intrinsic interest and motivation rather than because of external reinforcements and constraints. So, too, environments that allow people to be autonomous, related and competent will foster intrinsic motivation to engage in tasks present in that context.

People are considered to be self-determined when their thoughts and actions are well internalised and endorsed out of choice. For example, a student who works on an assignment because she chooses to do so, believes it is important and finds it enjoyable would be labelled as more strongly self-determined. In contrast, people are considered non–self-determined when their thoughts or actions are not internalised but are emitted out of internal or external pressure. For example, a student who works on an assignment because she feels forced to do so or fears the consequences of failure would be seen as non–self-determined. Motivation is, therefore, conceptualised as operating on a continuum ranging from fully self-determined (i.e., intrinsically motivated) to non–self-determined (i.e., externally regulated) and amotivated.

Self-determination theory has been applied to understanding motivation in a range of contexts, from work behaviour (Parker, Jimmieson and Amiot, 2010, 2013) to intergroup processes (Amiot, Sansfaçon and Louis, 2013), and experiences across the life span (Kasser and Ryan, 2001). Being self-determined is thought to be a positive state in and of itself, but it also has a variety of positive outcomes that range from greater well-being to improved performance. Having one's psychological needs met predicts higher well-being (Bettencourt and Sheldon, 2001; Kasser and Ryan, 2001; Reis, Sheldon, Gable, Roscoe and Ryan, 2001), enhanced cognitive persistence (Deci, Eghrari, Patrick and Leone, 1994), greater engagement in physical exercise (Daley and Duda, 2006) and better performance at work (Baard, Deci and Ryan, 2004).

Self-determination theory has also been applied to understanding of educational outcomes. In a study with French-Canadian high school students, Fortier, Vallerand and Guay (1995) found that the degree to which students felt autonomous, related and competent in the school setting predicted better academic performance across a range of subjects. Vallerand, Fortier and Guay (1997) extended this work to investigate high school dropout rates. Students who did not have their psychological needs met in the school environment showed greater dropout intentions and higher actual dropout rates compared with students whose needs were met.

The potential mediating role of identification in the process of need satisfaction is highlighted in Finn's (1989) participation–identification model. Finn notes that the self-esteem rates among school dropouts *and* non-dropouts are high. He argues this persistence of high self-esteem among dropouts is due to these individuals dis–identifying with the educational context and reidentifying within an alternative non-educational context, presumably one better able to fulfill the individual's basic psychological need requirements (see also Osbourne and Jones, 2011).

Combining self-determination and social identity approaches to education

Currently, we apply self-determination principles to understand how people come to identify with educational groups. We propose that individuals will be more likely to identify with educational groups when those groups satisfy members' motivational needs for autonomy, competence and relatedness. In turn, educational identification should mediate the positive impact of need satisfaction on a range of outcomes, including well-being and academic performance. As described below, we argue that psychological need satisfaction has positive effects on student outcomes by encouraging and strengthening the formation and development of educational social identity.

The university context may be particularly well suited to meeting one's psychological needs. Students transition from a highly structured environment in high school to an unregulated university environment that allows for independent working and choice in a range of learning opportunities, thus meeting the need for autonomy. More demanding curricula and course assessment give students the opportunity to experience and demonstrate competence. Finally, universities provide a range of opportunities for relatedness in the form of connections with other students and staff and in participation in extracurricular activities unrelated to the learning process.

Just as the university context can meet people's needs, groups, too, can provide a basis for need satisfaction. Indeed, groups provide individuals the possibility of bringing their own perspective to the collective (Jetten and Hornsey, 2011) – and, in this sense, support their autonomy and feelings of control (Cameron, 1999; Greenaway et al., 2015). Groups can also provide a blueprint for action and determine the rules to play by to function and become successful (Taylor, 2002) – hence fuelling competence. Finally, groups act as a fundamental source of belonging and relatedness (Baumeister and Leary, 1995). This suggests that groups can satisfy individuals' psychological needs. However, it also raises the possibility that groups that satisfy one's needs will be internalised to a greater degree in one's self-concept and will, hence, promote greater group identification. This is the main idea that we explore in this chapter.

In considering what factors might lead individuals to identify with educational groups, we propose that it is partly through satisfaction of one's autonomy, competence and relatedness needs that educational social identity is developed. This is a departure from the traditional emphasis in the social identity approach on socio-structural variables, such as status, legitimacy, stability and the permeability of group boundaries. For example, Ellemers, van Knippenberg, de Vries and Wilke (1988) found that individuals were particularly likely to identify with groups that possessed impermeable boundaries and high status. While acknowledging the importance of intergroup relations in social identification, a great deal of recent research in this area is consistent with the proposition advanced by Amiot, de la Sablonnière, Terry and Smith (2007) that, in addition to socio-structural beliefs, the satisfaction of individual needs feeds into group identification. From a social identity perspective, the concept of individual need satisfaction as an antecedent can perhaps be accommodated in the self-categorisation theory concept of perceiver readiness. This is simply the assumption that people (i.e., perceivers) vary as to how ready they are to identify with some groups rather than others (e.g., Turner, Oakes, Haslam and McGarty, 1994). We elaborate on this point below.

Early evidence relevant to the association between self-determination and identity was put forward by Barreto and Ellemers (2002). They found that individuals who were allowed to choose the group they joined were more highly identified and willing to cooperate with other group members compared to individuals who were not given the option of choosing their group. This work suggests that factors such as autonomy may play a role in directing the development of group identification. Similarly, Bettencourt and Sheldon (2001) found that individuals whose needs for autonomy and relatedness were met experienced more positive affect during a group task. Moreover, Sheldon and Bettencourt (2002) found that psychological need satisfaction predicted greater commitment towards the group, over and above other variables.

More recent research has applied self-determination principles directly to predicting social identification in groups. Self-determined motivation has been shown to predict stronger identification with national groups – Amiot and Sansfaçon (2011) found that, beyond any between-context influences on national identification (i.e., the specific type of intergroup relations; stronger cognitive category salience), citizens were more likely to identify strongly when they believed that their nationality affords them more choices and freedoms. Similarly, Amiot, Terry, Wirawan and Grice (2010) found that the degree to which the group was perceived as meeting needs for autonomy, competence and relatedness predicted greater identification among both university students and online gamers. In both groups, psychological need satisfaction operated through group identification to predict greater psychological well-being.

While a full elaboration of a theory of social identity development is beyond the scope of this chapter (see Amiot et al., 2007), it may be noted that contrasting individual need satisfaction and traditional social identity approaches to identification highlights two clear differences in emphasis. The present model generates a focus on motivation rather than cognition and a focus on individual differences rather than contextual factors (see also Monaghan and Bizumic, Chapter 14, this volume). To take the latter point first, the social identity analysis of contextual factors as the key drivers of group identification sits oddly with the common practice of operationalising social identification in terms of within-group, within-context individual differences (e.g., see Postmes and Branscombe, 2002). While intergroup relations clearly shape appraisals of identity between groups and make more or less salient particular social categories between contexts, the measurement of individual differences within groups and within contexts invites theoretical analysis of why such differences might emerge. Some of the individual differences in identification clearly derive from variation in cognitive appraisals of the intergroup relationship and in socio-structural beliefs (e.g., Johnson, Terry and Louis, 2005). However, motivational factors are, arguably, also relevant as previous research clearly demonstrates (Amiot and Sansfaçon, 2011; Amiot et al., 2010; Barreto and Ellemers, 2002; Bettencourt and Sheldon, 2001; Sheldon and

Bettencourt, 2002). Our theoretical model that individual differences in need satisfaction predict differences in identification, with important follow-on consequences in the educational context, is subjected to empirical testing below. Specifically, we tested the relationships between need satisfaction, educational social identification, and positive educational outcomes cross-sectionally and longitudinally, investigating the impact of need satisfaction via educational social identification on perceptions of identity conflict, conformity to group norms and academic satisfaction.

Model testing

We surveyed university students early in their university studies, most within the first semester of their first year of study. This is a critical transition period for university students in which they give up their secondary school identity and move to a new, more independent university social identity. What causes some people to embrace and adopt this new social identity more so than others? As highlighted above, we propose that it is in part the degree to which people perceive the new university group as meeting their needs for autonomy, competence and relatedness that determines the degree to which they develop identification and, so, reap the benefits of a strong student social identity (Amiot and Sansfaçon, 2011; Amiot et al., 2007, 2010). Students who feel more pressured or coerced in their choice of field or in their studies, along with students who feel socially isolated or incompetent in meeting university standards, would be expected to dis-identify and thereby to experience worse outcomes. We tested these hypotheses in two samples to investigate the development of student social identification over time and the role that psychological need satisfaction plays in this process.

We assessed four main outcome variables in this research, selected on the basis of their theoretical interest for scholars of university student integration and of identity and social influence more broadly. First, we measured two variables associated with strong group identification in past research on social influence: greater conformity to group norms and lower identity conflict. Considerable research within the social identity approach demonstrates that highly identifying individuals are more likely to conform to group norms (e.g., Terry and Hogg, 1996, 2001; see also Turner, 1991). In contrast, *identity conflict* is understood as the degree to which people perceive a group identity to conflict within their own personal self-concept. This failure to internalise a particular social identity, such as that of being a university student, manifests as a sense of inauthenticity; even if individuals enact a group identity, they experience the behaviours in that role as not reflecting who they perceive themselves as really being. We hypothesise that identity conflict should be lower if students embrace the educational social identity more strongly and internalise it into their own self-concept (e.g., Oyserman et al., 2006; see Amiot et al., 2007). Moreover, we hypothesised that, cross-sectionally and over time, psychological need satisfaction would predict greater student social identification which, in turn, would predict greater conformity to student norms and lower perceptions of identity conflict.

The final two constructs we examined were well-being and satisfaction with one's academic performance – two variables that illustrate students' successful or unsuccessful transition to university. Self-determined motivation and social identification have been shown in past research to converge by predicting, in separate studies, higher personal well-being and stronger academic performance (e.g., Bizumic *et al.*, 2009; Kasser and Ryan, 2001; Platow *et al.*, 2013; Reis *et al.*, 2001; Vallerand, Fortier and Guay, 1997). In the present research, we drew on these two theoretical approaches, hypothesising that psychological need satisfaction would predict greater student social identification, which in turn would predict greater well-being and academic satisfaction.

Model test 1: cross-sectional assessment of motivated identification

In our first test of our model, we sampled 521 University of Queensland (UQ) students (302 female, M_{age} = 19.08, SD = 4.25, age range 17–59) in the early stages of their university studies. Students were surveyed in first- and second-year lectures (30 per cent of the sample), approached in public areas on campus (55 per cent of the sample), or completed the survey in the lab for course credit (15 per cent of the sample). Approximately 24 per cent of the sample majored in the Sciences, 22 per cent in the Social Sciences, 16 per cent in Business, 14 per cent in the Arts, 11 per cent in Engineering, and 2 per cent in Physical Therapies. The remaining 11 per cent were unclassified.

Students reported the degree to which the group 'UQ students' supported their autonomy, competence and relatedness needs (e.g., 'How free and choiceful do you feel when being in this group?'; Sheldon and Bettencourt, 2002); their level of social identification as a UQ student (e.g., 'I have a lot in common with other UQ students'; Cameron, 2004); perceptions of identity conflict (e.g., 'Being a UQ student clashes with who I consider myself to really be'; see Smith, Amiot, Smith, Callan and Terry, 2013); personal well-being over the past two weeks (e.g., 'I felt alive and vital'; Ryan and Frederick, 1997); and academic satisfaction over the past two weeks (e.g., 'I achieved my goals academically during this time'). Perceived descriptive student norms and intentions were examined for five behaviours relevant to university students: studying, partying, trying to fit in, finishing their degree and valuing the university. Across the five items, the within-participant correlation between perceived norms and behavioural intentions was taken as an index of conformity. High positive correlations indicated that the behaviours participants rated as descriptively more normative (more commonly engaged in by other students) were also the behaviours they intended more strongly to engage in themselves. In contrast, scores of 'zero' indicated that there was no association between students' intentions and their perceptions of what other students did; and negative scores indicated that students intended to

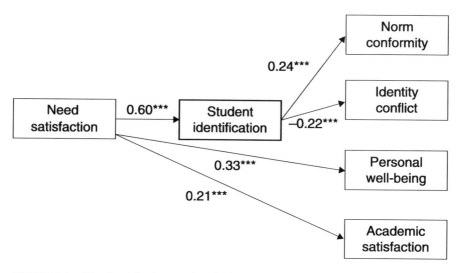

FIGURE 10.1 Need satisfaction predicts higher personal well-being and academic satisfaction directly, and higher conformity and lower identity conflict indirectly via student identification (Sample 1)

Note: standardised regression coefficients reported, ★★★$p < 0.001$

engage more in behaviours that they saw as being *less* normative (i.e., behaviours that were uncommon for other students).

Reported need satisfaction was modelled as an antecedent to student identification, which was in turn used to predict intentions to conform to student norms, identity conflict perceptions, academic satisfaction and personal well-being. The initial model provided a poor fit[1] to the data, $\chi^2(10) = 93.58$, $p < 0.001$; CFI = 0.794, RMSEA = 0.127, SRMR = 0.083, and modification indices revealed that two direct paths should be added from need satisfaction to personal well-being and to academic satisfaction. When these paths were included, the final model provided acceptable fit, $\chi^2(9) = 19.17$, $p = 0.024$; CFI = 0.975, RMSEA = 0.047, SRMR = 0.041. As shown in Figure 10.1, need satisfaction was associated with higher student identification, which in turn was associated with higher norm conformity and lower identity conflict, but not with personal well-being or academic satisfaction. Need satisfaction was directly associated with personal well-being and academic satisfaction. Bootstrap analyses using bias-corrected CIs with 10,000 resamples confirmed the significant indirect effects of need satisfaction via student identification on identity conflict and intentions to conform to student norms.

Model test 2: longitudinal assessment of motivated identification

In the second test of our model, we sampled 79 students who participated in our first model test (48 female, $M_{age} = 19.67$, $SD = 5.83$, age range 17–59); they were contacted approximately six weeks after the first questionnaire to complete a second wave of the survey. All students at Time 1 had been contacted if they had provided email addresses and indicated willingness, so the Time 2 sample represents significant attrition (> 80 per cent). Students completed the same survey as at Time 1, and their responses were matched via an anonymous code generated in the first survey.

At Time 2, residual scores were created to measure change by regressing Time 2 variables upon their Time 1 counterparts. Change in need satisfaction from Time 1 to Time 2 was then modelled as an antecedent of change in student identification, which was in turn used to predict changes in norm conformity, identity conflict, academic satisfaction and personal well-being. Identity conflict was allowed to covary with norm conformity and academic satisfaction.

The initial model provided acceptable fit, $\chi^2(8) = 11.57$, $p = 0.172$; CFI = 0.970, RMSEA = 0.076, SRMR = 0.068. As shown in Figure 10.2, increased need satisfaction was associated with increased student identification, which in turn was associated with increased personal well-being, academic satisfaction and decreased identity conflict perceptions. Increased identification was not significantly associated with conformity to student norms, however, despite a trend in the expected direction. As with the first model, bootstrap analyses using bias-corrected CIs with 10,000 resamples revealed significant indirect effects of increased need satisfaction via increased student identification on increased well-being, increased academic satisfaction, and decreased identity conflict. There was no significant indirect effect of increased need satisfaction via increased student identification on intentions to conform to student norms.

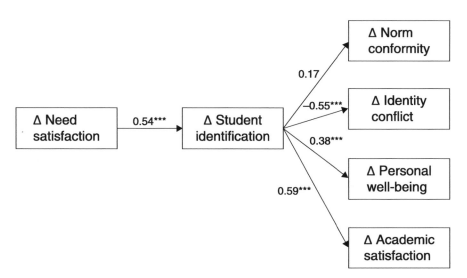

FIGURE 10.2 Change in need satisfaction indirectly predicts increased well-being and academic satisfaction and decreased identity conflict via change in student identification

Note: standardised regression coefficients reported, ★★★$p < 0.001$

Need satisfaction promotes educational identification with positive consequences for students

In this chapter, we united perspectives from the social identity and self-determination traditions to understand the development of educational social identity during critical transition phases for students. Previous research, and much of the work published in this volume, shows the benefit of identifying with educational groups for student well-being and academic outcomes. Our goal in this chapter was to explore, theoretically and empirically, the question of how students come to identify with educational groups, particularly in stages of transition that may otherwise undermine the development of group identification. We proposed that it is when educational groups support the psychological needs of their members that identification becomes internalised as a motivational force.

Consistent with our model, we confirmed that the degree to which the educational group met students' needs for autonomy, relatedness, and competence predicted greater group identification both in the short term and over the longer term. This is consistent with an emerging research agenda that applies self-determination principles to understanding intra-group and intergroup processes (e.g., Amiot and Sansfaçon, 2011; Amiot *et al.*, 2007, 2010, 2013; Legault, Green-Demers and Eadie, 2009; Legault, Green-Demers, Grant and Chung, 2007). This work unites two theoretical perspectives that are rooted in traditionally separate literatures of individual (self-determination theory) and group (social identity theory) functioning.

We examined, more specifically, how need satisfaction fuels social identification cross-sectionally and longitudinally. Linking these two variables lets us test explicitly if need satisfaction allows a new group identity to develop over time. Indeed, the sources of need satisfaction that are typically investigated in self-determination theory are located at the individual and interpersonal levels of analysis. As well, while self-determination theory incorporates self and identity processes in its theorising (e.g., Ryan, 1995; Ryan and Deci, 2003), these formulations have traditionally considered only the individual self. Investigating the effect of need satisfaction via the group in the context of social identity change also allows us to answer recent calls for research into: (1) how new social identities develop over time and (2) apart from the more cognitive processes accounted for by self-categorisation theory, what social and motivational factors fuel this sense of social identification over the long term.

We observed that the development of an educational social identity had a range of benefits for students at an early stage in their university schooling and up to six weeks later. To the degree that students felt self-determined in their educational group, they reported greater group identification and consequently higher well-being, greater academic satisfaction and less identity conflict. The importance of these positive outcomes for students' quality of life is self-evident. To the extent that universities and academics benefit from higher retention and more engaged students, or that societies benefit from more educated citizens and workers, the societal importance of the findings is also easy to argue.

The direction of the causal relationships is, of course, open to discussion. Cross-sectionally, greater identification was associated with conformity to student norms, which supports a long line of research demonstrating that identification encourages people to adopt and follow ingroup norms (e.g., Terry and Hogg, 1996, 2001). Interestingly, this trend was not borne out over time; change in identification was not associated with change in conformity to ingroup norms. More broadly, our research here focuses on identification as an outcome of need satisfaction and as mediating the impact of need satisfaction on other variables. However, in other past research, scholars have argued for the existence of positive feedback loops in the educational setting whereby educational identification leads to better academic outcomes and better academic outcomes feed educational identification (e.g., Platow *et al.*, 2013; Smyth *et al.*, 2013). We propose that this may occur, in part, through a process of enhanced self-determination. As needs of autonomy, competence and relatedness are met through the educational group, students become more intrinsically motivated to study, thus internalising the educational social identity more strongly into their self-concept. Future work could explore this feedback process more explicitly, including the possibility that stronger social identification leads to greater perceived need satisfaction (a reverse causality) or that need satisfaction moderates the association between identification and outcomes. Perhaps identification leads to higher well-being when needs are satisfied; but when needs are thwarted, social identification could be linked to lower well-being (see also, Haslam, Jetten, Postmes and Haslam, 2009), suggesting a more negative role for social identification under certain conditions. Here, social identification and need satisfaction were highly positively correlated ($rs >$ 0.50) as would be expected in permeable groups where dissatisfaction would lead to dropouts (Finn, 1989). Experimental research could be useful to clarify the nature of the interactions if identification and need satisfaction are independently manipulated.

The consistent pattern of results in our two samples combined with previous work showing a link between psychological need satisfaction and group identification (e.g., Amiot *et al.*, 2010) leads us to be optimistic about the generalisability of the findings. It should be acknowledged that both group identification and need satisfaction were considered at a global level, which might be interesting to unpack in future research. For example, need satisfaction could be assessed separately for competence, autonomy and relatedness in relation to separate dimensions of identification, such as cognitive centrality, affect and group ties (Cameron, 1999). It would not be surprising, for example, if satisfying group members' needs for relatedness was especially important in strengthening perceptions of group ties, while satisfying autonomy needs impacted particularly strongly on affect. If unique patterns emerged at this lower level of analysis, they might inform the development of tailored interventions where deficits are noted for marginalised groups of students.

Conclusions

This chapter represents one of the earliest attempts to combine the social identity and self-determination approaches and apply them to an educational context. Our theorising and findings have implications for uniting research perspectives from diverse theoretical backgrounds as well as practical implications for the well-being and performance of students during a critical transition to university. We hypothesised and found that as students come to internalise the educational social identity, they experience less identity conflict, which should ease the transition from secondary to tertiary education. The development of educational social identification also protected the well-being of students during this transition period. Finally, students who successfully developed strong group identification reported being more satisfied with their academic performance.

Understanding the factors that foster educational identification will contribute to the development of interventions designed to keep students achieving, happy and – perhaps most important of all – in school. Whereas interventions based on the self-determination theory approach in the context of education have beneficial outcomes for students' motivation and adjustment, we suggest that adding the group component into the equation further contributes to improving positive adjustment and academic outcomes.

Acknowledgements

Preparation of this paper was facilitated by an award to the lead author from the Canadian Institute for Advanced Research: Social Interactions, Identity and Well-being programme.

Note

1   Missing data were imputed using the expectation-maximisation maximum likelihood algorithm in SPSS version 20.0 (Gold and Bentler, 2000). Model fit was assessed using the comparative fit index (CFI), the root-mean-square error of approximation (RMSEA) and the standardised root mean residual (SRMR; see Hu and Bentler, 1998, for a discussion of fit indices). Based on the recommendations of Hu and Bentler (1999), the cut-off values employed for these indices were CFI > 0.95, RMSEA < 0.06, and SRMR < 0.08. We also report the results of the chi-square test (χ^2), but due to the sensitivity of χ^2 when used in large samples, we refer to practical fit indices to make our main judgements about model fit. To test for mediation, we used bias-corrected bootstrapping with 10,000 bootstrap resamples to generate estimates and 95 per cent confidence intervals (CIs) of indirect effects (Cheung and Lau, 2008; Shrout and Bolger, 2002).

References

Amiot, C. E. and Sansfaçon, S. (2011). Motivations to identify with social groups: A look at their positive and negative consequences. *Group Dynamics: Theory, Research and Practice*, 15(2), 105–27.

Amiot, C. E., De la Sablonnière, R., Terry, D. J. and Smith, J. R. (2007). Integration of social identities in the self: Toward a cognitive-developmental model. *Personality and Social Psychology Review*, *11*(4), 364–88.

Amiot, C. E., Sansfaçon, S. and Louis, W. R. (2013). Uncovering hockey fans' motivations behind their derogatory behaviors and how these motives predict psychological well-being and quality of social identity. *Psychology of Sport and Exercise*, *14*(3), 379–88.

Amiot, C. E., Terry, D. J., Wirawan, D. and Grice, T. A. (2010). Changes in social identities over time: The role of coping and adaptation processes. *British Journal of Social Psychology*, *49*(4), 804–26.

Antaki, C., Condor, S. and Levine, M. (1996). Social identities in talk: Speakers' own orientations. *British Journal of Social Psychology*, *35*(4), 473–92.

Baard, P. P., Deci, E. L. and Ryan, R. M. (2004). Intrinsic need satisfaction: A motivational basis of performance and well-being in two work settings. *Journal of Applied Social Psychology*, *34*(10), 2045–68.

Barreto, M. and Ellemers, N. (2002). The impact of respect versus neglect of self-identities on identification and group loyalty. *Personality and Social Psychology Bulletin*, *28*(5), 629–39.

Baumeister, R. F. and Leary, M. R. (1995). The need to belong: Desire for interpersonal attachments as a fundamental human motivation. *Psychological Bulletin*, *117*(3), 497–529.

Baumeister, R. F., Twenge, J. M. and Nuss, C. K. (2002). Effects of social exclusion on cognitive processes: Anticipated aloneness reduces intelligent thought. *Journal of Personality and Social Psychology*, *83*(4), 817–27.

Bettencourt, B. A. and Sheldon, K. (2001). Social roles as mechanisms for psychological need satisfaction within social groups. *Journal of Personality and Social Psychology*, *81*(6), 1131–43.

Bizumic, B., Reynolds, J. K., Turner, J. C., Bromhead, D. and Subasic, E. (2009). The role of the group in individual functioning: School identification and the psychological well-being of staff and students. *Applied Psychology: An International Review*, *58*(1), 171–92.

Bluic, A. M., Ellis, R. A., Goodyear, P. and Hendres, D. M. (2011). The role of social identification as university student in learning: Relationships between students' social identity, approaches to learning, and academic achievement. *Educational Psychology*, *31*(5), 559–74.

Cameron, J. E. (1999). Social identity and the pursuit of possible selves: Implications for the psychological well-being of university students. *Group Dynamics: Theory, Research, and Practice*, *3*(3), 179–89.

Cameron, J. E. (2004). A three-factor model of social identity. *Self and Identity*, *3*(3), 239–62.

Cheung, G. W. and Lau, R. S. (2008). Testing mediation and suppression effects of latent variables: Bootstrapping with structural equation models. *Organizational Research Methods*, *11*(2), 296–325. doi: 10.1177/1094428107300343

Daley, A. J. and Duda, J. L. (2006). Self-determination, stage of readiness to change for exercise, and frequency of physical activity in young people. *European Journal of Sport Science*, *6*(4), 231–43.

Deci, E. L., Eghrari, H., Patrick, B. C. and Leone, D. R. (1994). Facilitating internalization: The self-determination theory perspective. *Journal of Personality*, *62*(1), 119–42.

Deci, E. L. and Ryan, R. M. (1985). *Intrinsic motivation and self-determination in human behavior*. New York: Plenum.

Deci, E. L. and Ryan, R. M. (2000). The 'what' and 'why' of goal pursuits: Human needs and the self-determination of behavior. *Psychological Inquiry, 11*(4), 227–68.

Ellemers, N., van Knippenberg, A., de Vries, N. and Wilke, H. (1988). Social identification and permeability of group boundaries. *European Journal of Social Psychology, 18*(6), 497–513.

Finn, J. D. (1989). Withdrawing from school. *Review of Educational Research, 59*(2), 117–42.

Fortier, M. S., Vallerand, R. J. and Guay, F. (1995). Academic motivation and school performance: Toward a structural model. *Contemporary Educational Psychology, 20*(3), 257–74.

Gee, J. P. (2001). Identity as an analytic lens for research in education. In W. G. Secada (Ed.), *Review of research in education*, Vol. 25 (pp. 99–125). Washington, DC: American Educational Research Association.

Gold, M. S. and Bentler, P. M. (2000). Treatments of missing data: A Monte Carlo comparison of RBHDI, iterative stochastic, regression imputation, and expectation-maximization. *Structural Equation Modeling: A Multidisciplinary Journal, 7*(3), 319–55. doi: 10.1207/S15328007SEM0703_1

Greenaway, K. H., Haslam, S. A., Cruwys, T., Branscombe, N. R., Ysseldyk, R. and Heldreth, C. (2015). From 'we' to 'me': Group identification enhances perceived personal control with consequences for health and well-being. *Journal of Personality and Social Psychology, 109*(1), 53–74.

Haslam, S. A., Jetten, J., Postmes, T. and Haslam, C. (2009). Social identity, health and well-being: An emerging agenda for applied psychology. *Applied Psychology, 58*(1), 1–23.

Hu, L. and Bentler, P. M. (1998). Fit indices in covariance structure modeling: Sensitivity to underparameterized model misspecification. *Psychological Methods, 3*(4), 424–53. doi: 10.1037/1082-989X.3.4.424

Hu, L. and Bentler, P. M. (1999). Cutoff criteria for fit indexes in covariance structure analysis: Conventional criteria versus new alternatives. *Structural Equation Modeling, 6*(1), 1–55. doi: 10.1080/10705519909540118

Jetten, J. and Hornsey, M. J. (2011). *Rebels in groups: Dissent, deviance, difference, and defiance.* Oxford: Wiley-Blackwell.

Johnson, D., Terry, D. J. and Louis, W. R. (2005). Perceptions of the intergroup structure and anti-Asian prejudice among White Australians. *Group Processes and Intergroup Relations, 8*(1), 53–71.

Kasser, T. and Ryan, R. M. (2001). Be careful what you wish for: Optimal functioning and the relative attainment of intrinsic and extrinsic goals. In P. Schmuck and K. M. Sheldon (Eds), *Life goals and well-being: Towards a positive psychology of human striving* (pp. 116–31). Ashland, OH: Hogrefe and Huber Publishers.

Legault, L., Green-Demers, I. and Eadie, A. L. (2009). When internalization leads to automatization: The role of self-determination in automatic stereotype suppression and implicit prejudice regulation. *Motivation and Emotion, 33*(1), 10–24. doi: 10.1007/s11031-008-9110-4

Legault, L., Green-Demers, I., Grant, P. and Chung, J. (2007). On the self-regulation of implicit and explicit prejudice: A self-determination theory perspective. *Personality and Social Psychology Bulletin, 33*(5), 732–49. doi: 10.1177/0146167206298564

Mavor, K. I., McNeill, K. G., Anderson, K., Kerr, A., O'Reilly, E. and Platow, M. J. (2014). Beyond prevalence to process: The role of self and identity in medical student wellbeing. *Medical Education, 48*(4), 351–60.

Osborne, J. W. and Jones, B. D. (2011). Identification with academics and motivation to achieve in school: How the structure of the self influences academic outcomes. *Educational Psychology Review, 23*(1), 131–58.

Oyserman, D., Bybee, D. and Terry, K. (2006). Possible selves and academic outcomes: How and when possible selves impel action. *Journal of Personality and Social Psychology, 91*(1), 188–204. doi: 10.1037/0022-3514.91.1.188

Parker, S. L., Jimmieson, N. L. and Amiot, C. E. (2010). Self-determination as a moderator of demands and control: Implications for employee strain and engagement. *Journal of Vocational Behavior, 76*(1), 52–67. doi: 10.1016/j.jvb.2009.06.010

Parker, S. L., Jimmieson, N. L. and Amiot, C. E. (2013). Self-determination, control, and reactions to changes in workload: A work simulation. *Journal of Occupational Health Psychology, 18*(2), 173–90.

Platow, M. J., Mavor, K. I. and Grace, D. M. (2013). On the role of discipline-related self-concept in deep and surface approaches to learning among university students. *Instructional Science, 41*(2), 271–85.

Postmes, T. and Branscombe, N. R. (2002). Influence of long-term racial environmental composition on subjective well-being in African Americans. *Journal of Personality and Social Psychology, 83*(3), 735–51.

Reis, H. T., Sheldon, K. M., Gable, S. L., Roscoe, J. and Ryan, R. M. (2001). Daily well-being: The role of autonomy, competence, and relatedness. *Personality and Social Psychology Bulletin, 26*(4), 419–35.

Richardson, M., Abraham, C. and Bond, R. (2012). Psychological correlates of university students' academic performance: A systematic review and meta-analysis. *Psychological Bulletin, 138*(2), 353–87.

Ryan, R. M. (1995). Psychological needs and the facilitation of integrative processes. *Journal of Personality, 63*(3), 397–427.

Ryan, R. M. and Deci, E. L. (2003). On assimilating identities to the self: A self-determination theory perspective on internalization and integrity within cultures. In M. R. Leary and J. P. Tangney (Eds), *Handbook of self and identity* (pp. 253–72). New York: Guilford.

Ryan, R. M. and Frederick, C. (1997). On energy, personality, and health: Subjective vitality as a dynamic reflection of well-being. *Journal of Personality, 65*(3), 529–65.

Sheldon, K. M. and Bettencourt, B. A. (2002). Psychological need-satisfaction and subjective wellbeing within social groups. *British Journal of Social Psychology, 41*(1), 25–38.

Shrout, P. E. and Bolger, N. (2002). Mediation in experimental and nonexperimental studies: New procedures and recommendations. *Psychological Methods, 7*(4), 422–45. doi: 10.1037/1082-989X.7.4.422.

Smith, L. G. E., Amiot, C. E., Smith, J. R., Callan, V. J. and Terry, D. J. (2013). The social validation and coping model of organizational identity development: A longitudinal test. *Journal of Management, 39*(7), 1952–78.

Smyth, L., Mavor, K. I., Platow, M. J., Grace, D. M. and Reynolds, K. J. (2015). Discipline social identification, study norms and learning approach in university students. *Educational Psychology, 35*(1), 53–72.

Stephens, N. M., Fryberg, S. A., Markus, H. R., Johnson, C. S. and Covarrubias, R. (2012). Unseen disadvantage: How American universities' focus on independence undermines the academic performance of first-generation college students. *Journal of Personality and Social Psychology, 102*(6), 1178–97.

Taylor, D. M. (2002). *The quest for identity: From minority groups to Generation Xers*. Westport, CT: Praeger Publishers.

Terry, D. J. and Hogg, M. A. (1996). Group norms and the attitude-behavior relationship: A role for group identification. *Personality and Social Psychology Bulletin, 22*(8), 776–93.

Terry, D. J. and Hogg, M. A. (2001). Attitudes, behavior, and social context: The role of group norms and group membership in social influence processes. In J. P. Forgas and K. D. Williams (Eds), *Social influence: Direct and indirect processes* (pp. 253–70). Philadelphia, PA: Psychology Press.

Turner, J. C. (1991). *Social influence*. Belmont, CA: Thomson Brooks/Cole Publishing Co.

Turner, J. C., Oakes, P. J., Haslam, S. A. and McGarty, C. (1994). Self and collective: Cognition and social context. *Personality and Social Psychology Bulletin, 20*(5), 454–63.

Vallerand, R. J., Fortier, M. S. and Guay, F. (1997). Self-determination and persistence in a real-life setting: Toward a motivational model of high school dropout. *Journal of Personality and Social Psychology, 72*(5), 1161–76.

11

UNCERTAINTY IN TRANSITION

The influence of group cohesion on learning

*Tegan Cruwys, Amber M. Gaffney and
Yvonne Skipper*

As students move through the educational system, they will regularly face the challenge of transitioning to a new learning environment (e.g. transferring from primary to secondary school or entering university; see also in this volume, Greenaway, Amiot, Louis and Bentley, Chapter 10, and Jetten, Iyer and Zhang, Chapter 6). Previous research suggests that these transition points are 'high-risk' times for students and can lead to disengagement from the educational system (Benner, 2011; Taylor, 1991). This in turn can lead to a drop in grades and to poor long-term outcomes, such as social exclusion and poor mental health (Aronson, Quinn and Spencer, 1998; Henderson and Dweck, 1990). In this chapter, we outline and evaluate an uncertainty–identity (Hogg, 2000, 2007, 2012) model of educational transition. We propose that transitions are associated with significant *self-uncertainty* – that is, students can feel uncertain about themselves, their social groups and their competence in new learning environments (Arnett, 1999). These self-uncertainties motivate individuals to seek out and affiliate with groups that are particularly well suited for uncertainty reduction. Commonly, these are cohesive groups with clear norms prescribing behaviour (Hogg, 2014). However, not all cohesive groups value education. In fact, some such groups promote goals that de-prioritise educational goals in favour of other activities (e.g. sport, partying). Although affiliation with such groups may reduce self-conceptual uncertainty and provide individuals with other benefits of group memberships, conformity to anti-educational norms could compromise a student's success in his or her new learning environment. We provide evidence for this model in a sample of students transitioning to university and discuss the implications for learning interventions, emphasising the potential benefits of fostering cohesive groups with pro-education norms.

Educational transitions

Most students undergo at least two major educational transitions: from primary to secondary school, and from secondary school to university. Previous research suggests that transition points are times of high risk for students as they frequently involve discontinuity not only in their education but also in their physical environment, daily routine and, crucially, social relationships (Benner, 2011; Rutter, 1996). Transitions have, therefore, been associated with a wealth of negative outcomes, such as a drop in school grades (Otis, Grouzet and Pelletier, 2005; Simmons and Blyth, 1987), reduced academic motivation (Eccles and Midgley, 1989; Wigfield, Eccles, MacIver, Reuman and Midgley, 1991), increased stress and depressive symptoms (Rudolph, Lambert, Clark and Kurlakowsky, 2001), anxiety (Galton, Morrison and Pell, 2000; Jindal-Snape and Miller, 2008), and poor self-esteem (Fenzel, 2000). Furthermore, educational transitions exacerbate the risk of poor outcomes among already vulnerable students, such as those from a minority ethnic group or of low socio-economic status (Benner, 2011; Serbin, Stack and Kingdon, 2013). The way that young people respond to challenges in their new environment can set the pattern for how they will continue to respond throughout their education (Anderson, Jacobs, Schramm and Splittgerber, 2000). Given that success in schooling can predict social and occupational success across the life course (Alexander, Entwisle and Kabbani, 2001), it seems advantageous to build an understanding of how positive transition experiences can be facilitated.

Educational research has extensively documented the academic challenges that transitions create for students, such as facing new subjects with higher educational standards and greater workloads than they might have expected (Arthur and Hiebert, 1996; Elias, Gara and Ubriaco, 1985; Sirsch, 2003). However, the social challenges involved in transition have received less research attention. An educational transition requires a young person to meet new people, develop new social relationships and join new social groups. Such transitions of *social identity* entail a risk to mental health (Cruwys, Haslam, Dingle, Haslam and Jetten, 2014), particularly for students who do not identify with their new learning institution (Iyer, Jetten, Tsivrikos, Postmes and Haslam, 2009). Identity transitions in education are often high-stakes for students, with a low chance of achieving the identities to which they aspire (e.g. gaining access to professional training programmes or high-status learning institutions), and this may, in part, explain the higher risk of depression associated with such transitions (Cruwys, Greenaway and Haslam, 2015; Greenaway, Frye and Cruwys, 2015). Research with adults has suggested that many of the most stressful life events involve identity transition (e.g. changing jobs, moving cities; Cochrane and Robertson, 1973; Haslam *et al.*, 2008). We might, therefore, expect educational transitions to be one of the most stressful experiences of adolescent life.

Uncertainty and identification with cohesive groups

Research suggests that the transition from childhood to adulthood generates a great degree of uncertainty (see Bronfenbrenner, 1979; Erikson, 1968). Self-uncertainty can be uncomfortable and can create a negative drive state. In this situation, uncertainty–identity theory (Hogg, 2000, 2007, 2012) states that people are strongly motivated to reduce feelings of uncertainty, and group iden-tification provides a powerful means of uncertainty reduction. This is because when a person self-categorises as a group member, the beliefs and behaviours of the group become self-relevant (Turner, Hogg, Oakes, Reicher and Wetherell, 1987) and provide them with a clear image of precisely who they are (e.g. 'I *am* a member of Group X; we *believe* X, and we *do* X') and who they are not (e.g. 'I am *not* a member of Group Y, so I do *not* believe Y or *do* Y').

When people are uncertain, they identify more strongly with groups in which they are already members (Grieve and Hogg, 1999; Mullin and Hogg, 1998; see also Monrouxe and Rees, Chapter 17, this volume). However, during academic transitions, young people are in a new environment and often have limited continuity with previously existing groups that could have provided them with this stability. Therefore, they are likely to seek out new groups that will provide them with a guide to who they are and how they should behave. Not all of the potential new groups available to students will be equally likely to reduce uncer-tainty. Groups are more effective at reducing uncertainty when they are cohesive. A cohesive (or entitative) group is perceived to be an entity in its own right (Campbell, 1958), and group members are seen to share unity, coherence and organisation (Hamilton and Sherman, 1996). Cohesive groups have clearly defined and agreed-upon norms and group boundaries. People perceive cohesive groups as acting as a single unit; thus, they believe that the behaviour of members of cohesive groups is predictable (see Rydell and McConnell, 2005). By contrast, a nominal group may be viewed as a heterogeneous cluster of individuals who do not act 'as one' and, thus, may not be perceived to be a meaningful group at all. A cohesive group is particularly attractive to individuals experiencing uncer-tainty (Hogg, Sherman, Dierselhuis, Maitner and Moffitt, 2007). Cohesive groups reduce uncertainty by helping people to create an identity based on the clear behavioural and attitudinal norms of the group (Grieve and Hogg, 1999; Mullin and Hogg, 1998). Furthermore, when people experiencing uncertainty identify with a cohesive group, they are more likely to be subject to social influ-ence from fellow group members and act in line with their group's norms and values (Gaffney and Hogg, in press).

We argue that one reason educational transitions have been associated with poor outcomes is that sometimes the most cohesive groups available to adoles-cents during this uncertain period are ones that do not value education. In fact, it has even been suggested that in many adolescent peer groups, academic achieve-ment is so devalued as to be incompatible with high social status (Schwartz, Gorman, Nakamoto and McKay, 2006; Steinberg, Dornbusch and Brown, 1992;

Troop-Gordon, Visconti and Kuntz, 2011). This suggests that performing well in school is not necessarily associated with being socially *accepted* in school (Schwartz, Kelly and Duong, 2013). Research on adolescent health behaviour is replete with studies demonstrating that adolescents engage in risky behaviours such as inhalant use or smoking (e.g. Schofield, Pattison, Hill and Borland, 2001; Siegel, Alvaro, Patel and Crano 2009) to gain popularity in their peer groups. Moreover, engaging in such behaviours might actually gain them the admiration of their peers (e.g. Becker and Luthar, 2007) and provide them with distinctive labels that suggest a 'rebel' identity (e.g. Carroll, Houghton, Khan and Tan, 2008, p. 790). In schools, the presence of cohesive groups that devalue education (either implicitly or explicitly) is problematic because ingroup norms are a powerful influence on individual attitudes and behaviour (see, for example, in this volume, Jones, Livingstone and Manstead, Chapter 4, Smith, Louis and Tarrant, Chapter 9, and Smyth, Mavor, Platow and Grace, Chapter 13). As previously discussed, these group norms are likely to be even more powerful during periods of uncertainty.

Self-uncertainty is such a powerful force that it can even motivate people to identify with and join groups that may otherwise be seen as less appealing; for example, low-status groups (Reid and Hogg, 2005). Emler and Reicher (2005) suggest that young people often feel excluded from important social institutions such as the educational system. This motivates adolescents to join and form groups based on 'outsider' or 'delinquent' identities. Goldman, Giles and Hogg (2014) suggest that gangs, which are characterised by high cohesiveness and clearly defined norms, offer a family-like protection for people who experience uncertainty. This research suggests that people may join groups and comply with group norms even when such norms encourage behaviour that may be seen by others as extreme, antisocial or even maladaptive. We argue that this is more likely to occur when people feel a lack of clarity about their own identities because while these groups may encourage 'bad' behaviours, they do at least provide a sense of purpose, belonging and self-definition (Dingle, Stark, Cruwys and Best, 2015; Dingle, Cruwys and Frings, 2015). Indeed, Hogg, Siegel and Hohman (2011) explain the desire to engage in such behaviours through the lens of uncertainty–identity theory in that uncertainty can lead young people to join groups that advocate behaviours which others might believe are not in the young person's best interests. The model we propose is shown in Figure 11.1, and it states that a typical transitional experience for a student is as follows: a transition produces uncertainty that, in turn, leads to a desire to join a cohesive group; the norms of this group then influence behaviour, which may, depending on group norms, harm the student's long-term educational outcomes.

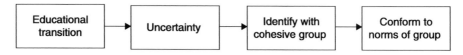

FIGURE 11.1 The proposed uncertainty–identity model of educational transition

This is not to say that all cohesive groups promote negative behaviours or that groups that promote education cannot be cohesive. In times of duress, people often seek groups that offer them support and clear guidelines for healthy and happy lifestyles (e.g. Alcoholics Anonymous, cancer support groups). Moreover, many young people join sports teams and academic clubs during times of transition, which provide them with this much-needed sense of 'belonging' to a group as well as a positive outlet and supportive peer environment. However, groups that value education may not be as visible or seem as cohesive as other available peer groups. Therefore, young people may be less likely to seek them out or to identify with them when they experience uncertainty. We argue that if cohesive groups that promote academic achievement are available, young people experiencing uncertainty may be interested in joining them. Such groups should reduce uncertainty and, through social identification, have a positive impact on academic achievement as young people engage in behaviours that are normative for these groups, such as attending class and studying. This could lead to higher academic achievement and, in turn, wider life choices in the future. Below, we present evidence that tests and illustrates these concepts; in particular, we evaluate a model of how students in transition respond when faced with a variety of groups that vary in their degree of cohesion as well as their group norms.

To test our model, we utilised an experimental design to assess the impact of uncertainty and cohesiveness on group identification and behavioural intentions among students transitioning from secondary school to university. Self-uncertainty was manipulated by asking students to write examples of what made them feel either more or less uncertain about this transition. Students were then presented with two groups – one 'party' group and one 'study' group. Students were randomly assigned to a condition in which the 'party' group was more cohesive or in which the 'study' group was more cohesive. Our first hypothesis from our model was that participants would prefer to affiliate (socially identify) with cohesive groups under conditions when self-uncertainty is high (relative to when self-uncertainty is low). Our second hypothesis from our model was that social identification with a particular group would, in turn, predict intentions to engage in behaviour consistent with that group's norms. Our model predicted that this will occur both for behaviours that are likely to lead to success at university (studying) and those which are less likely to lead to academic success (partying).

Model testing

To test our model, we sampled students who were transitioning to university during the week prior to classes commencing at an Australian university. We only sampled those students who were over 18 years of age, were commencing their first year of university study and were able to complete the full questionnaire in one sitting. Participants were 113 students (34 males) with a mean age of 19.68 ($SD = 3.50$). The study was administered online and was advertised as an investigation of 'Early experiences of university'; students received $10 or course credit for their participation. The study had a 2 (between-participants: high vs. low uncertainty) × 2 (within-participants: studying vs. partying group norms) × 2 (between-participants: study group cohesion high vs. low) mixed design. Participants were randomly assigned to one of the four between-participants conditions and all were presented with both a studying and partying group.

Uncertainty prime

The study commenced with an uncertainty prime adapted from previous research by Hogg and associates (e.g. Hohman and Hogg, 2011; Hohman, Hogg and Bligh, 2010). In the high uncertainty condition, a passage asked students to reflect on their first day at university and emphasised aspects of this experience that may have made them feel unsure or uncertain. Students were then asked to: 'List at least three things that make you feel insecure about forming relationships and about who you are'. In the low uncertainty condition, students were, instead, asked to reflect on how much more confident they were now compared to their first day at the university, emphasising things that made them feel confident. Students were then instructed to: 'List at least three things that make you feel secure about your relationships and about who you are'.

Cohesiveness manipulation and social groups

Students were introduced to two social groups, described as the main two groups of people at the university. Students were told:

> The groups tend to have some things in common, such as they are of equal status and both are known to be friendly. They also differ in many ways. For the purposes of this study, we have labelled these groups Yellow Group and Blue Group.

Two paragraphs were then used to describe each group. The first paragraph referred to the cohesiveness of each group. Although all participants read about both the party group (Blue) and the study group (Yellow), for some participants, the Blue group was described as relatively more cohesive, while for other participants, the Yellow group was described as more cohesive. This manipulation was informed by entitativity research, in particular the various components of entitativity as described by Campbell (1958) and confirmed experimentally by Haslam, Rothschild and Ernst (2000). The dimensions of entitativity included similarity, cohesion and informativeness (see Appendix A).

The second paragraph describing each group referred to the group norms. For the study group, the value of *education* was emphasised along with behaviours such as exchanging new ideas and discussing course material. Studying, going to lectures and learning were described as being common. For the party group, the value of *entertainment* was emphasised along with behaviours such as watching films and discussing television. Partying, going to bars and enjoying oneself were described as common (see Appendix A for the full manipulation).

Measures

To assess how successful the uncertainty manipulation had been in creating a sense of self-uncertainty, students were asked to complete the sentence 'Right now, I feel. . .'. using a seven-point response scale with anchors (1) 'uncertain of who I am' to (7) 'certain of who I am'.[1] Students' desires to join each of the two groups were then assessed using modified social identification scales (Leach *et al.*, 2008; Doosje *et al.*, 1995). For each group, students responded to seven items, such as 'It is likely that I would join the Blue/Yellow group' and 'I could fit in well with members of the Blue/Yellow group', on a seven-point scale from 'strongly disagree' to 'strongly agree'. The order in which participants saw each group was randomised. Students' behavioural intentions were also assessed to examine whether they were consistent with the norms of each of the two groups. For the study group, these behaviours were: regularly attend lectures, study in the evenings, exchange new ideas and discuss course material ($\alpha = 0.72$). For the party group, these behaviours were: regularly attend parties, go to bars, watch many films and discuss television shows ($\alpha = 0.71$). For each behaviour, students were asked, 'Please answer the following questions about what you personally intend to do in the next three months' with a response from a seven-point scale of 'definitely false' to 'definitely true'.

Outcomes of our model testing

Responses to the uncertainty manipulation check indicated that students were, indeed, somewhat less certain of themselves in the high uncertainty conditions ($M = 4.70$; $SD = 1.60$) than the low uncertainty conditions ($M = 5.30$, $SD = 1.20$; $t(111) = 1.99$, $p = 0.049$). To assess the impact of the manipulations on the relative affiliation with both groups, a $2 \times 2 \times 2$ ANOVA was conducted. This revealed a significant main effect of group, $F(1, 107) = 10.18$, $p = 0.002$; students identified more strongly with the study group than with the party group. However, this effect was qualified by a significant two-way interaction between uncertainty and entitativity, $F(1, 107) = 3.92$, $p = 0.050$. This occurred such that when uncertainty was high, students identified more strongly with the cohesive group (regardless of group norms). This interaction is depicted in Figure 11.2. Therefore, the first hypothesis of our model was supported.

Study-related behaviours had a mean of 6.26 on a seven-point scale ($SD = 0.76$), indicating a relatively high intention to engage in study behaviours in the sample overall. Party-related behaviours had a mean of 4.46 ($SD = 1.42$). The second hypothesis of our model was assessed using two moderated mediation statistical models (PROCESS, model 7; Hayes, 2012) where group cohesion was expected to indirectly predict normatively consistent behavioural

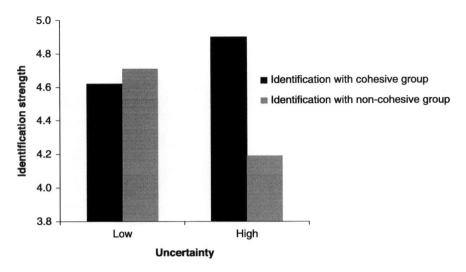

FIGURE 11.2 Interaction between uncertainty and group cohesion to predict social identification. When uncertainty is high, participants identify relatively more with groups that are cohesive (dark bars)

intentions via group identification, but *only* when self-uncertainty was high. Two moderated mediation models were assessed: one for party group identification and behaviour and one for study group identification and behaviour. Analyses were conducted with unstandardised variables to determine significance as recommended by Hayes (2012); however, standardised beta weights are presented here to aid interpretability. The two statistical models are collapsed and presented in Figure 11.3.

In the first statistical model, party group identification predicted intentions to engage in party behaviour ($\beta = 0.36$, $p < 0.001$). Party group identification was, in turn, predicted by party group cohesiveness condition, but *only* in the conditions in which self-uncertainty was high ($\beta_{high\ unc} = 0.32$, $p = 0.019$; $\beta_{low\ unc} = -0.15$, $p = 0.24$). Furthermore, the indirect effect of party group cohesiveness on party behaviour was significant only when self-uncertainty was high ($\beta = 0.12$; 95 per cent CI $= 0.02–0.27$) and not when self-uncertainty was low ($\beta = -0.05$; 95 per cent CI $= -0.17–0.02$).

In the second statistical model, study group identification predicted intentions to engage in study behaviour ($\beta = 0.25$, $p = 0.011$). Study group identification was, in turn, marginally predicted by study group cohesiveness condition, but *only* in the conditions in which self-uncertainty was high ($\beta_{high\ unc} = 0.25$, $p = 0.067$; $\beta_{low\ unc} = 0.10$, $p = 0.44$). Furthermore, the indirect effect of study group cohesiveness on study behaviour was significant only when self-uncertainty was high ($\beta = 0.07$; 95 per cent CI $= 0.01–0.18$) and not when self-uncertainty was low ($\beta = 0.03$; 95 per cent CI $= -0.04–0.09$).

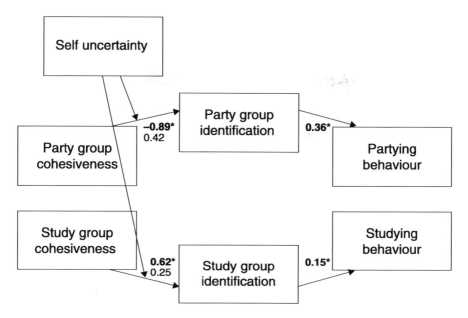

FIGURE 11.3 When uncertain, individuals identify more with cohesive groups and, in turn, intend to behave in ways consistent with group norms

Note: significance levels were assessed using unstandardised coefficients (cf. Hayes, 2012), but standardised beta weights are presented here to aid interpretation.

Therefore, the second hypothesis of our model was supported – social identification with cohesive groups was, in turn, associated with an increased intention to engage in behaviour consistent with the norms of the cohesive group, regardless of whether that behaviour was studying or partying.

Conclusions

In this chapter, we developed a model of student behaviour grounded in the research on social identity transitions and uncertainty–identity theory (Hogg, 2007, 2012). In doing so, we developed and evaluated two hypotheses, both of which we were able to support empirically. Specifically, we found that when uncertainty was high, students identified more strongly with the cohesive group relative to the non-cohesive group. Moreover, high affiliation with a group predicted intentions to act in line with group norms. This occurred both when group norms encouraged studying behaviours *and* when group norms encouraged partying behaviours.

Our empirical analysis provides support for the proposition that the experience of self-uncertainty (e.g. 'Who am I?'; 'How do I fit in?') prompts individuals to seek out or identify more strongly with cohesive groups. In fact, our work goes beyond previous authors' work by demonstrating that this increased desire to affiliate with cohesive groups applies regardless of the content of group norms. We also provide evidence suggesting that identifying with a group leads individuals to be influenced by that group in their own behavioural intentions.

In terms of the education literature, we provide further evidence that social psychological factors (in this case, self-uncertainty, group cohesion and social norms) are important determinants of motivation to engage in learning activities. Conceptually, our analysis is distinct in its framing of educational disengagement as psychologically meaningful – an adaptive response to self-uncertainty when the only cohesive groups available either do not explicitly value education or actively devalue it. The uncertainty–identity approach, therefore, provides an advance over other approaches that look to individual pathology (e.g. impulsivity, lack of empathy; Loney, Frick, Clements, Ellis and Kerlin, 2003; Moffitt, Caspi, Harrington and Milne, 2002) to explain why young people may disengage from education. Instead, we demostrate how this developmentally normal trajectory (Broidy et al., 2003) can emerge from uncertainty arising from an educational transition.

Even more importantly, the approach we have taken points to a solution to the problem of educational disengagement that makes use of this adaptive human drive for affiliation. That is, student engagement with education can be enhanced by means beyond attending to the 'usual suspects', such as quality of teaching. Instead, the cohesiveness of educational groups can influence the extent to which students are likely to affiliate with them, particularly at times of high uncertainty such as that experienced during educational transitions. From a practical perspective, these times of change are a significant opportunity for educators to capitalise on the potential for positive growth, and creating cohesive groups which value education may be a way to do this (see also, particularly, the chapter in this volume by Smyth, Mavor, Platow and Grace).

Our analysis suggests that individuals experiencing significant uncertainty are more likely to find academic groups (or other groups with 'learning-friendly' norms) more attractive to the degree that they are cohesive. We therefore suggest that interventions might feasibly target groups rather than individual students. By increasing the perceived cohesiveness of study groups and other groups that do not devalue education, educators can promote involvement in groups that facilitate, or at least do not hinder, academic success. We therefore expect that enhancing the cohesiveness of groups with norms that are learning-friendly may indirectly enhance studying (and other) behaviours that promote academic involvement and learning. Schools already invest significant resources in fostering sporting groups; and universities typically support clubs and societies representing a wide variety of interests and activities, some of which are closely aligned to specific discipline areas (e.g. the Engineering Students Society). Our research suggests that such investment can indirectly benefit educational outcomes as students will be more likely to affiliate with groups that have learning-friendly group norms when they are cohesive. Educational institutions might, thus, justify diversifying their social and recreational group offerings on educational grounds.

A potential limitation of our empirical analysis was that we measured only behavioural intentions rather than actual behaviours. The best (or worst) of intentions do not always translate into actions. However, the strong relationship previously found between behaviours and intentions (Armitage and Conner, 2001) strengthens our confidence in the likelihood that these findings would generalise to actual studying or partying behaviours. Another potential limitation was that students in our analysis were at relatively low risk of disengaging from the educational system. Although this provides a stringent test of the hypotheses, the greater challenge for educators is engaging young people who are already at substantial risk of disengagement due to a range of other risk factors as well as experiencing high self-uncertainty. Therefore, it is important that future investigation of our model prioritises research with these vulnerable populations.

Future avenues of investigation might include other educational transitions; for example, from primary to secondary school. The psychological processes we outline here may be even more pronounced in the primary to secondary transition as it has been suggested that adolescence is a critical period of identity development (for reviews, see: Bosma and Kunnen, 2001; Meeus, Iedema, Helsen and Vollebergh, 1999). Finally, it will be a task for future research to determine what an intervention to enhance group cohesion might entail and the feasibility of this in a variety of educational settings.

In sum, we have argued that a major contributor to educational disengagement at times of transition is uncertainty. Individuals are motivated to join cohesive groups to reduce this uncertainty. This increased affiliation with cohesive groups is not, in and of itself, problematic. However, highly identifying individuals are likely to converge upon group norms in terms of their own attitudes and behaviours. When and if it is the case that the most cohesive groups available have norms that are incompatible with academic success, then this places the individual at elevated educational risk.

Appendix A

Manipulations

Low cohesion

The Yellow Group is spread out all over campus, and many live far away from each other. Members of the Yellow Group are also very varied and different from one another – not only in terms of clothing styles and interests, but also in terms of goals and personalities. Members of the Yellow Group do not really spend that much time together. Because of this, finding out that someone is a member of the Yellow Group doesn't necessarily tell you much about what they're like. It often makes more sense to think of members of the Yellow Group as separate individuals than as a cohesive, identifiable group.

High cohesion

The Blue Group all hang out in the same area of campus and many live close to each other. Members of the Blue Group are more similar to one another than to members of other groups – not only in terms of clothing styles and interests, but also in terms of goals and personalities. Members of the Blue Group really spend a lot of time together. Because of this, finding out that someone is a member of the Blue Group can tell you a lot about what they are like. It often makes more sense to think of members of the Blue Group as a cohesive, identifiable group rather than as separate individuals.

Partying norms

The Blue Group really values entertainment; this is the main thing that they share. When they meet, they often watch films and discuss television, and they spend time partying and going to bars. Members of the Blue Group think it is really important to enjoy themselves.

Studying norms

The Yellow Group really values education; this is the main thing that they share. When they meet, they often exchange new ideas and discuss material from their courses, and they spend time studying and going to lectures. Members of the Yellow Group think it is really important to learn.

Note

1   Students were asked two questions to ensure they had read and understood the characteristics of each group: 'Which group valued education?' and 'Which group was the most cohesive?' For the uncertainty manipulation check, students responded to the following: 'Earlier in this study, you were asked to write about your experience at university. Think back to those questions. You were asked about experiences that made you feel . . .'. Response options were 'secure and certain of myself' and 'insecure and uncertain of myself'. Twenty-two participants failed one or more of these three manipulation checks and were excluded from analyses, yielding a final sample of 113 participants.

References

Alexander, K. L., Entwisle, D. R. and Kabbani, N. S. (2001). The dropout process in life course perspective: Early risk factors at home and school. *Teachers College Record*, *103*(5), 760–822.

Anderson, L. W., Jacobs, J., Schramm, S. and Splittgerber, F. (2000). School transitions: Beginning of the end or a new beginning? *International Journal of Educational Research*, *33*(4), 325–39.

Armitage, C. J. and Conner, M. (2001). Efficacy of the theory of planned behaviour: A meta-analytic review. *British Journal of Social Psychology*, *40*(4), 471–99.

Arnett, J. J. (1999). Adolescent storm and stress, reconsidered. *American Psychologist, 54*(5), 317–26.

Aronson, J., Quinn, D. M. and Spencer, S. J. (1998). Stereotype threat and the academic underperformance of minorities and women. In J. K. Swim and C. Stangor (Eds), *Prejudice: The target's perspective* (pp. 83–103). San Diego, CA: Academic Press.

Arthur, N. and Hiebert, B. (1996). Coping with the transition to post-secondary education. *Canadian Journal of Counselling, 30*(2), 93–103.

Becker, B. E. and Luthar, S. S. (2007). Peer-perceived admiration and social preference: Contextual correlates of positive peer regard among suburban and urban adolescents. *Journal of Research on Adolescence, 17*(1), 117–44.

Benner, A. (2011). The transition to high school: Current knowledge, future directions. *Educational Psychology Review, 23*(3), 299–328.

Bosma, H. and Kunnen, E. S. (2001). Determinants and mechanisms in ego identity development: A review and synthesis. *Developmental Review, 21*(1), 39–66.

Broidy, L. M., Nagin, D. S., Tremblay, R. E., Bates, J. E., Brame, B., Dodge, K. A., . . . Vitaro, F. (2003). Developmental trajectories of childhood disruptive behaviors and adolescent delinquency: A six-site, cross-national study. *Developmental Psychology, 39*(2), 222–45.

Bronfenbrenner, U. (1979). *The ecology of human development.* Cambridge, MA: Harvard University Press.

Campbell, D. T. (1958). Common fate, similarity, and other indices of the status of aggregates of persons as social entities. *Behavioral Science, 3*(1), 14–25.

Carroll, A., Houghton, S., Khan, U. and Tan, C. (2008). Delinquency and reputational orientations of adolescent at-risk and not-at-risk males and females. *Educational Psychology, 28*(7), 777–93.

Cochrane, R. and Robertson, A. (1973). The life events inventory: A measure of the relative severity of psycho-social stressors. *Journal of Psychosomatic Research, 17*(2), 135–9.

Cruwys, T., Greenaway, K. H. and Haslam, S. A. (2015). The stress of passing through an educational bottleneck: A longitudinal study of psychology honours students. *Australian Psychologist, 50*(5), 372–81.

Cruwys, T., Haslam, S. A., Dingle, G. A., Haslam, C. and Jetten, J. (2014). Depression and social identity: An integrative review. *Personality and Social Psychology Review, 18*(3), 215–38.

Dingle, G. A., Cruwys, T. and Frings, D. (2015). Social identities as pathways into and out of addiction. *Frontiers in Psychology, 6,* 1795.

Dingle, G. A., Stark, C., Cruwys, T. and Best, D. (2015). Breaking good: Breaking ties with social groups may be good for recovery from substance misuse. *British Journal of Social Psychology, 54*(2), 236–54.

Doosje, B., Ellemers, N. and Spears, R. (1995). Perceived intragroup variability as a function of group status and identification. *Journal of Experimental Social Psychology, 31*(5), 410–36.

Eccles, J. S. and Midgley, C. (1989). Stage-environment fit: Developmentally appropriate classrooms for early adolescents. In R. Ames and C. Ames (Eds), *Research on motivation in education* (pp. 139–86). New York: Academic Press.

Elias, M. J., Gara, M. and Ubriaco, M. (1985). Sources of stress and support in children's transition to middle school: An empirical analysis. *Journal of Clinical Child Psychology, 14*(2), 112–18.

Emler, N. and Reicher, S. (2005). Delinquency: Causes or consequences of social exclusion? In D. Abrams, M. A. Hogg and J. M. Marques (Eds), *The social psychology of inclusion and exclusion* (pp. 211–41). New York: Psychology Press.

Erikson, E. H. (1968). *Identity: youth and crisis*. New York: Norton.

Fenzel, L. M. (2000). Prospective study of changes in global self-worth and strain during the transition to middle school. *Journal of Early Adolescence, 20*(1), 93–116.

Gaffney, A. M. and Hogg, M. A. (in press). Social identity and social influence. In S. Harkins and K. D. Williams (Eds), *The Oxford handbook of social influence*. New York: Oxford University Press.

Galton, M., Morrison, I. and Pell, T. (2000). Transfer and transition in English schools: Reviewing the evidence. *International Journal of Educational Research, 33*(4), 341–63.

Goldman, L., Giles, H. and Hogg, M. A. (2014). Going to extremes: Social identity and communication processes associated with gang membership. *Group Processes and Intergroup Relations, 17*(6), 813–32.

Greenaway, K. H., Frye, M. and Cruwys, T. (2015). When aspirations exceed expectations: Quixotic hope increases depression among students. *PLOS ONE, 10*(9), e0135477.

Grieve, P. G. and Hogg, M. A. (1999). Subjective uncertainty and intergroup discrimination in the minimal group situation. *Personality and Social Psychology Bulletin, 25*(8), 926–40.

Hamilton, D. L. and Sherman, S. J. (1996). Perceiving persons and groups. *Psychological Review, 103*(2), 336–55.

Haslam, C., Holme, A., Haslam, S. A., Iyer, A., Jetten, J. and Williams, W. H. (2008). Maintaining group memberships: Social identity continuity predicts well-being after stroke. *Neuropsychological Rehabilitation, 18*(5–6), 671–91.

Haslam, N., Rothschild, L. and Ernst, D. (2000). Essentialist beliefs about social categories. *British Journal of Social Psychology, 39*(1), 113–27.

Hayes, A. F. (2012). PROCESS: A versatile computational tool for observed variable mediation, moderation, and conditional process modeling [white paper]. Retrieved from: www.afhayes.com/ public/process2012.pdf (accessed 1 September 2016).

Henderson, V. L. and Dweck, C. S. (1990). Motivation and achievement. In S. S. Feldman and G. R. Elliott (Eds), *At the threshold: The developing adolescent* (pp. 308–29). Cambridge, MA: Harvard University Press.

Hogg, M. A. (2000). Subjective uncertainty reduction through self-categorization: A motivational theory of social identity processes. *European Review of Social Psychology, 11*(1), 223–55.

Hogg, M. A. (2007). Uncertainty-identity theory. In M. P. Zanna (Ed.), *Advances in experimental social psychology* (Vol. 39, pp. 69–126). San Diego, CA: Academic Press.

Hogg, M. A. (2012). Uncertainty-identity theory. In P. A. M. Van Lange, A. W. Kruglanski and E. T. Higgins (Eds), *Handbook of theories of social psychology* (pp. 62–80). Thousand Oaks, CA: Sage.

Hogg, M. A. (2014). From uncertainty to extremism: Social categorization and identity processes. *Current Directions in Psychological Science, 23*(5), 338–42.

Hogg, M. A., Sherman, D. K., Dierselhuis, J., Maitner, A. T. and Moffitt, G. (2007). Uncertainty, entitativity, and group identification. *Journal of Experimental Social Psychology, 43*(1), 135–42.

Hogg, M. A., Siegel, J. T. and Hohman, Z. P. (2011). Groups can jeopardize your health: Identifying with unhealthy groups to reduce self-uncertainty. *Self and Identity, 10*(3), 326–35.

Hohman, Z. P. and Hogg, M. A. (2011). Fear and uncertainty in the face of death: The role of life after death in group identification. *European Journal of Social Psychology, 41*(6), 751–60.

Hohman, Z. P., Hogg, M. A. and Bligh, M. C. (2010). Identity and intergroup leadership: Asymmetrical political and national identification in response to uncertainty. *Self and Identity*, *9*(2), 113–28.

Iyer, A., Jetten, J., Tsivrikos, D., Postmes, T. and Haslam, S. A. (2009). The more (and more compatible) the merrier: Multiple group memberships and identity compatibility as predictors of adjustment after life transitions. *British Journal of Social Psychology*, *48*(4), 707–33.

Jindal-Snape, D. and Miller, D. J. (2008). A challenge of living? Understanding the psycho-social processes of the child during primary-secondary transition through resilience and self-esteem theories. *Educational Psychology Review*, *20*(3), 217–36.

Leach, C. W., van Zomeren, M., Zebel, S., Vliek, M. L. W., Pennekamp, S. F., Doosje, B. and Ouwerkerk, J. W. (2008). Group-level self-definition and self-investment: A hierarchical (multicomponent) model of in-group identification. *Journal of Personality and Social Psychology*, *95*(1), 144–65.

Loney, B. R., Frick, P. J., Clements, C. B., Ellis, M. L. and Kerlin, K. (2003). Callous-unemotional traits, impulsivity, and emotional processing in adolescents with antisocial behavior problems. *Journal of Clinical Child and Adolescent Psychology*, *32*(1), 66–80.

Meeus, W., Iedema, J., Helsen, M. and Vollebergh, W. (1999). Patterns of adolescent identity development: Review of literature and longitudinal analysis. *Developmental Review*, *19*(4), 419–61.

Moffitt, T. E., Caspi, A., Harrington, H. and Milne, B. J. (2002). Males on the life-course-persistent and adolescence-limited antisocial pathways: Follow-up at age 26 years. *Development and Psychopathology*, *14*(1), 179–207.

Mullin, B. and Hogg, M. A. (1998). Dimensions of subjective uncertainty in social identification and minimal intergroup discrimination. *British Journal Of Social Psychology*, *37*(3), 345–65.

Otis, N., Grouzet, F. and Pelletier, L. G. (2005). Latent motivational change in an academic setting: A 3-year longitudinal study. *Journal of Educational Psychology*, *97*(2), 170–83.

Reid, S. A. and Hogg, M. A. (2005). Uncertainty reduction, self-enhancement, and in-group identification. *Personality and Social Psychology Bulletin*, *31*(6), 804–17.

Rudolph, K. D., Lambert, S. F., Clark, A. G. and Kurlakowsky, K. D. (2001). Negotiating the transition to middle school: The role of self-regulatory processes. *Child Development*, *72*(3), 929–46.

Rutter, M. (1996). Transitions and turning points in developmental psychopathology: As applied to the age span between childhood and mid-adulthood. *International Journal of Behavioral Development*, *19*(3), 603–26.

Rydell, R. J. and McConnell, A. R. (2005). Perceptions of entitativity and attitude change. *Personality and Social Psychology Bulletin*, *31*(1), 99–110.

Schofield, P. E., Pattison, P. E., Hill, D. J. and Borland, R. (2001). The influence of group identification on the adoption of peer group smoking norms. *Psychology and Health*, *16*(1), 1–16.

Schwartz, D., Gorman, A. H., Nakamoto, J. and McKay, T. (2006). Popularity, social acceptance, and aggression in adolescent peer groups: Links with academic performance and school attendance. *Developmental Psychology*, *42*(6), 1116–27.

Schwartz, D., Kelly, B. M. and Duong, M. T. (2013). Do academically engaged adolescents experience social sanctions from the peer group? *Journal of Youth and Adolescence*, *42*(9), 1319–30.

Serbin, L. A., Stack, D. M. and Kingdon, D. (2013). Academic success across the transition from primary to secondary schooling among lower income adolescents:

Understanding the effects of family resources and gender. *Journal of Youth and Adolescence*, *42*(9), 1331–47.

Siegel, J. T., Alvaro, E. M., Patel, N. and Crano, W. D. (2009). '. . . you would probably want to do it. Cause that's what made them popular': Exploring perceptions of inhalant utility among young adolescent nonusers and occasional users. *Substance Use and Misuse*, *44*(5), 597–615.

Simmons, R. G. and Blyth, D. A. (1987). *Moving into adolescence: The impact of pubertal change and school context.* Hawthorne, NJ: Aldine.

Sirsch, U. (2003). The impending transition from primary to secondary school: Challenge or threat? *International Journal of Behavioral Development*, *27*(5), 385–95.

Steinberg, L., Dornbusch, S. M. and Brown, B. B. (1992). Ethnic differences in adolescent achievement: An ecological perspective. *American Psychologist*, *47*(6), 723–9.

Taylor, A. R. (1991). Social competence and the early school transition: Risk and protective factors for African-American children. *Education and Urban Society*, *24*(1), 15–26.

Troop-Gordon, W., Visconti, K. J. and Kuntz, K. J. (2011). Perceived popularity during early adolescence: Links to declining school adjustment among aggressive youth. *The Journal of Early Adolescence*, *31*(1), 125–51.

Turner, J. C., Hogg, M. A., Oakes, P. J., Reicher, S. D. and Wetherell, M. S. (1987). *Rediscovering the social group.* Oxford: Basil Blackwell.

Wigfield, A., Eccles, J. S., MacIver, D., Reuman, D. A. and Midgley, C. (1991). Transitions during early adolescence: Changes in children's domain-specific self-perceptions and general self-esteem across the transition to junior high school. *Development Psychology*, *27*(4), 552–65.

PART V

Approaches to learning and academic performance

12

THE ROLE OF STUDENTS' SOCIAL IDENTITIES IN FOSTERING HIGH-QUALITY LEARNING IN HIGHER EDUCATION

Ana-Maria Bliuc, Peter Goodyear and Robert A. Ellis

> Ultimately, the supercomplex world presents not challenges of knowing but of *being*. Traditionally, the main emphasis has been on intellectual development; but this is no longer enough. The human being consists of three distinct domains: knowing, self-identity, and action.
>
> (Barnett, 1999, p. 157)

To respond more effectively to the challenges of a world that is becoming increasingly 'supercomplex' on many levels, contemporary higher education needs to reconsider its position in relation to student learning. Efforts to ensure that students are well equipped only in their knowledge and skills leave them vulnerable in other respects; simply focusing on how students learn seems not to be sufficient anymore. The idea that being a university student entails more than learning while, at the same time, learning can be seen as a product of the whole experience of being a student builds into the argument that genuine higher education must go beyond student learning to accommodate a view centred on *the student as a whole* (Barnett, 2007, 2009). This view of higher education distinguishes between ontological learning (i.e., understanding being) and epistemological learning (i.e., understanding knowledge), suggesting that the focus should shift towards the former by valuing the process of *being and becoming* the student. This implies growth at a more holistic level as well as formation and nurturing of a will to learn and understand that later translates into a lifelong journey of learning and discovery (Blackie, Case and Jawitz, 2010; McCune and Entwistle, 2011). Drawing on these ideas, the broader question that we address in this chapter is *how student learning can be understood in a more holistic way* that would include aspects of both epistemological and ontological learning. At the same time, we seek to go beyond Barnett's philosophical argument by addressing the applicability in practice of these ideas.

Traditional models of student learning have been quite effective in informing research designed to identify key practices that teachers can approach differently to help students achieve high-quality learning outcomes – primarily, teaching in student-centred ways. However, these models of student learning have not been so impressive in terms of providing solutions to improve learning outcomes from a student's perspective. In the student-centred approach to teaching, learning outcomes are considered mostly as resulting from high-quality teaching. From the perspective of the students, the quality of learning outcomes is generally seen as being linked to a range of diverse factors, which can be broadly divided into *sociological factors* (e.g., socio-economic status, education, family, high school performance; Tinto, 1975, 1993) and *individual factors* (e.g., abilities, dispositions, academic motivation, goals; Eccles and Wigfield, 2002; Robbins, Lauver, Le, Davis, Langley and Carlstrom, 2004). Most of these sets of factors are not very flexible and, therefore, difficult, if not impossible, to alter through teaching interventions. Thus, according to this view, teachers rather than students have the power and, indeed, the responsibility to increase the quality of student learning outcomes.

The argument that we propose here, however, is that the manner in which students experience learning at university is not solely determined by the quality of the unit design or the teacher's talent to engage the students. While student-centred approaches to teaching are certainly very valuable in ensuring a high quality of the overall learning experience, we believe that students can have a more prominent role in their own learning – a role that is shaped by their level of self-investment and self-motivation to be successful in their chosen career pathway. If our aim is to find solutions to increase the quality of both learning experiences and outcomes, we need to focus not only on enriching the student learning experience through approaches to teaching but also on identifying aspects that can empower students in shaping their own learning experiences at university. We argue that this can be achieved through approaching research on student learning in a more comprehensive and holistic way – one that highlights the interconnected roles of the actor (the student), context (the university) and process (the learning).

There are several models of student learning that view this as a complex, multidimensional and interrelational process (e.g., Biggs, 1978; Prosser and Trigwell, 1999). Barnett's argument elaborates some of these ideas. He sees the university as fundamentally a place where old identities are enriched and transformed and new identities emerge and are enacted (Barnett, 2009). That is, learning and identity can be seen as being perpetually interlinked and feeding on each other as learning changes identities and identity (including self-investment) changes how and what we learn. These identities, and how they evolve, are crucial not only in shaping how students learn at university, but also for how they later adjust to professional lives. The idea that the learner identity (Mentowski, 2000) and the self-image of the learner as part of the learning context (Mezirow, 1991) are key to understanding the complexity of student experiences of learning has been briefly discussed in the higher education literature (Blackie *et al.*, 2010).

To be able to provide a comprehensive and relational perspective that includes the three key factors that come into play (i.e., the process of learning, the context of learning and aspects that form the background for individual identities), we integrate concepts from the student learning literature in higher education with key concepts from social identity theory in social psychology (Tajfel and Turner, 1979; Turner, Hogg, Oakes, Reicher and Wetherell, 1987).

By exploring the implications of interdisciplinary research that brings together ideas from both education and psychology, we propose a model of student learning at university that acknowledges that the quality of learning experience is shaped not only by the direct learning experiences of students, but also by factors such as student social identity (salient in a learning context). Further practical implications for educational designers and academics can be drawn on at least two levels.

1. *Quality of learning*
   Current models of learning suggest that one key way in which the quality of learning might be increased is by encouraging a deep approach to learning through supporting students to develop more cohesive conceptions about what they are learning and vice versa (for a review, see Prosser and Trigwell, 1999). To these, we seek to strengthen the role of student social identity in contributing to the quality of learning and learning outcomes. For example, by understanding how student social identity relates to learning (and how learning relates to student social identification) in the context of higher education, we can further explore ways of improving the quality of learning experience through the careful design of learning programmes that integrate identity and broader contextual issues in ways that are relevant for student learning.

2. *Psychological well-being and adjustment of students*
   Learning is part of university students' identity; but at the same time, the way students learn is influenced by their identity. Feelings of belonging to broader communities that share values, attitudes and beliefs have been shown to positively affect both learning and well-being (Bliuc, Ellis, Goodyear and Muntele Hendres, 2011a, 2011b; Iyer, Jetten, Tsivrikos, Postmes and Haslam, 2009). Understanding how these dimensions interconnect in university life can provide ways to design learning programmes with an increased awareness of students' psychological well-being.

To address these points further, the remainder of this chapter is structured into three sections. First, we briefly introduce the reader to one of the most widely used models of university student learning in education: the 3P model of student learning (Biggs and Tang, 2007; see also Smyth, Mavor, Platow and Grace, Chapter 13, this volume). Then we discuss the implications of findings from emerging research that adopts an interdisciplinary approach, strengthening the role of identity in the student experience of learning. Finally, integrating theory and evidence from across disciplines (Biggs and Tang, 2007; Bliuc *et al.*, 2011a,

2011b; Marton, 1981; Marton and Säljö, 1976, 1984; Prosser and Trigwell, 1999; Tajfel and Turner, 1979; Trigwell and Prosser, 1991; Turner *et al.*, 1987), we discuss the associations between learning outcomes, social identity and learning approaches, allowing us to focus on knowing, being/becoming and doing. Emphasising the associations amongst these variables connects outcomes to multiple sociological and individual factors so that student learning can be understood as part of an integrated system of knowledge, identity and behaviour.

How students learn: understanding student learning from the perspective of the relational student learning framework

Learning can be seen as a change in the way we conceptualise the world around us. The concept of approaches to learning: 'describes a qualitative aspect of learning. It is about how people experience and organise the subject matter of a task; it is about "what" and "how" they learn' (Ramsden, 2003, p. 41). The ways in which students approach learning are not seen as being dictated by fixed student characteristics, but, rather, they reflect *how* students learn at any given time, for a particular task.

To capture the dynamic relationships between 'student factors' and contextual factors of learning, Biggs (1978; see also Biggs and Tang, 2007) proposed the '3P model of student learning'. The model (see Figure 12.1) describes three connected aspects of the student experience:

1. *presage*: includes prior knowledge and learning experiences, current understandings of concepts and content, and contextual factors that shape learning (i.e., course design, teaching methods and assessment);
2. *process*: includes students' perceptions of their learning context and how they go about their learning (i.e., their approaches to learning);
3. *product*: refers to the outcomes from the experience of learning.

The 3P model is a dynamic model where the context of learning, approaches to learning and learning outcomes are all interrelated and influence each other through bidirectional relationships that play out over time. To be more specific, this model assumes that the *context of learning* is linked to students' approaches to learning which are seen as a function of students' learning orientation and their perceptions of the learning task. At the same time, perceptions of context (i.e., learning task) are influenced by contextual factors such as prior and current experiences of learning (Duff, Boyle, Dunleavy and Ferguson, 2004).

Student approaches to learning have also been shown to be significantly associated to learning outcomes, with qualitatively better approaches being linked to academic success and to more elaborate and coherent conceptions of learning (Marton and Säljö, 1976, 1984; Prosser and Trigwell, 1999). Many studies across different disciplinary areas have identified a clear association between the quality of the approaches to learning adopted by students and their

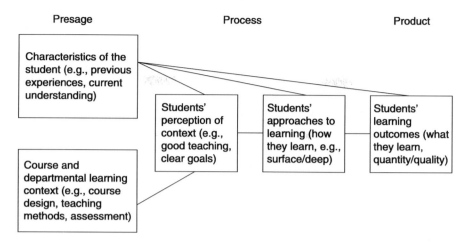

FIGURE 12.1   Biggs' 3P model of student learning

Source: Trigwell and Prosser (1997). Copyright © HERDSA, reprinted by permission of Taylor & Francis Ltd, www.tandfonline.com on behalf of HERDSA.

learning outcomes (e.g., Diseth, 2003, 2007; Diseth and Martinsen, 2003; Drew and Watkins, 1998; Entwistle and Ramsden, 1983; Swanberg and Martinsen, 2010; Trigwell and Prosser, 1991). The research distinguishes between deep, surface and strategic approaches to learning. A deep approach is characterised by attempts to understand the purpose of a task and to engage in higher-order thinking, with the aim of learning for understanding. Surface and strategic approaches typically fail to engage with the pedagogical purpose of a learning task as students focus on remembering surface details or optimising the balance between marks and effort. Deep approaches are empirically associated with higher-quality learning outcomes while surface approaches are associated with lesser-quality outcomes.

While the 3P model of student learning takes into consideration student factors (e.g., individual experiences of learning), little research has explored the interplay between aspects of student identity (or disciplinary social identification) and how these might relate to qualitatively different experiences of learning at university. By emphasising the variable of student social identity in the experience of learning at university, we hope to be able to provide a more complete perspective on student learning, a perspective that can lead to practical applications to support the achievement of high-quality learning outcomes. In the next section, we discuss some conceptual implications of applying social identity theory to student learning at university. Then, we focus on describing, in more detail, research that directly applies a social identity approach to education.

Integrating social identity theory and relational student learning research

Goodenow suggests that an ecologically valid psychology of education should include an integration between students' social identity and aspects of their learning:

> Though concepts of self and identity are receiving increased attention, research in educational psychology may benefit from exploring more explicitly the links between students' self-categorizations and group identities, on the one hand, and their behaviour, motivation and learning on the other. Research investigating the multiple meanings of social identities, and the factors that increase or decrease the salience of those dimensions of identity, may be an important part of the agenda for psychologists concerned with education.
>
> (1992, p. 182)

The research that we discuss here can be seen as a response to Goodenow's suggestion as it applies the concept of social identification – with its implications for group behaviour within the context of student learning in higher education. By using both the social identity approach and the relational student learning frameworks to explore university learning, the traditional focus of the latter on relationships between different aspects of learning is expanded to include subjective dimensions of (collective) self-definition as a student of a specific discipline at university (Cameron, 1999).

This approach to student learning is built around the concept of student identity as a *social identity* that encompasses those aspects of individuals' self-image that derive from meaningful social categories or groups to which he or she perceives himself or herself as belonging, together with the value and emotional significance attached to that category or group membership (Tajfel, 1981; Tajfel and Turner, 1979). The social identity approach to learning allows us to focus on powerful collective dynamics that are deeply interlinked to both context and enactment/ action. Within social identity theory, social identities have the adaptive function of producing social behaviour and attitudes (Turner, 1984). Research in various fields, including organisational and health psychology, shows that the way in which people define themselves as group members (a social identity) is central to understanding attitudes and behaviours (Ashforth and Mael, 1989; Jussim *et al.*, 2001) and is associated with psychological well-being and adjustment (Haslam *et al.*, 2009; Iyer *et al.*, 2009). A key proposition that we discuss here is whether the way in which students identify with different social categories at university (disciplinary or broader) contributes to qualitative variations in their experiences of learning.

Research by Bizumic, Reynolds, Turner, Bromhead and Subasic (2009) on the impact of school social identification on students' levels of psychological well-being indicates that social identification is connected to how students experience stress, positive affect, self-esteem, aggression and victimisation. Other examples of research that explores the effect of social identification with a learning community on the psychological well-being of students are studies by Cameron (1999), conducted in the context of learning at university. This research shows that the relationship between identification with the university student social category and well-being is mediated by self-esteem and perceptions of group efficacy. Such studies offer some insight into the usefulness of the social identity framework in relation to applications to education and, more specifically, to learning in the context of schools and universities.

Cross-disciplinary research that builds directly on the 3P model by applying principles of the social identity approach to learning at university examines the role of student social identity in relation to how students approach their learning and how these approaches are reflected in their learning outcomes (Bliuc *et al.*, 2011a, 2011b). In several studies across cultural and disciplinary contexts, we show that deep approaches to learning are positively associated with students' social identification as university students and that they positively predict academic achievement. At the same time, surface approaches to learning are negatively associated with students' social identification and negatively predict academic achievement. The mediational roles of deep and surface approaches to learning in the relationship between student social identity and academic achievement have also been explored. These findings indicate that for university students, strong social identification with the discipline tends to be linked to behaviours that are highly normative in a learning context (i.e., strong engagement with the disciplinary content), which is ultimately reflected in the type and the quality of approaches to learning that the students adopt.

This research shows that deep approaches to learning mediate the relationship between student social identity and learning outcomes; specifically, student social identification affects the quality of learning outcomes through its effect on deep approaches to learning (Bliuc *et al.*, 2011a). This finding is important at a practical level. It shows that by understanding how student identities are constructed and how they relate to what students *do* in the context of learning at university, we can effectively help students adopt qualitatively superior approaches to learning, thereby improving the quality and outcomes of their learning. In other words, looking at ways to increase disciplinary social identification can constitute an alternative route to improving the quality of learning – compared with the option of improving learning merely through teaching approaches. These studies highlight the value of integrating cross-disciplinary perspectives to further advance the understanding of student learning at university as they provide evidence of the interconnectedness between students' social identities in the context of learning at university and the ways in which they approach their learning, indirectly affecting the quality of learning outcomes.

Following on from the idea that changes in disciplinary identification can lead to changes in the quality of learning, there is existing research that indicates that this is, in fact, a viable option to pursue. Platow, Mavor and Grace (2013) propose a dynamic model, based on longitudinal research, where deep approaches to learning at Time

1 (semester 1 of the academic year) predict students' social identification with the discipline at Time 2 (semester 2). According to this model, an intrinsic interest in the discipline can lead to students adopting deep approaches to learning which, in the longer term, would produce a change at the level of their disciplinary self-concept (a stronger sense of disciplinary identity).

These two streams of research on student learning from a social identity perspective point to a circular relationship between student social identity, approaches to learning, and learning outcomes, with alternative pathways that indicate that student social identity can be both a predictor and an outcome of deep learning approaches. It is plausible that students in first-year units have emerging disciplinary student identities, and it is their interest in the subject that determines the quality of their learning approaches. As their disciplinary student identities further develop in the following years (through deep approaches to learning but possibly through other mechanisms), approaches to learning will also be shaped by students' shared disciplinary identity.

Research by Smyth, Mavor, Platow, Grace and Reynolds (2015; Smyth, Mavor, Platow and Grace, this volume), building on evidence from both these bodies of work, adds another layer of complexity to the picture painted so far by highlighting the importance of the meaning that students give to the groups they identify with. To be more specific, they found that student social identification with the discipline predicted student approaches in a range of different disciplines but, significantly, that perceived student norms moderated the effect. Thus, if the norms that students associate with a specific disciplinary identity are seen as promoting learning, it is more likely that students who strongly identify with the discipline will adopt deep approaches to learning.

Based on research to date, the emerging associations between key variables in a relational model of student learning (Biggs and Tang, 2007; Prosser and Trigwell, 1999) and the theoretical ideas drawn from the social identity approach (Turner et al., 1987) seem to be the *student* (as identity and enactment of identity), the *context* (as learning at university), and *student learning* (as learning approaches and outcomes), with different plausible causal pathways between them (see Figure 12.2). In Figure 12.2, disciplinary student social identity is situated in a central position in relation to learning outcomes and approaches because, as research shows, it plays an integrative role in the process of learning by linking approaches to learning and context (e.g., having a student of a specific discipline at a particular university) to the outcomes of learning.

Some implications of adopting an integrative approach to understanding student learning at university

Our proposed approach to research on student university learning represents a timely response to recent (and increasing) concerns about the future of higher education in the twenty-first century raised by prominent scholars in the field (see Barnett, 2007, 2009; McCune and Entwistle, 2011). In terms of theory

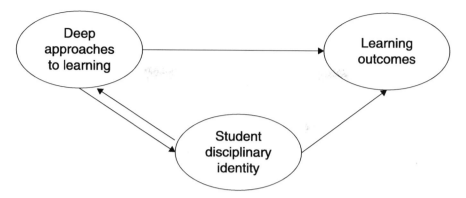

FIGURE 12.2   Relational pathways between student disciplinary identity, deep learning approaches, and learning outcomes

development, by understanding the role of student disciplinary social identity in learning more clearly, dimensions of the context of student learning can be investigated (e.g., how identity issues relate to lifelong learning, adjustment and psychological well-being; Cameron, 1999; Haslam *et al.*, 2009). From a more applied perspective, the findings of this research can help formulate specific principles and advice on improving the overall quality of the student learning experience at the university.

Moving to the implications of fostering strong student identities in the context of studying at the university, previous research has already found consistent evidence that the self-concept in the context of learning at different academic levels (i.e., secondary and tertiary levels) is central not only to the quality of learning but also to the mental health, stress levels and psychological well-being of students (Bizumic *et al.*, 2009; Cameron, 1999). Thus, in creating a strong sense of belongingness to a broader academic or disciplinary community, there are benefits to be gained in terms of quality of learning and contributing to a smooth adjustment to life as a university student (see also in this volume, Cruwys, Gaffney and Skipper, Chapter 11 and Reynolds, Subasic, Lee and Bromhead, Chapter 3).

In terms of further applications to improve the relevance and quality of university learning, the consistent finding that social identity and deep approaches to learning are dynamically interconnected suggests that higher levels of student engagement can be achieved by integrating learning activities that are linked to the actual professions. Thus, we suggest that learning tasks that are designed in alignment with career pathways and activities associated with specific degrees are likely to be more successful in achieving high-quality learning outcomes than perhaps the more traditional activities designed to simply consolidate basic concepts and the understanding of various theoretical perspectives. An approach to designing learning activities that ensures alignment between disciplinary student social identity and expected learning outcomes is likely to be beneficial in improving the quality of learning (ensuring that more students adopt qualitatively superior approaches to learning) as well as providing students with the basis for professional social identities that they could later fully adopt in their working lives. In this sense, a specific student social identity (social identification with the discipline of study) can be seen as acting as a transitory identity to a fully fledged professional identity.

At the same time, learning activities that bolster intrinsic interest in the discipline are important as they can ensure that curious, motivated students stay curious and motivated and, most importantly, come to see themselves in terms of specific disciplinary social identities. The fact that social identity seems to be the key factor that is closely related to learning approaches suggests that, ultimately, students' sense of who they are and where they want to be (i.e., their social identity, along with the values, beliefs and behaviours that it encapsulates) will shape their learning experience and outcomes in ways that are perhaps more powerful than teaching interventions that are not conceived from the student perspective.

To return to Barnett's quote from the beginning of this chapter, in the context of learning in and for a supercomplex world, student social identity provides an important bridge between 'knowing' and 'action'. That is, to understand student behaviour in the context of learning and, more importantly, post-university behaviour (i.e., developing pathways to professional careers), we need to recognise the importance of developing strong student social identities which are fully integrated with the experience of learning. Student social identities are transient, but this does not undermine their importance. A key point here is that student social identities evolve and become more sophisticated, enabling the transition from knowing about a subject to being a practitioner of that subject.

References

Ashford, B. E. and Mael, F. (1989). Social identity theory and the organization, *Academy of Management Review, 14*(1), 20–39.

Barnett, R. (1999). *Realizing the university in an age of supercomplexity.* Buckingham: Society for Research into Higher Education and the Open University Press.

Barnett, R. (2007). *A will to learn.* Maidenhead, UK: Society for Research into Higher Education and the Open University Press.

Barnett, R. (2009). Knowing and becoming in higher education. *Studies in Higher Education, 34*(4), 429–40.

Biggs, J. B. (1978). Individual and group differences in study processes. *British Journal of Educational Psychology, 48*(3), 266–79.

Biggs, J. B. and Tang, C. (2007). *Teaching for quality learning at university: What the student does* (3rd ed.). Maidenhead, UK: Open University Press.

Bizumic, B., Reynolds, K. J., Turner, J. C., Bromhead, D. and Subasic, E. (2009). The role of the group in individual functioning: School identification and the psychological well-being of staff and students. *Applied Psychology, 58*(1), 171–92.

Blackie, M. A., Case, J. M. and Jawitz, J. (2010). Student-centredness: The link between transforming students and transforming ourselves. *Teaching in Higher Education, 15*(6), 637–46.

Bliuc, A.-M., Ellis, R. A., Goodyear, P. and Muntele Hendres, D. (2011a). The role of social identification as a university student in learning: Relationships between students' social identity, approaches to learning, and academic achievement. *Educational Psychology, 31*(5), 559–75.

Bliuc, A.-M., Ellis, R. A., Goodyear, P. and Muntele Hendres, D. (2011b). Understanding student learning in context: Relationships between social identity, perceptions of the learning community, approaches to learning and academic performance. *European Journal of Psychology of Education, 26*(3), 417–33.

Cameron, J. (1999). Social identity and the pursuit of possible selves: Implications for the psychological well-being of university students. *Group Dynamics, 3*(3), 179–89.

Diseth, Å. (2003). Personality and approaches to learning as predictors of academic achievement. *European Journal of Personality, 17*(2), 143–55.

Diseth, Å. (2007). Approaches to learning, course experience and examination grade among undergraduate psychology students: Testing of mediator effects and construct validity. *Studies in Higher Education, 32*(3), 373–88.

Diseth, Å. and Martinsen, Ø. L. (2003). Approaches to learning, cognitive style, and motives as predictors of academic achievement. *Educational Psychology, 23*(2), 195–207.

Drew, P. Y. and Watkins, D. (1998). Affective variables, learning approaches and academic achievement: A causal modelling investigation with Hong Kong tertiary students. *British Journal of Educational Psychology, 68*(2), 173–88.

Duff, A., Boyle, E., Dunleavy, K. and Ferguson, J. (2004). The relationship between personality, approach to learning and academic performance. *Personality and Individual Differences, 36*(8), 1907–20.

Eccles, J. S. and Wigfield, A. (2002). Motivational beliefs, values, and goals. *Annual Review of Psychology, 53*, 109–32.

Entwistle, N. J. and Ramsden, P. (1983). *Understanding student learning.* London: Croom Helm.

Goodenow, C. (1992). Strengthening the links between educational psychology and the study of social contexts. *Educational Psychologist, 27*(2), 177–96. Reprinted by permission of the publisher (Taylor & Francis Ltd.)

Haslam, S. A., Jetten, J., Postmes, T. and Haslam, C. (2009). Social identity, health and well-being: An emerging agenda for applied psychology. *Applied Psychology, 58*(1), 1–23.

Iyer, A., Jetten, J., Tsivrikos, D., Postmes, T. and Haslam, S. A. (2009). The more (and the more compatible) the merrier: Multiple group memberships and identity compatibility as predictors of adjustment after life transitions. *British Journal of Social Psychology, 48*(4), 707–33.

Jussim, L., Ashmore, R. and Wilder, D. (2001). Introduction: Social identity and intergroup conflict. In R. D. Ashmore, L. Jussim and D. Wilder (Eds), *Social identity, intergroup conflict, and conflict resolution* (pp. 3–14). Oxford: Oxford University Press.

McCune, V. and Entwistle, N. (2011). Cultivating the disposition to understand in 21st century university education. *Learning and Individual Differences, 21*(3), 303–10.

Marton, F. (1981). Phenomenography: Describing conceptions of the world around us. *Instructional Science, 10*(2), 177–200.

Marton, F. and Säljö, R. (1976). On qualitative differences in learning: I. Outcome and process. *British Journal of Educational Psychology, 46*(1), 4–11.

Marton, F. and Säljö, R. (1984). Approaches to learning. In F. Marton, D. J. Hounsell and N. J. Entwistle (Eds), *The experience of learning* (pp. 36–55). Edinburgh: Scottish Academic Press.

Mentowski, M. (2000). *Learning that lasts: Integrating learning, development, and performance in college and beyond.* San Francisco: Jossey-Bass.

Mezirow, J. (1991). *Transformative dimensions of adult learning.* San Francisco, CA: Jossey-Bass.

Platow, M., Mavor, K. and Grace, D. (2013). On the role of discipline-related self-concept in deep and surface approaches to learning among university students. *Instructional Science, 41*(2), 271–85.

Prosser, M. and Trigwell, K. (1999). *Understanding learning and teaching: The experience in higher education.* Buckingham: Society for Research into Higher Education and the Open University Press.

Ramsden, P. (2003). *Learning to teach in higher education.* London: Routledge.

Robbins, S. B., Lauver, K., Le, H., Davis, D., Langley, R. and Carlstrom, A. (2004). Do psychosocial and study skill factors predict college outcomes? A meta-analysis. *Psychological Bulletin, 130*(2), 261–88.

Smyth, L., Mavor, K. I., Platow, M. J., Grace, D. M. and Reynolds, K. J. (2015). Discipline social identification, study norms and learning approach in university students. *Educational Psychology, 35*(1), 53–72.

Swanberg, A. B. and Martinsen, Ø. L. (2010). Personality, approaches to learning and achievement. *Educational Psychology, 30*(1), 75–88.

Tajfel, H. (1981). *Human groups and social categories: Studies in social psychology.* Cambridge: Cambridge University Press.

Tajfel, H. and Turner, J. C. (1979). An integrative theory of inter-group conflict. In W. G. Austin and S. Worchel (Eds), *The social psychology of intergroup relations* (pp. 33–47). Monterey, CA: Brooks/Cole.

Tinto, V. (1975). Dropout from higher education: A theoretical synthesis of recent research. *Review of Educational Research, 45*(1), 89–125.

Tinto, V. (1993). *Leaving college: Rethinking the cause and cures of student attrition* (2nd ed.). Chicago, IL: University of Chicago.

Trigwell, K. and Prosser, M. (1997). Towards an understanding of individual acts of teaching and learning. *Higher Education Research and Development, 16*(2), 241–52.

Trigwell, K. and Prosser, M. (1991). Improving the quality of student learning: The influence of learning context and student approaches to learning on learning outcomes. *Higher Education, 22*(3), 251–66.

Turner, J. C. (1984). Social identification and psychological group formation. In H. Tajfel (Ed.), *The social dimension*, Vol. 2. Cambridge: Cambridge University Press.

Turner, J. C., Hogg, M. A., Oakes, P. J., Reicher, S. and Wetherell, M. S. (1987). *Rediscovering the social group: A self-categorization theory.* Oxford: Blackwell.

13

UNDERSTANDING SOCIAL IDENTITY IN EDUCATION

The modifying role of perceived norms

Lillian Smyth, Kenneth I. Mavor, Michael J. Platow and Diana M. Grace

This chapter discusses the modifying effects that norms and group-based social influence processes have on the role of social identity in education. In particular, we discuss the way norms and social identity apply to the role of social influence in determining the learning approaches used by students. In simple terms, the work to be discussed draws together the emerging literature on social identification and learning approaches (Bliuc, Ellis, Goodyear and Hendres, 2011a, 2011b; Platow, Mavor and Grace, 2013) and existing literature on the self-categorisation theory analyses of social influence (Turner, 1991). The first of these bodies of work is built mainly on two streams of work, led by Bliuc and Platow, respectively (Bliuc *et al.*, 2011a, 2011b; Platow *et al.*, 2013). This work demonstrates the predictive value of discipline-related social identification in examining student learning approaches. These authors find a positive relationship between stronger student discipline-related social identification and a more fruitful approach to learning (see also Bliuc, Goodyear and Ellis, Chapter 12, this volume). Building on these analyses, we explore a dynamic, normative conceptualisation of student social identities to examine the normative-influence processes that determine the ways in which students approach learning. We propose an understanding of student self-concept based on the use of a self-categorisation theory (SCT) in which perceived norms modify the impact of social identification on student behaviour (Turner, 1991).

In line with that of Bliuc *et al.* (this volume), our analysis of student learning behaviour is driven by the concept of learning approaches. These 'approaches' are characterised in the literature as ways the learner can relate to the material to be learned (Biggs, 1979). These are the ways a learner experiences and organises the subject matter. The approach adopted can differ across learners, tasks and contexts (Ramsden, 2003). Learning approaches can be broadly divided into two types (described in in more detail below): deep learning (e.g., engaged, integrative, broad) and surface learning (e.g., rote memorisation; Biggs, 1999). They are, in essence, a typology of learning intentions, strategies and behaviours.

These approaches are, in the education literature, determined by a combination of student-specific (e.g., personality, motivation) and learning-context (e.g., assessment structure, workload) factors. This person-by-situation analysis of what drives learning approaches accounts quite well for much of the variation in student experience and actions (Baeten, Kyndt, Struyven and Dochy, 2010; Herman, 1995; Kek, Darmawan and Chen, 2007; Ramsden, 2003; Struyven, Dochy, Janssens and Gielen, 2006; Trigwell and Prosser, 1991; Yan and Kember, 2004). As such, it is necessary to consider what value the addition of social and normative-influence processes to educational models might have. We would argue that, where the traditional learning approach literature has accounted for both student attributes and the consequences of structural aspects of the tertiary learning experience, it has not yet fully explored the impact of other students and the student's own perceptions of them. In a face-to-face, course-based learning environment, mutual influence among students is inevitable. Further, this influence is dynamic and active throughout the learning process.

The aforementioned work linking discipline-related social identification and learning approaches (Bliuc *et al.*, 2011a, 2011b; Platow *et al.*, 2013) is an important advance towards fuller understanding of the student experience. What we aim to consider here, however, is an elaboration of this relationship between discipline-based identities and learning approaches, such that the norms students perceive to belong to their discipline are also considered. Using what we know from social-psychological research on the relationships between social identity, norms and behaviour (e.g., Baker, Little and Brownell, 2003; Hagger and Chatzisarantis, 2005; Louis, Davies, Smith and Terry, 2007), we can build a picture of whether and how these approaches are impacted by social normative processes among students.

A social understanding of tertiary education

The focus of this volume is on the role for social identity in models of education. The current chapter frames discussion in terms of adult education in the context of tertiary education (although some of the broader ideas discussed in the chapter also apply to other levels of education). To unpack the relevance of social identity to this educational context, it is necessary to consider the intentions of tertiary education. Drawing on existing literature, the nature of most tertiary education is such that it has three clear, yet non-independent, aims: (a) to prepare, train and impart relevant knowledge and 'marketable skills' (Mitchell and Forer, 2010, p. 78) to students for their intended profession or career; (b) to socialise the new generation into academia and the professional world (Mauranen, 2009); and (c) to develop self-direction, critical thinking and the capacity to understand (Watkins, 1982). We would argue that each of these aims can be conceptualised as a social process, susceptible to social influence to some degree. As such, we make a claim for a dynamic, social conceptualisation of tertiary education. In our view, all three of these aims are fundamentally associated with student self-concepts and their real and perceived relationships to others. The first of these aims reminds us that education serves as a method of preparing students for a career of their choosing. In selecting a career path and working towards acquiring the necessary skills, students are choosing an ideal self-image and a social role they intend to take on in a professional context. Thus, skill acquisition is a step on the path to changing themselves into a particular *self* with a particular social role.

The second aim (socialising new generations into the professional and academic world) is more explicitly social: teaching students to understand professional identities, norms and intergroup relationships. The third aim is about building agency and self-direction in students. The goal is to foster an understanding of the self that allows the student to solve problems, take initiative and think critically. This is a matter of socially driven self-perception as well as a socialisation process. In fostering students' self-direction and critical thinking, educators are encouraging students to see themselves (to self-categorise) as someone who has the skills and knowledge to adapt to their academic discipline. Further, the understanding of what it means to 'be critical' or 'solve problems' will depend on the norms of the particular social group (in this case, the relevant academic community). As demonstrated above in terms of the identified aims of tertiary education, who the students think they are and which groups they think they belong to is central to the experience of being tertiary students.

Further, challenges to effective teaching have arisen in tertiary education in response to the ever-increasing number of students and the ever-broadening range of student ability, background and prior knowledge. Traditional learning formats, such as the lecture/tutorial model, worked well for small groups of rigorously selected students in the past but no longer meet the needs of many tertiary students in a more accessible learning community (Biggs, 1999). What is needed is a reform of the way in which educators approach teaching and learning; and the concept of social identity has something to offer, both practically and theoretically, to this reform. Indeed, what can be seen throughout this volume is a synthesis of educational and social-psychological models that will allow for greater understanding of the processes at play and the practical avenues available for influencing students to engage in desirable learning behaviours.

The learning process

Before considering the social processes at play in learning, however, we must consider the existing literature on learning in a tertiary context. Biggs (1989) conceptualised learning in terms of the '3 Ps': *presage*, *procedure* and *product* (see also Bliuc *et al.*, this volume). In this model, learning is conceptualised, broadly, as a three-stage process. These stages divide the process into three categories: things that happen prior to, during and after learning. This model is the foundation of the learning approaches model in that the presage factors are expected to interact and produce a particular learning approach, or procedure. This learning approach then predicts the product, or outcome.

Presage

The first stage, the presage, is characterised as the factors that precede learning. These factors include both the properties of individual students and the structure and content of the learning context. For instance, conscientiousness has been demonstrated to bear a robust relation to both learning approaches and academic outcomes (Chamorro-Premuzic and Furnham, 2004, 2008; O'Connor and Paunonen, 2007; see also Monaghan and Bizumic, Chapter 14, this volume), and there is also some evidence that extraversion should predict deeper learning approaches (e.g., McManus, Keeling and Paice, 2004). Higher age is generally found to be a positive predictor of deep learning approaches and a negative predictor of surface learning approaches (e.g., Richardson, 1994). Gender effects often indicate that female students are more likely to report a deeper learning approach (e.g., Watkins and Hattie, 1981; alternatively, see Sadler-Smith, 1996). Some studies find that students from non-English-speaking backgrounds favour deeper learning approaches (Johnston, 2001), while other literature suggests that these students may favour a more surface-oriented approach (Bilbow, 1989). Some studies suggest that later-year students (as opposed to first-year students) may take deeper approaches (Newble and Clarke, 1986). Others suggest that, particularly in the sciences, a more surface-oriented approach is common in later years of study (Zeegus, 2001).

From a more environment-focused standpoint, there is literature considering ways to structure the learning context to maximise deep learning approaches. At a contextual level, factors can be broadly divided into dimensions that vary by discipline and structural variations. Discipline variations take the form of trends in delivery, content and class types (Kember and Leung, 2011; Laird, Shoup, Kuh and Schwarz, 2008; Lindblom-Ylänne, Trigwell, Nevgi and Ashwin, 2006; Neumann, Parry and Becher, 2002). Research has indicated there is substantive variation in style of teaching (Lindblom-Ylänne *et al.*, 2006), method of teaching, preparation time, hours of contact and research involvement (Neumann, 2001) as well in as the typical kinds of tasks involved in studying in a discipline (Ramsden, 2003).[1]

Structural variations refer to deliberate programmatic differences in class structure, such as using a problem-based learning approach (e.g., Norman and Schmidt, 1992) or structuring assessment as a learning portfolio (e.g., Zubizarreta, 2009). A key model in the area of course structure variation is the Biggs and Tang (2007b) model of constructive alignment, which focuses on ensuring a match between intended learning outcomes, learning activities and assessment. In this understanding, the impact of context is less contingent on variations in delivery and more dependent on a deliberate intellectual effort on the part of the educator to clarify and address intended learning outcomes. In a practical sense, this means: (1) generating clear, precise and measurable learning outcomes; (2) ensuring that learning activities address these learning outcomes; and (3) assessing student learning in such a way that students who have engaged in the activities and, therefore, achieved the learning outcomes will perform well (Biggs, 1999; Kember, 2009).

Procedure

The second stage of Biggs' conceptualisation – and the stage that is most pertinent to the current discussion – is the procedure stage, which captures the process and experience of learning. This was originally conceptualised simply as learning approaches, but it is here that the model has been developed to include social identity processes.

Learning approaches

The concept of learning approaches, originally proposed by Marton and Säljö (1976) and further developed by Biggs (1979, 1999), suggests that students relate to the task or subject material they are given in one of two ways: (1) engaging and seeking to understand intent and broader implications (i.e., deep learning approach) or (2) focusing on completion of task requirements and often resorting to memorisation (i.e., surface learning approach). This model has inspired a broad body of research on ways in which educators can shape these approaches and the relationships these approaches may have to crucial academic outcomes (e.g., Ramsden, 2003; Trigwell and Prosser, 1991; Zeegus, 2001).

In this literature, learning approaches themselves have been explored in depth (Baeten *et al.*, 2010; Biggs, 1979, 1999; Biggs, Kember and Leung, 2001; Biggs and Tang, 2007a, 2007b; Cassidy, 2004; Entwistle, 2000, 2005; Ramsden, 1991, 2003; Struyven *et al.*, 2006; Trigwell and Prosser, 1991; Walsh, 2007; Yan and Kember, 2004; Zeegus, 2001). Fundamentally, a learning 'approach' (as distinct from a learning 'style') is understood as something a student adopts, not something a student has. It is conceptually limited to a particular situation with a particular task. The approach is a way of organising, understanding and relating to a task (Biggs, 1999).

Students are described as adopting a *deep approach* to learning when focused on the intended learning outcomes of the task and how new information fits into their existing knowledge frameworks. In tertiary education students, this kind of approach is characterised by active integration of new knowledge, thinking critically, referring to a wide range of resources and questioning conclusions. In contrast, tertiary education students described as adopting a *surface approach* focus on completing task requirements and memorising what is necessary in the most efficient way possible. This kind of learning is generally characterised by a focus on isolated facts, rote memorisation strategies and selective information processing (Newble and Entwistle, 1986).

Product

The product stage, the final stage of Biggs' model, is described as the end product of education: the outcomes. As might be suggested by the kinds of learning activities associated with each approach, learning approaches have divergent impacts on both learning and academic outcomes. Deeper learning approaches are commonly associated with more positive educational outcomes, including development of professional identity, intention to continue study, long-term information retention and academic achievement level (e.g., Artino, Rochelle and Durning, 2010; Biggs, 1979; Lizzio, Wilson and Simons, 2002; Platow *et al.*, 2013; Richardson, Abraham and Bond, 2012; Walsh, 2007).

Learning approaches may also predict student perceptions of the course, overall course satisfaction and views of teaching quality (Lizzio *et al.*, 2002). This influence is a useful relationship to consider for two reasons. First, universities seek to maximise positive student experiences of courses, and, second, there is evidence that course satisfaction is related to higher grades and better long-term information retention (Ramsden, 1991).

Another valuable product of interest can be derived from modern pedagogical theory that suggests tertiary education should help initiate the student into a community of practice, not just transmit necessary knowledge to them (e.g., Barrie, 2006; O'Donnell and Tobbell, 2007). For this reason, intentions to continue to engage with this community (e.g., by continuing study, seeking relevant employment or finding out more about relevant topics) should also be considered an important academic outcome.

Social identity, norms and behaviour

Given that much of this literature is focused on predictors and consequences of particular learning behaviours and that we currently seek to unpack the social aspects of this process, we now turn to the relationship between social identity, norms and students' behaviours. Within social identity theory, an individual can be more or less identified with a particular group membership (e.g., van Rijswijk, Haslam and Ellemers, 2006). Identification is broadly conceptualised as the extent to which membership of a group, and the cognitive and emotional consequences of that membership, are central to self-perception (e.g., Cameron, 2004). The strength of this identification is a product of both the extent to which the identity is self-defining and the extent to which the individual is invested in this perception of himself or herself (Cameron, 2004; Leach *et al.*, 2008). This concept of strength of identification becomes particularly pertinent when we begin to consider the affective and behavioural impact social identities might have and the way in which identities can be used as a means of social influence.

Turner (1991) proposes a mechanism for identity-based social influence using this concept of social identification. This model, developed as an elaboration of self-categorisation theory (SCT; Turner, Hogg, Oakes, Reicher and Wetherell, 1987), proposes that when individuals perceive themselves as a members of a group (i.e., incorporate a social identity into their self-concept) and that identity is psychologically salient, they perceive themselves not as a unique individuals but, rather, as interchangeable members of the group. This perception carries with it a consequent internalisation of group prototypes, stereotypes, and cognitive, affective and behavioural norms. The stronger the identification becomes, the more these stereotypes and norms become central to the self and influence future behaviour.

The net effect of this is that every time an individual thinks of himself or herself as an 'engineering student' or a 'lawyer in training' or a 'member of the Monday-night tutorial' or even a 'night-before-the-exam crammer', these self-perceptions carry with them an understanding of a shared normative framework and regulations for what that means and ways 'people like me' behave (e.g., Haslam, Turner, Oakes, Reynolds and Doosje, 2002). This process is the mechanism through which social identification and group membership is thought to influence behaviour.

This model is both theoretically and practically important in that it provides one of the few available theoretical vectors from group membership to behaviour. This understanding allows us to disentangle instances of 'groupthink' (Turner, Pratkanis, Probasco and Leve, 1992), to promote sustainable organisational outcomes (Haslam, Powell and Turner, 2000), to disentangle intergroup conflict (Livingstone and Haslam, 2008) and to understand aspects of political influence (Greene, 2004). It also allows us to consider practical means for fostering collective action for positive social change (Bliuc, McGarty, Reynolds and Muntele, 2006; Haslam et al., 2002; McGarty, Bliuc, Thomas and Bongiorno, 2009; Musgrove and McGarty, 2008; Thomas, McGarty and Mavor, 2009a, 2009b) as well as methods of intervention to promote prosocial behaviour (Stürmer, Snyder and Omoto, 2005), healthy eating (e.g., Baker et al., 2003) and healthy eating intentions (Louis et al., 2007), and exercise behaviour (e.g., Hagger and Chatzisarantis, 2005), and environmental responsibility (e.g., littering: Kallgren, Reno and Cialdini, 2000; recycling: Terry, Hogg and White, 1999). This current volume aims to extend this literature into the domain of education.

Social identification and deep learning approaches

Previously, Bliuc et al. (2011a, 2011b; see also the chapter in this volume) have examined discipline-related social identity as a predictor of both learning approaches and academic achievement. The findings from their studies indicate that deep learning approaches are associated with better academic outcomes, and stronger identification with the discipline is associated with a deep learning approach. As hypothesised, there is also a significant indirect effect so that the relationship between discipline-related social identity and academic outcomes is mediated by the learning approach adopted by students.

In a parallel development, Platow et al. (2013) explored the relationship among social identification, learning approach and grades with a particular focus on the changes in self-concept associated with a course of study when adopting deep learning approaches. They argued that those who take a deep learning approach may experience a consequent change in their self-concept over time and have a stronger sense of shared social identity with other students in the same course or discipline. Reciprocally, they argued that those who identify more strongly as a student in their discipline may develop a stronger intrinsic interest in the course content as they are likely to perceive themselves as sharing the normative interests of students in the same discipline. The result of this stronger perceived interest would be a deep approach to learning. Platow *et al.*'s (2013) proposed model is, thus, a dynamic, cross-lagged one in which the discipline-related social identity and learning approach are related to each other and are reciprocally influential over time. Their data provided partial support for the model in that deeper learning approaches at Time 1 predicted increased identification levels, but the opposite path (Time 1 identification predicting changes in deeper learning approaches) was not significant.

Both the Bliuc *et al.* and Platow *et al.* models explore the relationships between discipline social identification and deep learning approaches, and their combined impact on outcomes. We currently build on these models in a key way. At a basic level, we take a more complex view of discipline social identification by taking account of what that identity *means* to its members. In a practical sense, that involves exploring the nature and strength of the norms that group members perceive as applying to the group as a whole as well as the impact these norms have on behaviour.

Using the SCT analysis of social influence as an organising framework, we suggest that the effect of group social identification (e.g., a shared discipline-based identity) on learning behaviour should be partially determined by the norms perceived to apply to the group in question. This model is one that the current authors have explored in a series of studies conducted in real-world academic contexts (e.g., Smyth, Mavor, Platow, Grace and Reynolds, 2015). These studies examine relationships between discipline-related social identification, perceived norms, learning approaches and outcomes, both at a single time point and longitudinally. Findings are supportive of the previous literature on identity in education (Bliuc *et al.*, 2011a, 2011b; Platow *et al.*, 2013) and, further, provide evidence for the proposed role of perceived norms. For the purposes of this chapter, we summarise the findings.

Discipline-based norms and learning approaches

Taken together, the line of work we have been doing has yielded three key findings pertinent to the current discussion. First, discipline social identification remains a positive predictor of deep learning approaches and a negative predictor of surface learning approaches even after controlling for a range of other pertinent variables such as language background, motivation, discipline area and year of study. Second, perceived norms have a moderating effect on this relationship such that students more strongly identified with students in their discipline are more likely to act in accordance with the norms they perceive for that discipline. Practically speaking, what this implies is that in instances where the perceived norms support deep learning, the identification–deep learning relationship is

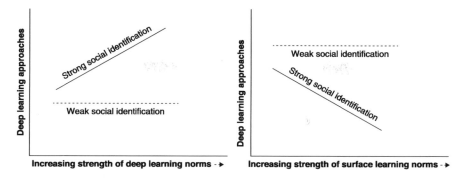

FIGURE 13.1 The conceptual interaction of discipline-related identification and perceived norms in predicting deep learning approaches

amplified. In situations where the perceived discipline norms support surface learning, the benefit of identification is undermined (in terms of deep learning as the outcome of interest; see Figure 13.1). In fact, given sufficiently strong surface learning norms, stronger identification may, then, also be associated with an increased use of a surface learning approach.

Third, educational products of interest (including course experience, intentions to continue in the field, academic performance) all demonstrated a positive relationship to deeper learning approaches. Often, we also found negative relationships with surface learning approaches. Further, many of these outcomes have significant positive relationships with discipline-related social identification and positive relationships of similar strength with one another.

A strength of this line of work is that it samples from a range of academic courses across a typical university and a range of year levels. Our approach has been to look for broad patterns of effects of identity and normative influence across the full range of courses.

Implications

Social identity, fostering norms and deep learning approaches

Aside from allowing a clearer and more veridical understanding of the student experience, the addition of the social influence model also has practical value. Our findings indicate a positive relationship between discipline-related social identification and deep learning approaches. In light of this, educators wishing to bolster deep learning approaches in their students may consider increasing discipline-related social identification as a means to this end. This finding offers an avenue, above and beyond constructive alignment, for encouraging a deep learning approach. There already exists literature on methodologies for systematically bolstering social identification and norms, owing to the practical value of these concepts in other domains. For example, Swaab and colleagues (Swaab, Postmes and Spears, 2008; Swaab, Postmes, van Beest and Spears, 2007) suggest a method for the formation and strengthening of a positive shared identity. In the context of multiparty negotiations, they describe a small-group interaction paradigm that allows group members the possibility to observe and communicate with one another. This paradigm means group members can inform themselves about certain group characteristics and attributes that allow them to induce a shared identity comprising stereotypes and norms for appropriate behaviour that is distinctive to the group.

To add a layer of complexity to this model, our findings also indicate the value of ensuring that the perceived discipline norms align with the intended learning approach. This idea is mirrored in newer developments in the applied social influence literature (e.g., Fekadu and Kraft, 2002; Hamilton and White, 2008; Louis et al., 2007; Terry et al., 1999; White, Smith, Terry, Greenslade and McKimmie, 2009) that model the moderating influence of norms on the link between social identification and behaviour. As such, practical methods for aligning desirable norms with social identification to promote action – such as those suggested by the opinion-based group literature (e.g., McGarty et al., 2009; Thomas et al., 2009a; see also Thomas, McGarty, Stuart, Lala and Pedersen, Chapter 8, this volume) – may also be of use. This literature has, at its core, an interaction-based model similar to that suggested by Swaab and colleagues. However, this paradigm also suggests that the nature of the norms that are formed in these small-group interactions can be shaped through a simple discussion-based intervention (Thomas et al., 2009a).

The intervention method described in this latter literature (e.g., Thomas et al., 2009a) involves two steps. First, participants must categorise themselves as a member of an opinion-based group (OBG). An OBG is a psychologically meaningful group defined by a shared opinion (Bliuc et al., 2006). In the educational context, this group could be something simple, such as 'students who are interested in taking a deep learning approach to this course' (or some more colloquial equivalent in a given context). We can invoke this identity by, for example, giving students a brief tutorial on the benefits (both educational and professional) of taking a deep learning approach and making clear that learning approaches are a choice they make. In this case, the implicit shared opinion is that 'deep learning approaches are desirable and I wish to take a deep learning approach to my learning tasks in this context'. Once they have explicitly perceived themselves as a member of this group, they are then involved in a 'group planning' discussion in which strategies to achieve group goals are discussed. In the current example, students can discuss study methods, habits and strategies that they think will assist them to take a deep learning approach. Through this process of strategising, group members are expected to construct norms for action (in this case, the action is learning) and consensualise on them as the norms for action that belong to their newly formed OBG identities (in this case, as students who wish to take a deep learning approach).

A crucial consideration in this interaction process is that, left unchecked, this could also be a thoroughly detrimental process that allows students to form meaningful norms for surface learning, contrary to the intention of the educator. This aspect is controlled through making deep learning an explicitly communicated goal of the group. This can be achieved through a brief explanation for students of the differences between deep and surface learning and their demonstrated effects on student performance. Armed with this information, students can then be asked to spend the interaction phase of the intervention generating strategies to achieve the group goal of engaging in deep learning to improve performance or 'do well'.

As described above, these concepts could plausibly be brought together to form a practically applicable intervention model for tertiary courses. Others have already explored the ways that educators can select particular students to maximise deep learning in their courses (see Newble and Entwistle, 1986, for a brief discussion of student selection and learning approaches in medical school) and methods for structuring courses to ensure there is no option but to take a deep approach (constructive alignment; Biggs and Tang, 2007b). However, the addition of social processes to the way we understand the student experience allows a further avenue for intervention.

Structuring the course to allow for a small-group interaction task based around the method described, early in the course, would be relatively achievable in most learning contexts. Providing that this task is carefully designed to bolster identification (through observation and communication; see Swaab et al., 2008) and shape the appropriate norms (through opinion-based norm consensualisation; see Thomas et al., 2009a), this would be a simple method that our work so far suggests would be effective in increasing deep learning approaches among students. Indeed, we are currently in the early stages of trying such methods, and more work is needed to ensure that the right facilitatory elements can be put in place to have such an intervention be effective.

Future directions

To conclude, it is crucial to consider ways in which we can further develop the ideas and models outlined in this chapter in order to provide yet further advances in the tools available to educators for shaping the ways students learn. The studies conducted and the current discussion open up some clear paths for future research in the area. Next, we discuss two key areas for further research and development: course design and norm perception.

Course design and norm perception

Taking this new role for norms into consideration, there are clear implications for course design. Perceived norms play a crucial role in our proposed model. These norms moderate the way in which discipline-related social identification impacts on student behaviour and cognition. Therefore, norms and social identification can be considered a useful tool to achieve educator aims through the shaping and bolstering of the social identity-related normative-influence processes described above. Yet there are further ways in which normative influence can be explored. In our research, when addressing the norms students perceived to be appropriate for their discipline, we asked only what they thought their fellow students would consider desirable. In a model of education such as ours that considers tertiary education as, at least in part, an induction into a community of practice (Barrie, 2006; O'Donnell and Tobbell, 2007), this is not a complete picture of the normative processes to which the student is subjected.

The course teaching team also has a role to play here, in two ways. First, they may engage in a direct attempt to influence, explaining to students the ways in which they are expected to learn and engage with the material. Second, however, the design of the course itself can also be considered an indication of normative expectations. The way in which the educator chooses to deliver the material, the class schedule and the assessment procedures suggest to the student the way the educator expects them to learn, and this impression can be modified or reinforced by assessment types, rubrics and feedback.

For example, in a course with frequent low-value assessment pieces based on factual recall (such as a weekly quiz on reading content), the structure conveys to the student that the educator expects them to read and memorise a large volume of information continuously throughout the semester. That performance on these assessment pieces would be contingent on factual recall further reinforces this impression. In this example, the educator is, perhaps unwittingly, communicating to the student that a surface learning approach is what is expected and rewarded in this course. This expectation will form part of the students' understanding of what it means to be a student in this discipline and, in turn, will shape what they perceive as normative for students in their discipline.

This concept of educator-instigated norms is entirely congruent with the constructive alignment model. Through constructive alignment, we contend that educators are not simply 'trapping' the student into deep learning through carefully structured activities and assessment. Based on the learning processes advanced in this chapter, these educators are also engaging in a normative-influence process that implicitly communicates to students that this is how 'we' engage in teaching and learning in this particular course or discipline.

Future research could explore these educator-instigated norms more fully, using experimental variation in key course and educator attributes to explore the impacts on student learning behaviour. From here, we can explore how strongly these aspects of course design and delivery affect student perceptions of norms. Furthermore, in the event that these educator-instigated norms (constructive alignment) are in conflict with student norms, there is evidence to suggest that this conflict can lead to more complex implications for the nature and strength of behavioural outcomes (McDonald, Fielding and Louis, 2013). The normative processes explored in this chapter open up a rich set of possibilities for future research examining identity-based referent social influence.

Conclusion

The current chapter offers ways, additional to those explored in several other chapters in this volume, in which perceived norms operate in conjunction with education-related social identities. We demonstrate the key moderating role that norms play in the relationship between discipline-based identity processes and learning approaches (deep and surface), and we suggest practical ways in which this can be harnessed for educational gain. Finally, we suggest further ways in which this already fruitful line of research can be expanded, which offer yet more ways in which the education and social identity literatures can inform each other to improve student learning.

Note

1   Academic disciplines can be categorised for this purpose using a Biglan–Becher-style typology of disciplines (Becher and Trowler, 2001; Biglan, 1973) in which they are divided along two dimensions: paradigm development and pragmatism (Umbach, 2007). This is a commonly used typology that was developed from Kolb's (1981) exploration of disciplinary difference in learning styles. This conceptualisation of the underlying differences between disciplines has formed the basis of much of the existing work on disciplinary variation in learning approaches (e.g., Kember and Leung, 2011; Laird *et al.*, 2008; Lindblom-Ylänne *et al.*, 2006; Neumann *et al.*, 2002).

References

Artino, A. R., Rochelle, J. S. L. and Durning, S. J. (2010). Second-year medical students' motivational beliefs, emotions and achievement. *Medical Education, 44*(12), 1203–12.

Baeten, M., Kyndt, E., Struyven, K. and Dochy, F. (2010). Using student-centred learning environments to stimulate deep approaches to learning: Factors encouraging or discouraging their effectiveness. *Educational Research Review, 5*(3), 243–60. doi: http://dx.doi.org/10.1016/j.edurev.2010.06.001

Baker, C., Little, T. and Brownell, K. (2003). Predicting adolescent eating and activity behaviors: The role of social norms and personal agency. *Health Psychology, 22*(2), 189–98.

Barrie, S. (2006). Understanding what we mean by the generic attributes of graduates. *Higher Education, 51*(2), 215–41. doi: 10.1007/s10734-004-6384-7

Becher, T. and Trowler, P. R. (2001). *Academic tribes and territories: Intellectual enquiry and the culture of disciplines* (2nd ed.). Buckingham: Society for Research into Higher Education and Open University Press.

Biggs, J. (1979). Individual differences in study processes and the quality of learning outcomes. *Higher Education, 8*(4), 381–94.

Biggs, J. (1989). Approaches to the enhancement of tertiary teaching. *Higher Education Research and Development, 8*(1), 7–25.

Biggs, J. (1999). What the student does: Teaching for enhanced learning. *Higher Education Research and Development, 18*(1), 57–75.

Biggs, J., Kember, D. and Leung, D. (2001). The revised two-factor study process questionnaire: R-SPQ-2F. *British Journal of Educational Psychology, 71*(1), 133–49.

Biggs, J. and Tang, C. (2007a). Teaching according to how students learn, in *Teaching for quality learning at university* (3rd ed., pp. 15–30). Maidenhead, UK: Open University Press.

Biggs, J. and Tang, C. (2007b). Using constructive alignment in outcomes-based teaching and learning, in *Teaching for quality learning at university* (3rd ed., pp. 50–63). Maidenhead, UK: Open University Press.

Biglan, A. (1973). The characteristics of subject matter in different academic areas. *Journal of Applied Psychology, 57*(3), 195–203.

Bilbow, G. T. (1989). Towards an understanding of overseas students' difficulties in lectures: A phenomenographic approach. *Journal of Further and Higher Education, 13*(3), 85–99.

Bliuc, A.-M., Ellis, R. A., Goodyear, P. and Hendres, D. M. (2011a). The role of social identification as university student in learning: Relationships between students' social identity, approaches to learning, and academic achievement. *Educational Psychology, 31*(5), 559–74. doi: 10.1080/01443410.2011.585948

Bliuc, A.-M., Ellis, R. A., Goodyear, P. and Hendres, D. M. (2011b). Understanding student learning in context: Relationships between university students' social identity, approaches to learning, and academic performance. *European Journal of Psychology of Education, 26*(3), 417–33. doi: 10.1007/s10212-011-0065-6

Bliuc, A.-M., McGarty, C., Reynolds, K. J. and Muntele, D. (2006). Opinion-based group membership as a predictor of commitment to political action. *European Journal of Social Psychology, 37*(1), 19–32.

Cameron, J. (2004). A three-factor model of social identity. *Self and Identity, 3*(3), 239–62.

Cassidy, S. (2004). Learning styles: An overview of theories, models, and measures. *Educational Psychology: An International Journal of Experimental Educational Psychology, 24*(4), 419–44.

Chamorro-Premuzic, T. and Furnham, A. (2004). A possible model for understanding the personality–intelligence interface. *British Journal of Psychology, 95*(2), 249–64. doi: 10.1348/000712604773952458

Chamorro-Premuzic, T. and Furnham, A. (2008). Personality, intelligence and approaches to learning as predictors of academic performance. *Personality and Individual Differences, 44*(7), 1596–1603. doi: 10.1016/j.paid.2008.01.003

Entwistle, N. (2000). Scoring key for the Approaches and Study Skills Inventory for Students (ASSIST) [online], *Enhancing Teaching-Learning Environments in Undergraduate Courses*. Retrieved from: www.etl.tla.ed.ac.uk/questionnaires/ASSIST.pdf (accessed 30 August 2010).

Entwistle, N. (2005). Contrasting perspectives on learning. In F. Marton, D. Hounsell and N. Entwistle (Eds), *The experience of learning: Implications for teaching and studying in higher education* (3rd [Internet] ed., pp. 3–22). Edinburgh: University of Edinburgh, Centre for Teaching, Learning and Assessment.

Fekadu, Z. and Kraft, P. (2002). Expanding the theory of planned behaviour: The role of social norms and group identification. *Journal of Health Psychology, 7*(1), 33–43.

Greene, S. (2004). Social identity theory and party identification. *Social Science Quarterly, 85*(1), 136–53.

Hagger, M. and Chatzisarantis, N. (2005). First and higher-order models of attitudes, normative influence and perceived behavioural control in the theory of planned behaviour. *British Journal of Social Psychology, 44*(4), 513–35.

Hamilton, K. and White, K. (2008). Extending the theory of planned behaviour: The role of self and social influences in predicting adolescent regular moderate-to-vigourous phsyical activity. *Journal of Sport and Exercise Psychology, 30*(1), 56–74.

Haslam, S. A., Powell, C. and Turner, J. (2000). Social identity, self-categorization and work motivation: Rethinking the contribution of the group to positive and sustainable organisational outcomes. *Applied Psychology: An International Review, 49*(3), 319–39.

Haslam, S. A., Turner, J. C., Oakes, P. J., Reynolds, K. and Doosje, B. (2002). From personal pictures in the head to collective tools in the world: How shared stereotypes allow groups to represent and change social reality. In C. McGarty, V. Y. Yzerbyt and R. Spears (Eds), *Stereotypes as explanations: The formation of meaningful beliefs about social groups* (pp. 157–85.). Cambridge: Cambridge University Press.

Herman, W. E. (1995). Humanistic influences on a constructivist approach to teaching and learning. Paper presented at the *Annual Meeting of the American Educational Research Association*, San Francisco, CA, April 18–22. Retrieved from: www.eric.ed.gov/PDFS/ED393814.pdf (accessed 1 September 2016).

Johnston, C. (2001). Student perceptions of learning in first year in an economics and commerce faculty. *Higher Education Research and Development*, 20(2), 169–84.

Kallgren, C. A., Reno, R. R. and Cialdini, R. B. (2000). A focus theory of normative conduct: When norms do and do not affect behavior. *Personality and Social Psychology Bulletin*, 26(8), 1002–12.

Kek, M. A. Y. C., Darmawan, I. G. N. and Chen, Y. S. (2007). Family, learning environments, learning approaches, and student outcomes in a Malaysian private university. *International Education Journal*, 8(2), 318–36.

Kember, D. (2009). Promoting student-centred forms of learning across an entire university. *Higher Education*, 58(1), 1–13.

Kember, D. and Leung, D. Y. (2011). Disciplinary differences in student ratings of teaching quality. *Research in Higher Education*, 52(3), 278–99.

Kolb, D. A. (1981). Learning styles and disciplinary differences. In A. W. Chickering (Ed.), *The modern American college*. San Francisco, CA: Jossey-Bass.

Laird, T. F. N., Shoup, R., Kuh, G. D. and Schwarz, M. J. (2008). The effects of discipline on deep approaches to student learning and college outcomes. *Research in Higher Education*, 49(6), 469–94.

Leach, C. W., van Zomeren, M., Zebel, S., Vliek, M., Pennekamp, S., Doosje, B., . . . Spears, R. (2008). Group-level self-definition and self-investment: A hierarchical (multicomponent) model of in-group identification. *Journal of Personality and Social Psychology*, 95(1), 144–65.

Lindblom-Ylänne, S., Trigwell, K., Nevgi, A. and Ashwin, P. (2006). How approaches to teaching are affected by discipline and teaching context. *Studies in Higher Education*, 31(3), 285–98.

Livingstone, A. and Haslam, S. A. (2008). The importance of social identity content in a setting of chronic social conflict: Understanding intergroup relations in Northern Ireland. *British Journal of Social Psychology*, 47(1), 1–21.

Lizzio, A., Wilson, K. and Simons, R. (2002). University students' perceptions of the learning environment and academic outcomes: Implications for theory and practice. *Studies in Higher Education*, 27(1), 27–49.

Louis, W., Davies, S., Smith, J. and Terry, D. (2007). Pizza and pop and the student identity: The role of referent group norms in healthy and unhealthy eating. *The Journal of Social Psychology*, 147(1), 57–74.

McDonald, R. I., Fielding, K. S. and Louis, W. R. (2013). Energizing and de-motivating effects of norm-conflict. *Personality and Social Psychology Bulletin*, 39(1), 57–72.

McGarty, C., Bliuc, A.-M., Thomas, E. and Bongiorno, R. (2009). Collective action as the material expression of opinion-based group membership. *Journal of Social Issues*, 65(4), 839–57.

McManus, I. C., Keeling, A. and Paice, E. (2004). Stress, burnout and doctors' attitudes to work are determined by personality and learning style: A twelve year longitudinal study of UK medical graduates. *BMC Medicine*, 2(29), 29. doi: 10.1186/1741-7015-2-29

Marton, F. and Säljö, R. (1976). On qualitative differences in learning – 1: Outcome and process. *British Journal of Educational Psychology*, *46*(1), 4–11.

Mauranen, A. (2009). Spoken rhetoric: How do natives and non-natives fare? In E. Suomela-Salmi and F. Dervin (Eds), *Cross-linguistic and cross-cultural perspectives on academic discourse* (pp. 199–218). Amsterdam: John Benjamins.

Mitchell, P. and Forer, P. (2010). Blended learning: The perceptions of first-year geography students. *Journal of Geography in Higher Education*, *34*(1), 77–89. doi: 10.1080/03098260902982484

Musgrove, L. and McGarty, C. (2008). Opinion-based group membership as a predictor of collective emotional responses and support for pro- and anti-war action. *Social Psychology*, *39*(1), 37–47.

Neumann, R. (2001). Disciplinary differences and university teaching. *Studies in Higher Education*, *26*(2), 135–46. doi: 10.1080/03075070124813

Neumann, R., Parry, S. and Becher, T. (2002). Teaching and learning in their disciplinary contexts: A conceptual analysis. *Studies in Higher Education*, *27*(4), 405–17. doi: 10.1080/0307507022000011525

Newble, D. I. and Clarke, R. (1986). The approaches to learning of students in a traditional and in an innovative problem–based medical school. *Medical Education*, *20*(4), 267–73.

Newble, D. I. and Entwistle, N. J. (1986). Learning styles and approaches: Implications for medical education. *Medical Education*, *20*(3), 162–75. doi: 10.1111/j.1365-2923.1986.tb01163.x

Norman, G. R. and Schmidt, H. G. (1992). The psychological basis of problem-based learning: A review of the evidence. *Academic Medicine*, *67*(9), 557–65.

O'Connor, M. C. and Paunonen, S. V. (2007). Big Five personality predictors of post-secondary academic performance. *Personality and Individual Differences*, *43*(5), 971–90.

O'Donnell, V. L. and Tobbell, J. (2007). The transition of adult students to higher education: Legitimate peripheral participation in a community of practice? *Adult Education Quarterly*, *57*(4), 312–28.

Platow, M. J., Mavor, K. I. and Grace, D. M. (2013). On the role of discipline-related self-concept in deep and surface approaches to learning among university students. *Instructional Science*, *41*(2), 271–85. doi: 10.1007/s11251-012-9227-4

Ramsden, P. (1991). A performance indicator of teaching quality in higher education: The Course Experience Questionnaire. *Studies in Higher Education*, *16*(2), 129–50.

Ramsden, P. (2003). Approaches to learning, in *Learning to teach in higher education* (pp. 39–61). London: Routledge.

Richardson, J. T. E. (1994). Mature students in higher education: I. A literature survey on approaches to studying. *Studies in Higher Education*, *19*(3), 309–25. doi: 10.1080/03075079412331381900

Richardson, M., Abraham, C. and Bond, R. (2012). Psychological correlates of university students' academic performance: A systematic review and meta-analysis. *Psychological Bulletin*, *138*(2), 353–87.

Sadler-Smith, E. (1996). Learning styles: A holistic approach. *Journal of European Industrial Training*, *20*(7), 29–36.

Smyth, L., Mavor, K. I., Platow, M. J., Grace, D. M. and Reynolds, K. J. (2015). Discipline social identification, study norms and learning approach in university students. *Educational Psychology*, *35*(1), 53–72.

Struyven, K., Dochy, F., Janssens, S. and Gielen, S. (2006). On the dynamics of students' approaches to learning: The effects of the teaching/learning environment. *Learning and Instruction*, *16*(4), 279–94.

Stürmer, S., Snyder, M. and Omoto, A. (2005). Prosocial emotions and helping: The moderating role of group membership. *Journal of Personality and Social Psychology, 88*(3), 532–46.

Swaab, R., Postmes, T. and Spears, R. (2008). Identity formation in multiparty negotiations. *British Journal of Social Pscyhology, 47*(1), 167–87.

Swaab, R., Postmes, T., van Beest, I. and Spears, R. (2007). Shared cognition as a product of, and precursor to, shared identity in negotiations. *Personality and Social Psychology Bulletin, 33*(2), 187–99.

Terry, D., Hogg, M. and White, K. (1999). The theory of planned behaviour: Self identity, social identity and group norms. *British Journal of Social Psychology, 38*(3), 225–44.

Thomas, E., McGarty, C. and Mavor, K. I. (2009a). Aligning identities, emotions and beliefs to create commitment to sustainable social and political action. *Personality and Social Psychology Review, 13*(3), 194–218.

Thomas, E., McGarty, C. and Mavor, K. I. (2009b). Transforming 'apathy into movement': The role of prosocial emotions in motivating action for social change. *Personality and Social Psychology Review, 13*(4), 310–33.

Trigwell, K. and Prosser, M. (1991). Improving the quality of student learning: The influence of learning context and student approaches to learning on learning outcomes. *Higher Education, 22*(3), 251–66.

Turner, J. (1991). *Social influence.* Milton Keynes: Open University Press.

Turner, J., Hogg, M., Oakes, P., Reicher, S. and Wetherell, M. (1987). *Rediscovering the social group: A self-categorization theory.* Oxford: Blackwell.

Turner, M. E., Pratkanis, A. R., Probasco, P. and Leve, C. (1992). Threat, cohesion, and group effectiveness: Testing a social identity maintenance perspective on groupthink. *Journal of Personality and Social Psychology, 63*(5), 781–96.

Umbach, P. D. (2007). Faculty cultures and college teaching. In R. P. Perry and J. C. Smart (Eds), *The Scholarship of teaching and learning in higher education: An evidence-based approach* (pp. 263–317). Dordrecht: Springer.

Van Rijswijk, W., Haslam, S. A. and Ellemers, N. (2006). Who do we think we are? The effects of social context and social identification on in-group stereotyping. *British Journal of Social Psychology, 45*(1), 161–74.

Walsh, A. (2007). An exploration of Biggs' constructive alignment in the context of work-based learning. *Assessment and Evaluation in Higher Education, 32*(1), 79–87.

Watkins, D. (1982). Identifying the study process dimensions of Australian university students. *Australian Journal of Education, 26*(1), 76–85.

Watkins, D. and Hattie, J. (1981). The learning processes of Australian university students: Investigations of contextual and personological factors. *British Journal of Educational Psychology, 51*(3), 384–93. doi: 10.1111/j.2044-8279.1981.tb02494.x

White, K., Smith, J., Terry, D., Greenslade, J. and McKimmie, B. (2009). Social influence in the theory of planned behaviour: The role of descriptive, injunctive, and in-group norms. *British Journal of Social Psychology, 48*(1), 135–51.

Yan, L. and Kember, D. (2004). Avoider and engager approaches by out-of-class groups: The group equivalent to individual learning approaches. *Learning and Instruction, 14*(1), 27–49.

Zeegus, P. (2001). Approaches to learning in science: A longitudinal study. *British Journal of Educational Psychology, 71*(1), 115–32.

Zubizarreta, J. (2009). *The learning portfolio: Reflective practice for improving student learning.* San Francisco, CA: John Wiley & Sons.

14

PERFORMANCE IN SMALL STUDENT GROUPS

Group personality, identity, and norms

Conal Monaghan and Boris Bizumic

> But, one might say, the individual is an effect, not a cause; he is a drop of water in the ocean; he does not act, he is acted upon, and it is the social environment which directs him. But what is this social environment made up of, if not of individuals? Thus we are at the same time actors and acted upon, and each of us contributes to forming this irresistible current which sweeps him along.
>
> (Durkheim, 1885, as quoted in Giddens, 1990, p. 140)

Organisations rely heavily on small groups to achieve a wide range of goals (Devine, Clayton, Philips, Dunford, and Melner, 1999). As a result, researchers have increasingly focused on the study of psychological factors that predispose these groups to be effective (e.g., Guzzo and Dickson, 1996; Halfhill, Sundstrom, Lahner, Calderone, and Nielsen, 2005). In education, academic curricula commonly include small-group work, although researchers have focused considerably less on psychological factors that influence how these small student groups perform.

Although there are many perspectives that offer an explanation of the psychological factors that contribute to the success of small student groups working on a project, this chapter focuses on two almost diametrically opposed approaches (for another related approach to examining social identification and individual differences, see Greenaway, Amiot, Louis, and Bentley, Chapter 10, this volume). These important approaches have not been extensively studied in relation to small-group performance in education. Furthermore, both have potential to provide useful information to educators. The first, the group personality approach, focuses on the influence of relatively stable personality traits of group members on group behaviour (e.g., McCrae and Costa, 2008). This approach argues that the average individual personalities of group members (i.e., group personality) influences group behaviour (cf. Cattell, 1951). The second, the social identity approach, argues that groups are qualitatively different to the mean of the individuals within them (i.e., population variables; Tajfel and Turner, 1979; Turner, 1982). It posits that once people are in groups with which they identify, they behave in accordance with the shared characteristics of that group membership. From this perspective, individual personality is fluid and adaptable. Therefore, it is not personality but group norms and group identification that influence group behaviour.

In this chapter, we review relevant personality and social identity theorising and research, and outline their potential points of integration in attempting to explain and predict the performance of small student groups. We illustrate the integration of both perspectives with a simulation analysis based on data from real small student groups that worked on a project over a period of one academic year. We conclude that to understand the dynamic nature of small-group work, researchers and educators need to consider the influence of both personality and social identity processes.

The group personality approach

Students bring their unique and idiosyncratic characteristics to the group environment. Consequently, each student group is distinctive as each group varies in membership. The differences between these students and, in turn, between groups can be explored in the context of the relative stability of particular individual characteristics. Researchers have shown that certain relatively stable characteristics relate to student performance, such as temperament (Martin, Olejnik, and Gaddis, 1994), emotional intelligence (Parker *et al.*, 2004), self-discipline (Duckworth and Seligman, 2005), autonomy (Miserandino, 1996), and intelligence or cognitive ability (Furnham and Chamorro-Premuzic, 2004; Furnham, Chamorro-Premuzic, and McDougall, 2003). Indeed, since the 1920s, psychologists have found that cognitive ability is unable to solely predict academic performance, meaning that researchers needed to turn to other important variables, such as personality traits, to explain performance (see Danziger, 1994). More recently, several researchers have suggested that personality traits may be as strong a predictor of academic performance as cognitive ability (Poropat, 2009), if not stronger and more informative than cognitive ability (Furnham *et al.*, 2003).

Although Allport (1937) distinguished between idiographic analyses, which focus on unique individual traits, and nomothetic analyses, which focus on individual traits common to all people, most researchers today tend to use the latter. The main line of research within the nomothetic approach attempts to capture all human personality differences within a small number of fundamental dimensions, known as personality traits (Digman, 1990; Goldberg, 1993). There are various models of personality traits, but over the last several decades, a model that postulates five basic traits, known as the Big Five, has emerged as the most influential (see Goldberg, 1993; McCrae and Costa, 1996). Theorists conceptualised these five personality traits as relatively consistent and enduring characteristics that underpin people's specific ways of thinking, feeling, and behaving across situations and time (Costa and McCrae, 1988; McCrae and Costa, 1996).

The Big Five personality traits are extroversion, neuroticism (often referred to by its converse – emotional stability), openness to experience, agreeableness, and conscientiousness (see Digman, 1990; Goldberg *et al.*, 2006; McCrae and Costa, 1996; McCrae and Terracciano, 2005). Extraversion refers to the degree to which individuals are outgoing, energetic, sociable, vigorous, and excitement seeking. Neuroticism refers to individuals' susceptibility to experience negative emotions, including anxiety, stress, anger, and depression. Openness to experience primarily refers to individuals' creativity, adventurousness, broad-mindedness, imagination, and artistic interests. Agreeableness, the main interpersonal component, refers to the degree to which an individual is cooperative, considerate, altruistic, modest, and trustful. Finally, conscientiousness refers to the degree to which individuals are responsible, hard-working, organised, and diligent.

According to personality trait theorists (e.g., McCrae and Costa, 2008), the Big Five are grounded in fairly stable biological mechanisms. Indeed, research suggests that the five traits are genetically based (e.g., Jang, Livesley, and Vemon, 1996; Loehlin, McCrae, Costa, and John, 1998; McCrae and Costa, 2008), are linked to specific neurological structures (DeYoung *et al.*, 2010), exist universally across cultures (McCrae and Costa, 1997), and appear to be relatively stable across one's lifespan (Costa and McCrae, 1988; McCrae *et al.*, 2000). These findings have led supporters of the approach to propose that personality traits appear almost independently of the environment (such as the social context).

Early research into the role of personality in both individual and group performance was impeded by the absence of modern meta-analytic methods and a widely accepted personality framework with which to focus and unify research (Barrick, Mount, and Judge, 2001; Guion and Gottier, 1965; Halfhill, Nielsen, Sundstrom, and Weilbaecher, 2005; Mann, 1959). As a result of advances in these areas, contemporary research has consistently shown that the Big Five personality traits are robust predictors of both individual and group performance (e.g., Barrick and Mount, 1991; Barrick *et al.*, 2001; De Raad and Schouwenburg, 1996; Halfhill, Sundstrom, *et al.*, 2005; O'Connor and Paunonen, 2007). Most studies have focused primarily on the role of the Big Five in organisations, although research has also shown that these personality traits are a significant predictor of academic performance (see De Raad and Schouwenburg, 1996; O'Connor and Paunonen, 2007; Poropat, 2011). The Big Five approach appears more suitable for predicting individual academic performance than alternative approaches to personality traits (see Poropat, 2011).

Personality researchers generally evaluate academic performance within a remarkably narrow scope that focuses on grade point averages, exam marks, and final course grades (e.g., Bauer and Liang, 2003; Chamorro-Premuzic and Furnham, 2003; O'Connor and Paunonen, 2007; Poropat, 2009, 2011). The focus on these specific performance criteria does not account for any contribution students may make to a teamwork environment or how the team as a whole performs. As project teams are regularly used in current educational curricula and play an important role in developing skills for later life (e.g., Johns-Boast and Flint, 2009), it is important to investigate academic performance specifically in terms of these student groups.

Group-level personality traits and performance

From the personality trait perspective, a small student group can be understood by focusing on the personalities of the group members. Although researchers have used various methods to capture the personality trait composition of small groups (see Halfhill, Sundstrom, *et al.*, 2005; Kramer, Bhave, and Johnson, 2014; Neuman, Wagner, and Christiansen, 1999), they typically calculate the average score of the group members' personality traits (Barrick, Stewart, Neubert, and Mount, 1998; Halfhill, Nielsen, *et al.*, 2005; Halfhill, Sundstrom, *et al.*, 2005; Peeters, van Tuijl, Rutte, and Reymen, 2006). This represents the group level of a trait (Halfhill, Sundstrom, *et al.*, 2005) that can be used to predict group behaviour (Cattell, 1951). For example, a group of introverted students will act, on average, in a more unsociable, reserved, and quiet way than a group of extraverted students (Neuman *et al.*, 1999).

In regards to group performance, groups will perform better when their membership has, on average, personality traits that positively influence performance. Average group personality traits have emerged as robust predictors of small-group performance (see Halfhill, Sundstrom, *et al.*, 2005), including the performance of groups in educational contexts (e.g., Bradley, Baur, Banford, and Postlethwaite, 2013; Monaghan *et al.*, 2015; Peeters, Rutte, Tuijl, and Reymen, 2008). More specifically, conscientiousness and agreeableness have repeatedly and consistently emerged as the two most important traits for prediction of small-group performance (Bell, 2007; Bradley *et al.*, 2013; Halfhill, Sundstrom, *et al.*, 2005; Neuman *et al.*, 1999; Peeters *et al.*, 2008).

Conscientiousness includes characteristics such as discipline, diligence, achievement striving, organisation, and hard work. These are highly desirable behaviours in the academic context as well as in organisations, and it is not surprising that researchers consider conscientiousness to be a global measure of performance, consistently predicting a wide range of performance indicators (Barrick and Mount, 1991; Furnham *et al.*, 2003; Hurtz and Donovan, 2000; O'Connor and Paunonen, 2007; Poropat, 2009). More importantly, these characteristics also benefit the performance of small groups. Conscientious group members tend to be highly motivated to work on behalf of the group and tend to engage more in teamwork than non-conscientious group members (Barrick and Mount, 1991; Barrick *et al.*, 1998; Le *et al.*, 2011).

Accordingly, groups with highly conscientious individuals (i.e., groups high on the average level of conscientiousness) tend to display similar beneficial behaviours, such as effective decision-making, extra-role behaviours, teamwork, and planning (Halfhill, Nielson, and Sundstrom, 2008; Peeters *et al.*, 2008). Research suggests that these behaviours, in turn, facilitate group performance. Indeed, group conscientiousness consistently predicts group performance in almost all organisational and academic environments (e.g., Barrick *et al.*, 1998; Halfhill *et al.*, 2008; Halfhill, Sundstrom, *et al.*, 2005; Monaghan *et al.*, 2015; Neuman *et al.*, 1999; Peeters *et al.*, 2008). The group's average level of conscientiousness, therefore, seems crucial to group performance.

Agreeableness captures characteristics related to work in interpersonal environments, such as being cooperative, personable, considerate, modest, and trusting. Consequently, agreeable individuals tend to display pro-group behaviours, such as cooperation, teamwork, consideration, and positive interpersonal interactions (e.g., Barrick *et al.*, 2001, 1998; De Raad and Schouwenburg, 1996; Hurtz and Donovan, 2000; LePine and Van Dyne, 2001; Mount, Barrick, and Stewart, 1998). Thus, agreeable individuals are particularly well suited to group environments where positive interpersonal behaviours play an instrumental role in the group's performance.

Due to the interpersonal and prosocial orientation of individuals high on agreeableness, agreeable groups can outperform disagreeable groups (Halfhill *et al.*, 2008; Halfhill, Sundstrom, *et al.*, 2005; Neuman *et al.*, 1999). Small groups that are more agreeable on average tend to have higher levels of cooperation, group cohesion, extra-role behaviours, communication, interpersonal facilitation, and workload sharing than small groups that are more disagreeable on average (Barrick *et al.*, 1998; Bradley *et al.*, 2013; Halfhill *et al.*, 2008; Neuman *et al.*, 1999; Peeters *et al.*, 2008). As agreeableness is not directly performance oriented, it appears that this facilitates performance in small groups to the extent that there is a need for contact and cooperation among group members.

It is, however, important to point out that group agreeableness does not always lead to higher group performance. For example, Bradley *et al.* (2013) studied group agreeableness in 107 small student groups working on a project. Although highly agreeable teams performed well in face-to-face situations, this did not happen when group members interacted through technologies. These findings suggest that when the direct interpersonal component is removed, agreeableness does not facilitate performance. This could explain why the relationship between highly agreeable groups and performance tends to be stronger outside the laboratory rather than within the laboratory (see Bell, 2007; Halfhill, Sundstrom, *et al.*, 2005) and why agreeableness is unrelated to performance measures that are not reliant on interpersonal interactions (e.g., De Raad and Schouwenburg, 1996; Furnham and Chamorro-Premuzic, 2004; Furnham *et al.*, 2003; O'Connor and Paunonen, 2007; Poropat, 2009). At times, agreeableness may pose a problem if the task requires individual, and not cooperative, efforts as agreeable teams may focus more on interpersonal relationships than the task at hand (Peeters *et al.*, 2008). In these situations, therefore, agreeableness may not facilitate group performance (e.g., Bradley *et al.*, 2013; Peeters *et al.*, 2008), and may even hinder performance (Monaghan *et al.*, 2015).

In summary, it appears that the personality perspective provides considerable insight into why students perform well, both individually and in groups.

Conscientiousness, as the studious and hard-working component of personality, and agreeableness, as the interpersonal component, appear central to group personality traits related to group performance. Research at the group level of analysis does reproduce many findings at the individual level, supporting the predictions of the personality trait perspective. There is, therefore, a strong empirical and theoretical framework to suggest that small student groups can, in part, perform well due to the intrinsic personality traits of their individual members.

The social identity approach

Theorists and researchers have criticised the trait perspective for being unable to explain why people often behave inconsistently across situations and for being dismissive of how and why people are affected by the external environment and social contexts (see Mischel, 1973). Additionally, since the beginnings of sociology, theorists have argued that a group is different from, if not greater than, the sum of its parts and that one cannot understand groups and group relations by focusing on the individuals within the group. Psychologists influenced by the sociological perspective have also espoused these ideas, and the social identity approach – consisting of social identity (Tajfel and Turner, 1979) and self-categorisation theories (Turner, Hogg, Oakes, Reicher, and Wetherell, 1987) – is today probably the dominant social-psychological perspective to argue against individualistic conceptions of groups and group behaviour.

According to the social identity perspective, individuals are more than their unique individual characteristics: they also integrate thoughts, feelings, and behaviours from their group memberships into their sense of 'self' (Hogg and Abrams, 1988; Tajfel and Turner, 1979; Turner, 1982; Turner, Reynolds, Haslam, and Veenstra, 2006). This perspective argues that group membership has a substantial psychological impact on individuals (Brown and Turner, 1981; Tajfel and Turner, 1979). When people define themselves more strongly as group members than as unique individuals, they become depersonalised, and their individual interests are replaced with the interests of the group (Haslam, 2004; Turner, Oakes, Haslam, and McGarty, 1994). Consequently, they shift from interacting with the world as individuals to interacting as self-stereotyped group members.

Small student groups are particularly conducive to social identity processes. Early social identity studies (e.g., Billig and Tajfel, 1973; Tajfel, Billig, Bundy, and Flament, 1971) suggest that social identity processes operate even when students are categorised into arbitrary groups. Thus, the simple act of assigning students into small student groups may be enough to mobilise social identity processes. In addition, small student groups often have other important aspects of groups that may further reinforce group memberships, such as interpersonal attraction, interdependence, common fate, social cohesion, and mutual interest (see Hogg and Abrams, 1988; Hogg and Turner, 1985; Turner, 1984).

The social identity perspective argues that personality is greatly variable and depends upon cognitive comparisons made within the social environment (Turner and Onorato, 1999). This is directly opposed to the personality trait approach, which proposes that individual behaviour in groups is underpinned by relatively stable and enduring individual characteristics. The social identity approach applied to small student groups, accordingly, would argue that it is primarily the strength of group identification and group norms (but not individual personalities) that shape students' behaviour in small groups and, ultimately, the behaviour of the whole group.

Group identification

The more individuals identify as group members, the more they define their sense of self in terms of that group membership. High identifiers are those individuals who strongly internalise a group as contextually self-defining, and low identifiers are those who do not. High identifiers, therefore, tend to care highly about their own group. They tend to see the world through that group membership and are likely to engage in pro-group behaviours and self-sacrifice for the group (Ellemers and Rink, 2005; van Knippenberg, 2000). For example, when compared to low identifiers, high identifiers show a greater adherence to the working style of the group (Barreto and Ellemers, 2000; McAuliffe, Jetten, Hornsey, and Hogg, 2003), and have less absenteeism as well as fewer thoughts about withdrawal from the group (van Knippenberg, van Dick, and Tavares, 2007). Group identification is also directly related to performance, predicting organisational citizenship behaviours (e.g., helping colleagues, acting beyond their assigned job), individual performance in the group, and the performance of the group as a whole (e.g., Christ, van Dick, Wagner, and Stellmacher, 2003; Tanghe, Wisse, and van der Flier, 2010; van Dick, Grojean, Christ, and Wieseke, 2006; also see van Knippenberg, 2000). Importantly, high identifiers are motivated to invest in the performance of the group regardless of their accountability within the group (Barreto and Ellemers, 2000).

Research suggests, therefore, that identification appears to be a key motivator for members of small groups, such as student groups, to perform on behalf of their groups because they internalise the group's interests and goals into their own self-representation. In other words, the more students identify with the group, the more they want to invest in the group's performance. Nevertheless, high identification is often not enough to increase performance, and the impact of identification may depend on the characteristics of the group, such as its group norms.

Group norms

Whereas the strength of identification relates to how much individuals perceive themselves as members of a group, group norms relate to the nature of that self-definition. When people identify with a group, they define themselves in terms of characteristics of that group membership (Hogg and Abrams, 1988; Turner, 1982). Group norms are the important characteristics of a group and express expected and desirable ways of thinking, feeling, and behaving. Group members tend to internalise group norms, which then form part of their social identity. Group norms provide a shared frame of reference (Brown and Turner, 1981) and homogenise group members around a particular style of operating and a shared level of performance. As such, identifying group members tend to see deviations from normative behaviours by other ingroup members as challenging their sense of self and, in turn, strive to uphold the norms and defend against norm violations (Biernat, Vescio, and Billings, 1999; Castano, Paladino, Coull, and Yzerbyt, 2002; Ellemers and Rink, 2005; Feldman, 1984).

Research suggests that group norms relevant to performance on a particular task may predict the actual performance within small student groups (Paulus and Dzindolet, 1993; Quinn and Spencer, 2001; Schmader, 2002; Spencer, Steele, and Quinn, 1999). Students in small student groups may internalise a wide range of group norms, including expected and desirable levels of performance, attendance, communication, sociability, and cooperation. Consequently, students who identify with particular groups behave according to salient group norms. For example, Shih, Pittinsky, and Ambady (1999) studied the effect of salient group norms surrounding a particular group identity on academic performance. These researchers identified two commonly held stereotypes in a sample of female Asian-American students: that women perform worse than men in mathematics; and that Asians perform better than members of other ethnic groups in mathematics. When students' identities as females were made salient, they performed significantly worse on a maths test than when their Asian identities were made salient. This research supports the view that students may internalise the performance norms of the salient social category and then behave in accordance with them (see also in this volume, Boucher and Murphy, Chapter 5, Cruwys, Gaffney, and Skipper, Chapter 11, and Smyth, Mavor, Platow, and Grace, Chapter 13). Additionally, this research suggests that making different group memberships and associated norms salient may profoundly change students' performance.

Students' group identification can both moderate and mediate effects of group norms on performance. In small student groups, students' identification with their group may determine the extent to which they adopt group norms, such as those associated with performance (cf. Barreto and Ellemers, 2000; Ellemers, De Gilder, and Haslam, 2004; Van Knippenberg and Ellemers, 2003). There is, therefore, a moderation effect as norms may play a role only for high identifiers, while they may be irrelevant for low identifiers.

On the other hand, the process of mediation suggests that group norms of performance may prescribe high levels of member involvement which can increase identification of students with the group; and this, in turn, may increase the actual performance of the group. For example, norms of high group-based performance require students to invest considerable time and energy into the group, leading it to play an important role in their identity. Conversely, norms of low group-based performance may foster a disregard for the performance of the group and little investment in the group's performance from student members. Accordingly, group identification plays the central role in group performance, mediating the relationship between the group norm of performance and the performance of that group. Thus, group norms may have a secondary, indirect effect on performance through their influence on group identification.

In summary, it appears that social identity variables, such as strong group identification and appropriate group norms, could foster student small-group performance. There is, therefore, a strong empirical and theoretical framework, consisting of two related theories – social identity and self-categorisation theories – which explain the performance of small student groups as the result of group processes.

Group personality, identification, and norms as complementary causes of performance

The group personality and social identity approaches offer two differing accounts of the performance of small student groups. On the one hand, the group personality approach suggests that individual dispositions (which are relatively stable and ultimately caused by genetic and biological factors) predispose people to behave in a particular way even when they are in groups with others. In contrast, the social identity approach argues that how individuals categorise themselves within a particular situation, the strength of group identification, and group norms determine both group behaviour and the behaviour of individuals in the group with which they identify. As this chapter has demonstrated, both approaches have empirical support. A question is, however, whether these perspectives can be reconciled.

Recently, together with a number of colleagues (Monaghan *et al.*, 2015), we have conducted a study that investigated the influence of both perspectives on group performance. We analysed a simulated data set that was based on real data from 80 students who worked in small student groups on one software engineering project over two semesters. Their performance was assessed through the mark that each group received. We used Monte Carlo simulation techniques to create a large sample of over 300 small student groups by extrapolating from the results of the original sample. This procedure allowed us to study both perspectives in a large data set.

The main findings of the study are presented in Figure 14.1. Results supported the influence of both group personality and group identification on group performance. Indeed, averages of both group conscientiousness and identification significantly increased the performance of the small student groups. This suggests that groups that had more conscientious individuals tended to perform better than groups with less conscientious individuals. Similarly, groups with which individuals tended to identify strongly also tended to perform well. In addition, there was a significant indirect effect of group norms of performance through group identification on group marks. This supports the mediation process; that is, group norms of performance increase people's identification with the group, which in turn predicts the actual, externally evaluated performance of the group. Interestingly, group norms of performance had a negative effect on group performance, once group identification was controlled for. This suggests that

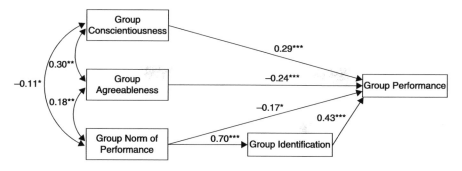

FIGURE 14.1 Path diagram showing effects of group-level measures of conscientious-ness, agreeableness, norm of performance, and identification on group performance. Presented coefficients are standardised

Source: Figure is adapted from Monaghan *et al.* (2015), p. 61. Copyright 2015 by Taylor and Francis. Reprinted with Permission. www.tandfonline.com.

Note: *$p < 0.05$; **$p < 0.01$; ***$p < 0.001$.

group norms of performance, without group identification, tend to lower performance. On the other hand, group agreeableness was a negative predictor of group performance, suggesting that cooperativeness, consideration, sympathy, and modesty at the group level may not necessarily translate into effective group performance, at least in a student software engineering group. The overall find-ings, nevertheless, suggest that social identity factors and personality traits play a complementary role in the performance of small student groups. (The modera-tion model, in which stronger group norms of performance affect performance only among more highly identified groups, was not supported.)

These findings along with the reviewed evidence from group personality and social identity approaches raise the question of the extent to which effects of group personality traits and social identity processes are contradictory and mutu-ally exclusive. The basic theoretical propositions are, indeed, contradictory. Whereas the personality trait perspective suggests that traits are biological, genetic, enduring, and resistant to environmental effects (McCrae and Costa, 2008), the social identity perspective assumes that personality traits are largely fluid and dynamic and can change relatively easily with changes in situations, groups, and meanings of group memberships (Turner, 1999; Turner and Onorato, 1999; Turner *et al.*, 2006). Both of these approaches appear too extreme or, at least, appear to overemphasise certain points and underemphasise others. Therefore, it is highly likely that any conceptualisation of the group that relies solely on either perspective is incomplete.

Studies suggest that personality traits may change over the course of a lifetime, probably due to diverse life experiences (see Caspi, Roberts, and Shiner, 2005; Hampson and Goldberg, 2006; Roberts, 1997; Roberts and DelVecchio, 2000; Roberts, Walton, and Viechtbauer, 2006). Nevertheless, despite these changes, personality traits do appear remarkably stable over many years, and changes tend to be very slow though they do accumulate over decades. These findings, therefore, suggest that people, although affected by experiences, situations, and groups, are not so malleable and easily transformed. Personality traits appear generally stable when individuals are in transitory groups, such as small student groups, and their personality traits, in part, can explain their behaviour in groups as well as the total behaviour of a group. In fact, the personality trait of conscientiousness is defined as the degree to which an individual is studious and hard-working across situations. Yet, people do modify their behaviour and performance due to environmental influences regardless of their personality traits (see Allport, 1937).

Although the social identity approach assumes a distinction between personal and social identities (Tajfel and Turner, 1979; Turner *et al.*, 1987), it has mainly studied and emphasised social identity at the expense of personal identity in both research and theory development (cf. Postmes and Jetten, 2006). However, personality traits (which this tradition sees as aspects of personal identity) may, in fact, influence social identity variables, such as group norms and identification. For example, when defining self in terms of a group membership, a student may infer characteristics of the group and its norms by observing the personality of other group members (indeed, this reasoning follows directly from the self-categorisation theory concept of meta-contrast; Turner *et al.*, 1987). Therefore, group personality acts as a key aspect of the group norm.

One must also consider that group members may, in fact, be more likely to associate and identify with a group that fits with their personality, and certain personality traits may predispose students to identify. For example, a recent longitudinal study of students found that over a period of one year, conscientiousness seemed to increase identification with their school, although identification did not have any causal effect on conscientiousness (Bizumic, Reynolds, and Meyers, 2012). These findings support the importance of personality traits as determinants of both group norms and identification and highlight avenues for further inquiry into predictors of performance in small student groups.

Findings such as these suggest that both the personality and social identity perspectives need to engage more with each other in order to achieve a more comprehensive explanation of group variables and group processes, including those pertaining to small student groups. For example, the social identity approach needs to explain how relatively stable and biologically based personality traits may shape behaviour in small student groups. On the other hand, the personality traits perspective has disregarded the social identity perspective and tends to neglect findings that group identities and norms can profoundly influence people's behaviour and potentially affect personality traits over a period of many years.

Conclusions

The group personality and social identity approaches offer very distinct explanations of what factors contribute to the success of small student groups. The group personality approach argues that personalities are important even in small student groups and that they play a key role in the performance of such groups. In contrast, the social identity approach argues that when students are categorised as group members, this membership has a real psychological impact on the students, modifying their thoughts, feelings, and behaviours. As a result, group behaviour cannot be sufficiently explained by the personality traits of its members. Instead, students' identification with their group and group norms are the key variables in small student group performance.

From both empirical and theoretical standpoints, the personality trait and social identity approaches can be considered complementary as long as they are not radically postulated. Personality traits do appear to predispose students to behave in a particular manner, and therefore traits may explain students' behaviour and may contribute to what the group will be. Similarly, group norms and identification may influence students' motivation to work on behalf of the group and specify the nature of students' contributions. The complex dynamic of small student group performance requires a joint perspective, with further pedagogical investigations focusing on potential points of integration.

We can conclude, by paraphrasing Durkheim's words at the beginning of the chapter, that students both act on their group (in terms of their personalities) and are acted upon by their group (in terms of their social identity). It is, indeed, both group personality and social identity processes that explain, at least in part, how students in these small groups will perform.

References

Allport, G. W. (1937). *Personality: A psychological interpretation*. New York: Henry Holt.

Barreto, M. and Ellemers, N. (2000). You can't always do what you want: Social identity and self-presentational determinants of the choice to work for a low-status group. *Personality and Social Psychology Bulletin, 26*(8), 891–906. doi: 10.1177/01461672002

Barrick, M. R. and Mount, M. K. (1991). The Big Five personality dimensions and job performance: A meta-analysis. *Personnel Psychology, 44*(1), 1–26. doi: 10.1111/j.1744-6570.1991.tb00688.x

Barrick, M. R., Mount, M. K. and Judge, T. A. (2001). Personality and performance at the beginning of the new millennium: What do we know and where do we go next? *International Journal of Selection and Assessment, 9*(1–2), 9–30. doi: 10.1111/1468-2389.00160

Barrick, M. R., Stewart, G. L., Neubert, M. J. and Mount, M. K. (1998). Relating member ability and personality to work-team processes and team effectiveness. *Journal of Applied Psychology, 83*(3), 377–91. doi: 10.1037/0021-9010.83.3.377

Bauer, K. W. and Liang, Q. (2003). The effect of personality and precollege characteristics on first-year activities and academic performance. *Journal of College Student Development, 44*(3), 277–90. doi: 10.1007/s11251-012-9259-9

Bell, S. T. (2007). Deep-level composition variables as predictors of team performance: A meta-analysis. *Journal of Applied Psychology, 92*(3), 595–616. doi: 10.1037/0021-9010.92.3.595

Biernat, M., Vescio, T. K. and Billings, L. S. (1999). Black sheep and expectancy violation: Integrating two models of social judgment. *European Journal of Social Psychology,*

29(4), 523–42. doi: 10.1002/(SICI)1099-0992(199906)29:4<523::AID-EJSP944> 3.0.CO;2-J

Billig, M. and Tajfel, H. (1973). Social categorization and similarity in intergroup behaviour. *European Journal of Social Psychology, 3*(1), 27–52. doi: 10.1002/ejsp.2420030103

Bizumic, B., Reynolds, K. J. and Meyers, B. (2012). Predicting social identification over time: The role of group and personality factors. *Personality and Individual Differences, 53*(4), 453–8. doi: 10.1016/j.paid.2012.04.009

Bradley, B. H., Baur, J. E., Banford, C. G. and Postlethwaite, B. E. (2013). Team players and collective performance: How agreeableness affects team performance over time. *Small Group Research, 44*(6), 680–711. doi: 10.1177/1046496413507609

Brown, R. J. and Turner, J. C. (1981). Interpersonal and intergroup behaviour. In J. Turner and H. Giles (Ed.), *Intergroup behaviour* (pp. 33–65). Oxford: Blackwell.

Caspi, A., Roberts, B. W. and Shiner, R. L. (2005). Personality development: Stability and change. *Annual Review of Psychology, 56*, 453–84. doi: 0.1146/annurev.psych. 55.090902.141913

Castano, E., Paladino, M. P., Coull, A. and Yzerbyt, V. Y. (2002). Protecting the ingroup stereotype: Ingroup identification and the management of deviant ingroup members. *British Journal of Social Psychology, 41*(3), 365–85. doi: 10.1348/014466602760344269

Cattell, R. B. (1951). New concepts for measuring leadership in terms of group syntality. *Human Relations, 4*(2), 161–84. doi: 10.1177/001872675100400203

Chamorro-Premuzic, T. and Furnham, A. (2003). Personality predicts academic performance: Evidence from two longitudinal university samples. *Journal of Research in Personality, 37*(4), 319–38. doi: 10.1016/S0092-6566(02)00578-0

Christ, O., Van Dick, R., Wagner, U. and Stellmacher, J. (2003). When teachers go the extra mile: Foci of organisational identification as determinants of different forms of organisational citizenship behaviour among schoolteachers. *British Journal of Educational Psychology, 73*(3), 329–41. doi: 10.1348/000709903322275867

Costa, P. T., Jr. and McCrae, R. R. (1988). Personality in adulthood: A six-year longitudinal study of self-reports and spouse ratings on the NEO Personality Inventory. *Journal of Personality and Social Psychology, 54*(5), 853–63. doi: 10.1037/0022-3514.54.5.853

Danziger, K. (1994). *Constructing the subject: Historical origins of psychological research.* Cambridge: Cambridge University Press. doi: 10.1017/CBO9780511524059.007

De Raad, B. and Schouwenburg, H. C. (1996). Personality in learning and education: A review. *European Journal of Personality, 10*(5), 303–36. doi: 10.1002/(SICI)1099-0984(199612)10:5<303::AID-PER262>3.0.CO;2-2

Devine, D. J., Clayton, L. D., Philips, J. L., Dunford, B. B. and Melner, S. B. (1999). Teams in organizations prevalence, characteristics and effectiveness. *Small Group Research, 30*(6), 678–711. doi: 10.1177/104649649903000602

DeYoung, C. G., Hirsh, J. B., Shane, M. S., Papademetris, X., Rajeevan, N. and Gray, J. R. (2010). Testing predictions from personality neuroscience: Brain structure and the Big Five. *Psychological Science, 21*(6), 820–8. doi: 10.1177/0956797610370159

Digman, J. M. (1990). Personality structure: Emergence of the five-factor model. *Annual Review of Psychology, 41*, 417–40. doi: 10.1146/annurev.ps.41.020190.002221

Duckworth, A. L. and Seligman, M. E. P. (2005). Self-discipline outdoes IQ in predicting academic performance of adolescents. *Psychological Science, 16*(12), 939–44. doi: 10.1111/j.1467-9280.2005.01641.x

Ellemers, N., De Gilder, D. and Haslam, S. A. (2004). Motivating individuals and groups at work: A social identity perspective on leadership and group performance. *Academy of Management Review, 29*(3), 459–78. doi: 10.2307/20159054

Ellemers, N. and Rink, F. (2005). Identity in work groups: The beneficial and detrimental consequences of multiple identities and group norms for collaboration and group performance. *Advances in Group Processes*, *22*, 1–41. doi: 10.1016/S0882-6145(05)22001-5

Feldman, D. C. (1984). The development and enforcement of group norms. *Academy of Management Review*, *9*(1), 47–53. doi: 10.2307/258231

Furnham, A. and Chamorro-Premuzic, T. (2004). Personality and intelligence as predictors of statistics examination grades. *Personality and Individual Differences*, *37*(5), 943–55. doi: 10.1016/j.paid.2003.10.016

Furnham, A., Chamorro-Premuzic, T. and McDougall, F. (2003). Personality, cognitive ability and beliefs about intelligence as predictors of academic performance. *Learning and Individual Differences*, *14*(1), 47–64. doi: 10.1016/j.lindif.2003.08.002

Giddens, A. (1990). Durkheim as a review critic. In P. Hamilton (Ed.), *Emile Durkheim: Critical assessments* (pp. 137–60). London: Routledge.

Goldberg, L. R. (1993). The structure of phenotypic personality traits. *American Psychologist*, *48*(1), 26–34. doi: 10.1037/0003-006X.48.1.26

Goldberg, L. R., Johnson, J. A., Eber, H. W., Hogan, R., Ashton, M. C., Cloninger, C. R. and Gough, H. G. (2006). The international personality item pool and the future of public-domain personality measures. *Journal of Research in Personality*, *40*(1), 84–96. doi: 10.1016/j.jrp.2005.08.007

Guion, R. M. and Gottier, R. F. (1965). Validity of personality measures in personnel selection. *Personnel Psychology*, *18*(2), 135–64. doi: 10.1111/j.1744-6570.1965.tb00273.x

Guzzo, R. A. and Dickson, M. W. (1996). Teams in organizations: Recent research on performance and effectiveness. *Annual Review of Psychology*, *47*, 307–38. doi: 10.1146/annurev.psych.47.1.307

Halfhill, T., Nielsen, T. M. and Sundstrom, E. (2008). The ASA framework: A field study of group personality composition and group performance in military action teams. *Small Group Research*, *39*(5), 616–35. doi: 10.1177/1046496408320418

Halfhill, T., Nielsen, T. M., Sundstrom, E. and Weilbaecher, A. (2005). Group personality composition and performance in military service teams. *Military Psychology*, *17*(1), 41–54. doi: 10.1207/s15327876mp1701_4

Halfhill, T., Sundstrom, E., Lahner, J., Calderone, W. and Nielsen, T. M. (2005). Group personality composition and group effectiveness: An integrative review of empirical research. *Small Group Research*, *36*(1), 83–105. doi: 10.1177/1046496404

Hampson, S. E. and Goldberg, L. R. (2006). A first large cohort study of personality trait stability over the 40 years between elementary school and midlife. *Journal of Personality and Social Psychology*, *91*(4), 763–79. doi: 10.1037/0022-3514.91.4.763

Haslam, S. A. (2004). *Psychology in organisations: The social identity approach* (2nd ed.). London: Sage.

Hogg, M. A. and Abrams, D. (1988). *Social identifications a social psychology of intergroup relations and group processes*. New York: Routledge. doi: 10.4324/9780203135457

Hogg, M. A. and Turner, J. C. (1985). Interpersonal attraction, social identification and psychological group formation. *European Journal of Social Psychology*, *15*(1), 51–66. doi: 10.1002/ejsp.2420150105

Hurtz, G. M. and Donovan, J. J. (2000). Personality and job performance: The Big Five revisited. *Journal of Applied Psychology*, *85*(6), 869–79.

Jang, K. L., Livesley, W. J. and Vemon, P. A. (1996). Heritability of the Big Five personality dimensions and their facets: A twin study. *Journal of Personality*, *64*(3), 577–92. doi: 10.1111/j.1467-6494.1996.tb00522.x

Johns-Boast, L. F. and Flint, S. (2009). Providing students with 'real-world' experience through university group projects. In S. Grainger and C. Kestell (Eds), *Engineering education: An Australian perspective* (pp. 87–96). Brentwood, UK: Multi-Science.

Kramer, A., Bhave, D. P. and Johnson, T. D. (2014). Personality and group performance: The importance of personality composition and work tasks. *Personality and Individual Differences, 58*, 132–7. doi: 10.1016/j.paid.2013.10.019

Le, H., Oh, I.-S., Robbins, S., Ilies, R., Holland, E. and Westrick, P. (2011). Too much of a good thing: Curvilinear relationships between personality traits and job performance. *Journal of Applied Psychology, 96*(1), 113–33. doi: 10.1037/a0021016

LePine, J. A. and Van Dyne, L. (2001). Voice and cooperative behavior as contrasting forms of contextual performance: Evidence of differential relationships with Big Five personality characteristics and cognitive ability. *Journal of Applied Psychology, 86*(2), 326–36. doi: 10.1037/0021-9010.86.2.326

Loehlin, J. C., McCrae, R. R., Costa, P. T., Jr. and John, O. P. (1998). Heritabilities of common and measure-specific components of the Big Five personality factors. *Journal of Research in Personality, 32*(4), 431–53. doi: 10.1006/jrpe.1998.2225

McAuliffe, B. J., Jetten, J., Hornsey, M. J. and Hogg, M. A. (2003). Individualist and collectivist norms: When it's ok to go your own way. *European Journal of Social Psychology, 33*(1), 57–70. doi: 10.1002/ejsp.129

McCrae, R. R. and Costa, P. T., Jr. (1996). Towards a new generation of personality theories: Theoretical contexts for the five-factor model. In J. S. Wiggins (Ed.), *The five-factor model of personality: Theoretical perspectives* (pp. 51–87). New York: The Guilford Press. doi: 10.5086/CHOICE.34-1846

McCrae, R. R. and Costa, P. T., Jr. (1997). Personality trait structure as a human universal. *American Psychologist, 52*(5), 509–16. doi: 10.1037/0003-066x.52.5.509

McCrae, R. R. and Costa, P. T., Jr. (2008). Empirical and theoretical status of the five-factor model of personality traits. In G. J. Boyle, G. Matthews and D. H. Saklofske (Eds), *The Sage handbook of personality theory and assessment: Vol 1 – Personality theories and models* (pp. 273–94). Thousand Oaks, CA: Sage. doi: 10.4135/9781849200462

McCrae, R. R., Costa, P. T., Jr., Ostendorf, F., Angleitner, A., Hrebickova, M., Avia, M. D., . . . Smith, P. B. (2000). Nature over nurture: Temperament, personality, and life span development. *Journal of Personality and Social Psychology, 78*(1), 173–86. doi: 10.1037/0022-3514.78.1.173

McCrae, R. R. and Terracciano, A. (2005). Universal features of personality traits from the observer's perspective: Data from 50 cultures. *Journal of Personality and Social Psychology, 88*(3), 547–61. doi: 10.1037/0022-3514.88.3.547

Mann, R. D. (1959). A review of the relationships between personality and performance in small groups. *Psychological Bulletin, 56*(4), 241–70. doi: 10.1037/h0044587

Martin, R. P., Olejnik, S. and Gaddis, L. (1994). Is temperament an important contributor to schooling outcomes in elementary school? Modeling effects of temperament and scholastic ability on academic achievement. In W. Carey and S. C. McDevit (Eds), *Prevention and early intervention: Individual differences as risk factors for the mental health of children: A festschrift for Stella Chess and Alexander Thomas* (pp. 59–68). New York: Brunner/Mazel.

Mischel, W. (1973). Toward a cognitive social learning reconceptualization of personality. *Psychological Review, 80*(4), 252–83. doi: 10.1037/h0035002

Miserandino, M. (1996). Children who do well in school: Individual differences in perceived competence and autonomy in above-average children. *Journal of Educational Psychology, 88*(2), 203–14. doi: 10.1037/0022-0663.88.2.203

Monaghan, C., Bizumic, B., Reynolds, K., Smithson, M., Johns-Boast, L. and Van Rooy, D. (2015). Performance of software development teams: The influence of personality and identifying as team members. *The European Journal of Engineering Education, 40*(1), 52–67. doi: 10.1080/03043797.2014.914156

Mount, M. K., Barrick, M. R. and Stewart, G. L. (1998). Five-factor model of personality and performance in jobs involving interpersonal interactions. *Human Performance, 11*(2–3), 145–65. doi: 10.1080/08959285.1998.9668029

Neuman, G. A., Wagner, S. H. and Christiansen, N. D. (1999). The relationship between work-team personality composition and the job performance of teams. *Group and Organization Management, 24*(1), 28–45. doi: 10.1177/1059601199241003

O'Connor, M. C. and Paunonen, S. V. (2007). Big Five personality predictors of post-secondary academic performance. *Personality and Individual Differences, 43*(5), 971–90. doi: 10.1016/j.paid.2007.03.017

Parker, J. D. A., Creque, R. E., Sr., Barnhart, D. L., Harris, J. I., Majeski, S. A., Wood, L. M., . . . Hogan, M. J. (2004). Academic achievement in high school: Does emotional intelligence matter? *Personality and Individual Differences, 37*(7), 1321–30. doi: 10.1016/j.paid.2004.01.002

Paulus, P. B. and Dzindolet, M. T. (1993). Social influence processes in group brain-storming. *Journal of Personality and Social Psychology, 64*(4), 575–86. doi: 10.1037/0022-3514.64.4.575

Peeters, M. A. G., Rutte, C. G., van Tuijl, H. F. J. M. and Reymen, I. M. M. J. (2008). Designing in teams: Does personality matter? *Small Group Research, 39*(4), 438–67. doi: 10.1177/1046496408319810

Peeters, M. A. G., van Tuijl, H. F. J. M., Rutte, C. G. and Reymen, I. M. M. J. (2006). Personality and team performance: A meta-analysis. *European Journal of Personality, 20*(5), 377–96. doi: 10.1002/per.588

Poropat, A. E. (2009). A meta-analysis of the five-factor model of personality and academic performance. *Psychological Bulletin, 135*(2), 322–38. doi: 10.1037/a0014996

Poropat, A. E. (2011). The Eysenckian personality factors and their correlations with academic performance. *British Journal of Educational Psychology, 81*(1), 41–58. doi: 10.1348/000709910X497671

Postmes, T. and Jetten, J. (Eds). (2006). *Individuality and the group: Advances in social identity.* Thousand Oaks, CA: Sage. doi: 10.4135/97811446211946

Quinn, D. M. and Spencer, S. J. (2001). The interference of stereotype threat with women's generation of mathematical problem-solving strategies. *Journal of Social Issues, 57*(1), 55–71. doi: 10.1111/0022-4537.00201

Roberts, B. W. (1997). Plaster or plasticity: Are adult work experiences associated with personality change in women? *Journal of Personality, 65*(2), 205–32. doi: 10.1111/j.1467-6494.1997.tb00953.x

Roberts, B. W. and DelVecchio, W. F. (2000). The rank-order consistency of personality traits from childhood to old age: A quantitative review of longitudinal studies. *Psychological Bulletin, 126*(1), 3–25. doi: 10.1037/0033-2909.126.1.3

Roberts, B. W., Walton, K. E. and Viechtbauer, W. (2006). Patterns of mean-level change in personality traits across the life course: A meta-analysis of longitudinal studies. *Psychological Bulletin, 132*(1), 1–25. doi: 10.1037/0033-2909.132.1.1

Schmader, T. (2002). Gender identification moderates stereotype threat effects on women's math performance. *Journal of Experimental Social Psychology, 38*(2), 194–201. doi: 10.1006/jesp.2001.1500

Shih, M., Pittinsky, T. L. and Ambady, N. (1999). Stereotype susceptibility: Identity salience and shifts in quantitative performance. *Psychological Science, 10*(1), 80–3. doi: 10.1111/1467-9280.00111

Spencer, S. J., Steele, C. M. and Quinn, D. M. (1999). Stereotype threat and women's math performance. *Journal of Experimental Social Psychology, 35*(1), 4–28. doi: 10.1006/jesp.1998.1373

Tajfel, H., Billig, M. G., Bundy, R. P. and Flament, C. (1971). Social categorization and intergroup behaviour. *European Journal of Social Psychology, 1*(2), 149–78. doi: 10.1002/ejsp.2420010202

Tajfel, H. and Turner, J. C. (1979). An integrative theory of intergroup conflict. In W. G. Austin and S. Worchel (Eds), *The Social Psychology of Intergroup Relations* (pp. 44–7). Monterey, CA: Brooks/Cole.

Tanghe, J., Wisse, B. and Van Der Flier, H. (2010). The formation of group affect and team effectiveness: The moderating role of identification. *British Journal of Management, 21*(2), 340–58. doi: 10.1111/j.1467-8551.2009.00656.x

Turner, J. C. (1982). Towards a cognitive redefinition of the social group. In H. Tajfel (Ed.), *Social identity and intergroup relations* (pp. 15–40). Cambridge: Cambridge University Press.

Turner, J. C. (1984). Social identification and psychological group formation. In H. Tajfel (Ed.), *The social dimension: European developments in social psychology* (Vol. 2, pp. 519–38). Cambridge: Cambridge University Press.

Turner, J. C. (1999). Some current issues in research on social identity and self-categorization theories. In N. Ellemers, R. Spears and B. Doosje (Eds), *Social identity: Context, commitment, content* (pp. 6–34). Oxford: Blackwell.

Turner, J. C., Hogg, M. A., Oakes, P. J., Reicher, S. D. and Wetherell, M. S. (1987). *Rediscovering the social group: A self-categorization theory.* Oxford: Basil Blackwell.

Turner, J. C., Oakes, P. J., Haslam, S. A. and McGarty, C. (1994). Self and collective: Cognition and social context. *Personality and Social Psychology Bulletin, 20*(5), 454–63. doi: 10.1177/0146167294205002

Turner, J. C. and Onorato, R. S. (1999). Social identity, personality, and the self-concept: A self-categorization perspective. In T. R. Tyler, R. M. Kramer and O. P. John (Eds), *The psychology of the social self* (pp. 11–46). Mahwah, NJ: Lawrence Erlbaum Associates. doi: 10.4324/9781315805689

Turner, J. C., Reynolds, K. J., Haslam, S. A. and Veenstra, K. E. (2006). Reconceptualizing personality: Producing individuality by defining the personal self. In T. Postmes and J. Jetten (Eds), *Individuality and the group: Advances in social identity* (pp. 11–36). Thousand Oaks, CA: Sage. doi: 10.4135/9781446211946

Van Dick, R., Grojean, M. W., Christ, O. and Wieseke, J. (2006). Identity and the extra mile: Relationships between organizational identification and organizational citizenship behaviour. *British Journal of Management, 17*(4), 283–301. doi: 10.1111/j.1467-8551.2006.00520.x

Van Knippenberg, D. (2000). Work motivation and performance: A social identity perspective. *Applied Psychology, 49*(3), 357–71. doi: 10.1111/1464-0597.00020

Van Knippenberg, D., van Dick, R. and Tavares, S. (2007). Social identity and social exchange: Identification, support, and withdrawal from the job. *Journal of Applied Social Psychology, 37*(3), 457–77. doi: 10.1111/j.1559-1816.2007.00168.x

Van Knippenberg, D. and Ellemers, N. (2003). Social identity at work: Developing theory for organisational practice. In S. A. Haslam, D. van Knippenberg, M. J. Platow and N. Ellemers (Eds), *Social identity and group performance: Identification as the key to group-oriented effort* (pp. 155–71). New York: Psychology Press.

15

STUDENT IDENTITY AND THE MARKETISATION OF HIGHER EDUCATION

Stefanie J. Sonnenberg

This chapter explores the role that wider socio-economic processes play in forging identities in higher education (HE). In particular, it considers the social-psychological consequences of students' positioning as 'customers' or 'consumers' in the wake of the current global trend towards the marketisation of HE provision (e.g., Brown and Carasso, 2013; Molesworth, Nixon and Scullion, 2009; Newman and Jahdi, 2009). In doing so, the chapter seeks to highlight the extent to which social identities in HE are not solely a function of intra-institutional or inter-institutional processes but, instead, are also determined by the political and ideological forces that shape the broader socio-economic contexts in which our HE institutions are embedded.

Across the globe, and particularly in the Anglo-Saxon world, HE provision is currently undergoing a profound change. Governments worldwide are placing increasing demands on universities to make a significant tangible (i.e., financial) contribution to the national economy and their nation's international competitive success (e.g., Brown, 2011; Collini, 2012; Foskett, 2011; Maringe, 2005). In response to these political/economic demands, the HE industry has been expanding steadily. For instance, not only are HE institutions now offering an unprecedented range of educational 'products' (Maringe, 2005), but there is also a growing number and greater variety of institutions with degree-conferring powers (e.g., Brown and Carasso, 2013). As a consequence, the present HE sector is characterised by rising levels of competition between institutions, both nationally and internationally. HE and its provision, in other words, have been subject to a process of ever-increasing marketisation (e.g., Brown and Carasso, 2013; Molesworth, Scullion and Nixon, 2011).

To date, one of the countries where the march of marketisation in HE appears most advanced is the UK (Brown and Carasso, 2013). UK universities are playing an increasingly prominent role in the nation's economic profile as well as within the global service sector (Foskett, 2011). Within the UK, universities are dedicating more and more resources to marketing, branding and overall 'customer service', with a particular focus on improving commercial and league table rankings (Brown and Carasso, 2013). Furthermore, during the past three decades, participation rates in English HE have more than tripled, increasing to 47 per cent in 2010–11 (Brown and Carasso, 2013).

The latest developments in the HE sector – especially in the aftermath of the so-called 'Browne report', to which we will turn shortly – have led to grave apprehensions about the direction tertiary education has taken in the UK, particularly in England. Here, serious concerns have been raised about the absence of any overt public and, indeed, academic debate on the question of what universities are (or perhaps should be considered to be) *for* in the first place (Collini, 2012; Love, 2008; Patrick, 2013). In other words, critics have argued that the changes recently implemented in English HE have been based neither on any meaningful prior discussion nor on any degree of general consent regarding the actual purpose(s) of university education (e.g., Collini, 2012; Furedi, 2009).

More specifically, recent developments in the UK's HE provision have led to much conjecture about the likely consequences the trend towards marketisation will have for university education in general and teaching and learning in particular (e.g., Molesworth, Scullion and Nixon, 2011; Newman and Jahdi, 2009). For instance, marketisation has raised significant concerns about the relationship between students and key representatives of HE institutions (e.g., academics). In particular, observers have argued that the marketisation process fundamentally redefines the relationship between academics and students insofar as universities and academics are increasingly regarded as 'service providers', whereas students have become defined as 'customers' or 'consumers' of educational services (e.g., Cheney, McMillan and Schwartzman, 1997; Furedi, 2011; Love, 2008; MacMillan and Cheney, 1996; Molesworth, Nixon and Scullion, 2009; Newman and Jahdi, 2009; Sander, Stevenson, King and Coates, 2000). The following question therefore arises: What are the consequences that students' positioning as 'consumers' – rather than, say, as 'learners' – within our broader political, socio-economic and institutional discourses may have for their educational identities and their experiences and expectations of HE?

There is increasing concern about the impact students' definition as consumers might have on learning and learning-related outcomes. For example, commentators speculate that students' depiction as customers or consumers is likely to alienate them from the learning process as it places them at the receiving end of educational instruction rather than at the centre of it (Maringe, 2011; McMillan and Cheney, 1996). Clayson and Hayley (2005), too, worry that such a depiction undermines students' responsibility for their own learning. Along similar lines, Newman and Jahdi (2009) argue that marketing rhetoric with its insistence on the student-as-customer is likely to lead students to expect a good degree whilst, at the same time, encouraging them to make external attributions for low academic achievement. In other words, the student-as-customer is likely to seek explanations for low attainment, or even failure, not in their own ability to meet the demands of the course but, instead, in the perceived deficiencies or failure of the institution, teaching or teaching staff; this, Newman and Jadhi suggest, might bring about an increase in student complaints.

There is some empirical evidence to indicate that such worries are not entirely unfounded and that students' approach to HE is becoming increasingly instrumental (e.g., Ottewill, 2003). For instance, Rolfe's (2002) analysis of interviews with university lecturers indicates that HE teachers have been observing gradual changes in student motivation for a while; these changes, in turn, tend to be attributed to the expansion of the HE sector and increased tuition fees. Observations made by Rolfe's interviewees included subtle shifts in students' underlying reasons for entering HE and for their choice of discipline, with an increasing emphasis on future employment and career prospects – rather than an inherent interest in learning or in a given subject matter. Moreover, lecturers described students as increasingly reliant on university staff and, correspondingly, displaying greater reluctance to engage in independent reading or study. Similar changes in students' motivations have been observed elsewhere (e.g., Bogler and Somech, 2002; Eagle and Brennan, 2007); these changes are interesting in terms of their potential effects on learning-related outcomes as well as in light of the growing literature on the negative impact extrinsic (versus intrinsic) goals or motivations can have on psychological well-being (e.g., Deci and Ryan, 2008; Schmuck, Kasser and Ryan, 2000; Vansteenkiste, Simons, Lens, Sheldon and Deci, 2004). Besides these observed changes in students' motivations, there is also some anecdotal support for the claim that student complaints have, indeed, been on the rise as a direct consequence of marketisation and the establishment of a consumer culture at universities (e.g., Abrams, 2014; Grove, 2014; Rotfeld, 1999).

In sum, there has been a considerable amount of speculation about the consequences that the marketisation of HE and, more specifically, the depiction of students as customers might have in the long run. The latter in particular, as some previous research indicates, seems to be associated with potential negative outcomes for universities and HE. Yet, to date, empirical evidence on this issue remains relatively sparse. Besides, from a UK perspective, the findings considered so far were obtained prior to some recent dramatic changes in English HE and its funding; it could thus be argued that the student-as-customer has only lately become fully legitimised in the UK and, therefore, warrants further investigation.

Most importantly, from a theoretical perspective, existing work has yet to provide a broader conceptual framework within which to account for the apparent shifts in students' approach to HE. So far, no explicit theoretical links have been made between marketisation on the one hand and the consumer as an educational *identity* on the other hand; or to put it slightly differently, the theoretical question of the mechanisms by which broader socio-economic processes (i.e., marketisation) shape and transform individuals' social-psychological realities (e.g., HE expectations and experiences as well as well-being in education) remains to be addressed. In the remainder of this chapter, my aim is to address this issue by arguing that students' positioning as consumers of educational services does, indeed, have consequences for their educational identities and, therefore, for their expectations and experiences of HE (including their well-being in a HE context).

In the following sections, I will, therefore, attempt to unpack this claim by considering some of the recent developments in the marketisation of the English HE sector. In particular, I will hone in on a UK government-commissioned review of the HE sector – the Browne report – which has had considerable impact on English HE provision in the last couple of years. The purpose of this specific focus is twofold: first, it will provide an explicit example of the nature of the broader forces that shape identities in HE and, as such, will enable me to trace some of the political rhetoric that has contributed to students' positioning as customers or consumers; second, it will provide a specific socio-economic context for examining some tentative empirical evidence regarding the social-psychological consequences that these broader forces, and such positioning, might have for students in HE.

Forging identities in higher education: the UK context

First, then, let us begin to trace some of the recent political forces that have established the student-as-customer in the UK and, in doing so, hone in on a specific key event that has accelerated the marketisation of English HE rather significantly. As we shall see, this political event stands out for several reasons that are pertinent for the current discussion of identity in HE.

The redefinition of English higher education in the wake of the Browne report

In 2009, the publication of a government White Paper (Department for Business, Innovation and Skills, 2009) urged the creation of closer links between the UK's HE institutions and the economy, particularly in regard to addressing the 'skills needs' identified by businesses. In the same year, the UK government initiated an independent review of the English HE system and its funding.[1] The review – led by former BP chief executive Lord Browne – not only aimed to assess the effects of previous legislation (i.e., the 2004 Higher Education Act), but also, most importantly, sought to explore ways to increase the contribution HE institutions make to the national economy and the country's international 'competitive edge' (Browne, 2010, p. 2). More specifically, the review's remit was to explore the changes that would be required to the then current system of HE funding and student finance to allow for further expansion and diversification of HE provision in England.

A year later, the review's proposals for the future sustainability of HE were published in the Browne report (2010). As already stated, the fundamental issue at the heart of the review concerned the financial viability and competitiveness of the HE sector – that is, the review's concerns were explicitly economic, rather than educational, in nature. The review's specific principles for HE reform were premised on the assertion that the private benefits derived from HE (measured in terms of graduates' higher lifetime earnings) by far exceed its public benefits. Indeed, it is on the back of this claim that Browne's suggested increase in university tuition fees was justified since, as the report states, 'it is reasonable to ask those who gain private benefits from HE to help fund it rather than rely solely on public funds collected through taxation from people who may not have participated in HE themselves' (2010, p. 21). As Collini — one of the most articulate critics of this trend in UK HE — observed at the time, Browne's stance 'signals a redefinition of higher education and the retreat of the state from financial responsibility for it' (2010, p. 23).

The student-as-consumer

One aspect of Browne's redefinition of HE as a private rather than a public good that is of particular relevance in the context of the present discussion is the accompanying definitive shift in the conception of the student — namely, to an explicit positioning as customer or consumer. This, in turn, is achieved by placing great emphasis on the notion of 'rational student choice'. As such, Browne's recommendations for HE reform are firmly rooted in free market ideology and rhetoric. For example, the review suggests that 'the money will follow the student' (2010, p. 4), emphatically insisting that student choice must be heeded and increased:

> Most of the investment in HE goes to institutions through a block grant and students have no sight of what it is buying.
> We want to put students at the heart of the system. Students are best placed to make the judgment about what they want to get from participating in higher education. [. . .]
> In our proposals, there will be more student places across the system as a whole. Relevant institutions will be able to expand faster to meet student demand; others will have to raise their game to respond. Students will be better informed about the range of options available to them. *Their choices will shape the landscape of higher education.*
>
> (2010, p. 25, emphasis added)

Here, student choice is not only seen as propelling the expansion of the HE sector but, crucially, also as determining educational content (i.e., the available 'range of options'). The HE landscape thus envisioned is one that is profoundly shaped by student demand (i.e., by the exertion of rational consumer choice). This choice, in turn, is supposedly based on price or value for money calculations to ensure that students can keep sight of what they are buying, to paraphrase Browne (2010, p. 25). In Browne's vision of HE, then, the supremacy of the consumer and his/her choice lies 'at the heart of the system'.[2]

To recap the most salient points for our discussion here, Browne's twin emphases on the importance of the HE sector's expansion and international competitiveness and on value for money calculations by students as customers clearly signal that HE provision in England should no longer be regarded as a public good

> articulated through educational judgement and largely financed by public funds. . . . Instead, we should think of it as a lightly regulated market in which consumer demand, in the form of student choice, is sovereign in determining what is offered by service providers (i.e., universities).
>
> (Collini, 2010, p. 23)

The recommendations for HE reform put forward by the Browne report were, by no means, without their criticisms. In fact, at the time of its publication, there was considerable opposition to the review and an expression of grave concerns over the potentially damaging impact its recommendations would have on the HE landscape (e.g., Collini, 2010; Evans, 2011). For instance, Evans argued that the implementation of Browne's proposals 'would alter fundamentally the pattern of checks and balances in HE in England' (2011, p. 121), especially since the proposals had substantial implications for how conflicts between students and HE institutions might be resolved in the future. In particular, Evans warned that Browne's overall vision unduly emphasised 'win or lose' outcomes in future dispute resolutions between students and universities (i.e., by explicitly pitting the student-as-consumer against his/her university) – which, Evans argued, would likely result in a broader culture of 'naming and shaming' HE institutions. Moreover, Evans expressed concern about the review's implication for academic content as

> the wording and general tenor of . . . the Report appears to envisage *direct intrusion into course design*, which could, for instance, include imposing a national curriculum for courses . . . with specified numbers of hours for 'delivery' of each part, to be reviewed if failing students expressed dissatisfaction and complained that they had failed because some element of the course had been inadequately 'delivered'.
>
> (2011, p. 125, emphasis added)

Yet, despite much well-articulated (academic) opposition, the review's overall vision of HE appeared to chime with policymakers. Indeed, many of the principles for reform suggested by Browne have since become translated into actual government policy. For example, state support for HE has been withdrawn significantly through a major cut in the annual government block grant to universities, which supports teaching; this teaching grant is expected to decline further over the next few years (see Brown and Carasso, 2013). As a consequence, undergraduate teaching in England is now mainly funded by student fees. Annual student fees, in turn, have almost tripled: the cap on fees of £3,375 per academic year set in 2006 was raised to £9,000 in September 2012.

Clearly, the apparent privatisation of English HE cannot be exclusively attributed to Browne's recommendations. In fact, it has been suggested that marketisation of HE in the UK was instigated by the Thatcher government's introduction of full-cost fees for overseas students in 1980 and that, since then, a series of key policy events under different governments has contributed to establishing the current state of affairs (see Brown and Carasso, 2013). Nevertheless, the previous coalition government's programme of HE reforms based on the Browne report, and its subsequent integration into another government White Paper (Department for Business, Innovation and Skills, 2011), has significantly accelerated the marketisation process; in fact, it has been described as 'the most radical [reform programme] in the history of UK higher education, and amongst the most radical anywhere' (Brown and Carasso, 2013, p. 1).

As several commentators have pointed out, there is little empirical evidence so far on the impact these changes in the English HE sector may have on the quality of student education (e.g., Brown and Carasso, 2013). In fact, in the UK, the term 'education' appears to be vanishing altogether from both political and university administrators' discourse. Instead, 'education' has been replaced by the rather vacuous 'student experience', which is, of course, far more compatible with the student-as-customer and his/her supposed rational choice based on value for money in HE. Since its commissioning by the Higher Education Funding Council for England (HEFCE) in 2005, the National Student Survey (NSS) – an annual survey of all final-year HE students – has functioned as the main gauge of this 'student experience'.[3] However, since Browne's review, its insistence on student choice and the subsequent changes in English HE, the NSS seems to have taken on another dimension of meaning: it is more palpably becoming a measure of consumer satisfaction and consumer demand. We will return to this issue below.

In summary, there have been seismic shifts in the marketisation of HE provision in the UK, particularly in England. As we have seen, the nature of the impetus behind this marketisation process has been a political/ideological one. It is by means of this impetus, and by drawing on a broader socio-economic discourse, that HE has been (re)defined as a private good and that the relationships between universities, their teaching staff and students have been readjusted. This, then, provides the wider context in which we now find ourselves positioned as service providers and customers, respectively. Let us now return to the question posed earlier: What are the social-psychological consequences of such positioning? In broader terms, what are the psychological mechanisms by which these socio-economic processes may come to transform individuals' experiences and expectations in the context of HE?

Beyond metaphors: the social-psychological consequences of students' positioning as customers/consumers

As already noted, there has been much speculation and concern about the consequences that the conception of students as customers or consumers may have for education – and these concerns are not new. For instance, as Cheney,

McMillan and Schwartzman (1997) warned nearly two decades ago, the widespread adoption of the student-as-consumer metaphor is suggestive of an undue distance between the student and his or her education; it is likely to dissociate students from their own learning – for example, by decreasing intrinsic motivation, increasing extrinsic motivation and undermining the active part students play in learning – thus hampering their critical engagement in the educational process (see also Molesworth *et al.*, 2011). McMillan and Cheney (1996) also worried that insistence on the student-as-consumer metaphor would undermine the importance of collaboration between universities and the sense of community within them (i.e., reinforcing individualism), thus requiring greater self-promotion on the part of academic faculty and encouraging an 'entertainment model' of classroom learning.

The use of metaphors in portraying students in HE is not new, and many different ones have been suggested over the years (e.g., Tight, 2013). However, it is my contention here that the student-as-consumer has moved beyond occupying purely metaphorical status – instead, it is now becoming an aspect of students' educational identity (at least in England). The basis for this claim is twofold. First, as we have seen in our discussion above, through the changes in English HE instigated by the Browne report, the sovereignty of students' consumer choice has now become fully embedded and legitimised within educational policy (i.e., in law). Second, alongside these HE policy changes, marketing theory has become prevalent in the management of HE institutions, and as a result, student (i.e., customer) satisfaction now represents a key output variable for universities' service provision (Moosmayer and Siems, 2012). The steady emergence of marketing practices – and associated customer satisfaction measures, league table rankings, and so on – thus bears further testimony to the fact that the student-as-consumer has transcended its use as a metaphor. In other words, the positioning of students as customers or consumers is now politically and institutionally enshrined.

From a theoretical perspective, it therefore seems plausible to argue that HE students in the UK, specifically in England, are likely to derive an aspect of their educational identity from being positioned as consumers. I will turn to discuss some preliminary evidence for this claim shortly. First, however, I will briefly outline the key theoretical points that are central to this claim. The social identity approach in social psychology (e.g., Haslam, 2004; Postmes and Branscombe, 2010; Tajfel and Turner, 1979; Turner *et al.*, 1987) provides a rich theoretical tradition – backed by an impressive range of empirical evidence – which suggests that our identities are crucial in determining our attitudes, behaviours and values. In other words, within this approach, people's values, attitudes and behaviours are regarded as a function of social identity processes (i.e., as contingent on their salient self-concepts); in fact, even our psychological well-being has been linked to social identification (e.g., Jetten, Haslam and Haslam, 2012; see also McNeill, Smyth and Mavor, Chapter 18, this volume). In the context of the current discussion, drawing on this particular theoretical perspective allows us to conceptualise political and socio-economic processes as forging identities in HE in two broad ways: (1) in terms of their capacity to frame *intergroup relations* both between insti-tutions and intra-institutionally (e.g., relations between universities as compet-itive rather than cooperative; students as customers and teaching staff as service providers; managers as business leaders and scholars as employees; see Reynolds, Subasic, Lee and Bromhead, Chapter 3, this volume); and (2) in terms of their ability to shape *individuals' self-understandings* in these educational contexts. I will now turn to consider the role these identity processes may play in HE. In partic-ular, I will focus on some preliminary evidence from the UK in order to examine the consequences that students' positioning as consumers may have for their HE experiences as well as for broader social-psychological outcomes.

Student identity and its correlates: some preliminary evidence from the UK

With increasing concerns about students' positioning as consumers – rather than, for instance, as learners – I examined, in a series of preliminary studies, the role such positioning may play in terms of students' educational identities and their experiences and expectations of HE in England (including learning-related indices) as well as in terms of broader psychological outcomes (e.g., well-being). Guided by the social identity approach, I assumed that students' positioning as consumers could be considered as a specific dimension of their educational social identity. By the same token, I assumed that being defined or positioned as learners constitutes another aspect of students' educational social identities.

As already stated, within the social identity approach, people's attitudes and values are seen as intrinsically linked to their self-concept(s); more specifically, attitudes and values are considered to be a function of social identity processes and, in line with more recent work, so too is psychological well-being. In the context of HE, there has been an increasing focus on students' attitudes and values over the past few years. More specifically, the emphasis on students as consumers of educational services has gone hand in hand with the requirement to understand consumers' attitudes, needs or demands – which, in turn, is achieved by means of measuring students' (dis)satisfaction with their HE 'experiences' (e.g., Newman and Jahdi, 2009).

In the UK, the annual NSS constitutes the principal measure of students' assessment of the quality of their HE experiences. As such, the NSS provides the HE sector's main gauge of consumer attitudes or consumer demand. Within the social identity approach, it can be argued that demand, too, is a function of iden-tity processes since 'what people want, and what they think they need, depends on who they think they are' (Haslam *et al.*, 2010, p. 372). On the basis of this theoretical model, then, the following series of studies explored whether identity processes do, indeed, play a role in students' assessment of the quality of their HE experience (i.e., consumer demand) as well as in other learning-related outcomes. We also considered student well-being in this context, based on the theoretical grounds outlined above as well as on existing work on goals and motivation which suggests that across various life domains, including in educational settings, intrinsic motivation and goals tend to be associated with better performance or outcomes (e.g., Vansteenkiste, Simons, Lens, Sheldon and Deci, 2004) and greater psychological health and well-being (Baker, 2004; Deci and Ryan, 2008; Schmuck, Kasser and Ryan, 2000).

Study 1

On the basis of previous speculations regarding the potential detrimental effects of conceptualising students as consumers/customers (e.g., Molesworth *et al.*, 2011), we hypothesised that students defined as consumers would be less satisfied with their HE experience than students defined as learners. In order to test this hypothesis, we manipulated these different dimensions of educational identity (Sonnenberg and Morris, 2011).

We asked 195 English undergraduate students to complete a brief survey consisting of the questions that constitute the NSS. The NSS comprises 22 attitude statements intended to measure final-year students' satisfaction with their chosen degree course. In addition to one general item tapping students' overall assessment of the quality of their chosen course ('Overall, I am satisfied with the quality of my course'), the NSS statements are designed to elicit students' evaluations of different aspects of HE provision – such as teaching (e.g., 'Staff have made the subject interesting'; 'Staff are good at explaining things'), assessment and feedback (e.g., 'Assessment arrangements and marking have been fair'), academic support (e.g., 'Good advice was available when I needed to make study choices'), organisation and management (e.g., 'The course is well organised') and learning resources – as well as personal development (e.g., 'My communication skills have improved').

The survey was completed under two experimental conditions that tapped different dimensions of students' educational identity – that is, participants were positioned either as 'learners' or as 'consumers'. Specifically, we manipulated the context in which the NSS questions were embedded with the aim of rendering different aspects of students' identities salient. The experimental manipulation simply consisted in varying the introduction to the NSS items (i.e., the cover sheets of the survey): in the 'learner' condition, the introduction comprised a brief paragraph that described HE as enabling the development of a set of skills and providing new learning opportunities, whereas, in the 'consumer' condition, the introductory text referred to the purpose of HE as delivering a set of products related to future employability and income. The phrasing of the NSS items was identical in both conditions.

The results of this relatively simple manipulation were rather striking, although perhaps not entirely surprising. In line with the prediction, when being positioned as 'consumers', participants' overall evaluation and satisfaction with their course was lower across all aspects of HE, including teaching, assessment and personal development (Sonnenberg and Morris, 2011). More specifically, the differences between the two experimental groups were statistically reliable for 16 out of the 22 NSS items: in comparison to students in the 'learner' group, those who were addressed as 'consumers' reported significantly lower levels of satisfaction with their 'student experience' on 16 NSS items. Crucially, this included a significant difference in students' responses to the general statement 'Overall, I am satisfied with the quality of my course', with 'consumers' reporting significantly lower overall satisfaction than 'learners'. This finding seems particularly noteworthy because, in the UK, students' responses to this general item are used as the basis of universities' national league table rankings in terms of student satisfaction. This preliminary experimental evidence suggests, then, that positioning students as consumers – as opposed to learners – can have negative consequences for the perceived quality of their HE experience (Sonnenberg and Morris, 2011).

Although we interpreted the differences in course satisfaction between 'consumers' and 'learners' as a direct function of identity processes, an explanation of these differences in terms of framing effects could not be entirely ruled out. In other words, this study did not provide any direct evidence for students' own endorsement of these two dimensions of educational identity as the key explanatory factor. The following questions, therefore, remained: To what extent do 'the learner' and 'the consumer' provide meaningful aspects of students' own educational identity or self-concept? Do students' own self-conceptualisations, in turn, play a role in their HE experience? We therefore addressed these questions in two subsequent correlational studies. In particular, we aimed to clarify the role that identity processes play in students' overall assessment of HE and their attitudes towards learning as well as in relation to psychological outcomes (i.e., subjective well-being).

Study 2

In an online survey, we asked 221 English undergraduate students to indicate the extent to which they regarded themselves as 'learners' or as 'consumers' (Sonnenberg and Fitzpatrick, 2012). To this end, we used a ten-item 'student identity' measure (adapted from Butler *et al.*, 2011, and Sonnenberg and Morris, 2011) in which five attitude statements tapped students' self-conceptualisation as learners (e.g., 'As a learner, I see higher education as providing an opportunity to enhance my understanding and ability to engage critically with the world') and the remaining items, their self-definition as consumers (e.g., 'As a student, I see myself as a consumer of the university's products and services'). Again, we measured students' overall satisfaction with the quality of their chosen course (i.e., using the general item from the NSS – 'Overall, I am satisfied with the quality of my course'). In addition, we included a measure of students' dedication to their course, which aimed to gauge students' commitment to their studies (e.g., 'How hard do you feel you have worked?'), as well as an overall well-being measure that tapped students' perceived satisfaction with their life in general (adapted from Diener, Emmons, Larsen and Griffin, 1985, and Lyubomirsky and Lepper, 1999).

On the whole, we found that students endorsed their identity as learners to a significantly greater extent than their identity as consumers (Sonnenberg and Fitzpatrick, 2012). However, we also found systematic and statistically reliable differences between students who defined themselves predominantly in terms of being a consumer and those for whom their identity as a learner was relatively more important. In particular, students who endorsed their identity as consumers to a greater extent than their identity as learners were less satisfied with their HE experience (i.e., the quality of their course) and also reported feeling less dedicated to their studies in general. Most importantly, in comparison to those who primarily identified as learners, consumers reported significantly lower well-being. Well-being, in turn, was significantly associated with greater overall course satisfaction. This finding seems particularly striking as it not only highlights the importance of identity-related processes for well-being in general (e.g., Jetten, Haslam and Haslam, 2012), but also draws specific attention to a possible relationship between student identity and well-being in the HE context.

The results of this study indicate that 'the learner' and 'the consumer' can, indeed, be considered as meaningful attributes of students' social identities in HE (although they do not appear to constitute entirely separate dimensions of educational identity). In line with our experimental findings, these results, thus, lend further support to the claim that identity processes are implicated in students' evaluation of the quality of their HE experience. Moreover, these findings suggest that students' educational self-concepts might have psychological consequences, not only in terms of how dedicated they are to their studies but also in regard to their overall well-being.

Study 3

Finally, in a follow-up survey of 181 English undergraduate students, we aimed to expand the above findings by examining: students' motivation for entering HE (e.g., 'The purpose of studying for a degree is to increase my knowledge' or 'The purpose of studying for a degree is to increase my employability'); students' attributions for their academic performance (e.g., 'When I get low marks, it tends to because of the quality of the teaching'); their self-assessment of the extent of their learning on their course (a two-item cognitive learning measure designed by McCroskey, Sallinen, Fayer, Richmond and Barraclough, 1996: 'How much do you think you have learnt/could have learnt during your course to date?'); as well as their view on whether their chosen degree course offered value for money (Sonnenberg, Perrett and Kelly, 2015). The sample included students who had commenced their degree course under an old tuition fee regime (i.e., up to £6,000 per academic year) as well as students who commenced their studies under a new fee regime (i.e., up to £9,000 per academic year). As previously, we also asked students to indicate the extent to which they regarded themselves as 'learners' or as 'consumers' and measured overall course satisfaction (e.g., 'Overall, I am satisfied with the quality of my course') and well-being (e.g., 'I am satisfied with my life').

Findings suggested a significant relationship between student social identity and motivations for entering HE: predictably, the more pronounced a student's self-definition as a consumer, the greater his/her extrinsic motivation for entering HE (e.g., 'A degree that does not enhance one's earning potential is not worth studying for'). In addition, we found that students' educational social identities were relevant for how they viewed their learning and academic achievement. In particular, the greater the extent to which students endorsed an identity as consumer, the more likely they were to attribute low attainment to external causes (e.g., lecturers). In other words, consumers were less likely to seek explanations for academic failure in their own lack of understanding or their particular approach to learning. Attributions for academic performance were, in turn, significantly related to perceived learning and overall well-being: the more external students' attributions were in terms of their achievement, the lower were the perceived extent of their learning and their reported well-being. Conversely, the greater students perceived their learning to be, the higher their well-being. As was the case in Study 2, we found that higher well-being was also associated with greater course satisfaction.

Interestingly, students' self-conceptualisations were also related to whether they perceived they got value for money from their respective degree course or university (i.e., 'Do you think you are getting good value for money at your university?'). More specifically, there was a significant difference between students for whom educational identity was primarily defined by being consumers and those who predominantly identified as learners: consumers' answers to the question of whether they received value for money tended to be 'no', whilst the reverse was the case for learners.

Finally, the study provided some tentative evidence to suggest that the recent increase in tuition fees in England has had a significant effect on students' educational identities (i.e., indicating that students' self-definitions are changing as a direct function of the new fee regime). In comparison to students who started their degree prior to the recent tuition fee increase (i.e., the 2011 cohort), we found that students' relative self-definition as consumers was significantly more pronounced under the new fee regime (i.e., in 2013). In other words, for post-fee increase students, educational social identity was more significantly defined in terms of being consumers. Interestingly, in comparison to those paying lower tuition fees, students paying higher fees also assessed their own learning as being significantly lower.

Taken together, the findings from this series of studies suggest that students' positioning as consumers does, indeed, have consequences not only for their educational social identity but also their expectations of HE, their learning and their well-being. The preliminary evidence outlined above indicates that 'the consumer' – at least in the UK context – can now be assumed to inhabit a part of students' selves; in other words, it constitutes a psychologically meaningful aspect of students' self-definition in HE. What is more, in line with previous speculations, our findings point to a range of potentially adverse outcomes in relation to students' self-conceptions as consumers. Conversely, this initial evidence also suggests that students' self-definition as learners might be associated with more positive outcomes (i.e., relating to course satisfaction, learning, motivation and even well-being; see also in this volume, Bliuc, Goodyear and Ellis, Chapter 12, and Smyth, Mavor, Platow and Grace, Chapter 13).

The above studies yield evidence in support of the claim that the student-as-consumer – in comparison to the student who predominantly defines herself/himself as a learner – is less satisfied with the quality of his/her HE experience. This, then, suggests that identity processes are likely to be implicated in current quality assessment practices and, therefore, in measuring consumer demand in HE. Crucially, as our experimental evidence shows (see Study 1), consumer demand can, in fact, be manipulated or influenced via students' positioning; that is, our experimental findings demonstrate that explicitly referring to students as consumers, as opposed to learners, can have a direct negative impact on their assessment of their courses and, thus, satisfaction with or attitudes towards their HE institutions.

This specific finding has wider-ranging implications for the measurement of student satisfaction or consumer demand in HE. In particular, our experimental evidence suggests that students' responses to the NSS might vary as a function of the broader context in which this satisfaction measure is presented. This, in turn, raises concerns about the validity of the NSS as a tool for gauging the quality of 'the student experience'. Perhaps more importantly, it also raises some unease about the potentially negative long-term impact that increased marketisation, with its discursive and political emphasis on students as consumers, might have on students' experiences and expectations of HE. Furthermore, as students' responses to the NSS now play a major role in UK universities' league table rankings, the current findings have practical implications insofar as relatively minor changes in students' satisfaction are likely to translate into comparatively large changes in such rankings. In sum, our studies are a first step in lending some tentative empirical support to previous speculations about the damaging consequences of marketisation and the (psychological) costs of students' positioning as consumers.

Concluding remarks

This chapter sought to engage with and inform contemporary discussion of the global trend towards marketisation of HE by drawing on principles from the social identity approach to self and identity (e.g., Haslam, 2004; Haslam et al., 2010; Tajfel and Turner, 1979; Turner et al., 1987). In doing so, and by focusing on the current UK context as an example, the chapter aimed to sketch some of the broader political and socio-economic forces by which identities in education – and specifically the student-as-consumer – are forged. In particular, I have attempted to illustrate, by means of preliminary evidence, that the marketisation process and its concomitant positioning of students as consumers is likely to have (adverse) consequences for students' self-definitions, experiences and expectations of HE and learning as well as for their well-being.

The commodification of HE has complex origins (e.g., Kaye, Bickel and Birtwistle, 2006), which renders the sketch presented in this chapter inevitably incomplete. For example, Kaye *et al.* (2006) argue that the seeds of the current mass education system, and thus modern consumerist attitudes to education, were sown within the 1948 Universal Declaration of Human Rights, which enshrined education as a human right. Since then, Kaye *et al.* maintain, the law and several legal developments have contributed to a focus on students and their (legal) rights, emphasising the contractual nature of the relationship between students and universities. According to Kaye *et al.*, it is this 'paradigm shift towards a "rights culture" [that] has led to the problem of consumerism in HE' (2006, p. 105). Students in HE now certainly seem to have an awareness of their 'customer rights', which are also made salient through universities' own feedback processes (Sander, Stevenson, King and Coates, 2000). Moreover, in the UK, the commodification of HE has gone hand in hand with an increasing loss of differentiation between education and (vocational) training (e.g., see Collini, 2012; Furedi, 2009; Kaye *et al.*, 2006).

Concerns about the commodification of HE are, therefore, not new. However, the commodification of HE associated with a mass education system is by no means synonymous with the marketisation of university education; in other words, defining education as a commodity or 'right' is not equivalent to the creation of a HE market (nor does it inevitably lead to the notion of students as customers). What *is* new, however, is the ever-increasing use of business analogies and the prevalence of marketing theory in the management of HE institutions (e.g., Collini, 2012; Furedi, 2009; Moosmayer and Siems, 2012) alongside an emphasis on economic viability and interinstitutional competition. The *overt* positioning and legitimisation of the student as customer or consumer – via recent government policy – is also new, as is the growing emphasis in the UK on value for money in HE. The latter is, of course, notoriously difficult to define as it is by no means clear what constitutes the 'product' in HE provision (e.g., Newman and Jahdi, 2009) or what, exactly, is being bought and sold (Foskett, 2011).

Yet, despite a lack of clear articulation (beyond rather simplistic references to 'contact hours') of what represents value for money in HE, in the wake of the recent increase of the tuition fee cap to £9,000 per year, a growing number of UK undergraduate students report receiving poor value for money from their universities (Bekhradnia, 2013; Kandiko and Mawer, 2013). From the standpoint of the student-as-consumer and, therefore, from an educational social identity perspective, this rise in discontent seems unsurprising. In fact, increasing student dissatisfaction seems a predictable consequence of ever-growing expectations in HE due to the rise in tuition fees – and in light of the infinite malleability of the concept of the 'student experience' (Moosmayer and Siems, 2012).

In conclusion, identities in HE are not shaped solely by inter- or intra-institutional processes but are also determined by the broader political and socio-economic context in which universities are embedded. In many countries, these broader contexts are now characterised by an increased focus on the marketisation of HE and its provision. In the UK, particularly in England, this marketisation process seems the most advanced, with recent government policy essentially signalling the privatisation of HE. Students' positioning as consumers – and their self-conceptualisations as such – can therefore be considered a function of the political/ideological redefinition of HE as a private rather than a public good. Such positioning, as we have seen, has consequences for students themselves as well as for society as a whole. As Collini, one of the most astute observers of HE in the UK, notes:

> In a climate where so much of the discussion of universities turns on questions of funding, it has come to seem almost inevitable that the only criterion of the expenditure of 'public money' assumed to command widespread acceptance where this ethos prevails is the consumerist one of increased prosperity. . . . This all too easily translates into the economistic philistinism of insisting that the activities carried on in universities need to be justified, perhaps can only be justified, by demonstrating their contribution to the economy. In the face of this, one has to make, over and over again, the obvious point that a society does not educate the next generation in order for them to contribute to its economy. It educates them in order that they should extend and deepen their understanding of themselves and the world, acquiring, in the course of this form of growing up, kinds of knowledge and skill which will be useful in their eventual employment, but which will no more be the sum of their education than that employment will be the sum of their lives.
>
> (2012, p. 91)

This, then, brings us back full circle to the question of what should be considered to be the primary purpose of education. According to Love (2008), contemporary discussions of HE are notable for their absence of articulation of any explicit educational ideals. The current lack of educational ideals, in turn, means that 'the economic threatens to eclipse all else, becoming the very raison d'être of educational institutions' (Love, 2008, p. 16). It has been the contention of this chapter that this state of affairs – manifest in the positioning of the student as consumer and the university as service provider – comes at a (psychological) cost, especially to students.

Notes

1   Within the UK, HE and its funding in Scotland, Wales and Northern Ireland have become increasingly divergent from England.
2   Such rhetoric patently draws on the *rational actor* – or *Homo economicus* – model of human action that lies at the root of neoclassical economic theory. This model is, of course, deeply problematic and has received widespread criticism throughout the social sciences (e.g., Etzioni, 1988; Sonnenberg, 2004; Zafirovski, 1999, 2000). We

cannot revisit these critiques here; for our present purposes, therefore, suffice it to note that Browne's recommendations, and the subsequent changes to HE they brought about, seem to be based on behavioural and psychological assumptions for which there is scant empirical support (e.g., Sonnenberg, 2004; Thaler, 1999, 2000; Tversky and Thaler, 1990).

3   This phrase is explicitly used by the HEFCE. The organisation's website states that the purpose of the NSS 'is to contribute to public accountability, help inform the choices of prospective students and provide data that assists institutions in enhancing the student experience' (see https://www.hefce.ac.uk/whatwedo/lt/publicinfo/nationalstudentsurvey/).

References

Abrams, F. (2014). University complaints by students top 20,000 [online], *BBC*, 3 June. Retrieved from: www.bbc.co.uk/news/education-27640303

Baker, S. R. (2004). Intrinsic, extrinsic, and amotivational orientations: Their role in university adjustment, stress, well-being, and subsequent academic performance. *Current Psychology*, *23*(3), 189–202.

Bogler, R. and Somech, A. (2002). Motives to study and socialization processes: The case of university students. *The Journal of Social Psychology*, *142*(2), 233–48.

Bekhradnia, B. (2013). *The Student Academic Experience Survey*. Joint report produced by the Higher Education Policy Institute and Which? Magazine. Retrieved from: www.hepi.ac.uk/wp-content/uploads/2014/02/1.Higher_Educational_Report.pdf (accessed 1 September 2016).

Brown, R. (2011). The march of the market. In M. Molesworth, R. Scullion and E. Nixon (Eds), *The marketisation of higher education and the student as consumer* (pp. 9–24). London: Routledge.

Brown, R. and Carasso, H. (2013). *Everything for sale? The marketisation of UK Higher Education*. London: Routledge.

Browne, J. (2010). *Securing a sustainable future for higher education: An independent review of higher education funding and student finance* [Browne report]. London: Department for Business, Innovation and Skills.

Butler, A., Lea, S. E. G. and Smith, J. (2011). The commercialisation of higher education in the UK: The effect of tuition fee payment on students' perception of their university. Paper presented at the *IAREP/SABE Annual Conference*, Exeter, UK, 12–16 July.

Cheney, G., McMillan, J. J. and Schwartzman, R. (1997). Should we buy the 'student-as-consumer' metaphor? *The Montana Professor*, *7*(3), 8–11.

Clayson, D. E. and Haley, D. A. (2005). Marketing models in education: Students as customers, products, or partners. *Marketing Education Review*, *15*(1), 1–10.

Collini, S. (2010). Browne's gamble. *London Review of Books*, *32*(21), 23–5.

Collini, S. (2012). *What are universities for?* London: Penguin.

Deci, E. L. and Ryan, R. M. (2008). Facilitating optimal motivation and psychological well-being across life's domains. *Canadian Psychology*, *49*(1), 14–23.

Department for Business, Innovation and Skills. (2009). *Higher Ambitions: The Future of Universities in a Knowledge Economy*. London: Department for Business, Innovation and Skills.

Department for Business, Innovation and Skills. (2011). *Higher Education: Students at the Heart of the System*. London: Department for Business, Innovation and Skills.

Diener, E. D., Emmons, R. A., Larsen, R. J. and Griffin, S. (1985). The satisfaction with life scale. *Journal of Personality Assessment*, *49*(1), 71–4.

Eagle, L. and Brennan, R. (2007). Are students customers? TQM and marketing perspectives. *Quality Assurance in Education, 15*(1), 44–60.

Etzioni, A. (1988). *The moral dimension: Toward a new economics.* New York: The Free Press.

Evans, G. R. (2011). The Browne review and the future of dispute resolution in higher education. *The Law Teacher, 45*(1), 121–30. © The Association of Law Teachers, reprinted by permission of Taylor & Francis Ltd, www.tandfonline.com, on behalf of The Association of Law Teachers.

Foskett, N. (2011). Markets, government, funding and the marketisation of UK higher education. In M. Molesworth, R. Scullion and E. Nixon (Eds), *The marketisation of higher education and the student as consumer* (pp. 25–38). London: Routledge.

Furedi, F. (2009). *Wasted: Why Education Isn't Educating.* London: Continuum.

Furedi, F. (2011). Introduction to the marketisation of higher education and the student as consumer. In M. Molesworth, R. Scullion and E. Nixon (Eds), *The Marketisation of Higher Education and the Student as Consumer* (pp. 25–38). London: Routledge.

Grove, J. (2014). Student complaints about assessment grow as fee levels rise. *Times Higher Education,* 23 January. Retrieved from: www.timeshighereducation.co.uk/news/student-complaints-about-assessment-grow-as-fee-levels-rise/2010711.article

Haslam, S. A. (2004). *Psychology in organizations: The social identity approach.* London: Sage.

Haslam, S. A., Ellemers, N., Reicher, S. D., Reynolds, K. J. and Schmitt, M. T. (2010). The social identity perspective tomorrow: Opportunities and avenues for advance. In T. Postmes and N. R. Branscombe (Eds), *Rediscovering social identity: Core sources* (pp. 357–79). New York: Psychology Press.

Jetten, J., Haslam, C. and Haslam, S. A. (Eds). (2012). *The social cure: Identity, health and well-being.* New York and Hove: Psychology Press.

Kandiko, C. B. and Mawer, M. (2013). *Student expectations and perceptions of higher education: Executive summary.* London: King's Learning Institute.

Kaye, T., Bickel, R. D. and Birtwistle, T. (2006). Criticizing the image of the student as consumer: Examining legal trends and administrative response in the US and the UK. *Education and Law, 18*(2–3), 85–129.

Love, K. (2008). Higher education, pedagogy and the 'customerisation' of teaching and learning. *Journal of Philosophy of Education, 42*(1), 15–34.

Lyubomirsky, S. and Lepper, H. S. (1999). A measure of subjective happiness: Preliminary reliability and construct validation. *Social Indicators Research, 46*(2), 137–55.

Maringe, F. (2005). Interrogating the crisis in higher education marketing: The CORD model. *International Journal of Educational Management, 19*(7), 564–78.

Maringe, F. (2011). The student as consumer: Affordances and constraints in a transforming higher education environment. In M. Molesworth, R. Scullion and E. Nixon (Eds), *The marketisation of higher education and the student as consumer* (pp. 142–54). London: Routledge.

McCroskey, J. C., Sallinen, A., Fayer, J. M., Richmond, V. P. and Barraclough, R. A. (1996). Nonverbal immediacy and cognitive learning: A cross-cultural investigation. *Communication Education, 45*(3), 164–75.

McMillan, J. J. and Cheney, G. (1996). The student as consumer: The implications and limitations of a metaphor. *Communication Education, 45*(1), 1–15.

Molesworth, M., Nixon, E. and Scullion, R. (2009). Having, being and higher education: The marketisation of the university and the transformation of the student into consumer. *Teaching in Higher Education, 14*(3), 277–87.

Molesworth, M., Scullion, R. and Nixon, E. (Eds). (2011). *The marketisation of higher education and the student as consumer.* London: Routledge.

Moosmayer, D. C. and Siems, F. U. (2012). Values education and student satisfaction: German business students' perceptions of universities' value influences. *Journal of Marketing for Higher Education, 22*(2), 257–72.

Newman, S. and Jahdi, K. (2009). Marketisation of education: Marketing, rhetoric and reality. *Journal of Further and Higher Education, 33*(1), 1–11.

Ottewill, R. M. (2003). What's wrong with instrumental learning? The case of business and management. *Education and Training, 45*(4), 189–96.

Patrick, F. (2013). Neoliberalism, the knowledge economy, and the learner: Challenging the inevitability of the commodified self as an outcome of education. *ISRN Education, 2013*, 108705. doi: 10.1155/2013/108705

Postmes, T. and Branscombe, N. R. (Eds.). (2010) *Rediscovering social identity: Core sources.* New York: Psychology Press.

Rolfe, H. (2002). Students' demands and expectations in an age of reduced financial support: The perspectives of lecturers in four English universities. *Journal of Higher Education Policy and Management, 24*(2), 171–82.

Rotfeld, H. J. (1999). Misplaced marketing: When marketing misplaces the benefits of education. *Journal of Consumer Marketing, 16*(5), 415–17.

Sander, P., Stevenson, K., King, M. and Coates, D. (2000). University students' expectations of teaching. *Studies in Higher Education, 25*(3), 309–23.

Schmuck, P., Kasser, T. and Ryan, R. M. (2000). Intrinsic and extrinsic goals: Their structure and relationship to well-being in German and U.S. college students. *Social Indicators Research, 50*(2), 225–41.

Sonnenberg, S. J. (2004). *Money and self: Towards a social psychology of money and its usage.* University of St. Andrews, unpublished PhD thesis.

Sonnenberg, S. J. and Fitzpatrick, L. (2012). The student as consumer, course satisfaction and well-being: The role of student identity in UK higher education. Paper presented at the *Conference of the International Association for Research in Economic Psychology (IAREP)*, Wroclaw, Poland, 5–8 September.

Sonnenberg, S. J. and Morris, P. (2011). Learners and consumers: Identity matters in higher education. Paper presented at the *Joint Conference of the International Association for Research in Economic Psychology (IAREP) and the Society for the Advancement of Behavioral Economics (SABE)*, Exeter, UK, 12–16 July.

Sonnenberg, S. J., Perrett, H. and Kelly, S. (2015). The student-as-consumer: Exploring student identity, learning and perceived value-for-money in UK higher education. Paper presented at the *Joint Conference of the International Association for Research in Economic Psychology (IAREP) and the Society for the Advancement of Behavioral Economics (SABE)*, Sibiu, Romania, 3–6 September.

Tajfel, H. and Turner, J. C. (1979). An integrative theory of intergroup conflict. In W. G. Austin and S. Worchel (Eds), *The social psychology of intergroup relations* (pp. 33–47). Monterey, CA: Brooks/Cole.

Thaler, R. H. (1999). Mental accounting matters. *Journal of Behavioral Decision Making, 12*(3), 183–206.

Tight, M. (2013). Students: customers, clients or pawns? *Higher Education Policy, 26*(3), 291–307.

Turner, J. C., Hogg, M. A., Oakes, P. J., Reicher, S. D. and Wetherell, M. S. (1987). *Rediscovering the social group: A self-categorization theory.* Oxford: Blackwell.

Tversky, A. and Thaler, R. H. (1990). Anomalies: Preference reversals. *Journal of Economic Perspectives, 4*(2), 201–11.

Vansteenkiste, M., Simons, J., Lens, W., Sheldon, K. M. and Deci, E. L. (2004). Motivating learning, performance, and persistence: The synergistic effects of intrinsic goal contents and autonomy-supportive contexts. *Journal of Personality and Social Psychology, 87*(2), 246–60.

Zafirovski, M. (1999). The 'unbearable lightness' of the economic approach to economic behavior in the social setting: Rational action and the sociology of the economy. *Journal for the Theory of Social Behaviour, 29*(3), 301–34.

Zafirovski, M. (2000). Extending the rational choice model from the economy to society. *Economy and Society, 29*(2), 181–206.

PART VI

Insights and applications from medical education

16

STEREOTYPING AND THE DEVELOPMENT OF CLINICIANS' PROFESSIONAL IDENTITIES

Bryan Burford and Harriet E. S. Rosenthal-Stott

In this chapter, we argue that professional identity can be seen as an instance of social identity. That is, professional identity is an individual's self-concept defined in terms of his or her membership of a professional group. First, we outline research that examines professional identity in the clinical education setting and discuss the parallels to, and applicability of, the social identity approach to this research. Second, we discuss issues surrounding stereotyping and how it relates to professional clinical identity. Third, we suggest how these issues are reflected in intergroup relations in the workplace. We link the theoretical issues to concrete examples of practice and potential educational impact throughout the chapter. Finally, we identify ways in which these issues may be applied to questions of educational practice and policy.

Professional identity and the social identity approach

The development of professional identity is considered an essential element of a medical student's transition into becoming a clinician. It has even been argued that an established professional identity is required in order for an individual to become a successful doctor because a strong professional identity results in individuals carrying out their jobs with confidence, eliciting confidence from others in turn (Monrouxe, 2010). In addition, a strong professional identity has been linked to medical student well-being as a moderating influence on the effects of stress (Mavor *et al.*, 2014; McNeill, Smyth and Mavor, Chapter 18, this volume).

From a social identity approach (Tajfel and Turner, 1979), the strength of individuals' professional identities is the extent to which they define themselves in terms of their professional group membership (e.g., the extent to which being a doctor or a nurse, a physician or a surgeon is an important element of their sense of self). However, while there is a body of work considering the relevance of social identity to health (Haslam, Jetten, Postmes and Haslam, 2009; Jetten, Haslam and Haslam, 2012) and some authors have applied the social identity approach to the clinical workplace (e.g., Burford, 2012a; Burford and Rosenthal-Stott, 2016; Carpenter, 1995; Mitchell, Parker and Giles, 2011; Willetts and Clarke, 2014), discussion of professional identity in medicine has tended to lack a coherent theoretical perspective. As such, ways of approaching, defining, and measuring professional identity vary within medical education.

However, conceptualisations of professional identity in the medical education literature do overlap with social identity theory. For example, professional identity has been examined in terms of commitment to the profession's values and goals (Niemi, 1997), changes in group identification from 'first-day student' to 'qualified doctor or nurse' as students progress through medical school (Crossley and Vivekananda-Schmidt, 2009), and changes in perceived traits as a medical student identity becomes established (Madill and Latchford, 2005). In addition, the concept of professionalism has been considered in ways that relate to professional identity. The three types of professionalism identified by Hodges *et al.* (2011) – individual, interpersonal, and societal/institutional – can be seen to reflect aspects of the social identity approach. Individual professionalism is defined as an individual's personality traits and behaviour, which could be construed as personal identity (Turner, Hogg, Oakes, Reicher and Wetherell, 1987), while interpersonal professionalism reflects relationships and behaviour between individuals framed within a medical context (i.e., interpersonal processes). Societal/institutional professionalism reflects the societal norms and expectations of the profession and is the result of interaction between different groups, thus highlighting the role of social identity, rather than personal identity, in establishing professionalism.

The social identity approach allows the development of identity to be viewed as dynamic and non-linear, with one's professional identity being more or less salient depending on context and the availability of other identities (e.g., Turner *et al.*, 1987). There may also be different levels of professional identity, with an individual belonging to different groups (e.g., medical student, doctor, surgeon). Multiple identities may be nested (hierarchical) or cross-cutting (Ashforth and Johnson, 2001), but often, one identity emerges as salient in a given context (Turner *et al.*, 1987).

In medical education, this issue has been considered by research examining progression or transition to the professional 'doctor' identity from the 'student' identity. Several studies present this progression as an implicitly dialectic process in which the student identity is in tension with the anticipated professional identity; education is, on the one hand, pushing the student forward into the identity of 'doctor' and, on the other hand, pulling them back into the identity of 'learner' (Shuval, 1975). This is reflected in the finding that students in their first clinical year initially feel like outsiders in the hospital setting (Pitkala and Mantyranta, 2003). Students may start with a model, or stereotype, of the professional role that they identify with, but experiences in practice challenge those preconceptions and cause their self-perception in relation to their emerging professional role to be reshaped (Monrouxe, 2009; Pratt, Rockman and Kauffman, 2006).

This change in identity from student to doctor was also identified by Weaver, Peters, Koch and Wilson (2011), who found that medical students experienced the transition as slowly feeling included as a member of their professional group while simultaneously feeling excluded from their student group membership. It has been suggested that medical students must either 'think like a student' or 'think like a doctor' (Lingard, Garwood, Schryer and Spafford, 2003), and these different modes of thinking are negotiated *in situ* in response to different contexts.

Overall, while approaches vary, work within the medical professional identity literature does appear to be compatible with the social identity approach, suggesting it may be a valid method for exploring professional identity within clinical education.

Stereotypes and identity

A stereotype is defined as the set of attributes believed to belong to members of a group (Oakes, Haslam and Turner, 1994) so that individuals are assumed to have those attributes based on their group membership. The literature on stereotyping is large and complex (Oakes *et al.*, 1994; Spears, Oakes, Ellemers and Haslam, 1997), and we focus on particular elements of this literature as it relates to the specifics of identity development.

Individuals concurrently belong to many social groups – such as their gender, ethnicity, nationality and religion. As established, some of these groups correspond to their profession – lecturer, teacher, student, doctor, nurse, and so forth. Self-categorisation theory describes how the salience of a particular identity at any particular time is dependent on perceiver readiness (initially framed as 'accessibility') and fit (Oakes, Haslam and Turner, 1994; Turner *et al.*, 1987; Turner, Oakes, Haslam and McGarty, 1994). An individual's readiness to use a category to define the self may come about through previous experience, current expectations, or his or her goals and motives. The social context and physical environment are important for readiness as people learn which categories are suitable for particular contexts; certain social and environmental cues increase readiness (Turner *et al.*, 1987). For example, being in a hospital is likely to make an emerging healthcare professional more ready to identify as a 'doctor' or 'nurse', in comparison to being in a lecture theatre where he or she may be more ready to adopt a 'student' identity.

However, there must still be sufficient fit for an identity to become salient. Fit contains two codependent elements. Comparative fit arises from the perceived difference between groups, while normative fit is the extent to which these differences are in line with prior beliefs associated with the categories (Turner *et al.*, 1994). Comparative fit relies on the meta-contrast ratio between two groups. Meta-contrast suggests that the distinctiveness of a group is maximised when there are greater differences between the groups (intergroup) than there are differences within the groups (intra-group; Turner *et al.*, 1987). The position where meta-contrast is maximised is the group prototype. Categorisation that maximises this meta-contrast is more likely to be salient.

As comparative fit varies according to which groups are cognitively accessible in a given context, prototypical positions and group boundaries may psychologically move. The most prototypical group member in one context may, therefore, be different to the most prototypical member in another context. Consequently, the extent to which an individual is representative of the group depends on the comparison outgroup. For example, in a doctor–patient interaction, the doctor who is knowledgeable and caring may be the most prototypical, while in a doctor–nurse context, a doctor who is assertive and confident may be viewed as the most prototypical. Importantly, comparisons made between groups rely, in part, on the stereotyped attributes of the group members – the more distinct these attributes are, the clearer the stereotype of the group will be (Turner *et al.*, 1987). For example, *ad hoc* task-oriented medical teams are common in clinical practice (Varpio, Hall, Lingard and Schryer, 2008), and the emergence of a team identity in such intergroup (i.e., inter-team) circumstances may be the result of enhanced comparative fit. This may have implications for the development of professional identities in both educational and clinical settings.

Normative fit, on the other hand, occurs where perceptions of an individual or oneself are in line with the perceived beliefs or attributes of a known and established group; for example, fitting the stereotype of a doctor. This process of comparison of self and stereotype may have consequences for individuals' perceptions of themselves (as discussed under 'Self-stereotyping and self-anchoring' below). Again, stereotypes may vary according to context and with the introduction of new information (Worchel and Rothgerber, 1997). Critically, as stereotypes entail attributes of group members, they also serve as the embodiment of social norms (e.g., who we are defines what we do; Oakes *et al.*, 1994), and so the existence and influence of professional stereotypes may have important cultural implications within the workplace.

Stereotypes in medicine

So far, there has been little work to formally describe the stereotypes surrounding clinical professions or to examine them within a comparative context. Bruhn and Parsons (1964) examined stereotypes held by preclinical and clinical students of four specialities. The most typical trait for each speciality was: (1) surgeon – 'domineering and arrogant'; (2) internist – 'sensitive to a wide range of factors when evaluating a medical problem'; (3) psychiatrist – 'emotionally unstable'/'deeply interested in intellectual problems'; (4) GP – 'friendly, pleasing personality' (Bruhn and Parsons, 1964, p. 42). It is worth noting that the speciality respondents planned to enter was viewed the most positively, which may suggest a degree of ingroup bias. Interestingly, Harris (1981) found similar results to Bruhn and Parsons (1964) when testing students both one week prior to starting medical school and five years later (before final exams). This suggests that these stereotypes are stable over time.

Similarly, in a sample of general medicine and surgery residents (Bellodi, 2004), the most typical trait for medicine was 'friendly and concerned' (note the parallels with Bruhn and Parsons, 1964), while the most typical trait for surgeons was 'objective and practical' (with arrogance also mentioned; cf. Bruhn and Parsons, 1964). This again suggests that these stereotypes are stable over time, which may have implications for the normative fit of identities related to these groups. Such association of traits and clinical speciality has been observed in relation to concrete examples as well as abstract groups. In a study of doctors' perceptions of GP and consultant colleagues, the ability of consultants was linked to their perceived clinical competence, while the ability of GPs was linked to effective communication with colleagues (Narayanan and Greco, 2007).

While these studies examine stereotypes relating to specialities, Carpenter (1995) considered the stereotypes held by medical and nursing students about their prospective professions. In line with the findings outlined above, doctors were viewed as confident, dedicated, decisive and arrogant, while nurses were viewed as good communicators, dedicated and caring. More recently, our own research (Burford and Rosenthal-Stott, 2016) explored stereotypes surrounding doctors and students and suggested that students (including medical students) view doctors as: kind; calm; considerate; knowledgeable; trustworthy; understanding; approachable; honest; professional; responsible; empathetic; patient; committed; compassionate; logical; reliable; and wealthy. Importantly, these positive traits are not shared in their perceived student stereotype.

The existence of these stereotypes has implications for the normative fit of professional identities and may influence the pursuit of a career in a particular speciality. Individuals may be more motivated to pursue a speciality where they feel there is good fit. This process may also have consequences for recruitment. Perceptions of medicine as a stereotypically 'posh' profession may be linked to the underrepresentation of lower socio-economic groups in medical degree programmes (Greenhalgh, Seyan and Boynton, 2004).

Self-stereotyping and self-anchoring

As previously stated, we hold stereotypes about our own social groups. According to self-categorisation theory (Turner et al., 1987), a shift from perceiving oneself as an individual to perceiving oneself as a member of a group (*depersonalisation*) results in individuals defining themselves in terms of their group membership and describing themselves in line with the stereotype of the group (the stereotype that is relevant to the current context). This is known as *self-stereotyping*.

Self-stereotyping was first established by Hogg and Turner (1987), who found that when gender was salient, women rated themselves in line with typical female traits and men rated themselves in line with typical male traits. This can be related to medical education in that a situation that makes medical students' 'doctor' identity salient could result in their perceiving themselves in more stereotypical ways (e.g., arrogant, considerate) compared to when their professional group membership is not salient. However, it has been suggested that people only self-stereotype in terms of the positive attributes of their group and do not describe themselves in terms of the negative attributes (Biernat, Vescio and Green, 1996), which protects their group identity. It has also been found that members of lower-status groups (e.g., women) self-stereotype more than members of higher-status groups (e.g., men), reflecting a larger overlap between cognitive representations of the self and the ingroup (sharing stereotypical traits) among members of lower-status groups (Latrofa, Vaes, Cadinu and Carnaghi, 2010). In the clinical environment, there are often *de facto* status differences between and within professional hierarchies, and this research suggests that lower-status professions and grades may self-stereotype more than higher-status professions.

This perception of overlap between the self and the ingroup is not limited to self-stereotyping. Group members may engage in *self-anchoring*, where individuals project their own attributes onto the ingroup (Cadinu and Rothbart, 1996). Importantly, it has been established that both self-stereotyping and self-anchoring can increase group identification; self-anchoring predicts identification in groups that are not clearly defined, and self-stereotyping predicts identification in clearly defined groups (van Veelen, Otten and Hansen, 2013). In addition, self-anchoring appears to promote identification for newcomers to a group, while self-stereotyping promotes identification for well-established group members (van Veelen, Hansen and Otten, 2014).

These points have important implications for medical education. They suggest that first-year medical students may engage in self-anchoring and project their own attributes onto their professional identity before beginning to self-stereotype as they progress through their education. However, our own research has actually found evidence for self-stereotyping and high identification as early as the first few weeks of medical school (Burford and Rosenthal-Stott, 2016). This suggests that the process of identifying as a doctor may actually begin prior to university and that self-anchoring may also occur prior to university. This is supported further by studies that have found evidence for identification in early stages of medical education (Carpenter, 1995; Coster *et al.*, 2008). This may illuminate the dialectic processes of identity transition identified earlier (e.g., from student to doctor; Pratt *et al.*, 2006), where the novel and sometimes unexpected qualities of the professional group require a modification of identity in order to accommodate the new stereotype. In the same way that self-stereotyping/self-anchoring may lead people to identify medicine as a potential career ('I am similar to a doctor'), it may influence speciality choice; for example, if individuals perceive themselves as having similar traits to a stereotypical surgeon or physician.

Stereotype threat

While self-stereotyping considers the attribution of characteristics of the group to the self, additional research has focused on how self-categorisation can affect behaviour. Focusing on the effects of a negative group membership, *stereotype threat*

(Steele and Aronson, 1995) is the fear of being judged by a negative ingroup stereotype; this can hinder performance and ultimately lead to underperformance in line with the negative stereotype. Stereotype threat has been established for a range of stereotypes, affecting a variety of group memberships; for example, African Americans and intelligence (Steele and Aronson, 1995), women and maths (Rosenthal and Crisp, 2006; Spencer, Steele and Quinn, 1999; see also Boucher and Murphy, Chapter 5, this volume), and low socio-economic status individuals and intelligence (Croizet and Claire, 1998).

This phenomenon is relevant to medical education for three reasons. First, as described above, negative stereotypes surround some medical professions. Stereotype threat may occur with individuals behaving in accordance with these stereotypes. For example, if a medical stereotype incorporates arrogance, a doctor may behave arrogantly when that identity is salient. As far as we are aware, there is no research examining stereotype threat within this context. Second, stereotype threat may affect patients such that they behave in line with negative stereotypes surrounding their group memberships (e.g., ethnic minorities), which could affect their treatment (see Aronson, Burgess, Phelan and Juarez, 2013). Third, medical professionals have other concurrent and cross-cutting non-professional group memberships, and negative stereotypes related to these groups could also affect performance (see Burgess, Warren, Phelan, Dovidio and van Ryn, 2010).

In line with theorising around this final point, a qualitative study concluded that negative stereotypes (e.g., poor patient communication; not vocal during clinical teaching) could be the reason for Asian (Indian/Pakistani/Bangladeshi heritage) medical students' underperformance (Woolf, Cave, Greenhalgh and Dacre, 2008), while an experimental study established that ethnic minority medical students underperformed compared to White medical students on a written assessment (Woolf, McManus, Gill and Dacre, 2009). Interestingly, this difference was reduced by the implementation of a self-affirmation task (writing about one's values), though this had the effect of reducing White students' perform-ance rather than improving minority students' performance. However, female student nurses under stereotype threat performed better on a maths test after receiving a self-affirmation task compared to a control task (Taillandier-Schmitt, Esnard and Mokounkolo, 2012). It has also been hypothesised that stereotype threat may explain women's underrepresentation in leadership roles within academic medicine (Burgess, Joseph, van Ryn and Carnes, 2012).

While stereotype threat highlights the adverse effects that negative stereotypes can have within medical education, it is worth noting that positive stereotypes can have a more reassuring effect. Following a meta-analysis of stereotype threat effects, Walton and Cohen (2003) concluded that such situations can actually improve the performance of members of the comparison group. For example, a stereotype threat situation that emphasises the women and maths stereotype could actually improve the maths performance of men in the same situation. This *stereotype lift* (or *stereotype boost*; Cheryan and Bodenhausen, 2000) effect tends to be less demonstrable than stereotype threat and often only exists as a trend (rather than a clearly evidenced pattern). However, some studies have found significant stereotype lift effects for certain stereotypes, such as White students and intellectual ability (Danso and Esses, 2001), men and navigation (Rosenthal, Norman, Smith and McGregor, 2012), and men and mental rotation (Hausmann, Schoofs, Rosenthal and Jordan, 2009).

Although no studies have examined stereotype lift effects within medical education (although perhaps work by Woolf et al., 2009, could be interpreted as stereotype lift), it appears to be relevant. For example, with their group membership and stereotype salient, GPs may behave in a friendlier manner. As such, the promotion of positive stereotypes may be beneficial for medical education and patient care.

Stereotype lift may, however, have less desirable implications during selection for medical school. Some countries use assessments of aptitude rather than knowledge as part of the selection process for medical school (e.g., the UK Clinical Aptitude Test) – the intention being to avoid biases present in knowledge-based tests (although there is evidence that such scores can vary similarly to academic scores; Tiffin et al., 2014). However, there is an additional risk that, in being explicitly framed as tests of clinical aptitude, those who belong to groups seen as typical of doctors (e.g., White, higher socio-economic status) may perform better than those who do not share such group memberships. In addition, stereotype threat may result in those not belonging to those typical groups (e.g., non-White, lower socio-economic status) underperforming on such tests. Thus, stereotype threat and lift may result in a gap in performance for these different groups, with negative implications for the agenda of widening participation in medical education.

Intergroup relations

The social identity approach also addresses intergroup relations, including intergroup conflict, which has implications for medical education. Issues arising from conflict and bias – for example, between professions, disciplines or medical specialities – may have consequences for clinical education by affecting learning, interpersonal communication and patient care (Burford, 2012b; Kreindler, Dowd, Star and Gottschalk, 2012).

Intergroup bias

Intergroup conflict is most apparent in the phenomena of ingroup favouritism and outgroup derogation (e.g., prejudice; see Hewstone, Rubin and Willis, 2002). This can be an expression of affect – simple like or dislike for others on the basis of their group membership – or may impact behaviour if there are opportunities to discriminate against outgroup members or favour ingroup members (e.g., Gagnon and Bourhis, 1996). In addition, information from ingroup sources is more influential than outgroup sources (Wilder, 1990).

Risks for workplace relations are evident here. One can easily imagine a situation where a nurse's accurate views about a patient are ignored by a surgeon because of pre-existing negative attitudes/stereotypes about nurses and expertise. Carpenter (1995) highlighted that contrasting professional stereotypes (e.g., nurses as caring; doctors as arrogant) could create intergroup tensions, although an interprofessional education initiative to reduce negative stereotyping was found to be moderately effective. Likewise, perceived racial bias within degree programmes has been suggested as an explanation for why Native Americans are underrepresented in nursing in the USA (Metz, Cech, Babcock and Smith, 2011).

Doctor–patient communication

Stereotyping and intergroup conflict may also influence doctor–patient relations. Doctors' implicit expectations of different groups may affect the way in which they perceive and treat patients. Patients' ethnicity and socio-economic status can affect physician perceptions and behaviour. One study found that Black patients were perceived more negatively than White patients (van Ryn and Burke, 2000), and race and patient behaviour has been found to influence prescription of opioids (Burgess et al., 2008). Patient gender can also influence diagnosis and management (e.g., Hamberg, Risberg, Johansson and Westman, 2002; Yourstone, Lindholm, Grann and Fazel, 2009). It is possible as well that intergroup bias between a patient and doctor could have consequences for adherence to treatment regimes (e.g., if the doctor is viewed as a negative outgroup by the patient).

Status and leadership

Status is an important aspect of intergroup relations. According to social identity theory, the desire for the ingroup to be different from and better than the outgroup (positive distinctiveness) is the result of a desire to see the ingroup positively, in part, to enhance self-esteem (Tajfel and Turner, 1979). However, if individuals are members of a lower-status group, they may boost their collective self-esteem by focusing on attributes of their group that they perceive as being positive (e.g., 'social creativity'; Tajfel and Turner, 1979).

In the clinical environment, hierarchical status differences between different professional groups exist (Nembhard and Edmondson, 2006) and can result in unfortunate consequences that can affect patient well-being. This was most clearly shown in a study where nurses were given instructions over the phone from an unknown doctor to administer an excessive amount of an unauthorised drug to a patient (Hofling, Brotzman, Dalrymple, Graves and Pierce, 1966). With 21 out of 22 nurses prepared to administer the drug, it shows the potential for negative consequences of obeying those of a higher perceived status, even if they may be perceived as outgroup members. Adhering to a hierarchy also appears to affect the learning and implementation of new clinical practices. Edmondson (2003) examined interdisciplinary operating room teams and established that successful implementation was the result of leaders breaking down perceptions of power and status in order to facilitate speaking out.

Leadership is generally identified as an important factor in healthcare systems for patient safety and staff well-being. Recent scandals in the UK have been linked to a failure of leadership (e.g., Francis, 2013). While the reasons for such failures are varied, there is a risk if individuals are in leadership positions over members of outgroups. Leadership, within the social identity approach, is exercised by those who hold the most prototypical position of a group (Turner, 2005), implying that leadership does not usually cross group boundaries (see Platow, Reicher and Haslam, 2009).

Superordinate identities

The creation of a team (or other collection of individuals) consisting of members of distinct outgroups (e.g., operating room teams) can result in the adoption of a common superordinate identity; for example, 'operating room team member' or, more generally, 'healthcare professional'. A common ingroup identity can facilitate leadership and reduce conflict (Brewer, 2000; Gaertner et al., 2000; Haslam and Platow, 2001). However, a common ingroup identity may also have the ironic effect of increasing intergroup bias. If different subordinate groups hold different stereotypes of the superordinate group – for example, Democrats and Republicans having different stereotypes of 'American' – then the effectiveness of the common identity is reduced when the superordinate identity is salient compared to when it is not (Rutchick and Eccleston, 2010). In the clinical context, this may mean that if doctors and nurses do not share a common view of 'healthcare professional' or physicians and surgeons do not share a common view of 'doctors', then the common ingroup identity will not have the desired effect of reducing intergroup conflict.

Superordinate identity may be felt to be a threat to a single professional identity (Crisp, Stone and Hall, 2006). For example, Mitchell et al. (2011) looked at the effect of a team identity on healthcare team effectiveness. They found that a more professionally diverse team was more effective than a less diverse one if there was a strong team identity rather than a weak one. However, they also found that the effect of diversity was moderated by identity threat, meaning that the beneficial effect was only present if the superordinate team identity did not challenge the original ingroup identity. If there was perceived identity threat, then team performance was undermined. The implication is that an interprofessional, superordinate team identity can be beneficial if it is sympathetic and complementary to the original ingroup. Along similar lines, Khalili, Orchard, Laschinger and Farah (2013) described an interprofessional education initiative that used social identity ideas to facilitate dual identity: original professional identity and a new 'interprofessional' identity.

Other research has explored the identity transition that occurs when a clinician moves from a clinical role to a management role. This research is interesting as it acknowledges that one may join a group where there was previous intergroup conflict and where tensions may still exist between the cross-cutting identities. Forbes and Hallier (2006; see also Hallier and Forbes, 2005) found that on becoming managers, some doctors were 'reluctant' and retained their clinical professional identity, using their membership of the clinical group to challenge undesired aspects of the managerial identity. They speculate that the transition is different for nurses because of the relative power imbalance between medicine and nursing. Similarly, Russell, Wyness, McAuliffe and Fellenz (2010) suggested that doctors who perceive the identity of 'manager' to have relatively low status will reinforce their clinician identity through the validation provided by the doctor–patient relationship. In line with this, Hotho found that GPs involved in management would describe themselves as 'clinicians first' (2008, p. 731).

Future directions for social identity and clinical education

So far, we have described how professional identity may be considered in social identity terms and how social identity and stereotyping effects may be relevant to clinical education and practice. As discussed, empirical work directly applying these theoretical concepts to clinical education is limited, although the social identity approach does appear to be emerging within the field. However, the question remains as to how this understanding can be used to inform innovative approaches in clinical education, and to what end.

There are a number of ways in which the approach discussed here could be applied to clinical education. A comprehension of social identity processes may help to understand the transitions experienced by individuals as they enter medical school and progress through undergraduate and postgraduate education. The social identity approach allows this to be seen not simply as a linear development but as an ongoing dynamic process shaped by context. A general understanding of this change may help shape induction and address the stresses students and trainees experience.

Social identity and stereotyping are means of transmitting and establishing group norms, which may represent the desired attitudes and behaviours of 'professionalism'. Understanding how group processes may lead to the transmission of adverse norms, and so have potentially negative consequences for patient care, may help to avoid instances of bad practice in the future.

Understanding group processes may similarly have benefits for team working. There are applications not just in interprofessional learning, where exploration of the concept of common ingroup identity has already begun (e.g., Khalili *et al.*, 2013), but also in terms of the operation of intra-professional hierarchies and the group processes at work between clinical specialties. The development of positive, shared stereotypes may have benefits for all groups and help to manage expectations of others.

The potential for stereotype threat and stereotype lift should be considered in the design of recruitment and assessment. In relation to the former, this is particularly with regard to widening participation in medical education and the recruitment of groups that are not seen as typical of the traditional medical group. This may also have relevance in the choice of career path. Diversity of personality types, as well as demographic characteristics, may be encouraged by challenging negative stereotypes and developing positive ones. In relation to formative assessment, such as multisource feedback, there is a risk of intergroup bias influencing both the feedback given and how it is perceived. Awareness and monitoring of this risk may help to ensure that feedback is given and received effectively.

It is also worth noting that the clinical education literature could draw on and apply research that is being carried out in more general education settings. For example, away from clinical education, social identity has been linked to learning approaches. Specifically, stronger group identification is associated with deep learning rather than surface learning (Bliuc, Ellis, Goodyear and Hendres, 2011a, 2011b; Platow, Mavor and Grace, 2013; Smyth, Mavor, Platow, Grace and Reynolds, 2015; see also in this volume, Bliuc, Goodyear and Ellis, Chapter 12, McNeill, Smyth and Mavor, Chapter 18, and Smyth, Mavor, Platow and Grace, Chapter 13). This strand of research may provide a greater illumination of *how* identification influences learning in clinical education.

So, a key question arising is how can we harness this understanding to improve learning and practice. The identity processes we have identified are embedded in individual cognition and group processes, so the challenge will be for curricula and educational initiatives to work with those processes in order to optimise the benefits and mitigate the adverse consequences.

It appears as though even first-year medical students identify with their future professional identities and the concomitant self-stereotype content of those identities. The stereotypes surrounding their group memberships may further affect their performance in their professional role as they may experience stereotype threat or lift effects. Finally, identification with their profession can result in intergroup conflict, which could affect relationships with patients and colleagues in different professions.

The clinical education field could also be informed by linking the social identity approach to other educational theories. For example, transformative learning theory considers how education changes the learner; this has been applied to a clinical education setting (for a review, see Taylor, 2007), but further research could explore whether transformative learning has an effect on professional social identities within the clinical education setting. Alternatively, threshold concepts (Meyer and Land, 2003, 2005; i.e., core transformational knowledge that is necessary to become expert in a discipline) and communities of practice (Lave and Wenger, 1991; workplace groups that have the potential to facilitate learning) could be explored as they may have implications for professional identities and clinical education.

Conclusion

In this chapter, we have discussed the role of the social identity approach and stereotype processes in the development of clinicians' professional identities. We have described how professional identity can be theorised as an instance of social identity – and so shaped by the processes described in social identity and self-categorisation theories – and how literature considering professional identity and professionalism can be viewed through a social identity lens.

Second, we have described the relationship between professional identity and stereotyping, illuminating the role of both self-anchoring and self-stereotyping as possible processes behind medical social identification. The role of stereotypes has been examined further through the exploration of stereotype threat and stereotype lift; stereotypes about one's group can affect behaviour such that individuals behave in line with those stereotypes.

Third, we have highlighted how issues of intergroup relations and conflict may affect the clinical workplace through bias, communication, status, leadership and the emergence of team and other superordinate identities. Finally, we have suggested ways in which the points raised throughout the chapter may be applied to clinical education.

Research examining the social identity approach in clinical education, including processes relating to stereotyping, is currently limited. However, it appears to be an important and worthwhile approach that researchers in the field of clinical education should embrace and incorporate into future research.

References

Aronson, J., Burgess, D., Phelan, S. M. and Juarez, L. (2013). Unhealthy interactions: The role of stereotype threat in health disparities. *American Journal of Public Health*, *103*(1), 50–6.

Ashforth, B. E. and Johnson, S. A. (2001). Which hat to wear? The relative salience of multiple identities in organisational contexts. In M. A. Hogg and D. J. Terry (Eds), *Social identity processes in organisational contexts* (pp. 31–48). Hove, UK: Psychology Press.

Bellodi, P. L. (2004). The general practitioner and the surgeon: Stereotypes and medical specialties. *Revista do Hospital das Clínicas*, *59*(1), 15–24.

Biernat, M., Vescio, T. K. and Green, M. L. (1996). Selective self-stereotyping. *Journal of Personality and Social Psychology*, *71*(6), 1194–209.

Bliuc, A.-M., Ellis, R. A., Goodyear, P. and Hendres, D. M. (2011a). Understanding student learning in context: Relationships between social identity, perceptions of the learning community, approaches to learning and academic performance. *European Journal of Psychology of Education*, *26*(3), 417–33.

Bliuc, A.-M., Ellis, R. A., Goodyear, P. and Hendres, D. M. (2011b). The role of social identification as a university student in learning: Relationships between students' social identity, approaches to learning, and academic achievement. *Educational Psychology*, *31*(5), 559–75.

Brewer, M. B. (2000). Superordinate goals versus superordinate identity as bases of intergroup cooperation. In D. Capozza and R. Brown (Eds), *Social identity processes: trends in theory and research* (pp. 118–33). London: Sage.

Bruhn, J. G. and Parsons, O. A. (1964). Medical student attitudes towards four medical specialties. *Journal of Medical Education*, *39*(1), 40–9.

Burford, B. (2012a). Group processes in medical education: Learning from social identity theory. *Medical Education*, *46*(2), 143–52.

Burford, B. (2012b). Conflict and power as intergroup processes: Not below the surface, but part of the fabric. *Medical Education, 46*(9), 830–2.

Burford, B. and Rosenthal-Stott, H. E. S. (2016). Self-stereotyping and professional identity in new medical students: A questionnaire study. Submitted for publication.

Burgess, D. J., Crowley-Matoka, M., Phelan, S., Dovidio, J. F., Kerns, R., Roth, C., . . . van Ryn, M. (2008). Patient race and physicians' decisions to prescribe opioids for chronic low back pain. *Social Science and Medicine, 67*(11), 1852–60.

Burgess, D. J., Joseph, A., van Ryn, M. and Carnes, M. (2012). Does stereotype threat affect women in academic medicine? *Academic Medicine, 87*(4), 506–12.

Burgess, D. J., Warren, J., Phelan, S., Dovidio, J. and van Ryn, M. (2010). Stereotype threat and health disparities: What medical educators and future physicians need to know. *Journal of General Internal Medicine, 25*(Suppl. 2), 169–77.

Cadinu, M. R. and Rothbart, M. (1996). Self-anchoring and differentiation processes in the minimal group setting. *Journal of Personality and Social Psychology, 70*(4), 661–77.

Carpenter, J. (1995). Doctors and nurses: Stereotypes and stereotype change in interprofessional education. *Journal of Interprofessional Care, 9*(2), 151–61.

Cheryan, S. and Bodenhausen, G. V. (2000). When positive stereotypes threaten intellectual performance: The psychological hazards of 'model minority' status. *Psychological Science, 11*(5), 399–402.

Coster, S., Norman, I., Murrells, T., Kitchen, S., Meerabeau, E., Sooboodoo, E. and d'Avray, L. (2008). Interprofessional attitudes amongst undergraduate students in the health professions: A longitudinal questionnaire survey. *International Journal of Nursing Studies, 45*(11), 1667–81.

Crisp, R. J., Stone, C. H. and Hall, N. R. (2006). Recategorization and subgroup identification: Predicting and preventing threats from common ingroups. *Personality and Social Psychology Bulletin, 32*(2), 230–43.

Croizet, J. C. and Claire, T. (1998). Extending the concept of stereotype threat to social class: The intellectual underperformance of students from low socioeconomic backgrounds. *Personality and Social Psychology Bulletin, 24*(6), 588–94.

Crossley, J. and Vivekananda-Schmidt, P. (2009). The development and evaluation of a Professional Self Identity Questionnaire to measure evolving professional self-identity in health and social care students. *Medical Teacher, 31*(12), e603–e607.

Danso, H. A. and Esses, V. M. (2001). Black experimenters and the intellectual test performance of White participants: The tables are turned. *Journal of Experimental Social Psychology, 37*(2), 158–65.

Edmondson, A. C. (2003). Speaking up in the operating room: How team leaders promote learning in interdisciplinary action teams. *Journal of Management Studies, 40*(6), 1419–52.

Forbes, T. and Hallier, J. (2006). Social identity and self-enactment strategies: Adapting to change in professional–manager relationships in the NHS. *Journal of Nursing Management, 14*(1), 34–42.

Francis, R. (2013). *Report of the Mid Staffordshire NHS Foundation Trust Public Inquiry.* London: The Stationery Office.

Gaertner, S. L., Davidio, J. F., Nier, J. A., Banker, B. S., Ward, C. M., Houlette, M. and Loux, S. (2000). The common intergroup identity model for reducing intergroup bias: Progress and challenges. In D. Capozza and R. Brown (Eds), *Social identity processes: Trends in theory and research* (pp. 133–48). London: Sage.

Gagnon, A. and Bourhis, R. Y. (1996). Discrimination in the minimal group paradigm: Social identity or self-interest? *Personality and Social Psychology Bulletin, 22*(12), 1289–301.

Greenhalgh, T., Seyan, K. and Boynton, P. (2004). 'Not a university type': Focus group study of social class, ethnic, and sex differences in school pupils' perceptions about medical school. *British Medical Journal, 328*(7455), 1541.

Hallier, J. and Forbes, T. (2005). The role of social identity in doctors' experiences of clinical managing. *Employee Relations, 27*(1), 47–70.

Hamberg, K., Risberg, G., Johansson, E. E. and Westman, G. (2002). Gender bias in physicians' management of neck pain: A study of the answers in a Swedish national examination. *Journal of Women's Health and Gender-Based Medicine, 11*(7), 653–66.

Harris, C. M. (1981). Medical stereotypes. *British Medical Journal, 283*(6307), 1676–7.

Haslam, S. A. and Platow, M. J. (2001). The link between leadership and followership: How affirming social identity translates vision into action. *Personality and Social Psychology Bulletin, 27*(11), 1469–79.

Haslam, S. A., Jetten, J., Postmes, T. and Haslam, C. (2009). Social identity, health and well-being: An emerging agenda for applied psychology. *Applied Psychology, 58*(1), 1–23.

Hausmann, M., Schoofs, D., Rosenthal, H. E. S. and Jordan, K. (2009). Interactive effects of sex hormones and gender stereotypes on cognitive sex differences: A psychobiosocial approach. *Psychoneuroendocrinology, 34*(3), 389–401.

Hewstone, M., Rubin, M. and Willis, H. (2002). Intergroup bias. *Annual Review of Psychology, 53*, 575–604.

Hodges, B. D., Ginsburg, S., Cruess, R., Cruess, S., Delport, R., Hafferty, F., . . . Wade, W. (2011). Assessment of professionalism: Recommendations from the Ottawa 2010 Conference. *Medical Teacher, 33*(5), 354–63.

Hofling, C. K., Brotzman, E., Dalrymple, S., Graves, N. and Pierce, C. M. (1966). An experimental study in nurse–physician relationships. *The Journal of Nervous and Mental Disease, 143*(2), 171–80.

Hogg, M. A. and Turner, J. C. (1987). Intergroup behaviour, self-stereotyping and the salience of social categories. *British Journal of Social Psychology, 26*(4), 325–40.

Hotho, S. (2008). Professional identity – product of structure, product of choice: Linking changing professional identity and changing professions. *Journal of Organizational Change Management, 21*(6), 721–42.

Jetten, J., Haslam, S. A. and Haslam, C. (Eds). (2012). *The social cure: Identity, health and well-being.* Hove, UK: Psychology Press.

Khalili, H., Orchard, C., Laschinger, H. K. S. and Farah, R. (2013). An interprofessional socialization framework for developing an interprofessional identity among health professions students. *Journal of Interprofessional Care, 27*(6), 448–53.

Kreindler, S. A., Dowd, D. A., Star N. D. and Gottschalk T. (2012) Silos and social identity: The social identity approach as a framework for understanding and overcoming divisions in health care. *Milbank Quarterly, 90*(2), 347–74.

Latrofa, M., Vaes, J., Cadinu, M. and Carnaghi, A. (2010). The cognitive representation of self-stereotyping. *Personality and Social Psychology Bulletin, 36*(7), 911–22.

Lave, J. and Wenger, E. (1991). *Situated learning: Legitimate peripheral participation.* Cambridge: Cambridge University Press.

Lingard, L., Garwood, K., Schryer, C. F. and Spafford, M. M. (2003). A certain art of uncertainty: Case presentation and the development of professional identity. *Social Science and Medicine, 56*(3), 603–16.

Madill, A. and Latchford, G. (2005). Identity change and the human dissection experience over the first year of medical training. *Social Science and Medicine, 60*(7), 1637–47.

Mavor, K., McNeill, K. G., Anderson, K., Kerr, A., O'Reilly, E., Platow, M. J. (2014). Beyond prevalence to process: The role of self and identity in medical student well-being. *Medical Education, 48*(4), 351–60.

Metz, A. M., Cech, E. A., Babcock, T. and Smith, J. L. (2011). Effects of formal and informal support structures on the motivation of Native American students in nursing. *Journal of Nursing Education*, *50*(7), 388–94.

Meyer, J. H. F. and Land, R. (2003). Threshold concepts and troublesome knowledge: Linkages to ways of thinking and practising within the disciplines. In C. Rust (Ed.), *Improving student learning: Theory and practice ten years on* (pp. 412–24). Oxford: Oxford Centre for Staff and Learning Development.

Meyer, J. H. F. and Land, R. (2005). Threshold concepts and troublesome knowledge (2): Epistemological considerations and a conceptual framework for teaching and learning. *Higher Education*, *49*(3), 373–88.

Mitchell, R. J., Parker, V. and Giles, M. (2011). When do interprofessional teams succeed? Investigating the moderating roles of team and professional identity in interprofessional effectiveness. *Human Relations*, *64*(10), 1321–43.

Monrouxe, L. V. (2009). Negotiating professional identities: Dominant and contesting narratives in medical students' longitudinal audio diaries. *Current Narratives*, *1*(1), 41–59.

Monrouxe, L. V. (2010). Identity, identification and medical education: Why should we care? *Medical Education*, *44*(1), 40–9.

Narayanan, A. and Greco, M. (2007). What distinguishes general practitioners from consultants, according to colleagues? *Journal of Management and Marketing in Healthcare*, *1*(1), 80–7.

Nembhard, I. M. and Edmondson, A. C. (2006). Making it safe: The effects of leader inclusiveness and professional status on psychological safety and improvement efforts in health care teams. *Journal of Organizational Behavior*, *27*(7), 941–66.

Niemi, P. M. (1997). Medical students' professional identity: Self-reflection during the preclinical years. *Medical Education*, *31*(6), 408–15.

Oakes, P. J., Haslam, S. A. and Turner, J. C. (1994). *Stereotyping and social reality*. Oxford: Blackwell.

Pitkala, K. H. and Mantyranta, T. (2003). Professional socialization revised: Medical students' own conceptions related to adoption of the future physician's role – a qualitative study. *Medical Teacher*, *25*(2), 155–60.

Platow, M. J., Mavor, K. I. and Grace, D. M. (2013). On the role of discipline-related self-concept in deep and surface approaches to learning among university students. *Instructional Science*, *41*(2), 271–85.

Platow, M. J., Reicher, S. D. and Haslam, S. A. (2009). On the social psychology of intergroup leadership: The importance of social identity and self-categorization processes. In T. Pittinsky (Ed.), *Crossing the divide: Intergroup leadership in a world of difference* (pp. 31–42). Cambridge, MA: Harvard Business School Press.

Pratt, M. G., Rockman, K. W. and Kauffman, J. B. (2006). Constructing professional identity: The role of work and identity learning cycles in the customization of identity among medical residents. *Academy of Management Journal*, *49*(2), 235–62.

Rosenthal, H. E. S. and Crisp, R. J. (2006). Reducing stereotype threat by blurring intergroup boundaries. *Personality and Social Psychology Bulletin*, *32*(4), 501–11.

Rosenthal, H. E. S., Norman, L., Smith, S. P. and McGregor, A. (2012). Gender-based navigation stereotype improves men's search for a hidden goal. *Sex Roles*, *67*(11), 682–95.

Russell, V., Wyness, L. A., McAuliffe, E. and Fellenz, M. (2010). The social identity of hospital consultants as managers. *Journal of Health Organisation and Management*, *24*(3), 220–36.

Rutchick, A. M. and Eccleston, C. P. (2010). Ironic effects of invoking common ingroup identity. *Basic and Applied Social Psychology*, *32*(2), 109–17.

Shuval, J. T. (1975). From 'boy' to 'colleague': Processes of role transformation in professional socialization. *Social Science and Medicine*, 9(8–9), 413–20.

Smyth, L., Mavor, K. I., Platow, M. J., Grace, D. M. and Reynolds, K. J. (2015). Discipline social identification, study norms and learning approach in university students. *Educational Psychology*, 35(1), 53–72.

Spears, R., Oakes, P. J., Ellemers, N. and Haslam, S. A. (1997). *The social psychology of stereotyping and group life*. Oxford: Blackwell.

Spencer, S. J., Steele, C. M. and Quinn, D. M. (1999). Stereotype threat and women's math performance. *Journal of Experimental Social Psychology*, 35(1), 4–28.

Steele, C. M. and Aronson, J. (1995). Stereotype threat and the intellectual test-performance of African-Americans. *Journal of Personality and Social Psychology*, 69(5), 797–811.

Taillandier-Schmitt, A., Esnard, C. and Mokounkolo, R. (2012). Self-affirmation in occupational training: Effects on the math performance of French women nurses under stereotype threat. *Sex Roles*, 67(1), 43–57.

Tajfel, H. and Turner, J. C. (1979). An integrative theory of intergroup conflict. In W. G. Austin and S. Worchel (Eds). *The social psychology of intergroup relations* (pp. 33–47). Monterey, CA: Brooks/Cole.

Taylor, E. W. (2007). An update of transformative learning theory: A critical review of the empirical research (1999–2005). *International Journal of Lifelong Education*, 26(2), 173–91.

Tiffin, P. A., McLachlan, J. C., Webster, L. A. D. and Nicholson, S. (2014). Comparison of the sensitivity of the UKCAT and A levels to sociodemographic characteristics: A national study. *BMC Medical Education*, 14(7).

Turner, J. C. (2005). Explaining the nature of power: A three-process theory. *European Journal of Social Psychology*, 35(1), 1–22.

Turner, J. C., Hogg, M. A., Oakes, P. J., Reicher, S. D. and Wetherell, M. S. (1987). *Rediscovering the social group: A self-categorization theory*. Oxford: Blackwell.

Turner, J. C., Oakes, P. J., Haslam, S. A. and McGarty, C. (1994). Self and collective: Cognition and social context. *Personality and Social Psychology Bulletin*, 20(5), 454–63.

van Ryn, M. and Burke, J. (2000). The effect of patient race and socio-economic status on physicians' perceptions of patients. *Social Science and Medicine*, 50(6), 813–28.

van Veelen, R., Hansen, N. and Otten, S. (2014). Newcomers' cognitive development of social identification: A cross-sectional and longitudinal analysis of self-anchoring and self-stereotyping. *British Journal of Social Psychology*, 53(2), 281–98.

van Veelen, R., Otten, S. and Hansen, N. (2013). Social identification when an ingroup identity is unclear: The role of self-anchoring and self-stereotyping. *British Journal of Social Psychology*, 52(3), 543–62.

Varpio, L., Hall, P., Lingard, L. and Schryer C. F. (2008). Interprofessional communication and medical error: A reframing of research questions and approaches. *Academic Medicine*, 83(Suppl. 10), S76–S81.

Walton, G. M. and Cohen, G. L. (2003). Stereotype lift. *Journal of Experimental Social Psychology*, 39(5), 456–67.

Weaver, R., Peters, K., Koch, J. and Wilson, I. (2011). 'Part of the team': Professional identity and social exclusivity in medical students. *Medical Education*, 45(12), 1220–9.

Wilder, D. A. (1990). Some determinants of the persuasive power of in-groups and outgroups: Organization of information and attribution of independence. *Journal of Personality and Social Psychology*, 59(6), 1202–13.

Willetts, G. and Clarke, D. (2014). Constructing nurses' professional identity through social identity theory. *International Journal of Nursing Practice*, 20(2), 164–9.

Woolf, K., Cave, J., Greenhalgh, T. and Dacre, J. (2008). Ethnic stereotypes and the underachievement of UK medical students from ethnic minorities: Qualitative study. *British Medical Journal, 337*(7670), a1220.

Woolf, K., McManus, I. C., Gill, D. and Dacre, J. (2009). The effect of a brief social intervention on the examination results of UK medical students: A cluster randomised controlled trial. *BMC Medical Education, 9*, 35. doi: 10.1186/1472-6920-9-35

Worchel, S. and Rothgerber, H. (1997). Changing the stereotype of the stereotype. In R. Spears, P. J. Oakes, N. Ellemers and S. A. Haslam (Eds), *The social psychology of stereotyping and group life* (pp. 72–93). Oxford: Blackwell.

Yourstone, J., Lindholm, T., Grann, M. and Fazel, S. (2009). Gender differences in diagnoses of mentally disordered offenders. *International Journal of Forensic Mental Health, 8*(3), 172–7.

17

HERO, VOYEUR, JUDGE

Understanding medical students' moral identities through professionalism dilemma narratives

Lynn V. Monrouxe and Charlotte E. Rees

Becoming a doctor entails assimilating a wide variety of knowledge, skills and attitudes required for clinical practice (General Medical Council, 2009, 2012). While necessary, in and of themselves, these are insufficient: to become a doctor, one must also develop a sense of oneself *as a doctor*. In other words, one must develop a sense of identity (Monrouxe, 2010, 2013). Part of this development includes developing a moral sense of oneself within the medical profession by learning professional codes of conduct (American Board of Internal Medicine Foundation, American College of Physicians–American Society of Internal Medicine Foundation, and European Federation of Internal Medicine, 2002; Australian Medical Association, 2015; Canadian Medical Association, 2005; Cruess and Cruess, 2006; General Medical Council, 2013; Hafferty, 2009). However, such codes are ever-changing. They are temporally and culturally specific (Chandratilake, McAleer and Gibson, 2012; Hafferty, 2006; Hafferty and Castellani, 2009; Hafferty and Levinson, 2008). What was acceptable professional practice for doctors 20 or 30 years ago is not necessarily acceptable today, or for future clinicians.

This acceptability, however, might be as much to do with how society is changing its expectations of medicine as a profession as it is with the actual changing of espoused professional values (Hafferty, 2000). Indeed, 2,500 years ago, the Hippocratic oath embodied a basic ethic that is still prevalent today, including that doctors should act in the best interests of their patients, acknowledge the limits of their own knowledge, recognise that there is an art to medicine with warmth and sympathy towards patients, and maintain patient confidentiality (Eva, 2014). However, like all humans, physicians are fallible and subject to strong socialising factors (Atkinson, 1984). Indeed, it has often been highlighted that 'the norms and value orientations encountered by students during their training are not always the standards medicine ritualistically identifies as defining medical practice' (Hafferty, 2000).

The moral milieu

The formal teaching of professionalism is a relatively recent phenomenon. So, in the past, by the time medical students graduated from medical school, they have been reported to suffer a form of 'ethical erosion' through witnessing or participating in professionalism lapses – witnessing or participating in something they believe to be unethical or 'wrong' – often encouraged by their seniors (Feudtner, Christakis and Christakis, 1994). For example, students might be told by their clinical teacher to perform, sometimes intimate, examinations or procedures on patients who have not given their explicit consent for them to do so (Rees and Knight, 2008; Rees and Monrouxe, 2011). Indeed, medical students attending the clinical workplace are often full of uncertainties around who they are and what activities are legitimate for them to engage in. In an attempt to reduce this uncertainty, and to 'fit in' within the clinical workplace (Hogg, 2012), students take cues from both the formal curriculum in which they are learning and from the observations of what *actually happens* within the clinical environment (the so-called informal and hidden curricula; Rees and Monrouxe, 2015).

Prior to the introduction of professionalism teaching within the formal curriculum, fitting in with other doctors often meant adopting habits and practices of senior members of the 'firm'. The result of this can be seen in a loss of trust by the public in medicine as a profession and the call for greater awareness of professionalism within the undergraduate curriculum. For example, in the UK, high-profile inquiries – such as the investigation of GP Harold Shipman and the Bristol inquiry – led to a lack of trust and a call for change (Greenhalgh, 2007; Kinnell, 2000; Smith, 1998). Furthermore, with more recent reports of serious quality of care failings – for example, at the Mid Staffordshire NHS Foundation Trust (Francis, 2013) – the formal teaching of professionalism remains high on the agenda.

The formal teaching of professionalism

Partly driven by society's diminishing trust in the profession and the increased public expectations of better medical care, the formal teaching of medical professionalism is now well established within medical school life. Indeed, the teaching and learning of professionalism has been deemed 'one of the most important topics in medical education today' (Sullivan, 2009, p. ix). Despite there being no single definition of 'medical professionalism' (Chandratilake *et al.*, 2012; Hafferty, 2006; Hafferty and Levinson, 2008; Monrouxe, Rees, and Hu, 2011; Shirley and Padgett, 2004), the topic has been, and continues to be, much debated. Amongst the issues debated include doctor–patient relationships, professional knowledge and development, the nature of autonomy, personal aspects of professionalism (e.g., altruism, respect, compassion), the assessment and evaluation of professionalism, and the issue of professionalism in relation to one's online behaviour (Chretien, Goldman, Beckman and Kind, 2010; R. L. Cruess, 2006; Cruess,

Cruess and Johnston, 2000; Cruess, Cruess and Steinert, 2009; Garner and O'Sullivan, 2010; Thistlethwaite and Spencer, 2008; Wear and Aultman, 2006). More recently, however, understandings about doctors and medical students having, or displaying, a professional and moral sense of self has gained importance (Holden, Buck, Clark, Szauter and Trumble, 2012). It is to this aspect that we now turn as we consider the various theoretical perspectives around the issues of the moral identity formation.

Theorising moral identities

Moral identities have been theorised in a number of different ways within the social sciences. Sometimes these identities are considered to be a property of the self. Elsewhere, identities are considered to emerge through social interaction. While on the face of it, these different theoretical perspectives come from different epistemological understandings of the world, the 'multiple components and processes of identity' (Schwartz, Luyckx and Vignoles, 2011, p. 933) captured across the complexity of these theories can be embraced in order to understand the messiness of what motivates us towards developing a sense of self and how we create and negotiate our identities.

When talking about self and identity, Leary (2004) highlights four different metaphors: 'self-as-knower', the 'I-self' (self-awareness), 'self-as-known', and 'self-as-decision-maker and doer'. Bamberg, de Fina and Schiffrin (2007) prefer the metaphors of 'self-as-speaker or narrator'. By drawing on a range of metaphors of identity and the self, we aim to understand how medical students construct their moral identities as they narrate professionalism lapses within the clinical environment as they learn to become doctors.

The moral self and personal identity

Individual perspectives on identity primarily draw on the metaphors of self-as-knower and as-known. While such perspectives suggest that identity resides within an individual's cognition – and so can be a *known* and, therefore, *knowable* fact – they also stress the interrelatedness of individuals and their social milieu (Marcia, Waterman, Matteson, Archer and Orlofsky, 1993). And within these individual perspectives resides the understanding of moral identity, which lies at the 'intersection of moral development and identity formation' (Hardy and Carlo, 2011, p. 495). This draws primarily on the metaphor of self-as-decision-maker and doer.

Set within an individual perspective of moral identity, Blasi's (1980, 1983) developmental model of moral selves identifies three key aspects that lead to moral behaviour: assuming responsibility, the centrality of our moral identity, and our drive for self-consistency. Thus, according to Blasi (1980, 1983), as we mature, we become more focused on our internal values rather than external appearances, and we gain a greater sense of agency. Simultaneously, we develop a strong need for self-consistency, and deviations from our ideal-selves can cause strong negative emotional reactions.

Moral identity and possible selves

Possible identities include a range of personal theories around whom we might become in the future. These possible identities can be both positive and negative, and can influence identity-based motivational actions (so, in the case of medical students, possible identity as a moral and accountable doctor might influence behaviours in the face of professionalism dilemmas). Again, self-consistency and the concept of a coherent self is an important factor as we project ourselves into our future identities (Oettingen and Mayer, 2002). Thus, we evaluate our present actions in terms of our future identities. And simultaneously, as highlighted earlier, these future identities can motivate us towards particular actions in the present to enable us to become like our 'true ideal' self (Kivetz and Tyler, 2007). Indeed, acting against one's ideal future self (e.g., actual-self versus ideal-self discrepancy) can lead to feelings of dejection and agitation (Gramzow, Sedikides, Panter and Insko, 2000).

Identity and uncertainty reduction

Uncertainty–identity theory suggests that we are fundamentally motivated to reduce uncertainty (Hogg, 2012; see also Cruwys, Gaffney and Skipper, Chapter 11, this volume). This uncertainty is contextually, rather than individually, dependent. Thus, uncertainty can arise when we find ourselves in situations that are unfamiliar. As mentioned above, medical students may be full of uncertainties within the clinical environment. For example, students often feel uncertain about their legitimacy within a clinical workplace designed to heal the sick rather than to teach the students. Thus, in such a situation, their student identities might cause uncertainty and anxiety. These feelings of uncertainty may be resolved in a number of ways, including identifying themselves *as doctors*. This enables them to feel legitimate within the clinical environment, and to *know* the types of behaviour they should engage in.

So, group identification is an effective method of reducing contextual uncertainty. When we identify with the group, we gain a sense of who we are – including what we should think, feel and do – and also it reduces uncertainty about others and how they will behave towards us. And finally, by identifying ourselves with a group, we validate our own world view and sense of self through that group, further reducing uncertainty. Because uncertainty drives this identifying process, the more uncertain people are within any context, the greater their desire is to identify with their desired group (Hogg, 2000). However, social categories such as 'doctor' also comprise prototypes containing ideal group attributes (e.g., being moral). When these ideals are challenged (such as during professionalism dilemmas), feelings of uncertainty can resurface. In such situations, students may be motivated to renegotiate their own and others' identities, and narratives of professionalism lapses can be seen as part of this identity (re)negotiation.

Narrating identities: plotlines, character tropes, positioning and moral selves

Discursive practice is a term used to describe the many ways in which individuals actively produce their social and psychological realities through talk (Davies and Harre, 2001). Discourse is multifaceted and includes narrative practices that comprise both the big autobiographical stories of our lives and the small stories of recent, or ongoing, or hypothetical events we share in everyday conversations through which meanings are dynamically achieved (Bamberg, 2006; Bamberg, Meister, Kindt, Schernus and Stein, 2004; Georgakopoulou, 2006, 2007). However, narrative theories of identity are far from homogeneous (Smith and Sparkes, 2008), ranging from identities as being a unique individual attribute or mental representation to identities being an emergent product of social-relational interaction in the moment and, therefore, not mentally represented. Again, a common characteristic of these theories is that of coherence. Narrative coherence is the artfully crafted telling of stories to enable a unified sense of self across time, which is thought to be beneficial for an individual's well-being (Frank, 1995; Smith and Sparkes, 2002).

Another common characteristic is our agency in the telling of stories: we invariably exercise choice with respect to how we tell our stories. For example, one choice we make is the position in which we locate ourselves when narrating events. By adopting certain positions within the events, we are able to see the world from that particular vantage point, drawing on (as we describe in detail below) common metaphors, character tropes (e.g., stereotypes of groups of people) and plotlines as we do so (Davies and Harre, 2001). It is through these discursive practices that our identities are brought to the fore.

From the perspective of Bamberg's metaphor of 'self-as-speaker or narrator' (Bamberg *et al.*, 2007), the identities we create through talk are not firmly fixed; rather, *who we are* is constituted and reconstituted through the variety of discursive practices in which we situate ourselves. From this perspective, while identities may have a cognitive component (i.e., internal to the self in terms of a belief or stance), identity is a process rather than a 'product' of the individual; so through interaction, a 'constellation' of identities are negotiated and contested (Bamberg, de Fina and Schiffrin, 2011). Therefore, our identities at any one time depend upon the positions that are available to us within our own discursive practices and within the practices of others (i.e., they are highly cultural). These are the cultural stories – the different discourses – through which we make sense of our own and others' lives. And it is within these stories that moral judgements are made.

The concept of *positioning* is by no means new. It has its roots in Foucault's (1969) notion of 'subject positions', which are made available and constrained by societal discourses. According to Foucault, discourses position subjects in terms of status, power, legitimate knowledge and the types of practices they are allowed to, and ought to, perform. Thereby, the discourses we draw upon in our narratives reflect how we wish ourselves to be interpreted and how we, in turn, interpret our (social) world and others (Foucault, 1969).

But we do not simply reproduce societal discourses to represent our own identities; rather, identity construction involves a number of complex processes. First, we need an understanding of the various categories, or groups of people, we might belong to. In the case of medical students, this involves the broad category of 'doctors', the more specific categories of 'specialties' (e.g., general practitioners, surgeons) and all the other professional and personal categories around them (e.g., gender, ethnicity). This understanding includes not only knowing who is included in and excluded from such categories, but also knowing the values through which those categories are understood. We also need to understand the discursive practices, including the cultural plotlines and character tropes within which we come to 'know' these groups and which give meaning to them. For example, medical students sometimes come to *know* what a doctor is through 'the good doctor' narrative: a discourse portraying doctors through an idealised notion that *all* doctors are good and do not possess negative personal qualities (Monrouxe, 2009). It is through our knowledge and adoption of these cultural storylines and character tropes that we might appropriate them for our own identity construction as we become members of those groups. Therefore, we position ourselves in terms of the groups within the storylines when we share our experiences with others, *belonging* to one category rather than another. Furthermore, such positioning enables us to display emotional commitment as part of this group and to develop our own moral code around this belonging (Monrouxe, 2009; Monrouxe and Rees, 2012; Monrouxe and Sweeney, 2010, 2013; Monrouxe, Rees, Endacott and Turnan, 2014).

However, as we develop our narrative sense of belonging, we need to negotiate ourselves amongst the myriad of contradictions about what it is *to be* as a member of that group; and in the case of medical students becoming doctors, as a *future self* (Monrouxe and Sweeney, 2010, 2013). This is particularly problematic when we engage in activities in which the dominant group members (e.g., senior clinicians) behave in ways that contradict our idealised moral sense of knowing (Monrouxe and Rees, 2012; Monrouxe *et al.*, 2014).

Identity construction and healthcare students' narratives of professionalism dilemmas

Since 2007, we have been researching healthcare students' experiences of professionalism dilemmas. Across a range of qualitative and quantitative studies with over 4,000 medical, dental, nursing, pharmacy and physiotherapy students, we have identified a common set of professionalism dilemmas that students experience across all years of their undergraduate education. These dilemmas include situations in which students are the victims of abuse, times when patient safety, dignity and consent are breached (by healthcare professionals and the students themselves), and issues around students raising concerns and challenging their seniors.

In addition to classifying the content of students' narratives, we have also analysed other aspects of these narratives, including negative emotional talk. An interesting finding across three studies examining medical, dental, nursing, pharmacy and physiotherapy students' oral and written narratives of professionalism dilemmas was that situations in which students witnessed healthcare professionals breach the safety and/or dignity of patients were narrated with significantly more negative emotional words (including anger) than when students narrated similar breaches by themselves (Monrouxe and Rees, 2012; Monrouxe *et al.*, 2014; Rees, Monrouxe and McDonald, 2013). Furthermore, our in-depth positioning analysis of two students' narratives (one medical and one nursing student) illustrated how the events were constructed in terms of assigning praise and blame within the narrative (indicating an ethical stance) and in terms of the narrative plotlines drawn upon as they told their stories to the researcher and sometimes to a group of other participants (e.g., a *regret* narrative and a *journey* narrative; see Monrouxe and Rees, 2012; Monrouxe *et al.*, 2014; Rees and Monrouxe, 2015; Rees, Monrouxe and Ajjawi, 2014; Rees *et al.*, 2013).

However, while we have touched upon the issue of plotlines and character positioning within the specific narratives presented, these were not elaborated on in terms of the patterns across our narrative data: the general tendencies within specific storylines that point to 'collective representations and inventories, which in turn can be related to wider social process such as economic and *cultural struggles*' (de Fina, 2013, p. 45, emphasis added). It is this deeper and 'collective' aspect of students' narratives that we now focus on as we specifically consider medical students' narratives of professionalism dilemmas and how narrators position themselves and others within a variety of culturally embedded plotlines and character tropes. In order to do this, we draw on Bamberg and Georgakopoulu's (2008) three levels of positioning (see Box 17.1 below).

BOX 17.1 THE THREE LEVELS OF POSITIONING ANALYSIS

Level 1 positioning: considers how the characters are portrayed and positioned *relationally* through the following devices: (1) the type of actions ascribed to the characters; (2) the motivations for those actions; and (3) the character tropes used.

Level 2 positioning: as positioning always occurs within the context of a specific *moral order* in talk (Moghaddam, 1999), this considers the 'interactional world' within which the narrative occurs and can shed light on how specific positioning practices are culturally embedded.

Level 3 positioning: identifies the wider social implications of how narrators 'fit in' with current ideologies around what it is to be a doctor.

We begin by outlining some of the most common narrative plotlines found across our data as medical students narrated the various patient safety and dignity breaches they witnessed in the clinical setting. We do so because these are the most common dilemmas narrated within our data and, following recent government reports (Francis, 2013), the most relevant in terms of students' identities as doctors of tomorrow. In doing so, we consider the character tropes employed for the various actors in these stories, specifically those attributed to the student narrator himself or herself and to doctors, patients and nurses.

Narrative plotlines

The plotline of a story comprises the logic of the story and attempts to explain why events happen. Medical students' narratives of patient safety and dignity breaches varied in tone according to how the different parties acted and reacted within the events portrayed. The most common plotlines were the *resistance* narrative, the *patient-advocate* narrative, the *passivity* narrative and the *regret* narrative. Thus, the different plotlines of each of the narrative types varied in terms of the actions of the narrator and the explanations for those actions rather than in terms of the actual breaches themselves. So similar breaches of patient safety or dignity – for example, healthcare professionals' inappropriate/inapt talk to or about patients such as calling a patient 'fat' to their face or using abusive language about a patient behind their backs – were narrated differently depending on how the student reacted during or after witnessing the breach (Table 17.1).

TABLE 17.1 The *resistance, patient-advocate, passivity* and *regret* narratives

Narrative plotline	Description	Brief illustration
Resistance	Students narrate agency and assume the right to act according to their moral conscience by challenging (directly or indirectly) inappropriate behaviours of others during the event.	"I had seen how uncomfortable the initial vaginal examination had been . . . she did not really want a further examination . . . I said that the patient looked uncomfortable and I wasn't going to perform the examination." (Female, Yr 4)
Patient-advocate	Students narrate their strong moral stance as they judge the perpetrator harshly. The narrator does not always actively resist during the event; resistance sometimes occurs in the act of narrating and sometimes in their actions after the event.	"doctor . . . causing patients physical pain and psychological distress for the point of demonstrating . . . one [patient] was on the verge of tears, one [patient] asked to stop . . . I reported the behaviour to the tutor at the university; it really upset me to see the patients treated badly for our learning." (Female, Yr 2)

Passivity	While recognising the professionalism lapse, students narrate inaction, either because they do not recognise their right to act or because they have no desire to act either now or in the future.	*"Well I was only in my first or second year; I knew she [doctor] should have washed her hands, but I didn't want to humiliate the GP . . . if I was in the situation again, I doubt I'd risk my neck to do the right thing."* (Male, Yr 3)
Regret	Students narrate inaction followed by a desire to have behaved differently. Sometimes the regret narrative includes a strong resolution to challenge similar behaviours in the future.	*"[I was] frustrated and a bit guilty that perhaps I should have raised my concerns afterwards at university."* (Female, Yr 2)

Character tropes

Character tropes are based on social stereotypes of groups of people who share similar characteristics, including manners of speaking and types of actions. These stereotypes can be defined as 'a set of consensual beliefs in one group about the attributes shared by members of another group' (Van Langenhove and Harre, 1999, p. 129). Thus, character tropes comprise 'fuzzy sets' of ideas about a character trope with no single representation being 'true'. We draw on these culturally defined character tropes within our narratives and are cognisant that no single character is recognisable without being represented alongside other characters within a moral story. For example, without a *villain* and a *victim*, there can be no *hero*; none of these characters can exist in a moral vacuum.

Within our data, we identified a range of different character tropes that students drew upon when narrating healthcare professionals' lapses of patient safety and dignity (see Table 17.2 for an overview). Each of these characters is ethically neutral, comprising both negative (shadow: the negative side of a character) and positive connotations. (We highlight the shadow aspect of the character in Table 17.2 only if it appears in our data.)

TABLE 17.2 The range of character tropes within students' oral narratives of patient safety and dignity breaches by healthcare professionals (in alphabetical order)

The advocate
Acts in defence of others (either an individual person or advocating the rights of specific minority/oppressed groups), often with the agenda of affecting broad social change.

The (deferential) apprentice
Acts to gain a mastery over the medical knowledge and practice that is lacking. This character is firmly positioned at the bottom of the hierarchy, deferring to the greater authority and knowledge of more powerful others, even when the character considers the actions of others to be unprofessional, unethical or wrong.

(Continued)

TABLE 17.2 (Continued)

The (eager) apprentice
Unlike the *deferential apprentice*, the *eager apprentice* character is often portrayed as being innocent about (or in ignorance of) professionalism lapses by themselves or others; this character is eager to learn irrespective of 'minor' behavioural lapses.

The (grateful) apprentice
This character is grateful to anyone who provides an opportunity for them to learn. When faced with a situation in which the *grateful apprentice* character witnesses or participates in a professionalism lapse, the character highlights issues of service–education tensions and how the added burden of teaching students can exasperate clinical situations (thereby indirectly blaming themselves for their seniors' lapses).

The (reluctant) apprentice
Portrayed as wishing only to learn 'ethically' with a fully consented patient and with appropriate supervision. This character's involvement in professionalism lapses is often constructed as someone being a reluctant participant who is 'dragged' or 'forced' into difficult situations by the clinical teacher.

The avenger
Acts to balance the scales of justice. The injustice can be against anyone deemed 'worthy' of defending. The perpetrator of the injustice can be other individuals, 'character tropes' or specific cultures (e.g. the ward culture). So the *avenger* could be avenging perceived unethical/unprofessional behaviour through any means. What differentiates the *avenger* from the *advocate* is the level of passion involved in the narrating of the 'injustices' done unto those being avenged. The *shadow* side of the avenger uses passive (e.g. leaving the scene) rather than active resistance.

The bully
Portrayed as overbearing, manipulating or abusing students. The *bully* character is often a senior clinician or other healthcare professional, and bullying is undertaken in order to maintain the power hierarchy within medicine.

The caregiver
Displays a desire to heal, care for and nurture others. Typical actions focus on the healing process, preserving patients' health and well-being that might be compromised by the actions of (less caring) others. The *shadow* of the *caregiver* appears to take advantage of the sick through an over-eagerness to heal by persisting in continuing a medical procedure against the will of the patient.

The (neglectful) caregiver
Rather than being constructed as deliberately destructive, this character is portrayed as being neglectful due to overwork or ignorance of the 'correct' procedure.

The coward
Avoids confrontation in situations where the right thing to do is known but the power hierarchy is such that this character feels unable – too 'scared' – to act. The *coward* is narrated as if the character agonises around inner fears of what might happen should a stand be made. The *coward* accepts the status quo rather than fighting inner fears to stand up for what he or she knows is right. Sometimes the coward reports the situation after the event, but not in an official capacity.

The dictator
Portrayed as behaving in a dictatorial manner, oppressing others with power portrayed as being used selfishly and without thought for others' feelings.

The diplomat

The *diplomat* can see the situation from many angles, trying not to 'judge' any party involved. This character might act in the manner of a diplomat to ease the situation and prevent any further issues.

The disciple

This character is linked to the *God* character. The *disciple* will follow that *God*, deferring to greater knowledge and power and accepting 'the way things are done here'. The *disciple* character might go against personal behavioural, ethical, and professional standards in order to do this.

The fool

Portrayed as one who brings forth an emotional reaction in others whilst displaying no emotions himself or herself. The *fool* character can include an element of social detachment whilst behaving in a manner that could be deemed inappropriate. Thus, others around this character might recognise the actions of the character as being like that of a fool, but the *fool* himself or herself might be portrayed as being oblivious.

The God

Constructed by the narrator as an unapproachable character set within a strict hierarchical system: the *God* is all knowing, in charge, obeyed, occasionally revered but more often is feared and never challenged. Mostly the *God* character is assigned to the other by the narrator, but sometimes is portrayed as the other assigning themselves as *God*.

The hero

Portrayed as being selfless, often overcoming their own personal fears in order to 'save' others. The *hero* narrates this as his or her 'cause' in their fight for 'rightness' and willingly sacrifices himself or herself for this cause. Sometimes this character is portrayed by the narrator as an intention for their own future action.

The (frustrated) hero

Also portrayed as selfless, overcoming personal fears to 'save' others. Unlike the *hero*, the *frustrated hero*'s efforts are, however, portrayed as fruitless, sometimes going unnoticed by the oppressor or the *victim* character (whom he or she is attempting to save).

The judge

The *judge* is the narrator, commenting on ethical or professionalism lapses of others whilst remaining silent on his or her own actions and personal responsibilities to act.

The liberator

The narrator portrays himself or herself as the *liberator* character within the narrative process itself. The reason for the *liberator*'s participation in the study is to share stories so that others might learn, thus liberating others from entrenched beliefs (e.g. the belief that students are disempowered and cannot act according to their own ethical standards).

The martyr

Portrayed as suffering for the sake of others with no personal gain. For example, this suffering might take the form of being the only person to speak out, thereby suffering the wrath of a senior clinician.

The prop

The *prop* character is portrayed as inactive in the events, almost non-human. The *prop* has no voice and is used by other characters in the story.

The shape-shifter

The *shape-shifter* character at first seems to be a good, honest and even heroic 'role model', but later turns out to behave in unprofessional or abusive ways.

(*Continued*)

TABLE 17.2 (Continued)

The slave
The *slave* character represents total absence of choice and self-authority in his or her actions. This character is enslaved by the 'master' who is outwardly obeyed but inwardly criticised.

The storyteller
Portrayed in the narrative itself – the narrator reveals how he or she, the *storyteller*, has become a 'better person' due to the events narrated. This is a story with a moral.

The (eager) teacher
Portrayed as being ignorant of today's professionalism code of conduct. The *eager teacher* character unwittingly asks students to participate in professionalism lapses because that is the way he or she learnt (e.g. examining patients without valid consent).

The victim
This character is narrated as an innocent and (sometimes) powerless *victim* of a stronger, more forceful tyrant. When narrated as powerless, the *victim* is vulnerable and might require rescuing.

The voyeur
This character manifests himself or herself as voyeuristic, albeit with good intentions. In order to learn, the *voyeur* character lurks in the background, not directly contributing to the situation, often witnessing professionalism lapses. Due to the voyeuristic nature of his or her presence, the *voyeur* character is unable to intervene to prevent any actions from occurring.

Narrative plotlines and character tropes

Similar characters were narrated across the various narrative plotlines within our data, although the patterns of positioning differed (see Table 17.3 below for the range of character tropes employed for student, doctor, patient and nurse). Unsurprisingly, the types of character tropes drawn upon tended to reflect the general plotline of the overall narrative itself. Thus, within the *passivity* and *regret* narratives, we see students portrayed as *cowards* and *victims* against the more powerful *dictator* or *bully*. Within the *resistance* narratives, however, students are positively portrayed as the *advocate*, *reluctant apprentice*, *diplomat* or *hero/heroine*. While sometimes doctors are negatively portrayed as a *dictator*, they are more often portrayed in ways that are culturally less 'evil' and, therefore, easier to resist; for example, the *eager teacher* who unwittingly breaches today's codes of professional conduct rather than an 'evil' perpetrator with malevolent intent. The importance of the different positions in which individuals' character tropes are portrayed within the narratives sheds light on the various identities narrators attribute to themselves and others. Such positioning can also influence (empowering and inhibiting) future social identities (possible selves) and, therefore, possibilities for behaving in the face of similar events.

TABLE 17.3 The range of character tropes used for students, doctors, nurses and patients within the common *narrative* plotlines

	Student	*Doctor*	*Nurse*	*Patient*
Resistance	Advocate; reluctant apprentice; avenger (and shadow); caregiver; diplomat; judge; hero	Eager teacher; neglectful caregiver; dictator; God	Avenger; coward; neglectful care-giver; victim	Martyr; prop; victim
Patient-Advocate	Reluctant, deferential, grateful and eager apprentice; avenger (shadow); caregiver; judge; hero and frustrated hero; slave; victim; voyeur	Bully; God; dictator	Caregiver (shadow); dictator	Prop; victim
Passivity	Reluctant, deferential, grateful and eager apprentice; coward; judge; slave; storyteller; voyeur	Bully; God; fool; shape-shifter	Dictator	Victim
Regret	Avenger (shadow); caregiver; coward; disciple; diplomat; judge; liberator; hero and frustrated hero; storyteller; voyeur	Bully; caregiver (shadow); dictator; fool; shape-shifter	Caregiver	Prop; victim

Having considered the common plotlines and character tropes within medical students' oral narratives of witnessing patient safety and dignity breaches, we now bring these together by presenting a positioning analysis of one narrative. This narrative was chosen as it: (a) contains a variety of character tropes; (b) portrays the student challenging the situation; (c) is based in a hospital setting (the most common setting for our students' professionalism dilemmas); and (d) involves a patient dignity breach involving older patients that was also common in our data and link to recent government reports of similar breaches (Care Quality Commission, 2011; Francis, 2013). Thus, it sheds light on a range of current contextual, personal and interpersonal issues that impact on the narrator's identity portrayal within his or her story world.

Example: positioning analysis of a patient-advocate narrative

The narrator is Billy (a pseudonym), a third-year medical student who sometimes works as a healthcare assistant (HCA) to supplement his income. The context is a busy ward in the early hours of the morning (see Box 17.2).

BOX 17.2 'I'M BIG ENOUGH AND UGLY ENOUGH'

1	Billy	I was going to say – what my thresholds were – where I did have
2		a discussion with the nurse in charge and it was quite similar . . .
3		poor chap, he was in a cubi* . . . he's got melaena,** but he also had
4		horrendous leg ulcers which were all dressed. The problem was that
5		he couldn't always get to the bell. He then tried to stand up. He
6		couldn't always make it to the toilet so he was forever um, you know,
7		defecating on his – on his dressings ((laughs)). And so I remember
8		you know I did about three – three dressings in – in the period of
9		about two hours, um and there's one time I was up somewhere else
10		sorting somebody else out and the bell's going and it's going and
11		going and I – and I looked at them and the nurse was sat in the centre
12		station and I thought *'oh yeah'* so I carried on with this person
13		'cause you know I – I can't remember what I was doing but it was –
14		I couldn't just leave him and then go off and do something else,
15		and um, I must have been there ten minutes and the bell was going
16		off the entire time and as I came out sort of – into the sluice – got rid
17		of all the stuff, this nurse said *'the chap down in one of the cubis*
18		*needs sorting out again',* and I says, *'well why haven't you gone and*
19		*done it?'* Well so uh, and so we had a bit of a discussion about you
20		know *'it doesn't matter what your role is or you know how important*
21		*you think you are or the fact that you're getting ready for your six*
22		*o'clock in the morning meds',* you know *'there's somebody there*
23		<u>*now'*</u> and – and you know *'distressed'* and they were, and of course
24		I get in there and he's sitting there at the end of the bed. He's trying
25		to get up, trying to make the toilet, hasn't made it so it's now all on
26		the floor ((said laughingly)) et cetera et cetera, and she still wouldn't
27		come in and help me, so it took me about an hour to eventually help
28		this guy onto the – back into bed, change him all, re-dress his legs, you
29		know, and then it was time to go home.
30	Lynn	But you challenged.
31	Billy	Oh yeah, well yes I'm – I'm big enough and ugly enough.

Notes: *'cubi' is short for cubicle; **melaena refers to black, 'tarry' feces associated with gastrointestinal haemorrhage.

The overall plotline centres around Billy and his actions as an advocate for the patient in the face of inaction from the nurse in charge and other ward nurses who must have also ignored the alarm bell (*neglectful caregivers*). So, in terms of the positioning of character tropes within the narrative (level 1 positioning), we begin by considering the types of action, motives for those actions and characteristics of the story figures (de Fina, 2013). Billy is attributed the actions of an *avenger*, passionately defending the rights of the passive (*victim*) patient (line 3, 'poor chap') against the injustice of a ward culture whereby patient care appears to come secondary to the general management of the ward (lines 21–22, preparing the 'six o'clock in the morning meds'). Not only does Billy defend the patient's rights by challenging the nurse, he does so through his dedication to attending to the patient's immediate needs (continually cleaning his dressings and providing continuity of care) while the nurse 'sits' in the centre station (lines 11–12).

The motive for Billy's actions is that a patient is in distress. The motive for the nurses' inaction is their higher status on the wards (compared with Billy, working as an HCA), their perceived importance (lines 20–21; Beer, 2013) and because they were busy on another job. This other job was deemed less important by Billy: not only did he fail to mention it until later in his narrative, but he also uses the evaluation device of *reported thought* to express a 'silent criticism' (Haakana, 2007) of the nurses' inaction (line 12, 'and I thought "*oh yeah*"').

The characteristic attributed to the patient is that of helpless *victim*. The characteristic of the nurse is mainly 'neglectful'. Indeed, throughout the narrative, the nurse is constructed as a *neglectful caregiver*, sitting at the station, refusing to assist the student as he repeatedly attended to the distressed patient. Thus, the characteristics attributed to Billy include him being a hard worker with strong morals and a caring attitude: an *avenger*, *patient-advocate* and *hero*.

We now turn to consider how the narrative was embedded in the surrounding talk (level 2 positioning). Billy's narrative was told in a mixed-gender group, comprising familiar co-participants, in which they were encouraged to talk about professionalism dilemmas to a social sciences researcher working at a different university. His story occurred around 27 minutes into the interview and directly followed another (female) student's narrative of working as an HCA on a stroke ward in which the nurses were sitting around drinking coffee, neglecting patients, leaving them undressed and crying (Beer, 2013). One nurse shouted at a patient, the student heard '*absolutely horrible crying*', and the nurse '*stomped away out of the ward*'. The female student did not challenge the nurse perpetrators directly because '*I didn't feel confident enough to*', instead preferring to attend to the patients and report the incident informally after the event. She later went home and cried for over an hour due to her own distressed state following the incident.

During the previous talk around professionalism dilemmas, Billy was an active participant in the evaluation of others' narratives, always holding a strong moral position whilst supporting his fellow group members in their (in)action (*avenger*). For example, 15 minutes into the interview, he commented on another student's narrative, saying '*and you should be, you know . . . empowered or brave enough or whatever to say "I don't like that, I don't think that's right" and regardless of who that person is*' (here, 'you' meaning 'we'; avenging the wrongs for all). Thus, we can see how Billy positions his identity as a moral and just person throughout the interview.

We now turn our focus to examine the wider implications of Billy's narrative in terms of how discourse and moral ideologies are relevant to the ways in which Billy positions himself and others in this particular narrative (level 3 positioning).

We therefore consider Billy's self-image, how this has been evoked and the wider social implications that arise from this (Potter and Wetherell, 1987). First, the group interview was held at a new medical school that has a strong professionalism curriculum, integrated across both university and clinical teaching settings, through which students are encouraged to explore professionalism issues in small-group settings. The professionalism discourses available to Billy were, therefore, wide-ranging (Monrouxe *et al.*, 2011), including the views that: (a) professionalism comprises a personal set of characteristics (morals and behaviours with a strong patient-centred focus) and (b) as future doctors, they have a contract with society to behave in patients' best interests, acting competently, altruistically and morally (S. R. Cruess, 2006).

The wider social implications of Billy embodying this professional identity are evident in his strong patient-centred actions and values as he directly challenges the nurse present in an attempt to shift the culture towards caring for patients as a priority over and above other ward activities (preparing medication). Indeed, both government and regulatory authorities are presently emphasising the role of medical students and trainees in the safeguarding of patients as they learn within the clinical environment (Francis, 2013). This safeguarding includes reporting deficiencies in the system, asserting that, whether qualified or in training, all doctors are under a moral obligation to protect patients (Francis, 2013). Billy seems to understand this and is willing to make a stand against those who do not. Ultimately, Billy appears to have embodied this moral ideology and seems unafraid to use it to affect cultural change.

Discussion

We have considered medical students' social identities as moral actors within their narratives of professionalism dilemmas encountered within the clinical workplace. We have highlighted the range of character tropes utilised within the four main plotlines identified in our data: the *resistance*, *patient-advocate*, *passivity* and *regret* narratives. Using positioning analysis, we have seen how various stereotypical characters have been narrated as medical students highlight their own moral selves as students of today, and as future doctors. We have highlighted how positioning analysis has enabled us to move from considering the various character tropes plotted within students' narratives and towards an understanding of the broader social meaning that such narrative constructions might have (de Fina, 2013). Set in the context of the current crisis in medicine around the working practices of some healthcare professionals, which compromise patient safety and dignity (Francis, 2013), these student narratives highlight ways in which the status quo is sometimes maintained (despite their inner moral anxieties, as in *regret* narratives) and sometimes contested (as in *resistance* narratives). Our work has implications in terms of the role of tomorrow's doctors in affecting cultural change and how we might facilitate future doctors' social identities of themselves as moral actors.

Across the data, we found a range of key character tropes for medical students, doctors, patients and nurses. Irrespective of the narrative plotline, the doctor character was frequently portrayed as *dictator, bully* or *God*; the nurse character was most often portrayed as *caregiver*; the patient character was mainly portrayed as *victim* or *prop*; and the student character was portrayed primarily as *judge, apprentice, avenger, caregiver, hero* or *voyeur*. Interestingly, both the range and frequency of character tropes drawn on to construct students' own identities was greater than those used to construct other characters in the narrative, with students sometimes drawing on a range of (mostly positive) character tropes at different points in the narrative (as illustrated in Box 17.2). The use of these multiple and positive characterisations of themselves serves to build up a bigger picture of the moral character of the narrator. This over-characterisation of their moral selves is most likely due to the process of narrating the self, ensuring a self-consistency across the narrative (and throughout the interview), along with the contextual need within the interviews to portray oneself in a positive light even in the face of inaction.

This brings us to consider the character tropes we identified in the different plotlines narrated. We found interesting patterns across the situations in which students typically challenged during the event (the *resistance* narrative) versus those in which students either challenged post-event or not at all (the *patient-advocate, passivity* and *regret* narratives) in terms of how they constructed themselves and the doctor character (for it was the doctor who they typically challenged). Thus, when students narrated a failure to challenge during the event, the doctor was most commonly characterised using the tropes of *bully, God, dictator* and *shape-shifter*, with the narrator as *voyeur, slave, apprentice, coward* and *frustrated hero/heroine*. However, when students narrated situations where they did challenge the perpetrator, the doctor character was narrated most frequently as an *eager teacher* or a *neglectful caregiver*, with themselves most commonly characterised as *advocate, caregiver, reluctant apprentice, diplomat* and *hero/heroine*.

The construction of the perpetrator within the narratives could be partly due to the different ways that they considered the people to be at the time, thereby influencing student action. For example, it is arguably easier to resist individuals who are more neglectful than malicious and scary. However, we must not forget that the narratives were part of a social act (which level 2 positioning focuses on). Therefore, such narrative constructions might also be face-saving for others within the group who narrated inaction in the face of a *dictator* consultant (softening their own heroism in the company of others who did not act). Conversely, some narrators might have actively constructed the doctor in certain ways (e.g., as *bully, dictator, God*) to account for their inaction in order to save their own face within the context of the focus group (Brown and Levinson, 1987). Indeed, it is rhetorically easier to maintain the status quo when faced with a *bully* or *dictator*.

The character tropes we have identified resonate with and expand upon others found in the literature. For example, we found patients used direct metaphoric expressions such as '*doctor as God*' alongside references to doctors being '*up there*' and patients being '*down here*' (Rees, Knight and Wilkinson, 2007). Other work examining attitudes to gender and nursing stereotypes have identified the tropes of 'angel', 'handmaiden', 'battleaxe' and 'whore' as being common in everyday imagery (Cunningham, 1999; Jinks and Bradley, 2004). Although we did not identify these in our data, probably because of the different focus of the two studies (professionalism versus gender), we did find the *dictator*, which is perhaps similar to but with more negative connotations of ill intent than the battleaxe trope with its connotations of 'bossiness' (Jinks and Bradley, 2004). We also found the *neglectful caregiver*, which resonates with current media concerns about nurses who are 'too posh to wash' (Beer, 2013). In our previous work examining narratives of professionalism dilemmas, we have commented on the construction of the patient as *victim* (Monrouxe and Rees, 2012; Monrouxe *et al.*, 2014; Rees and Monrouxe, 2015; Rees *et al.*, 2013, 2014). Furthermore, the *prop* character trope, exclusively used for patients, has also been identified in our earlier work examining doctor–patient–student interactions during bedside teaching examinations (Monrouxe, Rees and Bradley, 2009; Rees, Ajjawi and Monrouxe, 2013). Here, patients were sometimes used as props for students to learn on rather than being included in the 'learning team' as active participants. Although the limited character tropes identified for patients have been reported on before, to our knowledge, apart from the broad character trope of *hero,* there has been no work examining the wider range of tropes medical students use to highlight their own social and moral identities within talk. We believe that this work makes an original contribution in this respect and develops our knowledge in terms of understanding the various ways in which students construct their own (and others') identities in the face of professionalism dilemmas. These constructions have implications in terms of students' beliefs about their legitimacy in the clinical workplace, their roles as patient advocates and the actions that are permissible or available to them.

Understanding how medical students narrate their moral identities, therefore, has implications for medical educators in their role of facilitating students' good ethical practice. Although narratives are personal constructions of events, as opposed to the events themselves, characters portrayed – and the social order of those characters – have a certain *social reality* within our minds. Furthermore, understanding narratives through positioning analysis enables us to make sense of narrators' sense of self in the social world – their larger social identity – beyond the context of the telling. It is here we can see how students' discourses of *who they are* sometimes resonate with wider discourses around *who they should be*: *avengers* for the rights of patients (Francis, 2013). However, let us not forget that sometimes students narrate themselves less favourably; for example, as *cowards.*

Previous research has used video reflexivity to develop participants' awareness of their own interactions within clinical settings to facilitate aspects such as patient safety (Iedema and Carroll, 2011). Other work has utilised the reflexive process in order to 'open up' participants' narratives around their online activities by playing back excerpts from narratives recorded earlier, providing them with the opportunity to expand upon and, therefore, 're-narrate' the reasons for certain actions. Such reflexivity, therefore, enables individuals to (re)position themselves in empowered ways (Georgakopoulou, 2013). Using similar methodologies, alongside organisational support for cultural change, we believe that medical students might benefit from engaging in a reflexive process around the times in which they failed to act in patients' best interests, despite their inner desires to do so. Part of this reflexivity might be to highlight the legitimacy of the student in the clinical workplace, thus reducing uncertainty around their self-identity as future doctors (Hogg, 2000) and their own moral commitment to protect patients, thus facilitating students to act according to their 'true ideal' future selves (Kivetz and Tyler, 2007).

References

American Board of Internal Medicine Foundation, American College of Physicians–American Society of Internal Medicine Foundation, and European Federation of Internal Medicine. (2002). Medical professionalism in the new millennium: A physician charter. *Annals of Internal Medicine, 136*(3), 243–6.

Atkinson, P. (1984). Training for certainty. *Social Science and Medicine, 19*(9), 949–56.

Australian Medical Association. (2015). Medical Professionalism – 2010. Revised 2015 [online], *AMA*, 12 October. Retrieved from: https://ama.com.au/position-statement/medical-professionalism-2010-revised-2015

Bamberg, M. (2006). 'Stories: Big or small: Why do we care?' *Narrative Inquiry, 16*, 139.

Bamberg, M. and Georgakopoulou, A. (2008). Small stories as a new perspective in narrative and identity analysis. *Text and Talk, 28*(3), 377–96.

Bamberg, M., de Fina, A. and Schiffrin, D. (2007). *Selves and identities in narrative and discourse.* Amsterdam: John Benjamins.

Bamberg, M., de Fina, A. and Schiffrin, D. (2011). Discourse and identity construction. In K. Luyckx, S. J. Schwartz and V. L. Vignoles (Eds), *Handbook of identity theory and research*, Vol. 1 (pp. 177–200). New York: Springer.

Bamberg, M., Meister, T., Kindt, W., Schernus, W. and Stein, M. (2004). Narrative discourse and identites. In J. C. Meister (Ed.), *Narratology beyond literary criticism* (pp. 213–37). Berlin and New York: Walter de Gruyter.

Beer, G. (Ed.). (2013). *Too posh to wash? Reflections on the future of nursing.* London: 2020health.org. Retrieved from: www.2020health.org/dms/2020health/downloads/reports/2020tooposh_06-02-13.pdf. London 2020health.org (accessed 1 September 2016).

Blasi, A. (1980). Bridging moral cognition and moral action: A critical review of the literature. *Psychological Bulletin, 88*(1), 1–45.

Blasi, A. (1983). Moral cognition and moral action: A theoretical perspective. *Developmental Review, 3*(2), 178–210.

Brown, P. and Levinson, S. C. (1987). *Politeness: Some universals in language usage.* Cambridge: Cambridge University Press.

Canadian Medical Association. (2005). *Medical professionalism (Update 2005).* Ottowa: CMA. Retrieved from: http://policybase.cma.ca/dbtw-wpd/Policypdf/PD06-02.pdf (accessed 1 September 2016).

Care Quality Commission. (2011). *Dignity and nutrition inspection programme.* Newcastle upon Tyne: Care Quality Commission.

Chandratilake, M., McAleer, S. and Gibson, J. (2012). Cultural similarities and differences in medical professionalism: A multi-region study. *Medical Education, 46*(3), 257–66. doi: 10.1111/j.1365-2923.2011.04153.x

Chretien, K. C., Goldman, E. F., Beckman, L. and Kind, T. (2010). It's your own risk: Medical students' perspectives on online professionalism. *Academic Medicine, 85*(10 Suppl.), S68–S71.

Cruess, R. L. (2006). Teaching professionalism: Theory, principles, and practices. *Clinical Orthopaedics and Related Research, 449,* 177–85. doi: 110.1097/1001.blo.0000229274. 0000228452.cb.

Cruess, R. L. and Cruess, S. R. (2006). Teaching professionalism: General principles. *Medical Teacher, 28*(3), 205–8.

Cruess, R. L., Cruess, S. R. and Johnston, S. E. (2000). Professionalism: An ideal to be sustained. *Lancet, 356*(9224), 156–9.

Cruess, R. L., Cruess, S. R. and Steinert, Y. (Eds). (2009). *Teaching Medical Professionalism.* Cambridge: Cambridge University Press.

Cruess, S. R. (2006). Professionalism and medicine's social contract with society. *Clinical Orthopaedics and Related Research, 449,* 170–6. doi: 10.1097/01.blo.0000229275. 66570.97

Cunningham, A. (1999). Nursing stereotypes. *Nursing Standard, 13*(45), 46–7.

Davies, B. and Harre, R. (2001). Positioning: The discursive production of selves. In M. Wetherell, S. Taylor and S. J. Yates (Eds), *Discourse theory and practice: A reader* (pp. 261–71). London: Sage and the Open University.

de Fina, A. (2013). Positioning level 3: Connecting local identity displays to macro social processes. *Narrative Inquiry, 23*(1), 40–61.

Eva, K. W. (2014). Trending in 2014: Hippocrates. *Medical Education, 48*(1), 1–3.

Feudtner, C., Christakis, D. A. and Christakis, N. A. (1994). Do clinical clerks suffer ethical erosion? Students' perceptions of their ethical environment and personal development. *Academic Medicine, 69*(8), 670–9.

Foucault, M. (1969). *The archaeology of knowledge.* (A. M. Sheridan Smith, Trans.). London and New York: Routledge, 2002.

Francis, R. (2013). *Report of the the Mid Staffordshire NHS Foundation Trust Public Inquiry.* London: The Stationery Office.

Frank, A. W. (1995). *The wounded storyteller: Body, illness and ethics.* Chicago, IL: Chicago University Press.

Garner, J. and O'Sullivan, H. (2010). Facebook and the professional behaviours of undergraduate medical students. *Clinical Teacher, 7*(2), 112–15.

General Medical Council. (2009). Tomorrow's Doctors [online], *GMC.* Retrieved from: www.gmc-uk.org/education/undergraduate/tomorrows_doctors_2009.asp (accessed 30 October 2009).

General Medical Council. (2012). *Good Medical Practice 2012.* Manchester: General Medical Council.

General Medical Council. (2013). *Good Medical Practice 2013.* Manchester: General Medical Council.

Georgakopoulou, A. (2006). Thinking big with small stories in narrative and identity analysis. *Narrative Inquiry, 16*(1), 122–30.

Georgakopoulou, A. (2007). *Small stories, interaction and identities.* Amsterdam: John Benjamins.

Georgakopoulou, A. (2013). Building iterativity into positioning analysis: A practice-based approach to small stories and self. *Narrative Inquiry, 23*(1), 89–110.

Gramzow, R. H., Sedikides, C., Panter, A. T. and Insko, C. A. (2000). Aspects of self-regulation and self-structure as predictors of perceived emotional distress. *Personality and Social Psychology Bulletin, 26*(2), 188–205. doi: 10.1177/0146167200264006

Greenhalgh, T. (2007). Can you trust a doctor? *Accountancy, 140*(1368), 67.

Haakana, M. (2007). Reported thought in complaint stories. In E. Holt and R. Clift (Eds), *Reporting talk: Reported speech in interaction* (pp. 120–49). Cambridge: Cambridge University Press.

Hafferty, F. W. (2000). In search of a lost chord: Professionalism and medical education's hidden curriculum. In D. Wear and J. Bickel (Eds), *Educating for professionalism: Creating a culture of humanism in medical education* (pp. 11–34). Iowa City, IA: University of Iowa Press.

Hafferty, F. W. (2006). Definitions of professionalism: A search for meaning and identity. *Clinical Orthopaedics and Related Research, 449*, 193–204. doi: 10.1097/01.blo. 0000229273.20829.d0

Hafferty, F. W. (2009). Professionalism and the socialization of medical students. In R. L. Cruess, S. R. Cruess and Y. Steinert (Eds), *Teaching medical professionalism* (pp. 53–72). New York: Cambridge University Press.

Hafferty, F. W. and Castellani, B. (2009). A sociological framing of medicine's modern-day professionalism movement. *Medical Education, 43*(9), 826–8.

Hafferty, F. W. and Levinson, D. (2008). Moving beyond nostalgia and motives: Towards a complexity science view of medical professionalism. *Perspectives in Biology and Medicine, 51*(4), 599–615.

Hardy, S. A. and Carlo, G. (2011). Moral identity. In S. J. Schwartz, K. Luyckx and V. L. Vignoles (Eds), *Handbook of identity theory and research* (pp. 495–513). New York: Springer Science and Business Media.

Hogg, M. (2000). Subjective uncertainty reduction through self-categorisation: A motivational theory of social identity processes. *European Review of Social Psychology, 11*(1), 223–55.

Hogg, M. (2012). Uncertainty-identity theory. In P. A. M. Van Lange, A. W. Kruglanski and E. Tory Higgens (Eds), *Handbook of theories of social psychology*, Volume 2 (pp. 62–80). London: Sage.

Holden, M., Buck, E., Clark, M., Szauter, K. and Trumble, J. (2012). Professional identity formation in medical education: The convergence of multiple domains. *HEC Forum, 24*(4), 245–55. doi: 10.1007/s10730-012-9197-6

Iedema, R. and Carroll, K. (2011). The 'clinalyst' institutionalizing reflexive space to realize safety and flexible systematization in health care. *Journal of Organizational Change Management, 24*(2), 175–90. doi: 10.1108/09534811111119753

Jinks, A. M. and Bradley, E. (2004). Angel, handmaiden, battleaxe or whore? A study which examines changes in newly recruited student nurses' attitudes to gender and nursing stereotypes. *Nurse Education Today, 24*(2), 121–7.

Kinnell, H. G. (2000). Serial homicide by doctors: Shipman in perspective. *BMJ, 321*(7276), 1594–7.

Kivetz, Y. and Tyler, T. R. (2007). Tomorrow I'll be me: The effect of time perspective on the activation of idealistic versus pragmatic selves. *Organizational Behavior and Human Decision Processes, 102*(2), 193–211.

Leary, M. (2004). Editorial: What is the self? A plea for clarity. *Self and Identity, 3*(1), 1–3.

Marcia, J. E., Waterman, A. S., Matteson, D. R., Archer, S. and Orlofsky, J. L. (1993). *Ego identity: A handbook for psychsocial research*. New York: Springer.

Moghaddam, F. M. (1999). Culture and private discourse. In R. Harre and L. Van Langenhove (Eds), *Positioning theory: Moral contexts of intentional action* (pp. 74–86). Oxford: Blackwell.

Monrouxe, L. V. (2009). Negotiating professional identities: Dominant and contesting narratives in medical students' longitudinal audio diaries. *Current Narratives*, *1*(1), 41–59.

Monrouxe, L. V. (2010). Identity, identification and medical education: Why should we care? *Medical Education*, *44*(1), 40–9.

Monrouxe, L. V. (2013). Identity, self and medical education. In K. Walsh (Ed.), *Oxford Textbook of medical education* (pp. 113–23). Oxford: Oxford University Press.

Monrouxe, L. V. and Rees, C. E. (2012). 'It's just a clash of cultures': Emotional talk within medical students' narratives of professionalism dilemmas. *Advances in Health Science Education*, *17*(5), 671–701.

Monrouxe, L. V., Rees, C. E. and Bradley, P. (2009). The construction of patients' involvement in hospital bedside teaching encounters. *Qualitative Health Research*, *19*(7), 918–30. doi: 10.1177/1049732309338583

Monrouxe, L. V., Rees, C. E., Endacott, R. and Turnan, E. (2014). 'Even now it makes me angry': Healthcare students' professionalism dilemma narratives. *Medical Education*, *48*(5), 502–17.

Monrouxe, L. V., Rees, C. E. and Hu, W. (2011). Differences in medical students' explicit discourses of professionalism: Acting, representing, becoming. *Medical Education*, *45*(6), 585–602.

Monrouxe, L. V. and Sweeney, K. (2010). Contesting narratives: Medical professional identity formation amidst changing values. In S. Pattison, B. Hannigan, H. Thomas and R. Pill (Eds), *Emerging professional values in health care: How professions and professionals are changing* (pp. 61–77). London and Philadelphia: Jessica Kingsley.

Monrouxe, L. V. and Sweeney, K. (2013). Between two worlds: Medical students narrating identity tensions. In C. R. Figley, P. Huggard and C. E. Rees (Eds), *First do no self-harm: Understanding and promoting physician stress resilience* (pp. 44–66). Oxford: Oxford University Press.

Oettingen, G. and Mayer, D. (2002). The motivating function of thinking about the future: Expectations versus fantasies. *Journal of Personality and Social Psychology*, *83*(5), 1198–1212.

Potter, J. and Wetherell, M. (1987). *Discourse and social psychology*. London: Sage.

Rees, C. E., Ajjawi, R. and Monrouxe, L. V. (2013). The construction of power in family medicine bedside teaching: A video observation study. *Medical Education*, *47*(2), 154–65.

Rees, C. E. and Knight, L. V. (2008). Thinking 'no' but saying 'yes' to student presence in general practice consultations: Politeness theory insights. *Medical Education*, *42*(12), 1152–4.

Rees, C. E., Knight, L. V. and Wilkinson, C. E. (2007). Doctors being up there and we being down here: A metaphorical analysis of talk about student/doctor-patient relationships. *Social Science and Medicine*, *65*(4), 725–37.

Rees, C. E. and Monrouxe, L. V. (2011). Medical students learning intimate examinations without valid consent: A multicentre study. *Medical Education*, *45*(3), 261–72. doi: 10.1111/j.1365-2923.2010.03911.x

Rees, C. E. and Monrouxe, L. V. (2015). Professionalism education as a jigsaw: Putting it together for nursing students. In T. Brown and B. Williams (Eds), *Evidence-based education: Promoting best practice in the teaching and learning of health professional students* (pp. 96–110). London: Radcliffe Publishing.

Rees, C. E., Monrouxe, L. V. and Ajjawi, R. (2014). Professionalism in workplace learning: Understanding interprofessional dilemmas through healthcare student narratives. In D. Jindal-Snape and E. Hannah (Eds), *Exploring the dynamics of ethics in practice: Personal, professional and interprofessional dilemmas* (pp. 295–310). Bristol: Polity Press.

Rees, C. E., Monrouxe, L. V. and McDonald, L. A. (2013). Medical students' most memorable professionalism dilemmas: Narrative, emotion and action. *Medical Education*, *47*(1), 80–96.

Schwartz, S. J., Luyckx, K. and Vignoles, V. L. (Eds). (2011). *Handbook of identity theory and research*. London: Springer.

Shirley, J. L. and Padgett, S. M. (2004). Profesionalism and discourse: But wait, there's more! *The American Journal of Bioethics*, *4*(2), 36–8.

Smith, B. and Sparkes, A. C. (2002). Men, sport, spinal cord injury and the construction of coherence: Narrative practice in action. *Qualitative Research*, *2*(2), 143–71. doi: 10.1177/146879410200200202

Smith, B. and Sparkes, A. C. (2008). Contrasting perspectives on narrating selves and identities: An invitation to dialogue. *Qualitative Research*, *8*(1), 5–35. doi: 10.1177/1468794107085221

Smith, R. (1998). All changed, changed utterly. *BMJ*, *316*(7149), 1917–18.

Sullivan, W. M. (2009). Foreword. In R. L. Cruess, S. R. Cruess and Y. Steinert (Eds), *Teaching medical professionalism* (pp. ix–xvi). New York: Cambridge University Press.

Thistlethwaite, J. and Spencer, J. (2008). *Professionalism in medicine*. Oxford: Radcliffe Publishing Ltd.

Van Langenhove, L. and Harre, R. (1999). The production and use of stereotypes. In R. Harre and L. Van Langenhove (Eds), *Positioning theory: Moral contexts of intentional action* (pp. 127–37). Oxford: Blackwell.

Wear, D. and Aultman, J. M. (Eds). (2006). *Professionalism in medicine: Critical Perspectives*. New York: Springer-Verlag.

18

THE COMPLEXITY OF MEDICAL EDUCATION

Social identity and normative influence in well-being and approaches to learning

Kathleen G. McNeill, Lillian Smyth and Kenneth I. Mavor

In examining educational processes, researchers often seek to provide general models that can be applied in a broad range of learning contexts. While this is a useful pursuit, the current chapter addresses some of the problems inherent in this approach. We investigate the specific context of medical education to demonstrate that the application of general models of education may, at times, be complex. Medical education is often treated as a special case in tertiary education. This is because it differs from other disciplines in terms of the breadth of content to be covered, the ways in which the content is taught and the social norms that are prevalent in the medical education setting. These differences mean that commonly used educational processes and models may produce counter-intuitive outcomes in the context of medical education. The current chapter focuses on two broad types of outcomes: student well-being and student learning. These outcomes are the subject of much debate in medical education and represent concrete examples of areas in which educational models do not apply in the manner we might expect. Our current examination of medical education demonstrates the importance of considering specific contextual complexities and social influence processes in applying general educational models.

Student well-being, learning approaches and social identity

Medical training is widely understood to be a stressful experience. Medical students face a wide range of stressors, both personal and academic, that influence student outcomes, both academically and with regard to health and well-being (O'Reilly, McNeill, Mavor and Anderson, 2014). Many of these stressors are unique to the experience of medical education and are unlike the stressors experienced by other students. As such, medical education is a unique environment in which student groups tend to become highly exclusive as students work to acquire medical knowledge and skills and to develop a professional identity as medics (see also Monrouxe and Rees, Chapter 17, this volume). Medical students are likely to have a high level of social identification (a sense of belonging and being part of the medical student group) and strong group cohesion (mutual social attraction or positive regard towards the group). There may be many positive outcomes from being involved in such a group. Indeed, in other chapters in this volume, we have seen that social identity and related processes play an important role in learning approaches (in this volume, Bliuc, Goodyear and Ellis, Chapter 12, and Smyth, Mavor, Platow and Grace, Chapter 13) and well-being (e.g., Smith, Louis and Tarrant, Chapter 9, this volume) in a general university context.

In the current chapter, however, we discuss not only the benefits but also the pitfalls of applying these general insights in the specific context of medical education. We consider the potential role of identity in promoting professional development, learning and well-being amongst medical students. We also consider several norms associated with the medical student social identity that may be detrimental for students in terms of their professional development, learning and well-being. Thus, we examine the paradoxes associated with how social-psychological processes may both facilitate and potentially undermine medical student outcomes.

The context of medical education

Medical education differs significantly from general university education. Medical students face additional stressors that are specific to their training, including having to perform cadaver dissection, being exposed to illness and suffering and having to pass high-stakes barrier exams (Daly and Willcock, 2002; Dyrbye, Thomas and Shanafelt, 2005; Sreeramareddy et al., 2007). Many medical students feel they have little time for pursuits outside of medical school (Finlay and Fawzy, 2001) and often lose touch with old friends who do not study medicine (Laidlaw, McLellan and Ozakinci, 2016). Thus, medical students are set apart from other students in terms of a more limited social network (Blakey, Blanshard, Cole, Leslie and Sen, 2008) and a highly intensive training programme.

While some degree of stress is considered helpful in motivating students to function to their best ability, the levels of stress observed amongst medical students are often detrimental to their well-being and academic performance. Stress of this severity impairs students' functioning and is considered problematic. Indeed, medical students show poorer well-being than is seen in the general population. They show high levels of problematic stress (Daly and Willcock, 2002; Radcliffe and Lester, 2003) and fatigue (Squires, 1989), and they exhibit poor health habits, such as little exercise, poor diet and unhealthy sleep routines (Ball and Bax, 2002; Keller, Maddock, Laforge, Velicer and Basler, 2007). There is also significant concern in the literature about medical students engaging in alcohol and substance abuse (Granville-Chapman, Yu and White, 2001; Newbury-Birch, White and Kamali, 2000; Takeshita and Morimoto, 1999), although the prevalence may be similar for university students more generally (e.g., in Australia, Wu, Ireland, Hafekost and Lawrence, 2013). Medical students show a heightened prevalence of mental illnesses, such as depression and anxiety (Dyrbye et al., 2006, 2011), and may be at increased risk of suicide (Hays, Cheever and Patel, 1996; Hem, Grłnvold, Aasland and Ekeberg, 2000; Pepitone-Arreola-Rockwell, Rockwell and Core, 1981).

In a similar vein, there is a unique set of educational factors, including diversity of content, vocational applicability and the theory and practice divide, which mean, for medical students, university education is not conducted in the same way as it is more generally. Broadly applied models of learning, such as learning approaches and constructive alignment (Biggs, 1996), become problematic when applied in an educational setting as complex as medical education. An understanding of the best ways to communicate content and assess student learning is not straightforward when students are exposed to a wide variety of content domains and academic ideologies. The multifaceted nature of medicine (spanning physical sciences like anatomy and pathology; social sciences like population health and epidemiology; applied vocational training like clinical skills and the curious mix of law, ethics, culture and humanities that characterises education under the banner of professionalism) means that medical education, as a whole, defies traditional academic discipline typologies (e.g., Becher and Trowler, 2001; Biglan, 1973).

In fact, the ways in which learning outcomes, educational activities and assessment items can be aligned by educators to foster desirable learning approaches are not clear in medical education. Medical educators seek to impart an in-depth, integrated theory-and-evidence-based understanding of the function and dysfunction of the human body as well as providing a practical, applied, procedure-based aspect to the learning of medicine. The theory-and-evidence-based component of medical education lends itself very clearly to traditional conceptualisations of a deep learning approach, as characterised by integrating information into a network, critically evaluating evidence and constructing consolidated understanding of concepts in a broader framework. The applied, practice-based component, however, would be ineffective and potentially dangerous if pursued in a student-led, constructivist manner. The high-stakes, rigidly regulated and procedural nature of physical examinations, investigations and even history-taking skills requires a certain level of *rote* learning, repetition and teacher-led activities (often associated with a more surface learning approach). As such, it is often difficult to design learning activities and, indeed, assessment regimes that can adequately balance these two competing sides of the curriculum.

Medical education is, thus, often a rather idiosyncratic educational environment. Institutions often employ a mix of methods (e.g., a curriculum driven by problem-based learning [PBL] with additional lectures and a separate clinical skills programme) and a mix of very diverse assessment tasks (e.g., written exams and assignments, Objective Structured Clinical Examinations, oral exams and peer evaluations of PBL participation). As a result of these complex learning and assessment environments, capturing the ways in which medical students learn *when studying medicine* is difficult.

The benefits of group membership: well-being, learning and professional development

We have explored the ways in which the environment of medical education differs from other disciplines. In such an intense and unique learning environment, students can become distant from non-medical student friends and may interact more exclusively with medical student peers (Blakey *et al.*, 2008; Weaver, Peters, Koch and Wilson, 2011). We now consider how this social environment and associated group-based processes may influence medical student outcomes.

Social-psychological literature has demonstrated that there are important consequences of group membership. When people take on a social identity (i.e., a group becomes psychologically meaningful to them), they perceive other group members as similar to themselves, while adopting the goals, values and norms of the group (Tajfel and Turner, 1979). Recent literature in social psychology has emphasised the health and well-being benefits of this process (see Jetten, Haslam and Haslam, 2012). In this section, we discuss the role of social identity in learning, well-being and professional development and explore how this role might apply in the context of medical education.

Identity enhances well-being

Group membership provides an opportunity for giving and receiving social support in times of stress (Haslam, O'Brien, Jetten, Vormedal and Penna, 2005). More than that, it appears that being involved in a group can provide individuals with the practical and psychological resources to endure more pain (Jones and Jetten, 2010) and cope with the stress of life transitions (Iyer, Jetten, Tsivrikos, Postmes and Haslam, 2009). Membership in groups has also been demonstrated to alleviate the symptoms of depression and protect against future relapse (Cruwys *et al.*, 2013). Research also supports the notion that group membership may improve one's physical health (Knight, Haslam and Haslam, 2010). Accordingly, medical students' well-being is likely to benefit from membership in such a highly cohesive group where fellow group members tend to have a mutual positive regard for the group. Indeed, a recent study found that medical students who had a higher level of social identification with the medical student group showed greater well-being than those with lower levels of identification (McNeill, Kerr and Mavor, 2014). This initial evidence, taken with the general findings from social psychology, would suggest that it is in the interests of medical students' well-being to be highly involved and connected within their student group.

Identity can enhance learning

One of the most popular conceptions of the ways in which students experience and behave in learning environments is that of learning approaches. The model proposed by Marton and Säljö (1976) and developed by Biggs (1979, 1999) suggests that students relate to the task or subject material they are given in one of two ways: (1) engaging and seeking to understand intent and broader implications (known as a 'deep' learning approach) or (2) focusing on completion of task requirements and often resorting to memorisation (known as a 'surface' learning approach). This model has inspired considerable research regarding the ways in which educators can shape these approaches and the relationships these approaches may have to crucial academic outcomes (e.g., Ramsden, 2003; Trigwell and Prosser, 1991; Zeegus, 2001). In broad terms, deep learning approaches are more desirable, from an educator perspective, as they are associated with more positive educational outcomes, including development of professional identity, intention to continue with study, long-term information retention and academic achievement level (e.g., Artino, La Rochelle and Durning, 2010; Biggs, 1979; Platow, Mavor and Grace, 2013; Richardson, Abraham and Bond, 2012; Walsh, 2007). In this literature, the best way for educators to facilitate this deeper learning approach is by employing the principle of 'constructive alignment' (Biggs, 1996). In this principle, the educator must align intended learning outcomes with learning activities and assessment items.

Some recent developments in the learning approaches literature are informed by the social identity approach (Bliuc, Ellis, Goodyear and Hendres, 2011a; Platow et al., 2013; Smyth et al., 2015). This literature suggests that student social identification with students in their discipline has a direct positive relationship with deep learning approaches and that deep learning is the driving force behind the established link between stronger identification and better grades (Bliuc et al., 2011a, 2011b). In addition, this line of work has demonstrated a longitudinal relationship between social identification and deep learning approaches, both of which have a role in determining student grades and intentions to continue (Platow et al., 2013). Finally, the role of student social norms has been demonstrated to place a qualification on the social identification–deep learning relationship. That is, in instances where students perceive deep learning norms, the link between identification and the deep learning approach link is amplified. In situations where students perceive surface learning norms, the identification–deep learning link can be attenuated or reversed (Smyth et al., 2015).

Identity is essential for professional development

As medical students progress through their education, in addition to being connected to the other medical students, they also begin to feel connected to medical professionals more broadly. Students are taught about the moral and ethical framework of being a doctor and are encouraged to take this on from even the earliest stages of training. Thus, medical students begin to develop a medical professional identity that is broader than their identity as a medical student (Monrouxe, 2009). It has been argued that the development of this professional identity is as important an outcome of medical training as skills and knowledge acquisition (Jarvis-Selinger, Pratt and Regehr, 2012; see also, in this volume, Burford and Rosenthal-Stott, Chapter 16, and Monrouxe and Rees, Chapter 17).

Developing a medical professional identity involves students taking on the ethics, values and norms of the medical profession. This is important if medical students are to operate effectively within the hospital system and to interact with other medical professionals. Thus, in addition to obtaining the knowledge and skills of a medic, students are also faced with the personal challenge of learning to see themselves as a medical professional and thinking and behaving in ways that are consistent with this new identity. This might be particularly challenging for students for whom there is discord between existing identities and the new, professional identity (Costello, 2005).

Identity-potent stressors

Mavor and McNeill (2014) recently argued that we must look further at the dynamic association between stress itself and medical professional identity. Some forms of stress are not only an important part of medical training but, indeed, become embedded in the medical social identity itself. Many stressors cannot be separated from the experience of being a doctor or a member of a medical specialisation. Emergency medicine, for example, involves high-pressure, quick decisions, a diversity of presenting problems, and exhaustion (Heyworth, 2004; Ratzan, 2014). Oncology involves delivering poor prognoses to patients and accompanying them in their fight for both health and dignity (Manochakian, 2014). This does not diminish the potential impact but acknowledges that some stressors are identity-potent: they are given special meaning in the professional identity formation process (Mavor and McNeill, 2014). Thus, some stressors might have a direct negative effect on well-being (O'Reilly *et al.*, 2014) but may also have an additional indirect effect on well-being through increasing identification with being a medical student (Laidlaw *et al.*, 2016), a doctor or a member of a relevant specialty (e.g., a 'badge of honour' in emergency medicine – Heyworth, 2004; 'a privilege' in oncology – Manochakian, 2014). That is, given the many benefits of identification, stressors that are identity-potent for medical students and doctors may have an indirect positive effect on well-being through strengthening identification with the profession (see Figure 18.1a). Figure 18.1b demonstrates this process in the example of emergency medicine, showing that a stressor such as high pressure might reinforce the sense of professional identity, which in turn reduces the impact of stress and improves well-being. In contrast, stressors that do not have any special meaning in the context of the professional identity, such as the burden of paperwork or interpersonal conflicts with co-workers, are likely to have a simple negative effect on well-being.

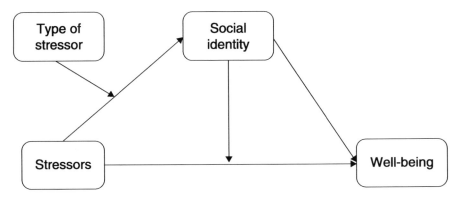

FIGURE 18.1a Schematic representation of the impact of stressors and identity on well-being

Note: perpendicular arrow represents a moderation relationship (interaction).

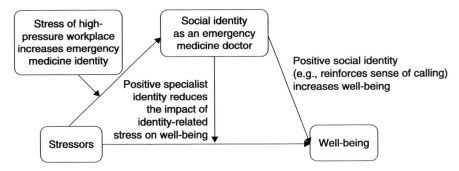

FIGURE 18.1b Schematic representation of the impact of the stress of a high-pressure environment on social identity and well-being

The potential costs of social identity in medical education: problematic norms

We have seen that social identity processes are important in general and are likely to play an important role for medical student well-being, learning and professional development. A strong sense of being 'one of the group' is likely to assist medical students to cope with stress, to facilitate a deeper learning approach and to assist them to take on the identity of a medical professional. In addition, identifying with a group involves taking on the goals of the group and behaving in ways that are consistent with the groups' values and norms. Thus, the more strongly people identify with their group, the more likely they are to engage in behaviour that they perceive as normative for the group (Terry and Hogg, 1996). This has been demonstrated for a range of behaviours, including both healthy and unhealthy eating choices (Cruwys et al., 2012; Louis, Davies, Smith and Terry,

2007; see also Smith, Louis and Tarrant, Chapter 9, this volume) and intentions to binge drink (Johnston and White, 2003).

In many cases, it may be desirable for medical students to adhere to the norms of their group, such as when these norms prescribe ethical conduct and a professional attitude. However, this adherence to norms may be less desirable when the norms associated with the medical student identity (and the medical professional identity more generally) are potentially detrimental for learning, professional development or well-being. Indeed, there is evidence that there are several unhealthy and counterproductive norms amongst medical students that may impact upon their functioning, both academic and psychological. In the following sections, we explore the dilemmas associated with these norms and the potential impacts on students' learning and well-being. We consider three broad categories of norms that are relevant to the medical education setting: social exclusivity norms, health and well-being norms and learning norms.

Social exclusivity norms

Medical students appear to be more socially exclusive than other students. Many medical students often lose contact with old (non-medical-student) friends throughout their training, and they more often live with, date and play sports with fellow students than do students of other disciplines (Blakey *et al.*, 2008). This social exclusivity has been attributed, in part, to the high workload and number of contact hours required for medical training and the physical location in which training takes place (Blakey *et al.*, 2008; Weaver *et al.*, 2011). Since stress is seen as being inherent to the study of medicine, students tend not to complain about their high workload to non-medical peers (Laidlaw *et al.*, 2016), which may further isolate them from those peers. In addition, there may be a perception amongst medical students that it is normative to reduce one's involvement in friendships and activities outside of medical school and to dedicate oneself fully to the pursuit of becoming a doctor (Finlay and Fawzy, 2001).

This social exclusivity may be problematic for medical students' acquisition of important skills and knowledge. Indeed, there is an emphasis on doctors being able to communicate effectively with a range of people, both patients and other professionals. The social exclusivity observed during medical training is unlikely to assist students to develop these important communication skills (Blakey *et al.*, 2008). A medical student from Bristol University describes this notion:

> A combination of time pressures and lack of enthusiasm to cultivate other interests has meant that [medical students] have become narrower people during their time at medical school, their perception of themselves as a 'medic' vastly overshadowing any other facets of their identity – a sad irony considering that diversity of interest and understanding makes a good clinician.

(Finlay and Fawzy, 2001, p. 92)

In addition, it has been suggested that a narrow focus on medical school may lead to some medical students being more vulnerable to the effects of stress (Mavor *et al.*, 2014). Indeed, there is a range of evidence to suggest that diversity of roles, relationships and group memberships improves one's ability to cope with stressful life events and enhance psychological well-being (Brook, Garcia and Fleming, 2008; Jones and Jetten, 2010; Linville, 1985, 1987). This tension between adopting the high-value but exclusive medical identity and gaining broader experiences and greater integration is likely to have consequences for how medical professionals deal with stress and for the quality of patient care (Fahrenkopf *et al.*, 2008; Shanafelt *et al.*, 2010; Shanafelt, Bradley, Wipf and Back, 2002; Wallace, Lemaire and Ghali, 2009; West *et al.*, 2006).

Health and well-being norms

There are several concerning health-related norms associated with medical students. The first of these is alcohol abuse, which is common amongst this group. Estimates range from 21 per cent to 52 per cent of medical students consuming alcohol at problematic levels (Keller *et al.*, 2007; Newbury-Birch *et al.*, 2000; Wu *et al.*, 2013). Alcohol intake appears to increase during the first semester of medical school and remain high thereafter (Ball and Bax, 2002). In addition to the likely detrimental health effects, this misuse of alcohol has been demonstrated to lead to medical students missing out on study, engaging in more sexual activity than they normally would, and becoming involved in physical fights and arguments (Newbury-Birch *et al.*, 2000). It is concerning that medical students view this drinking behaviour as normative. Indeed, medical students tend to overestimate the amount fellow medical students drink (Keller *et al.*, 2007), indicating that there is a perception amongst medical students that members of their group tend to drink heavily. This norm of drinking is problematic due to its influence on medical students' own behaviour. Indeed, in a general student population, perceptions of other students' attitudes towards drinking has been shown to be strongly associated with students' own alcohol consumption (Perkins and Wechsler, 1996). Within the social identity approach, we would expect that it is those medical students who identify most strongly with their group who would be most influenced by their group's norms (Terry and Hogg, 1996). Indeed, in a recent study, we found that medical students who were most highly identified with their group most strongly described themselves as wanting to 'party hard to blow off steam' (McNeill *et al.*, 2014, p. 105). Thus, medical students' level of identification with their student group may place them at risk for alcohol misuse and its associated problems.

Another health-related norm that may be problematic for medical student well-being is the reluctance of students to seek help for mental health complaints. This norm appears to be strong in the medical profession in general, with beliefs about the stigma of mental illness being held by doctors and students alike (Wu *et al.*, 2013). Medical students report being reluctant to speak up about stress and mental health problems due to a belief that it would have a negative impact on career prospects (Chew-Graham, Rogers and Yassin, 2003). Approximately half of a large sample of Australian medical students believed that if they experienced depression or anxiety, it would be a sign of personal weakness; and 10 per cent believed that a history of anxiety or depression would make a person a less reliable doctor (Wu *et al.*, 2013). Unfortunately, medical students' perceptions of the stigma association with mental illness are not unfounded: 59 per cent of Australian doctors believe that being a patient themselves is embarrassing, and 40 per cent believe that a history of mental illness would reflect on perceptions of their competence (Wu *et al.*, 2013). Similarly, a sample of United Kingdom general practitioners confirmed a high perception of stigma amongst other medical professionals, with over 96 per cent agreeing that doctors feel they should portray a healthy image (Adams, Lee, Pritchard and White, 2010). Medical students are unlikely to feel encouraged to seek help for themselves when their professional role models and supervisors are reluctant to do so (Brimstone, Thistlethwaite and Quirk, 2007).

Medical students may also be reluctant to seek help for mental health problems because stress itself may be seen as normative for medical professionals. Medical students, as they undertake their various rotations and placements in hospitals, are being introduced to the medical profession and the values and norms associated with it. Certainly, if medical professionals appear to value stress and see it as a normative component of their occupation, then this is the norm to which medical students become acclimatised. It is not surprising, then, that medical students are reluctant to seek help for their stress and related mental health problems. Rather than seeing this stress as concerning, they may see it as an indication that they are becoming medical professionals. Furthermore, any simple intervention aimed at reducing students' stress could inadvertently undermine students' professional identities.

Paradoxically, we know that it is vital for medical students to develop a professional identity in order to become doctors (Jarvis-Selinger *et al.*, 2012; Monrouxe, 2010), although there may be several norms associated with this that are detrimental to students' health and well-being. Thus, social identity as a doctor may both facilitate and undermine professional development during the course of medical training. Identifying the stressors that are inherent to developing professional identities and those that are not will be an important step in disentangling the complicated normative processes that impact on well-being.

Learning norms

Medical student discipline norms are similarly problematic in the academic domain. Although research has indicated that social identification is broadly related to deep learning approaches (e.g., Bliuc *et al.*, 2011a) and, by extension, with better academic achievement and engagement with the discipline, this is not always the case in a medical education setting. Learning norms among medical students, at least in our data, seem to be firmly in favour of surface learning approaches and surface learning strategies (see below). We would contend that this effect can be traced to the complex, high-stakes, workload-heavy and domain-diverse context in which students are trying to learn. Owing to the extreme difficulty faced in trying to constructively align a medical education environment, students may find that a surface approach is, in fact, the most adaptive. As a result, stronger identification with the discipline can, in fact, drive students to adopt a less conceptually engaged learning approach and may undermine academic outcomes.

In a pilot study of discipline identification, perceived norms and learning approaches in first-year medical students, we do, in fact, find evidence of this potentially harmful pattern. Eighty-three[1] graduate students from the first year of a relatively small PBL-based medical programme at an Australian university were surveyed at the conclusion of lecture sessions. Data were collected at a single time point in the semester: midway through the first term of their first year of medical school. In this survey, students were asked to report on the extent to which they identified with their fellow medical students, the norms they perceived to belong to the group 'medical students', and their own learning approaches when it came to studying medicine.

Results broadly indicated that student identification was relatively strong and was associated with perceived surface learning norms and the adoption of a surface learning approach. These results make sense in the special context of medical education. These same students reported their perceived workload was significantly higher ($M = 6.48$ on a seven-point scale) than students from other disciplines (as compared to a cross-disciplinary sample of 400 students across 14 disciplines, $M_{comp} = 5.55$, $t = 7.241$, $p < 0.001$). This is in keeping with the high workload noted above (Blakey *et al.*, 2008) and has been demonstrated in the education literature to be associated with students adopting a surface learning approach (Biggs, 1999; Ramsden, 2003).

However, this finding could also be indicative of a potential identity-related problem in medical education. In our sample, the norms associated with being a medical student were supportive of prioritising effeciency over effectiveness, minimising student time, working only to complete task requirements (rather than master content), and memorising key information instead of trying to fit new knowledge in a framework. Medical students perceived that these learning behaviours were both commonly performed by and valued by other medical students. This presents a problem for educators when we consider the effect these perceptions have on the way students approach learning.

The paradoxes of medical education

We have highlighted in this chapter the special case of medical education as a setting where certain social-psychological processes play out in paradoxical ways. Whilst identification with fellow students may be beneficial for medical students' well-being, strong identification may also place students at greater risk of conforming to unhealthy norms that affect well-being. We have seen that although a strong medical professional identity is important in order for a student to become a doctor, the norms associated with this identity may also put individuals' health and well-being at risk. We also know that high levels of identification with one's student group are generally helpful for facilitating deep learning of course materials. However, predominant surface learning norms among medical students may mean that higher identifiers are more likely to take this approach over an arguably more desirable deep learning approach. Thus, there is a tension between the benefits of social identification and the costs of problematic norms for medical students. This is displayed schematically in Figure 18.2a. Figures 18.2b and 18.2c demonstrate these processes in the examples of help seeking and surface learning norms respectively.

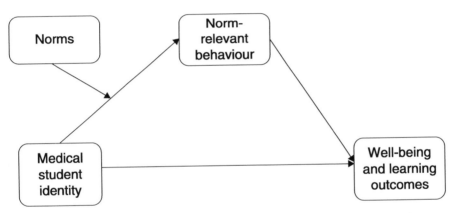

FIGURE 18.2a Schematic representation of the effect of social identification and norms on well-being and learning outcomes

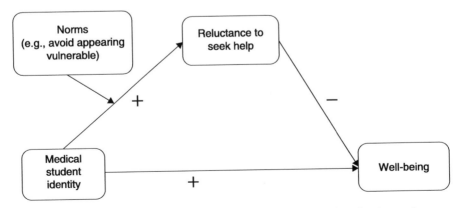

FIGURE 18.2b Schematic representation of the effect of social identification and norms on well-being

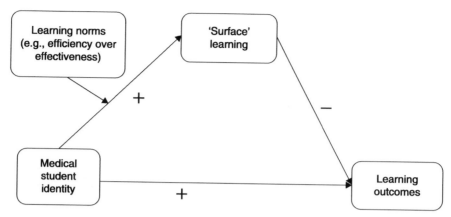

FIGURE 18.2c Schematic representation of the effect of identity and surface norms in learning outcomes

Whilst we have discussed several norms of medical schools that are concerning, we may reasonably expect the specific norms of medical student groups to vary somewhat between medical schools and between different groups of students within these schools. Therefore, the balance between the benefits and costs of identification with the medical student group are likely to vary along with these norms. Specifically, when there are strong norms for behaviour that under-mine well-being or learning (such as a strong norm of alcohol abuse), then identification with that student group may be detrimental to students' well-being and learning. In contrast, in medical schools where these norms are less strongly perceived or where the norms prescribe less problematic behaviour, students' well-being and learning may benefit from identification with their student group.

Broader application of these paradoxes

The current chapter explored the paradoxes associated with norms and identity in the context of medical education, where commitment to the group and the professional identity tends to be strong (Burford, 2012) and several of the norms are understood to be unhealthy (Keller et al., 2007). This description would arguably apply to medical professionals at any stage of their careers; therefore, it is likely that these paradoxes would be of use to understanding well-being and professional development issues in the broader context of medical profes-sionals. There may be several other groups or social categories for which this also applies. Indeed, we might consider these issues in any profession that involves a high level of personal commitment, such as specialised groups within the police force, mental health workers and the armed forces. Certainly, recent media coverage has raised grave concern about some of the norms regarding the mistreatment of women in the Australian Defence Force (Department of Defence, 2012). Thus, we might expect that young members of the Defence Force face a similar paradox of wanting to belong to the group and, facing pressure due to norms and practical constraints, to reduce diversity of social contact and engage in unhealthy practices.

Conclusions

Medical education can be considered a complex system in which multiple factors interact. Several key paradoxes arise from this system in a way that has important implications for the way we think about medical education and how we conduct research in this area. In the specific context of medical education, the influences of group membership may sometimes be both facilitative and detrimental to students' functioning. This highlights the need for medical educators to consider carefully the group influences on their students and, where possible, to take steps to influence these processes in positive ways. It also provides a framework for examining other specific groups for whom social-psychological processes may present similar paradoxes. Finally, our analysis highlights the utility of social identity theory in contributing to understanding processes involved in well-being, learning and professional identity in a complex environment.

Note

1   The programme has year-level cohorts of around 90 students so the responses represent a large proportion of the available population (92 per cent).

References

Adams, E., Lee, A. J., Pritchard, C. W. and White, R. J. E. (2010). What stops us from healing the healers: A survey of help-seeking behaviour, stigmatisation and depression within the medical profession. *The International Journal of Social Psychiatry, 56*(4), 359–70. doi: 10.1177/0020764008099123

Artino, A. R., La Rochelle, J. S. and Durning, S. J. (2010). Second-year medical students' motivational beliefs, emotions, and achievement. *Medical Education, 44*(12), 1203–12.

Ball, S. and Bax, A. (2002). Self-care in medical education: Effectiveness of health-habits interventions for first-year medical students. *Academic Medicine: Journal of the Association of American Medical Colleges, 77*(9), 911–7.

Becher, T. and Trowler, P. (2001). *Academic tribes and territories: Intellectual enquiry and the culture of disciplines.* Philadelphia, PA: McGraw-Hill International.

Biggs, J. (1979). Individual differences in study processes and the quality of learning outcomes. *Higher Education, 8*(4), 381–94.

Biggs, J. (1996). Enhancing teaching through constructive alignment. *Higher Education, 32*(3), 347–64. doi: 10.1007/BF00138871

Biggs, J. (1999). What the student does: Teaching for enhanced learning. *Higher Education Research Development, 18*(1), 57–75.

Biglan, A. (1973). The characteristics of subject matter in different academic areas. *Journal of Applied Psychology, 57*(3), 195–203.

Blakey, H., Blanshard, E., Cole, H., Leslie, F. and Sen, R. (2008). Are medical students socially exclusive? A comparison with economics students. *Medical Education*, *42*(11), 1088–91. doi: 10.1111/j.1365-2923.2008.03126.x

Bliuc, A., Ellis, R. A., Goodyear, P. and Hendres, D. M. (2011a) The role of social identification as university student in learning: Relationships between students' social identity, approaches to learning, and academic achievement. *Educational Psychology*, *31*(5), 559–74. doi: 10108001443410585948

Bliuc, A., Ellis, R. A., Goodyear, P. and Hendres, D. M. (2011b). Understanding student learning in context: Relationships between university students' social identity, approaches to learning, and academic performance. *European Journal of Psychology of Education*, *26*(3), 417–33. doi: 101007s1021201100656

Brimstone, R., Thistlethwaite, J. E. and Quirk, F. (2007). Behaviour of medical students in seeking mental and physical health care: Exploration and comparison with psychology students. *Medical Education*, *41*(1), 74–83. doi: 10.1111/j.1365-2929.2006.02649.x

Brook, A. T., Garcia, J. and Fleming, M. (2008). The effects of multiple identities on psychological well-being. *Personality and Social Psychology Bulletin*, *34*(12), 1588–600. doi: 10.1177/0146167208324629

Burford, B. (2012). Group processes in medical education: Learning from social identity theory. *Medical Education*, *46*(2), 143–52. doi: 10.1111/j.1365-2923.2011.04099.x

Chew-Graham, C. A., Rogers, A. and Yassin, N. (2003). 'I wouldn't want it on my CV or their records': Medical students' experiences of help-seeking for mental health problems. *Medical Education*, *37*(10), 873–80.

Costello, C. Y. (2005). *Professional identity crisis: Race, class, gender and success at professional schools*. Nashville, TN: Vanderbilt University Press.

Cruwys, T., Dingle, G. A., Haslam, C., Haslam, S. A., Jetten, J. and Morton, T. A. (2013). Social group memberships protect against future depression, alleviate depression symptoms and prevent depression relapse. *Social Science and Medicine*, *98*, 179–86. doi: 10.1016/j.socscimed.2013.09.013

Cruwys, T., Platow, M. J., Angullia, S. A., Chang, J. M., Diler, S. E., Kirchner, J. L., . . . Wadley, A. L. (2012). Modeling of food intake is moderated by salient psychological group membership. *Appetite*, *58*(2), 754–7. doi: 10.1016/j.appet.2011.12.002

Daly, M. G. and Willcock, S. M. (2002). Examining stress and responses to stress in medical students and new medical graduates. *The Medical Journal of Australia*, *177* (Suppl. July), S14–S15.

Department of Defence. (2012). *Pathway to change: Evolving defence culture*. Canberra: Commonwealth of Australia.

Dyrbye, L. N., Harper, W., Durning, S. J., Moutier, C., Thomas, M. R., Massie, F. S., . . . Shanafelt, T. D. (2011). Patterns of distress in US medical students. *Medical Teacher*, *33*(10), 834–9. doi: 10.3109/0142159X.2010.531158

Dyrbye, L. N., Thomas, M. R., Huschka, M., Lawson, K. L., Novotny, P. J., Sloan, J. A. and Shanafelt, T. D. (2006). A multicenter study of burnout, depression, and quality of life in minority and nonminority US medical students. *Mayo Clinic Proceedings*, *81*(11), 1435–42.

Dyrbye, L. N., Thomas, M. R. and Shanafelt, T. D. (2005). Medical student distress: Causes, consequences, and proposed solutions. *Mayo Clinic Proceedings*, *80*(12), 1613–22. doi: 10.4065/80.12.1613

Fahrenkopf, A. M., Sectish, T. C., Barger, L. K., Sharek, P. J., Lewin, D., Chiang, V. W. and Landrigan, C. P. (2008). Rates of medication errors among depressed and burnt out residents: Prospective cohort study. *British Medical Journal*, *336*(7642), 488–91.

Finlay, S. E. and Fawzy, M. (2001). Becoming a doctor. *Journal of Medical Ethics: Medical Humanities*, *27*(2), 90–2.

Granville-Chapman, J. E., Yu, K. and White, P. D. (2001). A follow-up survey of alcohol consumption and knowledge in medical students. *Alcohol and Alcoholism*, *36*(6), 540–3.

Haslam, S. A., O'Brien, A., Jetten, J., Vormedal, K. and Penna, S. (2005). Taking the strain: Social identity, social support, and the experience of stress. *The British Journal of Social Psychology*, *44*(3), 355–70. doi: 10.1348/014466605X37468

Hays, L. R., Cheever, T. and Patel, P. (1996). Medical student suicide, 1989–1994. *The American Journal of Psychiatry*, *153*(4), 553–5.

Hem, E., GrŁnvold, N. T., Aasland, O. G. and Ekeberg, O. (2000). The prevalence of suicidal ideation and suicidal attempts among Norwegian physicians. Results from a cross-sectional survey of a nationwide sample. *European Psychiatry: The Journal of the Association of European Psychiatrists*, *15*(3), 183–9.

Heyworth, J. (2004). Stress: A badge of honour in the emergency department? *Emergency Medicine Australasia*, *16*(1), 5–6.

Iyer, A., Jetten, J., Tsivrikos, D., Postmes, T. and Haslam, S. A. (2009). The more (and the more compatible) the merrier: Multiple group memberships and identity compatibility as predictors of adjustment after life transitions. *The British Journal of Social Psychology*, *48*(4), 707–33. doi: 10.1348/014466608X397628

Jarvis-Selinger, S., Pratt, D. D. and Regehr, G. (2012). Competency is not enough: Integrating identity formation into the medical education discourse. *Academic Medicine*, *87*(9), 1185–90. doi: 10.1097/ACM.0b013e3182604968

Jetten, J., Haslam, C. and Haslam, S. A. (Eds). (2012). *The social cure: Identity, health and wellbeing*. Hove and New York: Psychology Press.

Johnston, K. L. and White, K. M. (2003). Binge-drinking: A test of the role of group norms in the theory of planned behaviour. *Psychology and Health*, *18*(1), 63–77.

Jones, J. M. and Jetten, J. (2010). Recovering from strain and enduring pain: Multiple group memberships promote resilience in the face of physical challenges. *Social Psychological and Personality Science*, *2*(3), 239–44. doi: 10.1177/1948550610386806

Keller, S., Maddock, J. E., Laforge, R. G., Velicer, W. F. and Basler, H.-D. (2007). Binge drinking and health behavior in medical students. *Addictive Behaviors*, *32*(3), 505–15. doi: 10.1016/j.addbeh.2006.05.017

Knight, C., Haslam, S. A. and Haslam, C. (2010). In home or at home? How collective decision making in a new care facility enhances social interaction and wellbeing amongst older adults. *Ageing and Society*, *30*(8), 1393–1418. doi: 10.1017/S0144686X10000656

Laidlaw, A., McLellan, J. and Ozakinci, G. (2016). Understanding undergraduate student perceptions of mental health, mental well-being and help-seeking behaviour. *Studies in Higher Education*, *41*(12), 2156–68. doi: 10.1080/03075079.2015.1026890

Linville, P. W. (1985). Self-complexity and affective extremity: Don't put all of your eggs in one cognitive basket. *Social Cognition*, *3*(1), 94–120.

Linville, P. W. (1987). Self-complexity as a cognitive buffer against stress-related illness and depression. *Journal of Personality and Social Psychology*, *52*(4), 663–76.

Louis, W., Davies, S., Smith, J. and Terry, D. J. (2007). Pizza and pop and the student identity: The role of referent group norms in healthy and unhealthy eating. *The Journal of Social Psychology*, *147*(1), 57–74. doi: 10.3200/SOCP.147.1.57-74

McNeill, K. G., Kerr, A. and Mavor, K. I. (2014). Identity and norms: The role of group membership in medical student wellbeing. *Perspectives on Medical Education*, *3*(2), 101–12. doi: 10.1007/s40037-013-0102-z

Manochakian, R. (2014). My first year as an oncologist. *Journal of Palliative Medicine*, *17*(6), 636–7.

Marton, F. and Säljö, R. (1976). On qualitative differences in learning: Outcome and process. *British Journal of Educational Psychology*, *46*, 4–11.

Mavor, K. I. and McNeill, K. G. (2014). Moving toward a complex systems view in medical student well-being research. *Medical Education*, *48*(10), 941–3.

Mavor, K. I., McNeill, K. G., Anderson, K., Kerr, A., O'Reilly, E. and Platow, M. J. (2014). Beyond prevalence to process: The role of self and identity in medical student wellbeing. *Medical Education*, *48*(4), 351–60.

Monrouxe, L. V. (2009). Negotiating professional identities: Dominant and contesting narratives in medical students' longitudinal audio diaries. *Current Narratives*, *1*(1), 41–59.

Monrouxe, L. V. (2010). Identity, identification and medical education: Why should we care? *Medical Education*, *44*(1), 40–9. doi: 10.1111/j.1365-2923.2009.03440.x

Newbury-Birch, D., White, M. and Kamali, F. (2000). Factors influencing alcohol and illicit drug use amongst medical students. *Drug and Alcohol Dependence*, *59*(2), 125–30.

O'Reilly, E., McNeill, K. G., Mavor, K. I. and Anderson, K. (2014). Looking beyond personal stressors: An examination of how academic stressors contribute to depression in Australian graduate medical students. *Teaching and Learning in Medicine*, *26*(1), 56–63. doi: 10.1080/10401334.2013.857330

Pepitone-Arreola-Rockwell, F., Rockwell, D. and Core, N. (1981). Fifty-two medical student suicides. *The American Journal of Psychiatry*, *138*(2), 198–201.

Perkins, H. and Wechsler, H. (1996). Variation in perceived college drinking norms and its impact on alcohol abuse: A nationwide study. *Journal of Drug Issues*, *26*(4), 961–74.

Platow, M. J., Mavor, K. I. and Grace, D. M. (2013). On the role of discipline-related self-concept in deep and surface approaches to learning among university students. *Instructional Science*, *41*(2), 271–85. doi: 10.1007/s11251-012-9227-4

Radcliffe, C. and Lester, H. (2003). Perceived stress during undergraduate medical training: A qualitative study. *Medical Education*, *37*(1), 32–8.

Ramsden, P. (2003). *Learning to Teach in Higher Education* (Approaches to learning, pp. 39–61). London: Routledge.

Ratzan, R. M. (2014). 'Lives there who loves his pain?': Empathy, creativity, and the physician's obligation. *The Hastings Center Report*, *44*(1), 18–21.

Richardson, M., Abraham, C. and Bond, R. (2012). Psychological correlates of university students' academic performance: A systematic review and meta-analysis. *Psychological Bulletin*, *138*(2), 353–87.

Shanafelt, T. D., Balch, C. M., Bechamps, G., Russell, T., Dyrbye, L., Satele, D. and Freischlag, J. (2010). Burnout and medical errors among American surgeons. *Annals of Surgery*, *251*(6), 995–1000.

Shanafelt, T. D., Bradley, K. A., Wipf, J. E. and Back, A. L. (2002). Burnout and self-reported patient care in an internal medicine residency program. *Annals of Internal Medicine*, *136*(5), 358–67.

Smyth, L., Mavor, K. I., Platow, M. J., Grace, D. M., Reynolds, K. J., Trigwell, K. and Prosser, M. (2015). Discipline social identification, study norms and learning approach in university students. *Educational Psychology*, *35*(1), 251–66.

Squires, B. P. (1989). Fatigue and stress in medical students, interns and residents: It's time to act! *Canadian Medical Association Journal*, *140*(1), 18–9.

Sreeramareddy, C. T., Shankar, P. R., Binu, V. S., Mukhopadhyay, C., Ray, B. and Menezes, R. G. (2007). Psychological morbidity, sources of stress and coping strategies among undergraduate medical students of Nepal. *BMC Medical Education*, 7(1), 26. doi: 10.1186/1472-6920-7-26

Tajfel, H. and Turner, J. C. (1979). An integrative theory of intergroup conflict. In *The social psychology of intergroup relations* (pp. 33–47). Monterey, CA: Brookes/Cole.

Takeshita, T. and Morimoto, K. (1999). Self-reported alcohol-associated symptoms and drinking behavior in three ALDH2 genotypes among Japanese university students. *Alcoholism, Clinical and Experimental Research*, 23(6), 1065–9.

Terry, D. J. and Hogg, M. A. (1996). Group norms and the attitude-behavior relationship: A role for group identification. *Personality and Social Psychology Bulletin*, 22(8), 776–93. doi: 10.1177/0146167296228002

Trigwell, K. and Prosser, M. (1991). Improving the quality of student learning: The influence of learning context and student approaches to learning on learning outcomes. *Higher Education*, 22(3), 251–66.

Wallace, J. E., Lemaire, J. B. and Ghali, W. A. (2009). Physician wellness: A missing quality indicator. *Lancet*, 374(9702), 1714–21.

Walsh, A. (2007). An exploration of Biggs' constructive alignment in the context of work-based learning. *Assessment Evaluation in Higher Education*, 32(1), 79–87.

Weaver, R., Peters, K., Koch, J. and Wilson, I. (2011). 'Part of the team': Professional identity and social exclusivity in medical students. *Medical Education*, 45(12), 1220–9. doi: 10.1111/j.1365-2923.2011.04046.x

West, C. P., Huschka, M. M., Novotny, P. J., Sloan, J. A., Kolars, J. C., Habermann, T. M. and Shanafelt, T. D. (2006). Association of perceived medical errors with resident distress and empathy: A prospective longitudinal study. *JAMA – Journal of the American Medical Association*, 296(9), 1071–8.

Wu, F., Ireland, M., Hafekost, K. and Lawrence, D. (2013). *National mental health survey of doctors and medical students*. N.p: Beyond Blue.

Zeegus, P. (2001). Approaches to learning in science: A longitudinal study. *British Journal of Educational Psychology*, 71(1), 115–32.

PART VII

Making connections

19

THE SOCIAL CONSTRUCTION OF TEACHERS' IDENTITIES

Finding connections in social identity and post-structuralist perspectives

Emma Rich, Kenneth I. Mavor and Louisa Webb

Preamble

The story of this chapter begins with two siblings – academics with a common interest in the nature of *identity*, but from very different backgrounds: Ken Mavor in social psychology and Louisa Webb in teacher education and physical education pedagogy. Ken's background is in social identity theory (SIT) and self-categorisation theory (SCT) approaches, and Louisa worked from a Foucauldian, post-structuralist perspective – two approaches which might be experienced as mutually incomprehensible given different traditions, methods and terminology.

In trying to understand each other's perspectives, we repeatedly found, after unpacking the terminology and seeking a mutually intelligible way of expressing the core concepts and assumptions, that there were actually many things in common. Though living at that time on opposite sides of the globe, we enjoyed the discoveries of mutual perspectives and looked forward to being able to share our ideas with each other (and perhaps others) more easily.

Unfortunately, this intellectual project had barely begun when Louisa became quite ill and eventually succumbed to cancer in 2012. The conversations carried on close to the end, chatting during her treatments or while walking in the woods near Loughborough. This chapter is a first tentative effort to honour those conversations, and in collaboration with Louisa's friend and colleague Emma Rich, to explore the complexity of teacher identity, very much embedded in a world of social meanings and power relations. In this chapter, we draw heavily on the post-structuralist work in this area and try to make a few tentative connections with the SIT/SCT concepts. We hope that readers with social identity, post-structuralist or symbolic interactionist backgrounds will also start to see the glimmer of common ground and see this as an invitation to explore this topic more and with mutual respect to these traditions.

Introduction

Within this chapter, we sketch out some emerging perspectives on the social construction of teacher identities. The research we present below is largely focused on teachers' identities in school-based contexts, although many of the insights would apply to those who need to construct a teacher identity in other contexts. *Identity* is a heavily used concept that has been conceptualised across a range of different theories and analytical traditions. We will not unpack them all here, but in line with the themes of the book, we do distinguish between perspectives that see identity as being synonymous with the personal or individual and perspectives that consider the 'social' to have a core place in the understanding of identity (Blumer, 1969; Foucault, 1980, 1982; Turner, Oakes, Haslam and McGarty, 1994; see also in this volume, Platow, Mavor and Bizumic, Chapter 1, and Haslam, Chapter 2). In recent years, accounts of teacher identity have challenged perspectives that place the 'individual self' at the centre. Following a line of inquiry grounded in post-structuralist theory, more recent literature has focused on teachers' subjectivities and the constitution of identities as more *socially contingent*. We consider how these post-structuralist accounts can inform our understanding of the relationship between the self, social identity, and education.

Teacher identity has received little attention from a specifically social identity approach, but social identity theory is also heavily grounded in a meta-theory that sees identity as socially defined as well as socially embedded. Historically, social identity theory (and self-categorisation theory) emerged broadly from an interactionist perspective, which has been influential in social psychology as well as in sociology (see Reynolds, Turner, Branscombe, Mavor, Bizumic and Subasic, 2010; Turner and Oakes, 1986; Turner, Oakes, Haslam and McGarty, 1994). Although *social identity* has become a rather mainstream concept in some ways, we argue that it is in its more strident elements of social analysis that the social identity approach has some important points of resonance with the interests of many post-structuralist researchers in education.

The purpose of the current chapter – embedded as it is in a book largely focused on social identity – is primarily to introduce a number of ways of exploring the nature of teacher identities from a post-structuralist perspective and to encourage readers from varied perspectives to look for new ways to ask questions of interest in this domain. Rather than defining post-structuralism formally here, we explore comparative examples throughout the chapter. We finish the chapter with some reflections on what is lost when we create silos of thought around methodology rather than looking to learn from shared intuitions about the nature of the self.

Teachers' identities

First, we begin with an account of various attempts to characterise teacher identity. In recent years, the conceptualisation of teachers' identities has gathered increasing attention across a range of disciplinary fields. The trajectory towards theories of the social construction of teachers' identities has, in part, emerged because of the need for a more complex reading of identity than those driven by the fundamental values of a humanistic self, which conceptualises the teacher as having a fixed and constant identity. In contrast, perspectives that focus on the socially constructed nature of identities invite a view of the self that is more contingent, emerging and fluid. This focus on teacher identities moves away from the concept of a *fixed self* and the *individual* and moves, instead, towards an understanding of teacher identities as socially constituted and negotiated (Miller and Marsh, 2002).

Rather than assuming a core inner self that is autonomous and fixed, these perspectives acknowledge that teachers, in the constant process of becoming a 'teacher', negotiate multiple identities. The extent to which we can think of identity as fluid, shifting and socially constructed varies, and there is not space here to examine the nuances of the varied ontological and epistemological differences within this body of work. Indeed, the analytical traditions and conceptual foci employed in attempts at understanding teachers' identities are varied. Furthermore, the concept of *self* is a complex and contested issue within the literature on teachers' identities and teacher education, and as Beauchamp and Thomas suggest,

> One must struggle to comprehend the close connection between identity and the self, the role of emotion in shaping identity, the power of stories and discourse in understanding identity, the role of reflection in shaping identity, the link between identity and agency, the contextual factors that promote or hinder the construction of identity.
>
> (Beauchamp and Thomas, 2009, p. 176)

However, perhaps what is common to these approaches is that the idea of a 'coherent, bounded' (Rose, 1998, p. 3) and stable self has certainly been called into question. Collectively, this work points to the complex relationalities through which previous depictions of identity have been rendered more fluid, contingent and always in a process of *becoming*. In this vein, there are a number of different ontological and epistemological approaches to understanding self and identity that acknowledge its socially constructed nature but that might go about studying this in different ways, from those that focus on the narratives of self that teachers construct (Brown and Rich, 2002; Connelley and Clandinin, 1999) and their life stories (Munroe, 1988) through to an examination of the discourses through which teachers' identities as 'subjectivities' are constituted (see Alsup, 2006).

To this list, we could easily flag the potential for more contributions from a social identity approach, which might examine how group-level interactions also provide a context in which teachers develop a sense of 'what it means' to be a teacher. Teachers must develop their sense of identity in contrast to student identities, discipline-based differences among teachers, alignments or conflicts with parents (collectively or individually), school administrations, and the larger political contexts of education as a social institution (see also in this volume, Jetten, Iyer and Zhang, Chapter 6, Reynolds, Subasic, Lee and Bromhead, Chapter 3, and Sonnenberg, Chapter 15). This approach, which emphasises the intergroup context that is salient as teachers negotiate different parts of their identity, could usefully complement these other social constructionist perspectives.

We will not exhaust the entirety of this spectrum of approaches but seek to elaborate further on the contemporary debates. The next section of this chapter examines the literature that speaks specifically to the discursive constitution of identities.

The discursive constitution of teachers' subjectivities

Self as process through discourse

> Post-structuralist discourse entails a move from the self as a noun (and thus stable and relatively fixed) to the self as a verb, always in process, taking its shape in and through the discursive possibilities through which selves are made.
>
> (Davies, 1997, p. 274)

Claims pertaining to the literature that focuses on identity as a sociocultural perspective (Olsen, 2008) point towards the emergence of teachers' multiple identities across different contexts. However, other approaches go further than this in their questioning of the very concept of identity. Instead of 'identity', post-structuralist writers promulgate the concepts of *subject* and *subjectivity*, which can be seen to 'mark a crucial break with humanist conceptions of the individual' (Weedon, 1987, p. 32). Post-structuralist theories have begun to examine more closely the ways in which selves are constituted through social relations, specifically those framed with relations of power-knowledge. Often drawing from the work of Foucault, these approaches utilise the concept of *discourse* and discourse analysis to better understand the power relations between education, identity and teachers' lives.

For Foucault, discourses are: 'practices that systematically form the objects of which they speak. Discourses are not about object; they constitute them and in the practice of doing so conceal their own intervention' (1972, p. 49). Thus, the rejection of a fixed self and the application of these concepts within educational research have given way to a focus on how teachers are being *constituted* within contemporary educational contexts. This set of literature acknowledges identities as multiple and always in a process of possibly being 'displaced/replaced' (Lather, 1991, p. 118). This is, in part, because subjectivity is constantly being produced through a range of discourses, producing tensions, contradictions and complexities. In this vein, post-structuralist notions of subjectivity, power and discourse draw attention to the contingent and relational processes through which teachers are constituted, drawing attention to the significance of language:

> Who we are, our subjectivity, is spoken into existence in every utterance not just in the sense that others speak us into existence and impose unwanted structures on us, as much feminist writing presumed, but, in each moment of speaking and being, we each reinvent ourselves inside the male/female dualism, socially, psychically, and physically.
>
> (Davies, 1992, p. 75)

The concept of subjectivity, thus, provides a further theoretical lens through which to examine teachers' experiences, of what is elsewhere described in terms of 'identity', as fluid, contradictory, complex and in flux. As Davies and Banks suggest, 'from a post-structuralist perspective, subjectivity is formulated through discourses, given substance and pattern through storyline and deployed in social interaction' (1992, p. 3). The implications for research are clear: researchers might explore how teachers make sense of themselves as particular kinds of teachers (child-centred, professional, student teacher, etc.) and identify the various discourses through which this occurs. As Wright articulates it, 'the notion of discourse provides a means to understand what resources are available to individuals as they make sense of the world and themselves in the world' (2004, p. 20). In understanding 'teachers' identities' in this way, we can begin to register the 'constitutive effects' of the various 'discursive practices' that teachers might be exposed to (Davies, 1993).

Self as process through salience

Self-categorisation theory also adopts a fluid and contextual understanding of the self and, importantly, explicitly positions *social* selves as essential and real aspects of the self along with *personal* selves (Turner, Hogg, Oakes, Reicher and Wetherell, 1987). Indeed, although SCT makes a personal/social distinction in order to focus attention on the reality of the social aspects of self, it also argues that all selves are, in important ways, socially derived (Oakes, Haslam and Turner, 1994; Turner *et al.*, 1994). A key strength of the *self-categorisation* part of the theory is that it provides a model which integrates cognitive aspects (memories, expectations; formally *perceiver readiness*) with the perceived social context (changes in the patterns or alignments of social interactions; formally *comparative fit* and *normative fit*) to explain why different understandings or aspects of self come to be salient at any given moment (Oakes, 1987; Oakes, Turner and Haslam, 1991; Turner *et al.*, 1994). The *salience model* proposes that these three elements (perceiver readiness, comparative fit and normative fit) operate in conjunction such that certain identities are more likely to come to the fore and determine how we see the world if we are predisposed or cued to think in those terms, or if the nature of comparisons being made in the current context highlight certain identities as more meaningful than others. One could imagine how the discursive processes that *constitute* certain identities could be seen as operating through something like the salience model.

The SCT salience model is a powerful tool for understanding both how the self can be so fluid and how stable patterns of interaction can lead to apparently stable experiences of self. We argue that there are some potential points of connection between the social identity/self-categorisation and post-structuralist perspectives and that, at least in some cases, the meta-theoretical point being made about the dynamic, social and contextual construction of identities can find common ground across both of these perspectives.

Power and institutions

Our focus on fluidity is not to suggest that individuals are simply free to choose what kinds of subjects they want to be. Rather, possibilities emerge within particular relationalities of power, or as Davies articulates it, 'if you are constituted as a powerful agent you may well be able to act powerfully' (1997, p. 272). In other words, post-structuralist analyses offer a way to examine how particular subject positions (e.g., the 'professional teacher') are constituted within complex systems of power-knowledge (Foucault, 1980, p. 82). From this perspective, a number of studies have focused on the impact of subjectivities on teachers' work (McWilliam, 1999). Through a focus on discourse and relationalities of power, one can also begin to ask a different set of questions about the social conditions through which some are privileged and others are marginalised:

> Female teachers and small girls . . . are not unitary subjects uniquely positioned, but produced as a nexus of subjectivities, in relations of power that are constantly shifting, rendering them at one moment powerful and at another powerless.
>
> (Walkerdine, 1990, p. 1)

Drawing on these theories of language, subjectivity and discourse, one can understand the power relations through which teachers' sense of themselves and others are constituted. As Weeden makes clear, different discursive fields of teaching offer the individual 'a range of modes of subjectivity' as they 'consist of competing ways of giving meaning to the world and of organizing social institutions and processes' (1987, p. 35). The concept of *discursive positioning* offers further clarity in terms of how teachers might 'take up' these particular positions within storylines of what, for example, makes a 'good' or 'professional' teacher. As Schick contends, 'the norm of teacher is accomplished by a set of practices and discourses marked by identities within race, gender, class, sexual orientation' (2000, p. 301). As Davies argues:

The personal histories of being positioned in particular ways and of inter-preting events through and in terms of familiar story lines, concepts and images that one takes up as one's own effectively constitute the meness of me separate from others. To the extent that one takes oneself up in terms of these familiar positionings and story lines, then they have become part of the subjectivity of that person.

(Davies, 1992, p. 57)

To this end, subjectivities are not located in the individual, but are represent-ations, subject positions made available in and through discourses (see Wright, 2004). From this interpretation of identity, one can more fully appreciate the complexity of teachers' lives and their situatedness in complex relations of power. For instance, a number of feminist educational researchers draw on these theor-etical perspectives in their exploration of gender and identity (e.g., Davies 1989a, 1989b, 1989c; Jones, 1989, 1993; Kenway, Willis, Blackmore and Rennie, 1994; Walkerdine, 1989, 1990). The concepts of positioning and subjectivity, therefore, provide an understanding of how teachers 'become gendered' (Jones, 1993) through the binary language used to describe 'masculine' and 'feminine' styles of pedagogy.

These approaches have also informed the work examining professional iden-tities and modes of state regulation, making visible how teachers' subjectivities are shaped by neoliberal discourses of individualism, efficiency, performativity and productivity, and their impact on teacher authenticity (Mahony and Hextall, 1997). In such contexts, teachers may come to be *positioned* within these discourses as knowing, rational, consumer-oriented professionals and as instrumental in the process of achieving success in an education 'marketplace' (see also Sonnenberg, this volume). Writing about how teachers' identities have been affected by reforms that have moved schools towards 'self-managing schools in the era of new managerialism', Smyth argues,

what is going on here is clearly to some degree at least . . . a process of rein-venting teacher identities—some of it being driven by processes of external policy formation, but other aspects being contributed to in the way in which teachers themselves interpret, react to and adapt to the wider policy reform process.

(Smyth, 2002, p. 468)

The tensions between often contradictory discourses is indicative of under-standing a teacher's political identity, not as a 'rational entity' but as 'a complex subjective and multifaceted phenomenon which is embedded in the tension between the desire for political agency and the necessity for mutual recognition (see Benhabib, 1997; Weir, 1997) in diverse and social contexts' (Dillabough, 1999, p. 388).

Bringing identities into being

Other work has attended to the way in which language brings teachers' identities into being. Weedon's work, for example, has been important in setting out this post-structuralist relationship between experience and language: 'As we acquire language, we learn to give voice – meaning – to our experience and to understand it according to particular ways of thinking, particular discourses, which predate our entry into language' (1987, p. 33). Thus, rather than reflecting a standpoint epistemology (Harding, 1991; Stanley and Wise, 1990), these perspectives consider identity as being constituted in and through an engagement with language. Thus, how teachers talk about their professional and personal lives is constitutive of their identities: 'As individuals construct past events and actions in personal narratives they engage in a dynamic process of claiming identities, selves and constructing lives' (Sparkes, 1999, p. 18).

The narratives teachers construct about their lives, selves and practices are, therefore, seen to be of significance in understanding teachers' identities. It is through language and narrative that we are able to construct particular identities as meaning is articulated through language. Such discursive analytical techniques have 'enabled us to attend to the ways in which language traps us, for example, into binary forms of thought' (Davies, 1997, p. 272). Importantly, the analytical techniques of post-structuralism can help teachers, as subjects, identify the constitutive forces of particular discourses in the shaping the self.

For example, in their research on teachers' life histories, Brown and Rich (2002) analyse identities from the position of gender stories that men and women (re)construct about themselves as a result of previous, current and future-anticipated life experiences. This way, the narration of an apparently stable gender identity can be understood, in part, as an effect of normalisation within discourse itself; in other words, a humanistic discourse of neoliberalism in education demands a 'coherent self'. Moreover, whilst subjectivity understands experience of ourselves as fragmented, shifting and often contradictory, many authors observe the discourses that encourage us to search for a stable, coherent identity (Edley, 2001; Rich, 2001; St. Pierre, 2000) in the process of constituting an identity.[1] One of the key arguments in this body of work is that the conceptualisation of identity as rational, coherent and stable masks inequalities, insofar as individuals may be constituted differently through discursive practices of gender, race, class, ethnicity, and so forth. For instance, Rich, through a feminist post-structuralist analysis, reveals the extent to which student teachers of physical education construct narratives which attempted to appear consistent in 'self production' (2001, p. 132), albeit within social boundaries of particular gendered power relations. Reflecting on the language teachers use to talk about girls and boys or what it means to be a 'professional' or 'child-centred' teacher can make recognisable the very discourses through which they are constituted.

Embodied and emotional selves

Collectively, this work reveals the importance of understanding subjectivities in making visible the effects of particular discourses that may also be important in terms of the 'health lifeworld' of teachers; this is a concept used by Webb, McCaughtry and MacDonald to 'symbolise a broad perspective of health and takes into account some areas of thinking about teachers' work that often have not explicitly been framed in terms of health, such as occupational satisfaction and attrition' (2004, p. 207).

A growing body of work has begun to register the ways in which discourses can produce normalising, surveillant and regulating effects on teachers' subjectivities and practices. Often drawing from Foucault's (1977) work in *Discipline and Punish*, it has been recognised that particular discourses work in such a way as to shape, train and govern teachers' bodies and are produced within relations of power. In their work on surveillance as a technique of power in the context of physical education, Webb *et al.* (2004) reveal that surveillance does act as a technique of power and influences the embodied subjectivities of teachers in physical education. Their use of subjectivity 'recognises the embodiment of experience and ways of being that are fluid and shifting rather than fixed' (Webb *et al.*, 2004, p. 208). Similarly, Foucault's concept of 'technologies of self' has been deployed in research on teachers to better understand their 'operations on their own bodies and souls, thoughts, conduct and way of being' (1997, p. 225). Moreover, the idea that teachers' *emotions* are something internal and located in the individual has also been disrupted through the conceptual possibilities of discursive constitution.

Post-structural perspectives of emotions identify the place of emotion in identity formation as constantly embedded in 'power relations, ideology and culture' (Zembylas, 2003, p. 213). The work of Zembylas has highlighted how 'a discursive understanding of emotion in teaching provides a useful theoretical tool in analysing the place of emotion in the constitution of teacher identity' (2005, p. 936). For example, this work has examined how teachers resist or participate in the 'emotion discourses' of teaching (2002b). This understanding also offers educators a perspective that draws attention to the complexities of 'emotional rules' (Zembylas, 2002a) and how teacher identity is constituted through these practices.

While the social identity approach has not yet been used to explore this particular territory of emotion and embodied self in teacher identity, there are some broad connections to be made. Work on intergroup emotions emphasises that emotions go beyond the individual and can also be experienced as part of the social self (see Mackie, Smith and Ray, 2008). Several lines of work also show the role of social identities in moderating health effects (Jetten, Haslam and Haslam, 2012; Mavor, McNeill, Anderson, Kerr, O'Reilly and Platow, 2014) and that the effect of the social self is not only psychological but can be embodied in crowds and collectives (e.g., Hopkins and Reicher, 2016; Hopkins, Reicher, Khan, Tewari, Srinivasan and Stevenson, 2016). Insights from these areas could well intersect with the emerging ideas from post-structuralist thought to further inform our understanding of the 'health lifeworld' of teachers (see Webb *et al.*, 2004).

Conclusion

The above has provided an introduction into the theoretical approaches to understanding how teachers are spoken into existence through relations with others and positioning within particular discourses. The various contributions explored in this chapter recognise that 'subjectivities are not things that people have' (Webb *et al.*, 2004, p. 208) and, instead, seek to understand the social and cultural forces that come to constitute particular kinds of subjects. As we have outlined, much of the work focusing on how identities are socially constructed does so through a Foucauldian lens, revealing the many discourses at work in education and the multiple subjectivities that are constituted through relations of power. Whilst many of these authors draw from the work of Foucault, there is a wide range of theoretical, conceptual and analytical techniques that could be brought to bear – beyond those which are limited to Foucault yet sharing a similar orientation to the social nature of the self.

In exploring these theoretical frameworks, one might ask: Why does subjectivity matter in the context of understanding teachers? Why should educational research concern itself with the subjectivities of teachers? Decades on since some of the very influential work of feminist post-structuralist writers revealed the significance of understanding how we become gendered in education, we are still struck by the gendered binaries through which teachers and students understand particular *subjects* in the classroom. Elsewhere, research that focused on the damaging impact of the increasing levels of performativity in education revealed the constitutive effects of neoliberal discourses in making up teachers' subjectivity. We could write much more here about the power relations that guide teachers' practices, institutional practices, and issues of inclusion and exclusion; our point, however, is that the focus on teachers' subjectivity also reveals the powerful workings of discourses in the study of salient issues of teachers' lives. These tools provide powerful possibilities for revealing the processes through which teachers are constituted as particular kinds of subjects and the power relations that come to bear upon how teachers understand themselves.

Post-structural readings of the subject are also important not only because they reveal the forces through which people become certain subjects but also because they help to resist and make visible the power relations through which some are marginalised and others are privileged. For Davies, agency lies in the 'reflexive awareness of the constitutive power of language that becomes possible through post-structuralist theory' (1997, p. 272).

Avoiding methodological and linguistic silos of thought

A reading of the basic tenets of post-structuralism and self-categorisation theory (as well as the social interactionist perspective that also informs much work on identity in education) shows that these perspectives do share an important understanding of the phenomenal reality of the social world and its impact on our self-definitions. Yes, there are important differences (for example, in emphasis on the role of *mind* and in the nature of social interaction), but they nonetheless could find important intellectual resonances and be sources of new and interesting insights across perspectives. However, these research communities often glare at each other across the apparent chasms of language and method.

It would be easy to point particularly at post-structuralism (and related social constructionist rhetorical forms) as having a very distinctive linguistic style that is capable of hiding intellectual weaknesses as well as illuminating insights. The fairly well known 'Sokal hoax' in which a physicist submitted a nonsensical article to the journal *Social Text* (Hilgartner, 1997; Sokal, 1994) is an easy example. However, other domains are not immune to such challenges. Epstein (1990) expressed concerns about confirmation bias in sociology journals, and psychology has recently been rocked by concerns about replicability of key 'effects' as well (Open Science Collaboration, 2015). For our purpose here, the point is that all research domains have a language and terminology that outsiders can criticise as being opaque and which insiders can use to obfuscate, however unintentionally. Even in a less dramatic way, the use of particular technical terms operates as a means to define our intellectual ingroups and outgroups (see Coupland and Giles, 1988; Gallois and Giles, 2015; Petronio, Ellemers, Giles and Gallois, 1998), whether it be understanding the technical sense of the term 'intersubjectivities' or the terms 'moderators' and 'mediators'.

While method is often a discourse marker of the boundaries of intellectual inclusion and exclusion, we argue that it need not always be one of exclusion. Some researchers may pursue a particular method because they believe it to be the only way to get at the truth of interest to them; however, in many cases, the choice of method can be based on the audience to whom the insight is addressed or, indeed, selected to create a contrast with what might be seen as a problem.

As an example of this dynamic, it seems to us that there is nothing in the core historical tenets of symbolic interactionism that necessarily requires that these issues be interrogated using qualitative, idiographic or discursive methods; yet we can see the roots of this focus in the early writings of Blumer, who helped to define the methods of symbolic interactionism (Blumer, 1969). Blumer saw the danger in contemporary psychological methods that treated the social as the sum of individual parts (cf. Allport, 1924). Blumer writes:

> the conception of human association as a compound of the psychological makeup of the participating individuals becomes an obstacle to the study of such association. This is undeniably the most unfortunate consequence – a consequence which is always ready to plague social psychology and cut at its very roots.
>
> (1953, as cited in Blumer, 1969, p. 104)

These are words that would also resonate with social identity researchers since social identity theory also emerged from the same concerns (e.g., Turner and Oakes, 1986). And yet, while social identity researchers largely sought to make their point within the methodological traditions of those they critiqued, Blumer (1969) saw the methods of the time as too far removed from the actual experience of group life. Blumer exhorted researchers to immerse themselves more deeply in the actual social world that they were studying rather than being driven by abstract models and theories and fitting the data to these. In making such exhortations, Blumer helped to define the methodological traditions of researchers in the domain. However, using particular methods is no guarantee of achieving the degree of immersion that Blumer sought. All methodological silos run that risk because all of our abstractions (including mental states, discourses, intersubjectivities, etc.) can be imposed on our subjects of study in ways that can distort our understanding of their experiences as well as illuminate them.

Summary

We set out with goals on multiple levels: to explore the nature of teacher identity primarily from the perspective of post-structuralism; to highlight some points of resonance between these approaches and self-categorisation theory such that an SIT/SCT researcher might fruitfully draw from this existing literature in seeking to further explore the nature of teacher identity; and finally, to make a meta-point about the way we might approach research across fuzzy boundaries of method and meta-theory. We hope that researchers might find some useful insights here that will allow a richer understanding of the social construction of teachers' selves and identities.

Looking to the wider context of the whole book in which this chapter is embedded, we hope that the reader will also take this message of connection to heart. We encourage researchers to look beyond silos of method and historical boundaries and to seek out common ground among the broader family of researchers who share a view of the self as fluid, socially constructed, and brought into being through our social perceptions and experiences of the world.

Note

1 Davies (1993) further explores this relationship between the subject constituted through humanist discourses and how it is read through post-structuralist theory discourse.

References

Allport, F. H. (1924). *Social psychology*. Boston: Houghton Mifflin.
Alsup, J. (2006). *Teacher identity discourses: Negotiating personal and professional spaces*. Mahwah, NJ: Lawrence Erlbaum.

Beauchamp, C. and Thomas, L. (2009) Understanding teacher identity: An overview of issues in the literature and implications for teacher education. *Cambridge Journal of Education, 39*(2), 175–89.

Blumer, H. (1969). *Symbolic interactionism: Perspective and method.* Berkeley, CA: University of California Press.

Brown, D. and Rich, E. (2002). Gender positioning as pedagogical practice in teaching physical education. In D. Penney (Ed.), *Gender and physical education: Contemporary issues and future directions* (pp. 80–100). London: Routledge.

Connelly, M. and Clandinin, J. (1999). *Shaping a professional identity: Stories of educational practice.* London, Ontario: The Althouse Press.

Coupland, N. and Giles, H. (1988). Introduction: The communicative contexts of accommodation. *Language and Communication, 8*(3–4), 175–82. doi: 10.1016/0271-5309(88)90015-8

Davies, B. (1989a). Education for sexism: A theoretical analysis of the sex/gender bias in education. *Educational Philosophy and Theory, 21*(1), 1–19.

Davies, B. (1989b). *Frogs and snails and feminist tales. Preschool children and gender.* Sydney: Allen and Unwin.

Davies, B. (1989c). The discursive production of the male/female dualism in school settings. *Oxford Review of Education, 15*(3), 229–41.

Davies, B. (1992) Women's subjectivities and feminist stories. In C. Ellis and M. Flaherty (Eds), *Investigating subjectivity: Research on lived experience* (pp. 53–67). Newbury Park, CA: Sage.

Davies, B. (1993) *Shards of glass: Children reading and writing beyond gendered identity.* Sydney: Allen & Unwin.

Davies, B. (1997) The subject of post-structuralism: A reply to Alison Jones. *Gender and Education, 19*(3), 271–83.

Davies, B. and Banks, C. (1992) The gender trap: A feminist poststructuralist analysis of primary school children's talk about gender. *Journal of Curriculum Studies, 24*(1), 1–25.

Dillabough, J. (1999). Gender politics and conceptions of the modern teacher: Women, identity and professionalism. *British Journal of Sociology of Education, 20*(3), 373–94.

Edley, N. (2001) Analysing masculinity: Interpretive repertoires, ideological dilemmas and subject positions. In M. Wetherell, S. Taylor and S. J. Yates (Eds), *Discourse as data: A guide for analysis* (pp. 189–228). London: Sage in association with the Open University.

Epstein, W. M. (1990) Confirmational response bias among social work journals. *Science, Technology and Human Values, 15*(1), 9–38.

Foucault, M. (1972). *The archaeology of knowledge.* (A. Sheridan, Trans.). New York: Pantheon Books.

Foucault, M. (1977). *Discipline and punish: The birth of the prison.* (A. Sheridan, Trans.). New York: Pantheon Books.

Foucault, M. (1980) *Power/knowledge: Selected interviews and other writings, 1972–1977.* New York: Pantheon.

Foucault, M. (1982) The subject and power. In H. Dreyfus and P. Rabinow (Eds), *Beyond Structuralism* (pp. 208–26). Chicago, IL: University of Chicago Press.

Foucault, M. (1997). Technologies of the self. In P. Rabinow (Ed.), *Michael Foucault: Ethics, subjectivity and truth* (pp. 223–54). New York: The New Press.

Gallois, C. and Giles, H. (2015). Communication accommodation theory. In K. Tracy (Ed.), *The international encyclopedia of language and social interaction* (pp. 1–18). Chichester, UK: Wiley Blackwell.

Harding, S. (1991). *Whose science? Whose knowledge? Thinking from women's lives.* Ithaca, NY: Cornell University Press.

Hilgartner, S. (1997) The Sokal affair in context. *Science, Technology and Human Values,* 22(4): 506–22.

Hopkins, N. and Reicher, S. (2016). The psychology of health and well-being in mass gatherings: A review and a research agenda. *Journal of Epidemiology and Global Health,* 6(2), 49–57. doi: 10.1016/j.jegh.2015.06.001

Hopkins, N., Reicher, S. D., Khan, S. S., Tewari, S., Srinivasan, N. and Stevenson, C. (2016). Explaining effervescence: Investigating the relationship between shared social identity and positive experience in crowds. *Cognition and Emotion,* 30(1), 20–32. doi: 10.1080/02699931.2015.1015969

Jetten, J., Haslam, C. and Haslam, S. A. (Eds). (2012). *The social cure: Identity, health and wellbeing.* Hove, UK: Psychology Press.

Jones, A. (1989). The cultural production of classroom practice. *British Journal of Sociology of Education,* 10(1), 19–31.

Jones, A. (1993) Becoming a 'girl': Post-structuralist suggestions for educational research. *Gender and Education,* 5(2), 157–67.

Kenway, J., Willis, S., Blackmore, J. and Rennie, L. (1994). Making 'hope practical' rather than 'despair convincing': Feminist post-structuralism, gender reform and educational change. *British Journal of Sociology of Education,* 15(2), 187–210.

Lather, P. (1991) *Getting smart: Feminist research and pedagogy with/in the postmodern.* New York: Routledge.

Mackie, D. M., Smith, E. R. and Ray, D. G. (2008) Intergroup emotions and intergroup relations. *Social and Personality Psychology Compass,* 2(5), 1866–80. doi: 10.1111/j.1751-9004.2008.00130.x

McWilliam, E. (1999) *Pedagogical pleasures.* New York: Peter Lang.

Mahony, P. and Hextall, I. (1997). Sounds of silence: The social justice agenda of the Teacher Training Agency. *International Studies in Sociology of Education,* 7(2), 137–56.

Mavor, K. I., McNeill, K. G., Anderson, K., Kerr, A., O'Reilly, E. and Platow, M. J. (2014). Beyond prevalence to process: The role of self and identity in medical student well-being. *Medical Education,* 48(4), 351–60.

Miller Marsh, M. (2002) The shaping of Ms. Nicholi: The discursive fashioning of teacher identities. *Qualitative Studies in Education,* 15(3), 333–47.

Munroe, P. (1988) *Subject to fiction: Women teachers' life history narratives and the cultural politics of resistance.* Buckingham, UK: Open University Press.

Oakes, P. J. (1987). The salience of social categories. In J. C. Turner, M. A. Hogg, P. J. Oakes, S. D. Reicher and M. S. Wetherell (Eds), *Rediscovering the social group: A self-categorisation theory* (pp. 117–41). Oxford: Blackwell.

Oakes, P. J., Haslam, S. A. and Turner, J. C. (1994). *Stereotyping and social reality.* Oxford: Blackwell.

Oakes, P. J., Turner, J. C. and Haslam, S. A. (1991). Perceiving people as group members: The role of fit in the salience of social categorizations. *British Journal of Social Psychology,* 30(2), 125–44.

Olsen, B. (2008). *Teaching what they learn, learning what they live.* Boulder, CO: Paradigm Publishers.

Open Science Collaboration. (2015). Estimating the reproducibility of psychological science. *Science,* 349(6251). doi: 10.1126/science.aac4716

Petronio, S., Ellemers, N., Giles, H. and Gallois, C. (1998). (Mis)communicating across boundaries: Interpersonal and intergroup considerations. *Communication Research,* 25(6), 571–95.

Reynolds, K. J., Turner, J. C., Branscombe, N. R., Mavor, K. I., Bizumic, B. and Subasic, E. (2010). Interactionism in personality and social psychology: An integrated approach to understanding the mind and behaviour. *European Journal of Personality, 24*(5), 458–82. doi: 10.1002/per.782

Rich, E., 2001. Gender positioning in teacher education in England: New rhetoric, old realities. *International Studies in Sociology of Education, 11*(2), 131–56.

Rose, N. (1998). *Inventing our selves: Psychology, power and personhood.* Cambridge: Cambridge University Press.

Schick, C. (2000). White women teachers accessing dominance. *Discourses: Studies in the Cultural Politics of Education, 21*(3), 299–309.

Smyth, J. (2002) Unmasking teachers' subjectivities in local school management. *Journal of Education Policy, 17*(4), 463–82. Reprinted by permission of the publisher, Taylor & Francis Ltd, www.tandfonline.com.

Sokal, Alan D. (1994). Transgressing the boundaries: Towards a transformative hermeneutics of quantum gravity. *Social Text, 46/47,* 217–52.

Sparkes, A. (1999). Exploring body narratives. *Sport, Education and Society, 4*(1), 17–30.

St. Pierre, E. A. (2000) Poststructural feminism in education: An overview. *Qualitative Studies in Education, 13*(5), 477–515.

Stanley, L. and Wise, S. (1990). Method, methodology and epistemology in feminist research processes. In L. Stanley (Ed.), *Feminist praxis* (pp. 20–60). London: Routledge.

Turner, J. C., Hogg, M. A., Oakes, P. J., Reicher, S. D. and Wetherell, M. S. (1987). *Rediscovering the social group: A self-categorisation theory.* Oxford: Basil Blackwell.

Turner, J. C. and Oakes, P. J. (1986). The significance of the social identity concept for social psychology with reference to individualism, interactionism and social influence. *British Journal of Social Psychology, 25*(3), 237–52.

Turner, J. C., Oakes, P. J., Haslam, S. A. and McGarty, C. (1994). Self and collective: Cognition and social context. *Personality and Social Psychology Bulletin, 20*(5), 454–63.

Walkerdine, V. (1989). *Counting girls out: Girls and mathematics.* London: Virago.

Walkerdine, V. (1990). *Schoolgirl fictions.* London: Verso.

Webb, L., McCaughtry, N. and MacDonald, D. (2004) Surveillance as a technique of power in physical education. *Sport, Education and Society, 9*(2), 207–22.

Weedon, C. (1987). *Feminist practice and poststructuralist theory.* Cambridge, MA: Blackwell.

Wright, J. (2004) Post-structural methodologies: The body, schooling and health. In J. Evans, B. Davies and J. Wright (Eds), *Body knowledge and control: Studies in the sociology of physical education and health* (pp. 19–31). London: Routledge.

Zembylas, M. (2002a). Constructing genealogies of teachers' emotions in science teaching. *Journal of Research in Science Teaching, 39*(1), 79–103.

Zembylas, M. (2002b). 'Structures of feeling' in curriculum and teaching: Theorizing the emotional rules. *Educational Theory, 52*(2), 187–208.

Zembylas, M. (2003). Emotions and teacher identity: A poststructural perspective. *Teachers and Teaching: Theory and Practice, 9*(3), 213–38.

Zembylas, M. (2005) Discursive practices, genealogies, and emotional rules: A poststructualist view on emotion and identity in teaching. *Teaching and Teacher Education, 21*(8), 935–48.

INDEX

Note: italics denote figures; bold denotes tables.

Taylor & Francis eBooks

Helping you to choose the right eBooks for your Library

Add Routledge titles to your library's digital collection today. Taylor and Francis ebooks contains over 50,000 titles in the Humanities, Social Sciences, Behavioural Sciences, Built Environment and Law.

Choose from a range of subject packages or create your own!

Benefits for you
- » Free MARC records
- » COUNTER-compliant usage statistics
- » Flexible purchase and pricing options
- » All titles DRM-free.

REQUEST YOUR FREE INSTITUTIONAL TRIAL TODAY

Free Trials Available
We offer free trials to qualifying academic, corporate and government customers.

Benefits for your user
- » Off-site, anytime access via Athens or referring URL
- » Print or copy pages or chapters
- » Full content search
- » Bookmark, highlight and annotate text
- » Access to thousands of pages of quality research at the click of a button.

eCollections – Choose from over 30 subject eCollections, including:

Archaeology	Language Learning
Architecture	Law
Asian Studies	Literature
Business & Management	Media & Communication
Classical Studies	Middle East Studies
Construction	Music
Creative & Media Arts	Philosophy
Criminology & Criminal Justice	Planning
Economics	Politics
Education	Psychology & Mental Health
Energy	Religion
Engineering	Security
English Language & Linguistics	Social Work
Environment & Sustainability	Sociology
Geography	Sport
Health Studies	Theatre & Performance
History	Tourism, Hospitality & Events

For more information, pricing enquiries or to order a free trial, please contact your local sales team: **www.tandfebooks.com/page/sales**

 Routledge Taylor & Francis Group | The home of Routledge books

www.tandfebooks.com

Printed in Great Britain
by Amazon

47533816R00215